TOWARD A SOCIOLOGY OF WOMEN

Peter J. M.
6-5-72

Toward a Sociology
of Women

CONSTANTINA SAFILIOS-ROTHSCHILD

Wayne State University

Xerox College Publishing

Lexington, Massachusetts / Toronto

Preface

During the last two or three years a number of books have appeared about the Women's Liberation Movement, women, and their "sisterhood." Some of these books, however, have been either historical treatises on "feminism" and the status of women through the ages, or rather emotional tracts permeated with the anger that is currently filling American women. And for these reasons, they may not have reached and influenced a wide public of *men and women,* a public whose level of awareness must be raised considerably before significant social and cultural changes can take place.

I undertook the editing of this book convinced that it is extremely important to reach as many undergraduate and graduate students and laymen (laywomen) as possible and to educate them, by offering them a good balance of research data and conclusions (presented in an uncomplicated manner), accounts of personal experiences, and remarks, theories, and projections for the future. Another basic concern of mine has been the establishment of some cornerstones for building a sociology of women, or a sociology of sex roles, as it is called by some social scientists, and, hopefully, this volume will provide a foundation for this new, important sociological field.

Furthermore, it is my sincere hope that this reader as well as other works relating to women and sex roles may lead to the reformulation of existing sociological theories and the development of new ones that will extend our ability to understand and to explain social relationships and related phenomena.

Students and laymen alike have often observed that while sociologists have many interesting things to say, they usually choose the dullest and least imaginative way to say them. Keeping this frequent criticism in mind, I have selected the articles in this volume not only for their interest and quality of content but also for their vividness, clarity, and style of presentation, so that the readers of this collection may be entertained as well as educated on one of the most crucial themes of our era: men and women. Furthermore, adhering to the principle that such a collection is useful only if it brings to students material to which they are not normally exposed or do not have access, I have included here articles either specially commissioned for this volume (eleven out of a total of thirty-one articles) or reprinted in most cases from journals that are rarely read by students, such as *Michigan Law Review, The Humanist, The Futurist, Social Policy, Acta Sociologica,* and *Journalism Quarterly.*

Being socialized in the Greek culture and by a remarkably "liberated" mother, I could never comprehend (at least emotionally) the "women's problem" and the "women's conflict" in the United States. I have been teaching undergraduate and graduate students family courses related to the sociology of women at the Merrill-Palmer Institute and Wayne State University since the fall of 1963 (when I began to teach), and while at that time I was usually thought to have quite "radical" views on the subject of women, social changes have caught up with me. By now, I may even be accused by some radicals of being "conservative" on the same issues.

I would like to thank, first of all, my good friend, Theodore Caris, President of Xerox College Publishing, who invited me and urged me to prepare this reader. Also I would like to thank the following men who helped me through endless discussions, sometimes sociological and sometimes introspective, to become even more aware of and sensitive to the issues concerning sex roles, discrimination against women, and the relationships between men and women: my husband, Walter G. Rothschild; Jan Trost; Jacques Dofny; and S. M. Miller.

Finally, I would like to thank Irene Zak, my good friend and tireless secretary, and my assistants Marina Mariadou and George Bakopoulos for their help with the endless details of book preparation.

CONSTANTINA SAFILIOS-ROTHSCHILD

Acknowledgments

JESSIE BERNARD, "Women, Marriage, and the Future." Reprinted by permission of the author and the journal from *The Futurist*, vol. 4 (April 1970).

LAURA BERGQUIST, "How Come a Nice Girl Like You Isn't Married?" Reprinted by permission of the editors from the January 11, 1966, issue of *Look* magazine. Copyright 1965 by Cowles Communications, Inc.

CAROLINE BIRD, "Let's Draft Women Too!" Reprinted by special permission of the Saturday Post Company. Copyright © 1966 by The Curtis Publishing Company.

DANA DENSMORE, "On the Temptation to Be a Beautiful Object." Reprinted by permission of the author and the journal from *No More Fun and Games. A Journal of Female Liberation*, issue 2 (February 1969), pp. 43–48.

"Dialogue-Focuser: Women." Reprinted from *Dialogue on Women* (Indianapolis: The Bobbs-Merrill Company, 1967), pp. 11–17.

ALTHEA JOMPEN DREW, ". . . Femininity Is About as Ambiguous a Matter as Patriotism . . ." Reprinted by permission of the author from *Mademoiselle* (February 1970), pp. 185, 265–267.

PHILIP GOLDBERG, "Are Women Prejudiced Against Women?" Reprinted by permission of the journal from *Trans-Action*, vol. 5, no. 5 (April 1968), pp. 28–30.

GAEL GREENE, "A Vote Against Motherhood: A Wife Challenges the Importance of Childbearing." Reprinted by permission of the Harold Matson Company, Inc., and The Saturday Post Company. Copyright © 1963 by Gael Greene.

PATRICIA ALBJERG GRAHAM, "Women in Academe." Reprinted by permission of the author and the journal from *Science*, vol. 169 (September 25, 1970), pp. 1284–1290. Copyright 1970 by the American Association for the Advancement of Science.

ELINA HAAVIO-MANNILA, "Sex Roles in Politics." Reprinted in an abridged form by permission of the author and the journal from *Scandinavian Political Studies*, vol. 5 (1970), pp. 209–216, 226–238.

HARRIET HOLTER, "Sex Roles and Social Change." Reprinted by permission of the author and the journal from *Acta Sociologica*, vol. 14, nos. 1/2 (1971), pp. 2–12.

MARGARET B. LEFKOWITZ, "The Women's Magazine Short-Story Heroine in 1957 and 1967." Reprinted by permission of the journal from *Journalism Quarterly*, no. 2 (Summer 1969), pp. 364–366.

Lyrics from "Love and Marriage" reprinted by permission of Barton Music Corporation.

MARGARET MEAD, "Is College Compatible with Marriage?" Reprinted by permission of the Editorial Projects for Education, Inc., from *Ohio State University Monthly*.

S. M. MILLER, "The Making of a Confused Middle-aged Husband." Reprinted by permission of the author and International Arts and Sciences Press from *Social Policy*, vol. 2 no. 2 (July/August, 1971), pp. 33–39.

RHONA RAPOPORT and ROBERT N. RAPOPORT, "The Dual-Career Family: A Variant Pattern and Social Change." Reprinted by permission of the authors and the journal from *Human Relations*, vol. 22, no. 1 (January 1969).

ALICE S. ROSSI, "Sex Equality: The Beginnings of Ideology." This article first appeared in *The Humanist*, vol. 29 (September/October 1969), pp. 3–6, 16, and is reprinted by permission of the author and the journal. "Women in Science: Why So Few?" Reprinted by permission of the author and the journal from *Science*, vol. 148 (May 28, 1965), pp. 1196–1202. Copyright 1965 by the American Association for the Advancement of Science.

CONSTANTINA SAFILIOS-ROTHSCHILD, " 'Honor' Crimes in Contemporary Greece." Reprinted by permission of *The British Journal of Sociology*, vol. 20, no. 2 (June 1969), pp. 205–218.

JAMES J. WHITE, "Women in the Law." Reprinted in abridged form by permission of the author and the Michigan Law Review Association from the *Michigan Law Review*, vol. 65, no. 6 (April 1967), pp. 1051–1122.

MARTHA S. WHITE, "Psychological and Social Barriers to Women in Science." Reprinted by permission of the author and the journal from *Science*, vol. 170 (October 23, 1970), pp. 413–416. Copyright 1970 by the American Association for the Advancement of Science.

Contents

CHAPTER 3 Money, Sex and Women

CHAPTER 4 The Options of Women

CHAPTER 5 On Combining a "Deviant" and a Conventional Option

CHAPTER 6 Women in "Deviant" Occupations

CHAPTER 7 Projections About the Women's Liberation Movement and the Future of Men and Women

The Making of Men and Women

DIANA W. WARSHAY

Sex Differences in Language Style*

This study examines sex differences in language style as an example of the general behavioral differences found between the sexes. Male and female are here seen as social statuses for which differing value systems are prescribed and which require different behavioral orientations for their occupants. Language as socially conditioned organized behavior should be consonant in style with other behaviors expected from the occupants of a particular status and reflective of cultural values prescribed for that status. Using a traditional distinction that has also been theoretically extended and empirically supported by studies of sex differences, this study expects men to be more likely to use an instrumental language style and women an affective language style.

The Instrumental-Affective Dimension

Summaries of studies of sex differences have shown males to be more aggressive and domineering (Anastasi and Foley 1949, pp. 671–672), in expectation as well as in actuality (Kagan 1964, p. 139), to see the world as a hostile environment requiring the developing of weapons and skills so as to tear success and reward from it (Bennett and Cohen 1959, pp. 139, 148), and thus to stress achievement and independence needs (Douvan and Adelson 1966, pp. 494–495). Females differ from males by having a more social orientation (Anastasi and Foley, op. cit.), being more concerned with development of their interpersonal skills, having a greater need for love (Douvan and Adelson, op. cit.), and showing a preoccupation with people and harmonious interpersonal relations coupled with greater dependency, conformity, and a greater emphasis on caring for and relating to others (Kagan, op. cit.). Feeling themselves to be generally helpless, timid, and the weaker of the two sexes, women see the world as relatively benevolent and manageable by greater dependency and gregariousness, and they view success as achievable through love and luck, without independent effort (Bennett and Cohen, op. cit., pp. 125, 130, 148).

The previous statements imply an active and instrumental attitude on the part of the male that is related to his view of the world as something requiring conquest or manipulation by means of competitive skills and resources. The

---

* This article incorporates portions of papers read at the 1971 annual meetings of the Southwestern Sociological Association and the Ohio Valley Sociological Society.

female, by comparison, tends to a passive and affective attitude that is related to her view of the world as requiring placating and cultivation through nurturance and cooperation.

In relations between the sexes, it is the male who initiates activity, is deferred to, has his interests as primary, and can act directly to further them. The female keeps herself responsive to the male (Douvan and Gold 1966, p. 525), is sensitive to his needs and wants, puts her own interests second, and uses indirection in the gaining of her own ends.

In 1951, Talcott Parsons distinguished between instrumental and expressive aspects of social action. Instrumental social action is consciously planned behavior that is directed toward the achievement of a goal. Expressive social action, by contrast, is oriented toward the emotional gratification that may be a concomitant of behavior (Parsons 1951, pp. 48–49). Later, Parsons characterized the husband's status within the family as fulfilling an instrumental function, that of adaptation (i.e., responding to exigencies outside the family such as making a living), and the wife's family status as fulfilling a consummatory function, that of integration within the family (i.e., dealing with internal problems such as keeping the family cohesive and efficiently run) (Parsons 1959, pp. 6–7; 1964, pp. 48–49). This age-old distinction between action and emotion, usually attached to male-female differences, also appears in the works of many classical writers, such as Comte, Toennies, and Durkheim, as well as in those of contemporary sociologists.

Cultural Expectations for Sex Statuses

Equality, achievement, and individualism have been regarded as the predominant American values since colonial times (Lipset 1963, p. 101). Robin Williams has a similar description of major American values as centered around the idea of the responsible individual whose accomplishments result from his own initiative and industry and whose achievements are judged by the same standards as are those of everyone else. However, Williams also finds alternate themes to the major American values of individualism, instrumentalism, and universalism. These alternate themes in American society are organized around the idea of status—who one is carries more importance than what one has accomplished. They also contain a particularistic ethic with a closed world view that emphasizes group identity, traditionalism, contemplation, affect, and the passive acceptance of experience (Williams 1970, pp. 501–502). However, these alternate themes do not comprise a coherent system. Rather, they represent either deviance from or adjustments to particular social roles and situations (Williams, *op. cit.*, p. 575). Apparently, to Williams, there is but one coherent value system in American society, alternates to it being situational adjustments.

In contrast, the foregoing alternate themes in American society are seen by Florence Kluckhohn as forming a coherent value system, albeit a variant of the dominant one. Kluckhohn pictures the dominant American value system very much the way Williams does. In her view, the dominant American value orientations are an emphasis upon the future, autonomy, individualistic achievement externally evaluated, and an instrumental mode of behavior capable of overcoming obstacles (Kluckhohn 1955, pp. 347–352). Further, Kluckhohn sees the dominant American value system as prescribed only for those of higher rank within American society—for example, only for American males. For females and others of lower status in American society, the variant system of value orientations is the appropriate one. This variant value system prescribes collaterality in social relations (i.e., one's loyalties and duties are to one's kin), a "being-in-becoming" mode of activity (that is, an emphasis on existence rather than on action), harmony with the world, and a present time orientation. That is, the goals and welfare of the laterally expanded group rather than of the individual are prime, emphasis is on self-realization through acceptance of existence, and there is a concern for what the individual is and not for what he can accomplish (Kluckhohn, op. cit., pp. 350–352).

Thus, not only do male-female differences in behavioral style result from situational differences (role behavior) but this difference is buttressed and legitimized by more general cultural value orientations applicable to the two sexes (status behavior). Men and women are therefore occupants of different sex statuses with differential rank, these differences being supported by differing cultural expectations that not only legitimize differential behavior for occupants of adult sex statuses but also supply differential cultural expectations for adolescents and children.

The Study

The present study is focused on instrumental and affective language attached to sex status rather than to more situationally specific role behavior. That is, it was not intended to measure speech as used in interaction with others but to see, instead, how one uses language (i.e., writes) when more or less free from the requirements of a particular social situation. A setting maximizing the language peculiarities of each subject and, consequently, reflecting his past experiences was wanted.

Hence, a comparatively anonymous setting was used, large university classes during the first week of an academic year. Then, a reasonably unstructured instrument devised by the investigator for the collection of language samples was administered. This was the Important Events Test (IET), which asks the subject to write down all the events in the past important to him.

The lack of structure in the IET enables language to be emitted relatively spontaneously, thereby increasing its representativeness as language relevant to social status. Furthermore, the focus of the test on past events detaches the subject from the present role situation. Thus, the IET, by transcending the testing situation, should enable generalization beyond particular role interactions to social status.

The language samples for this study were obtained from 263 subjects who were middle-class, white, native-born students at a large midwestern state university. The data from these subjects were grouped for statistical purposes not only by sex, but also by age (under twenty, and twenty and over), previous research indicating that age may be a significant factor (cf. Lawton 1963, pp. 123–133).

The language samples elicited by the IET consisted of 3311 separate events, which were analyzed using categories derived from the descriptions of dominant (or major) and variant (or alternate) value orientations as set forth by Kluckhohn and by Williams. In devising these variables, the aim was to deal with language from the standpoint of grammar as well as from the more usual approaches of content analysis and word count. The individual variables and their rationales are discussed in the following section, along with the findings in this study.

The Findings

1. *Active versus passive orientation.* The form of reference to the event, that is, whether the event is signified by a verb form or a noun, should be indicative of an active or a passive orientation, respectively.

Charles W. Morris's description of the value dimensions of the stages of an act has a linguistic change associated with moving from the manipulatory stage of action (having dominance as its value) to the consummatory stage (which has dependence as its value). In describing this movement, Morris's word use changes from verb to noun (1964, p. 23). In value orientation terms, signifying an event by a verb would imply Williams's "active mastery" and Kluckhohn's "doing" orientation; by contrast, use of a noun would imply Williams's "passive acceptance" and Kluckhohn's "being" orientation. American males would be expected to use more predicate verbs or gerunds (e.g., "graduated," "graduating"), whereas women would be expected to use relatively more nouns (e.g., "graduation").

In the samples studied, males used a significantly higher proportion of verb forms to signify an event than did females. This was true of both older and younger samples. (See Item 1 in Data Table 1.)

2. *Individualism versus collaterality.* Inclusion of personal happenings (e.g., "when I graduated," "my graduation") and emphasis upon one's involvement in the events (e.g., "Sister's wedding was important to me," "when I heard of Kennedy's assassination") imply individualism both in the sense of interest in oneself and one's achievements, and in the focus upon "individual personality rather than group identity and responsibility" (Williams, *op. cit.*, p. 502). Hence, American males would be expected to give more individualistic references. In contrast, references to others generally as well as to those with whom one usually interacts (e.g., "brother's wedding," "fishing with Jim") imply collaterality. A higher proportion of these references would be expected from American females.

Reflecting an individualistic orientation, the older males in this study, as compared with the older females, had significantly higher proportions of their total events located in the Personal Sphere than in the Interacting Community; they also displayed a significantly greater involvement in their events. The females leaned more toward a collateral orientation. While only the older females were significantly more likely to locate events in the Interacting Community than were older males, females at both age levels had significantly higher means for Numbers of "Others" Referenced than did males. (See Item 4 in Data Table 1.)

3. *Time orientation.* The dominant value system prescribed for American

males embodies in its instrumentalism a future time orientation with a concomitant de-emphasis upon the past. In the present study, two opposing bases for prediction existed. On the one hand, males should make fewer time references, since the IET asked them to focus on past events; on the other hand, to the degree that the respondent "transported" himself to the past to "act out" the event in memory, it was now for him in the present. Further, the tendency to focus on time is a characteristic of modernism and hence should be more characteristic of males since stereotypically men are expected to be more modern than women.

The results generally supported the connection between Total Time References and maleness, though they were statistically significant only for the younger samples. (See Item 5 in Data Table 1.)

Further analysis of time references was made by dividing Total Time References into three types: Date, Dated, and Vague. *Date* refers to time itself as an event (e.g., "December 25, 1965," "seventeenth birthday," "year in the army"). *Dated* refers to the specific placing of the event in time or to the

Data Table 1   Results on Important Events Test by Sex-Age Category

Item	Older Males (N = 60)	Older Females (N = 66)	Younger Males (N = 32)	Younger Females (N = 105)
1.	Ratio of Verb to Noun Form of Reference to Event:			
	2.4	1.3*	2.7	1.9*
2.	Ratio of Personal Sphere to Interacting Community Events:			
	25.1	6.6*	13.1	9.3
3.	Percentage of Total Events Showing Involvement:			
	91.0	80.8*	84.8	83.3
4.	Mean Number of "Others" Referenced:			
	5.8	8.4*	5.0	9.2*
5.	Percentage of Total Events with a Time Reference:			
	24.6	22.1	29.4	23.1*.
6.	"Date" Percentage of Total Time References:			
	13.3	19.0	9.2	20.4*
7.	"Dated" Percentage of Total Time References:			
	67.7	71.5	58.6	49.6
8.	"Vague" Percentage of Total Time References:			
	19.0	9.5*	32.2	30.1*
9.	Mean Number of Words:			
	85.8	96.3*	71.9	98.6*
10.	Mean Number of Events:			
	10.7	13.7*	9.2	14.0*
11.	Mean Response Rate (words/event/subject):			
	9.9	8.4	9.3	8.9

* Indicates $p < .05$, two-tailed. Significance tests based upon chi-square except for Items 4, 9, 10, and 11 where critical ratios were used. All comparisons are between males and females of the same age grouping. Hence, asterisks appear only in the second column (to indicate a significant difference between older males and females) and in the fourth column (to indicate a significant difference between younger males and females).

clear indication of its duration (e.g., "June 23, 1964, the day I was married," "living with a French family for six weeks last summer"). Finally, *Vague* refers to a vague or nonspecific indication of time location or duration (e.g., "when I met Jim," "every time my friends get together"). Male instrumentalism should militate against seeing time as an event in itself (Date), for the accomplishing of an act is what is rewarded, not the experiencing of it. Hence, male instrumentality should lean, more than would female affectivity, toward dating events (Dated) and perhaps even toward making nonspecific (Vague) time references.

The results give some support to the above. As expected, females gave a higher proportion of Date references than did males, and males had a higher proportion of Vague references than did females. However, in the case of Dated references, only the younger males gave a higher proportion than the younger females. (See Items 6, 7, and 8 in Data Table 1.)

4. *Fluency.* Instrumentalism in behavior implies an efficient use of resources and a conserving of them for maximum future use instead of an expenditure of them in present (consummatory) gratification. Affectivity, on the contrary, implies greater immediate, direct gratification. When it comes to language, one would expect males, who are more instrumental, activist, and future-oriented, to be conserving of words and sentences and to use them as they would tools. In contrast to males, females would be expected to be more fluent in words and in sentences, being more inclined to use them for direct gratification and as substitutes for unavailable gratifying action. This reasoning therefore became the basis for expecting the females to write more events and more words than the males.

The results upheld the predictions, in that both the older and the younger female samples wrote significantly higher mean numbers of events and of words than did the older and younger males, respectively. These findings are given greater weight since there was no significant difference in the mean length of event (i.e., the number of words per event per subject) between the sexes. Furthermore, given the fact that females wrote more events, one might have expected them to write fewer words per event; the lack of significant male-female differences in length of event thereby attests all the more to the females' greater fluency. (See Items 9, 10, and 11 in Data Table 1.)

Summary and Conclusion

In short, males tended to write with less fluency, to refer to the events in a verb phrase, to be time-oriented (in a particularly vague manner), to involve themselves more in their references to the events, to locate the event in their personal sphere of activity, and to refer less to others. Thus, the male is shown to be more active, more ego-involved in what he does, and less concerned about others. His achievements are personal, underscoring and rewarding his individuality.

Females, in contrast to males, were more fluent, referred to events in a noun phrase, were less time-oriented (except where the date was the event), and tended to be less involved in their event references, to locate the event in their Interacting Community, and to refer more to others. The female adult thus exhibits concern with "being." Blocked or largely excluded from public achievement, she seeks satisfaction in primary relations and in the local community.

The previously discussed results, deriving from the present study of male-female language-style differences, support the picture of men and women yielded by the many earlier studies of overt and covert behavior.

References

ANASTASI, A., and FOLEY, J. P., JR. *Differential Psychology*. New York: The Macmillan Company, 1949.

BENNETT, E. M., and COHEN, L. R. "Men and Women: Personality Patterns and Contrasts." *Genetic Psychology Monographs* 59 (1959): 100–153.

DOUVAN, E., and ADELSON, J. *The Adolescent Experience*. New York: John Wiley & Sons, 1966.

DOUVAN, E., and GOLD, M. "Modal Patterns in American Adolescence." In *Review of Child Development Research*, edited by L. W. Hoffman and M. L. Hoffman, vol. 2, pp. 469–528. New York: Russell Sage, 1966.

KAGAN, J. "Acquisition and Significance of Sex Typing and Sex Role Identity." In *Review of Child Development Research*, edited by M. L. Hoffman and L. W. Hoffman, vol. 1, pp. 137–168. New York: Russell Sage, 1964.

KLUCKHOHN, F. "Dominant and Variant Value Orientations." In *Personality in Nature, Society, and Culture*, edited by C. Kluckhohn and H. A. Murray. 2nd ed., pp. 342–357. New York: Alfred A. Knopf, 1955.

LAWTON, D. "Social Class Differences in Language Development: A Study of Some Samples of Written Work." *Language and Speech* 6 (1963) (part 3): 120–143.

LIPSET, S. M. *The First New Nation*. New York: Basic Books, 1963.

MORRIS, C. W. *Signification and Significance*. Cambridge, Mass.: M.I.T. Press, 1964.

PARSONS, T. *The Social System*. Glencoe, Ill.: The Free Press, 1951.

———. "General Theory in Sociology." In *Sociology Today*, edited by R. K. Merton, L. Broom, and L. S. Cottrell, Jr., pp. 3–38. New York: Basic Books, 1959.

———. *Social Structure and Personality*. New York: Free Press, 1964.

WILLIAMS, R. *American Society*. 3rd ed. New York: Alfred A. Knopf, 1970.

PHILIP GOLDBERG

Are Women Prejudiced Against Women?

"Woman," advised Aristotle, "may be said to be an inferior man."

Because he was a man, Aristotle was probably biased. But what do women themselves think? Do they, consciously or unconsciously, consider their own sex inferior? And if so, does this belief prejudice them against other women —that is, make them view women, simply because they *are* women, as less competent than men?

According to a study conducted by myself and my associates, the answer to both questions is Yes. Women *do* consider their own sex inferior. And even when the facts give no support to this belief, they will persist in downgrading the competence—in particular, the intellectual and professional competence —of their fellow females.

Over the years, psychologists and psychiatrists have shown that both sexes consistently value men more highly than women. Characteristics considered male are usually praised; those considered female are usually criticized. In 1957 A. C. Sheriffs and J. P. McKee noted that "women are regarded as guilty of snobbery and irrational and unpleasant emotionality." Consistent with this report, E. G. French and G. S. Lesser found in 1964 that "women who value intellectual attainment feel they must reject the woman's role"—intellectual accomplishment apparently being considered, even among intellectual women, a masculine preserve. In addition, ardent feminists like Simone de Beauvoir and Betty Friedan believe that men, in important ways, are superior to women.

Now, is this belief simply prejudice, or are the characteristics and achievements of women really inferior to those of men? In answering this question, we need to draw some careful distinctions.

Different or Inferior?

Most important, we need to recognize that there are two distinct dimensions to the issue of sex differences. The first question is whether sex differences exist at all, apart from the obvious physical ones. The answer to this question seems to be a unanimous Yes—men, women, and social scientists agree that, psychologically and emotionally as well as physically, women *are* different from men.

But is being different the same as being inferior? It is quite possible to perceive a difference accurately but to value it inaccurately. Do women automatically view their differences from men as *deficiencies?* The evidence is that they do, and that this value judgment opens the door to anti-female prejudice. For if someone (male or female) concludes that women are inferior, his perceptions of women—their personalities, behavior, abilities, and accomplishments—will tend to be colored by his low expectations of women.

As Gordon W. Allport has pointed out in the *Nature of Prejudice,* whatever the facts about sex differences, anti-feminism—like any other prejudice—*distorts perception and experience.* What defines anti-feminism is not so much believing that women are inferior, as allowing that belief to distort one's perceptions of women. More generally, it is not the partiality itself, but the distortion born of that partiality, that defines prejudice.

Thus, an anti-Semite watching a Jew may see devious or sneaky behavior. But, in a Christian, he would regard such behavior only as quiet, reserved, or perhaps even shy. Prejudice is self-sustaining: it continually distorts the "evidence" on which the prejudiced person claims to base his beliefs. Allport makes it clear that anti-feminism, like anti-Semitism or any other prejudice, consistently twists the "evidence" of experience. We see not what is there, but what we *expect* to see.

The purpose of our study was to investigate whether there is real prejudice by women against women—whether perception itself is distorted unfavorably. Specifically, will women evaluate a professional article with a jaundiced eye when they think it is the work of a woman, but praise the same article when they think its author is a man? Our hypotheses were:

1. Even when the work is identical, women value the professional work of men more highly than that of women.
2. But when the professional field happens to be one traditionally reserved for women (nursing, dietetics), this tendency will be reversed, or at least greatly diminished.

Some 140 college girls, selected at random, were our subjects. One hundred were used for the preliminary work; 40 participated in the experiment proper.

To test the second hypothesis, we gave the 100 girls a list of fifty occupations and asked them to rate "the degree to which you associate the field with men or women." We found that law and city planning were fields strongly associated with men, elementary-school teaching and dietetics were fields strongly associated with women, and two fields—linguistics and art history—were chosen as neutrals, not strongly associated with either sex.

Now we were ready for the main experiment. From the professional literature of each of these six fields, we took one article. The articles were edited and abridged to about 1500 words, then combined into two equal sets of booklets. The crucial manipulation had to do with the authors' names—the same article bore a male name in one set of booklets, a female name in the other set. An example: if, in set one, the first article bore the name John T. McKay, in set two the same article would appear under the name Joan T. McKay. Each booklet contained three articles by "men" and three articles by "women."

The girls, seated together in a large lecture hall, were told to read the articles in their booklets and given these instructions: "In this booklet you will find excerpts of six articles, written by six different authors in six different professional fields. At the end of each article you will find several questions. . . . You are not presumed to be sophisticated or knowledgeable in all the fields. We are interested in the ability of college students to make critical evaluations. . . ." Note that no mention at all was made of the authors' sexes. That information was contained—apparently only by coincidence—in the authors' names. The girls could not know, therefore, what we were really looking for.

At the end of each article were nine questions asking the girls to rate the articles for value, persuasiveness, and profundity—and to rate the authors for writing style, professional competence, professional status, and ability to sway the reader. On each item, the girls gave a rating of from 1 (highly favorable) to 5 (highly unfavorable).

Generally, the results were in line with our expectations—but not completely. In analyzing these results, we used three different methods: We compared the amount of anti-female bias in the different occupational fields (would men be rated as better city planners, but women as better dieticians?); we compared the amount of bias shown on the nine questions that followed each article (would men be rated as more competent, but women as more persuasive?); and we ran an overall comparison including both fields and rating questions.

Starting with the analysis of bias by occupational fields, we immediately ran into a major surprise. (See box below.) That there is a general bias by women against women, and that it is strongest in traditionally masculine fields, was clearly borne out. But in other fields, the situation seemed rather confused. We had expected the anti-female trend to be reversed in traditionally feminine fields. But it appears that, even here, women consider themselves inferior to men. Women seem to think that men are better at *everything*—including elementary-school teaching and dietetics!

Law: A Strong Masculine Preserve

These are the total scores the college girls gave to the six pairs of articles they read. The lowest possible score—9—would be the most favorable; the highest possible score—54—the most critical. While male authors received more favorable ratings in all occupational fields, the differences were statistically significant only in city planning, linguistics, and—especially—law.

Field of Article	MEAN	
	Male	Female
Art history	23.35	23.10
Dietetics	22.05	23.45
Education	20.20	21.75
City planning	23.10	27.30
Linguistics	26.95	30.70
Law	21.20	25.60

Scrutiny of the nine rating questions yielded similar results. On all nine questions, regardless of the author's occupational field, the girls consistently found an article more valuable—and its author more competent—when the article bore a male name. Though the articles themselves were exactly the same, the girls felt that those written by the John T. McKays were definitely more impressive, and reflected more glory on their authors, than did the mediocre offerings of the Joan T. McKays. Perhaps because the world has accepted female authors for a long time, the girls were willing to concede that the female professionals' writing styles were not *far* inferior to those of the men. But such a concession to female competence was rare indeed.

Statistical analysis confirms these impressions and makes them more definite. With a total of 6 articles, and with 9 questions after each one, there were 54 points at which comparisons could be drawn between the male authors and the female authors. Out of these 54 comparisons, 3 were tied, 7 favored the female authors, and the number favoring the male authors was 44!

Clearly, there is a tendency among women to downgrade the work of professionals of their own sex. But the hypothesis that this tendency would decrease as the "femaleness" of the professional field increased was not supported. Even in traditionally female fields, anti-feminism holds sway.

Since the articles supposedly written by men were exactly the same as those supposedly written by women, the perception that the men's articles were superior was obviously a distortion. For reasons of their own, the female subjects were sensitive to the sex of the author, and this apparently irrelevant information biased their judgments. Both the distortion and the sensitivity that precedes it are characteristic of prejudice. Women—at least these young college women—are prejudiced against female professionals and, regardless of the actual accomplishments of these professionals, will firmly refuse to recognize them as the equals of their male colleagues.

Is the intellectual double-standard really dead? Not at all—and if the college girls in this study are typical of the educated and presumably progressive segments of the population, it may not even be dying. Whatever lip service these girls pay to modern ideas of equality between men and women, their beliefs are staunchly traditional. Their real coach in the battle of the sexes is not Simone de Beauvoir or Betty Friedan. Their coach is Aristotle.

Is the Grass Greener on the Other Side?

The first role a person acquires in any society is a sex role. This role is ascribed, in that infants are not free to choose one sex role over the other, and is considered a basic role, in that it limits and determines other roles that the individual may achieve (Banton 1965). From the time the pink or blue blanket is placed on the newborn baby, he begins to receive differential attention and reinforcement from others in his environment. As he matures, these reinforcements gradually shape an individual's behavior into the appropriate sex role as defined by society. Little boys are expected to engage in behaviors labeled masculine which train them for male adult roles, while little girls are expected to display feminine characteristics aligned with adult female roles.

Societies tend to assume innate differences, beyond the biological, between the sexes as a way of legitimating differential behavioral expectations for women and men. However, in contemporary American society, and to some extent in other parts of the world, the traditional roles of men and women are being called into question, largely by the individuals who are experiencing frustrations, anxieties, and pressures with present sex-role definitions. In particular, the Women's Liberation Movement, which has been a vanguard in this area, has pointed out that the male role in society is the more dominant and prestigious. The structure of present-day society creates a high status for being male and, as a residual effect, a low status for being female. Many of the efforts of the women's movement are directed at opening the more prestigious roles to women or at least at creating a structure in which prestigious roles are considered as a viable alternative for women as well as for men. The demands being made by women focus very heavily on the advantages of the male role. However, it is reasonable to assume that there are certain negative aspects associated with the male role. In response to these, small numbers of men have begun to express dissatisfaction with the traditional male role and to join in the attempt to change sex-role definitions.

In this paper we shall explore, in light of these challenges to traditional role definitions, the extent to which each sex perceives the advantages and disadvantages of the opposite sex roles. The answer to this question should have serious implications for orientations to change. There are several possible findings. To the extent that individuals are dissatisfied with their own sex role, they may have a tendency to focus more heavily on the advantages than on the disadvantages of the role which they are restricted from occupying. This would indicate an interest by both sexes in role reversal. However, to the extent that women are correct in asserting the dominance or superior prestige of the male role, we may find that they are disproportionately aware of the advantages which accrue to males, while males are disproportionately aware of the disadvantages which accrue to females. Such a finding would indicate general agreement that the male role is more advantageous, in addition to agreement on the desirability of any given characteristic for all individuals regardless of sex. This would suggest that the female role should move closer to the traditional male role. A third possible finding is that each sex, believing in the superior advantages of its own role, will assign a disproportionate number of disadvantages relative to advantages to the opposite sex. This finding would indicate that both sexes would prefer to maintain the status quo in terms of role division. Lastly, when both the advantages and disadvantages of the opposite sex role are seen in approximately equal proportions, the appropriateness of sex as a role category can be questioned. The demand for equality as an orientation for change rests on the assumption that both men and women have something to gain by changing society's reliance on sex-role differentiation, i.e., members of each sex should be able to gain by fusing the advantages of both sex roles and discarding the disadvantages of each.

Design

Over the past two years we have had the opportunity in both social psychology and sex-role courses to gather information about students' evaluations of both sex roles. Opinions were gathered in five different courses from 250 students, representing an age range from 19 to 50 as well as a conglomeration of ethnic backgrounds and social classes. This paper will focus primarily on sex role as perceived by members of the opposite sex, in an attempt to gain insight into the questions raised above. Information on sex role as perceived by members of the same sex will be mentioned where appropriate.

Working in same-sex groups of five or six, students were asked to list as many advantages and disadvantages of the opposite sex role as possible, based on common cultural definitions of this role. In addition to shedding light on the questions we have raised, these data can help verify or disprove the generality of sex-role stereotypes. However, it should be kept in mind that although stereotypes exert an influence on the choice of behaviors in a situation (cf. Goffman 1959), the individuals polled may not assume normative sex-role definitions for themselves or others in any particular situation.

Presentation of Data

The simplest way to look at our observations is to compare the advantages listed for one sex with the disadvantages listed for the opposite sex. In the first half of Table 1, females' perceptions of the advantages of the male role are compared with males' perceptions of the disadvantages of the female role. In the second half of the table, males' perceptions of the advantages of the female role are compared with females' perceptions of the disadvantages of the male role. The information is organized so that advantages and disadvantages that center around different aspects of a similar characteristic are listed next to each other.°

° Cases where the commonality of a characteristic is not clear as the basis for pairing need further clarification. "Interaction taken seriously," a male advantage, is

In most cases, the relationship between the advantages for one sex compared with the disadvantages for the opposite sex is one of complementarity. Items which are listed as advantages for either sex generally have corresponding disadvantages for the opposite sex which take the form of an opposite characteristic or opposing quality of the same characteristic. The extent to which this relationship exists strongly suggests that there is general agreement on the desirable characteristics for any individual, regardless of sex.

In some cases, *opposite* characteristics were assigned to each sex as an advantage or to each as a disadvantage, suggesting disagreement between the sexes on the desirability of the characteristic. For example, an advantage for males is "able to take initiative" while an advantage for females is "don't have to initiate relationships." On the disadvantage side, "restrictions on taking initiative" is listed for the female role, while "risk of initiating relationships" is listed for the males. Taking these four characteristics together, the apparent disagreement vanishes: both sexes agree that an individual should have the opportunity to initiate relationships, but should not have sole responsibility for this behavior. Other apparent contradictions in the table resolve in a similar manner.

The most important insight suggested by Table 1 concerns the relative desirability of the male and female roles. Women see more advantages than

Table 1 Perceptions of the Advantages and Disadvantages of Opposite Sex Roles

Advantages of the Male Role (as seen by females)	Disadvantages of the Female Role (as seen by males)
Higher pay	Low pay
Greater educational opportunity	Less educational opportunity
No domestic work	Domestic responsibilities
Power and decision making	Deprived of authority positions
Less responsibility for children	Time spent raising children
Independence	Dependence
Interaction taken seriously	Ideas seen as emotional
Mobility	Restricted mobility
Able to take initiative	Restrictions on taking initiative
Less emphasis on appearance	Emphasis on physical appearance

paired with the female disadvantage of "ideas seen as emotional," since both refer to an underlying rational–emotional continuum. Another male advantage, "women build up ego," is paired with the female disadvantage, "weak ego identity," because it seems likely that weak egos in women can be seen in part as a consequence of the nonreciprocity of ego-flattering behavior. Lastly, the female advantage, "protected by men," is paired with the male disadvantage, "trying to keep women happy," because the latter is seen as one form of protection men give women.

Table 1 (Cont.)

Advantages of the Male Role (as seen by females)	Disadvantages of the Female Role (as seen by males)
Opportunity for self-actualization	Lack of opportunity for self-actualization
Not seen as a sex object	Seen as a sex object
Sexual freedom	Sexual restrictions
Women build up ego	Weak ego identity
Occupational choice	(Limited occupational choice) *
Dominance	(Expected not to be dominant)
Aggressiveness	(Expected not to be aggressive)
Less pressure to marry	(Pressure to marry)
Free of birth-control responsibility	(Responsible for birth control)
	Pressure to give up career
	Act like a lady

Advantages of Female Role (as seen by males)	Disadvantages of the Male Role (as seen by females)
Freedom from the draft	Draft
Less pressure to work	Pressure to work
No financial responsibility	Financial responsibility
Flexible workday	Inflexible workday
Free to express emotions	Emotional suppression
Don't have to initiate relationships	Risk of initiating relationships
Sexual passivity	Sexual performance pressure
No responsibility for use of power	Responsiblity for use of power
Protected by men	Trying to keep women happy
Less pressure to be dominant	(Pressure to be dominant)
Dates paid for	(Cost of paying for dates)
Influence on children	(Little influence on children)
	Forced competition
	Have to prove masculinity

* In cases in which the opposite sex did not state a corresponding disadvantage, we have inferred what it might be and listed it in parentheses. Fortunately, we have information from individuals as to the aspects of their own roles which bother them personally. In each case, the inferred disadvantage is actually listed by individuals as a negative aspect of their own role.

disadvantages for the male role, while men see more disadvantages than advantages for the female role. Although these findings must be interpreted with caution, since no attempt has been made to insure that the items listed for each sex are of equal generality and weight, it would appear that both sexes perceive women as getting the worst end of the division of sex-role expectations. This relationship tends to be confirmed by individual data collected separately. Students were asked to list the disadvantages which they personally experienced in their sex role. Women listed an average of 30 percent more disadvantages than did men.

These findings tend to confirm the belief that the male role is seen as more prestigious and advantageous by both sexes, and would indicate that pressure for change in sex roles is likely to take the form of moving women's roles toward greater similarity with traditional male roles. This may partially explain why women have been more active in a movement for change than men. On the other hand, men listed a substantial number of advantages for the female role, while females listed a sizable number of disadvantages for the male role. This fact indicates that although there may be less pressure on males for role change, males do have something to gain potentially from a redefinition of their role.

Emphasis on Sex Identity

Two items that appear in Table 1 deserve further comment. "Have to prove masculinity" and "act like a lady," while both listed as disadvantages for the appropriate sex, differ from the other items in their level of generality with respect to behavioral choices. These characteristics can be seen as emphasizing the process of gaining a sex identity. Despite the fact that the dichotomous nature of sex as a characteristic creates the impression that sex is extremely concrete in definition, establishing and maintaining a sex identity is a complex process for most individuals. To the extent that biological differences are used as the bases for categorization, the definition is concrete. Thus, by the time a child is five or six, he is fairly confident of which sex he is (Kohlberg 1966). However at adolescence and in adulthood, the emphasis shifts from the biological fact of sex to the sex role as a source of identity for the individual. When the society adheres to a strict sex-role definition based on cultural stereotypes, it creates the assumption that males and females are very different beings beyond basic biological differences, and it provides positive social sanctions for behaviors which conform to the role and negative sanctions for behaviors which do not. Through this differential reinforcement process, both males and females come to have a fairly clear understanding of what is expected of them in their sex role. However, since it is impossible for any individual to conform completely to the cultural stereotypes, an awareness of the tendency to have some characteristics or behaviors of the opposite sex is a threat to the individual's confidence in his own sex identity. The fear and anxiety that many individuals experience with respect to their perception of their sex identity is coupled with the strong desire to have others perceive them as members of their appropriate sex category. This creates pressure on an individual to conform to the cultural stereotypes even in those respects in which his personality is incongruent with the social expectations.

In addition, this pressure is magnified by the fact that most of the expectations for both sexes are very general qualities, which leave the individual unclear as to the point at which he has adequately demonstrated his adherence to the expectations. For example, if males are expected to be independent, in what way can an individual man prove that he is truly independent? To the extent that he feels or exhibits *any* dependence (and all people do), he may feel that he is not living up to the expectation of his role, and may begin to question his masculinity. On the other hand, a woman who exhibits independence in any area may begin to see herself (and be seen by others) as less than ideally feminine. In this way, the conversion of biological characteristics to associated role expectations leaves individuals in a perpetual state of ambiguity about their sex identity.

A more specific example of these pressures on identity is found in the fact that "dominance" was listed as an advantage for males, while "less pressure to be dominant" was an advantage of the female role. One advantage of dominance, for men, is that it can be seen as helpful in establishing a male sex identity. However, males who are continually unsure of having established a strong sex identity will be under constant pressure to assert dominance. This type of pressure reduces some of the otherwise advantageous aspects of the characteristic; therefore, males see "less pressure to be dominant" as an advantage for females.

Rights, Obligations, and Proscriptions

We may take the data from Table 1 and categorize them in another way to further understand the nature of sex-role divisions. Sales and Gleason (1968) have pointed out that roles consist of rights, obligations, and proscriptions for the behavior of the role occupant. Rights are differentiated from obligations and proscriptions in that there are no punishments associated with behavioral choices. Rights allow the individual the freedom to commit an act or refrain from an act without receiving sanctions for either choice. For example, the advantage of "mobility" listed for males may be seen as a right: men are given the freedom to be mobile; at the same time they are not punished if they choose not to be mobile. While obligations and proscriptions both involve negative social sanctions, they differ in the way behavior is emphasized. Obligations involve pressures to commit an act, whereas proscriptions involve pressures to refrain from an act. In both cases, punishments in the form of negative social sanctions result from failure to comply with the appropriate pressures. The domestic responsibility of women can be seen as an obligation, while the expression of emotions for men is a proscription.

On the surface, the advantages of a sex role can be seen as rights, while the disadvantages can be seen in terms of obligations and proscriptions. This makes sense intuitively, since advantages should not involve social sanctions, while disadvantages should involve something negative such as punishments. While it is possible to categorize all of the disadvantages listed for both sex roles in terms of obligations and proscriptions, the designation of rights for all advantages is somewhat misleading. In many cases what can be perceived as a right is actually an obligation or proscription of the role. For example, men have the right to be independent; however, men who are not independent tend to be punished by disapproval. Therefore, independence is an obligation of the male sex role rather than a right. In a similar way, "less responsibility for children," which is listed as an advantage, can be interpreted as a proscription rather than a right of the male sex role since there are pressures for men to refrain from taking responsibility for child care, even on the part of their wives.*

Certain items listed as advantages cannot be seen in terms of any of the above categories. Therefore, in addition to rights, obligations, and proscriptions, we have devised a fourth category which is labeled "structural benefits."

Table 2 *Advantages and Disadvantages of Female and Male Roles by Category*

ADVANTAGES	
Female	Male
	Rights
	Mobility
	Less emphasis on appearance
	Opportunity for self-actualization
	Sexual freedom
	Less pressure to marry
	Free of birth-control responsibility
	Structural Benefits
Freedom from the draft	Higher pay
Flexible workday	Greater educational opportunity
Protected by men	Interaction taken seriously
Dates paid for	Not seen as a sex object
	Women build up ego
	Occupational choice
	Obligations
Free to express emotions	Power and decision making
Sexual passivity	Independence
Influence on children	Able to take initiative
	Dominance
	Aggressiveness
	Proscriptions
Less pressure to work	No domestic work
No financial responsibility	Less responsibility for children
Don't have to initiate relationships	
No responsibility for use of power	
Less pressure to be dominant	

---

* See Constantina Safilios-Rothschild, "Companionate Marriages and Sexual Inequality: Are They Compatible?" in Chapter 2 of this book.

Table 2 (Cont.)

DISADVANTAGES

Female	Male

Obligations

Female	Male
Domestic responsibilities	Draft
Time spent raising children	Pressure to work
Emphasis on physical appearance	Financial responsibility
Seen as a sex object	Risk of initiating relationships
Act like a lady	Sexual performance pressure
(Pressure to marry)	Responsibility for use of power
(Responsible for birth control)	Trying to keep women happy
	(Pressure to be dominant)
	(Cost of paying for dates)
	Forced competition
	Have to prove masculinity

Proscriptions

Female	Male
Low pay	Inflexible workday
Less educational opportunity	Emotional suppression
Deprived of authority positions	(Little influence on children)
Ideas seen as emotional	
Restricted mobility	
Restrictions on taking initiative	
Lack of opportunity for self-actualization	
Sexual restrictions	
Weak ego identity	
(Limited occupational choice)	
(Expected not to be dominant)	
(Expected not to be aggressive)	
Pressure to give up career	
Dependence	

The items in this category refer not to behavioral expectations for role occupants but rather to advantages derived from the social structure or from actions of others. "Higher pay" for men and "freedom from the draft" for women are examples of the former type, while the male advantage "not seen as a sex object" and the female advantage "protected by men" are examples of the latter. Structural benefits which are listed as an advantage for one sex tend to create either obligations or proscriptions for the opposite sex. For example, freedom from the draft is a structural benefit for women, while the draft is an obligation for men.

Table 2 presents each advantage and disadvantage listed in the previous table in terms of whether it is a right, structural benefit, obligation, or proscription.

The most striking feature of the table is that men have six rights while women have none. Since a right provides behavioral alternatives, it appears that men have more freedom than women. It should be remembered at this point, however, that we are working with cultural role expectations rather than with actual behaviors or with expectations in a given situation and that most individuals have more leeway in their actual role behaviors (that is, more rights) than the cultural role expectations customarily grant. The data discussed thus far do not shed light on who has more freedom in actual practice. However, when asked about obligations or proscriptions of their roles which actually bother them, women in our classes indicate that they feel more constrained in practice than do men.

If we examine this table further, it becomes clear that the female role is characterized heavily by proscriptions in both advantages and disadvantages, while the male role is characterized heavily by obligations. This suggests that the male role consists largely of action, while the female role consists largely of refraining from action. This may be the origin of the idea that men are active while women are passive, a key dimension of the sex-role stereotype in our society. It is also a part of what Simone de Beauvoir (1953) meant when she pointed out that the role of woman is to be "the other." Men and their activities are defined; women are simply counterposed to this definition—they are "other than men." Apparently this is still the case, since most of the advantages listed for females are seen as either proscriptions or structural benefits. In the former case, women are prevented from doing things which men are obliged to do, while in the latter, women are put into the role of passive recipients.

The fact that women are defined largely in terms of what they should not do or be does not necessarily mean that they are at a greater disadvantage than men. For one of the things which has become clear through our classes is that men suffer considerably from the continual pressure on them to live up to the obligations of the male role. This fact, that male roles are characterized by obligations, indicates that men are under greater pressure than are women. The reason for this is that these obligations create the male identity. Therefore, a male is under pressure to live up to his obligations in order to prove his masculinity to himself and to others. Proscriptions also are related to identity formation. They are tied into the fear of losing an appropriate sex identity by suggesting ways of avoiding behaviors that are used by the opposite sex to achieve an identity. Since the female role is composed most heavily of proscriptions, the chief identity pressure on a woman is on not losing a feminine identity by inappropriate action. For the man, however, the pressures of obligations operate to force him continually to attempt to gain a masculine identity by attempting to meet these expectations.

Implications

These findings have several implications for social change. As has been pointed out, the data strongly indicate that the male role is seen by both sexes as being more advantageous and having more freedom than the female role, leading to the conclusion that women will have more interest in change than will men. This is true despite the fact that there are disadvantages to the male role, especially in the pressures on men to act to achieve a masculine identity.

If pressures for changes in sex-role definitions succeed in opening up more leeway in the feminine role, women may find themselves in a relatively advantageous position, for by getting rid of the proscriptions of their role, they gain freedoms in areas which may still be regarded as obligatory for men. For example, as women win the freedom to work and earn money, these will be rights to the extent that there are no sanctions either for or against their working. Meanwhile, men may still retain the obligation to work and to be financially responsible for the family as a pressure to prove masculine identity. In fact, to the extent that women win freedoms in the areas in which men still retain obligations, the pressure on male identity may even be increased.

Since social trends appear to be moving in the direction of increasing freedom for women, it would seem that it is highly important that men begin to recognize the costs to them of pressures to demonstrate masculine identity by fulfilling the many obligations upon them. Men, too, have a vested interest in eliminating inequalities between the sexes and in abolishing sex-role stereotypes, thus increasing the freedom of both sexes.

References

BANTON, MICHAEL P. *Roles: An Introduction to the Study of Social Relations.* New York: Basic Books, 1965.

BEAUVOIR, SIMONE DE. *The Second Sex.* New York: Alfred A. Knopf, 1953.

GOFFMAN, ERVING. *Presentation of Self in Everyday Life.* Garden City, N.Y.: Doubleday & Co., 1959.

KOHLBERG, LAWRENCE. "A Cognitive-Developmental Analysis of Children's Sex-Role Concepts and Attitudes." In *The Development of Sex Differences,* edited by Eleanor Maccoby. Stanford, Cal.: Stanford University Press, 1966.

SALES, S. M., and GLEASON, T. C. "On Role Theory." Unpublished manuscript, University of Michigan, 1968.

...*Femininity is About as Ambiguous a Matter as Patriotism*...

I am a living American female, east of the Mississippi and a little bit east of the Hudson. I earn my own keep, as I have for some years, and relish among other things the company of men. When I don't have access to baritone voices, or countertenor ones anyway, I felt unhappy and incomplete, I believe that men and women define each other and most assuredly, in any number of ways, need each other. But it isn't easy, in these convulsive Aquarian times, being a woman among men. Or maybe I should say it isn't so easy being a *feminine* woman, which is something I always hope I am but sometimes I'm not.

"But how ridiculous!" a loyal friend protests. "Of course you're feminine. One doesn't wonder whether one is, one just *is.*" I envy her that certainty. It seems to me that femininity is about as ambiguous a matter as patriotism, now that women no more depend on men's brute force than men depend on women to weave, and now that our most banal cliché is "any more it's gettin' so you can't tell the girls from the boys."

It is getting that way, even for those of us too old or too reserved to wear "unisex" hair styles and clothes, even for those of us who have no yen whatever to switch genders. Femininity, that nebulous quality, can suggest simpering fluffiness, or funky bosomy earth mothers with soil from the garden under their nails, or madonnalike docility, or kohl-eyed vamps swinging their provocative hips and swinging in a more contemporary sense as well. A hint of what it means to me floated up from my subconscious in an unusually vivid dream I had a year or so ago. All there was in that dream was one big image: a large barn, like one drawn with a child's crayon, on which was superimposed a gigantic apple, both scaled to the same size.

I succumbed, in trying to puzzle the meaning, to the sort of Freudian glibness I normally deplore, and concluded that the dream's message to me, its audience, was YOU ARE A GIRL—a source of shelter (the barn), and nourishment (the apple), and supreme lack of logic (their juxtaposition). I think I had the dream because I needed reassurance of my own femininity.

By femininity I mean neither femaleness, which is a matter of plain biology, nor feminism, which is a matter of politics and which has many people confused these days. Feminism is a radical movement dedicated to finishing the work the early suffragettes began. I agree with some of its tenets. I agree that men shouldn't be paid more than women are to do exactly the same work, or promoted farther and faster. I agree that there still prevails an outdated "nigger mentality," whereby the inferiority of women is as wrongly accepted as the ugliness of black skin. I agree that society is unfair to permit a man's role, but not a woman's, to transcend the functions of the body. I detest being called a "career girl," and wonder why, if I have to be that, my male colleagues aren't "career boys."

But I don't feel personally oppressed by men, nor do I wish to burn my brassiere in protest of Miss America contests or anything else, nor to storm the Oak Room of the Plaza Hotel at lunchtime or any other all-male sanctuary. I do not yearn for the "convenience" of extrauterine pregnancies, and I don't want to do away with love, sex, and marriage. I require love and sex as I require Vitamin C, often wish I were married, and if I were never to feel a baby swelling in my belly, I should feel very much cheated. I don't want to threaten men, or deprive them of anything they have. Most particularly, I deny that even in the most metaphorical, abstract sense I have any wish to "castrate" them—an ambition often glibly attributed to all women whose work is competitive or responsible. God forbid.

So militancy doesn't define femininity for me, any more than does the giggling Distaff Side vapidity that characterized the sorority house I never quite summoned the nerve to resign from in college. Those years gave me so suffocating an overdose of all-girl gatherings that to this day I won't have lunch (if I can help it) with more than two other women at a time, not even if they're my best friends, and I'd sooner go to a dogfight than most bridal or baby showers.

We owe the ladies'-luncheon mentality to the generation before us, nowhere better described than in Evan Connell's fine novel *Mrs. Bridge*, whose pitiful heroine sums up everything the feminists decry. Some of this mentality filtered down to me from the very first woman I ever met, who obliged, when I asked how she defined femininity, with the following list: "Charming, dainty, attractive to men, fresh and pretty, with a light touch, flirty, and with some brains back there, too." All worthy qualities, I guess, but isn't there something wrong with the order? We can't blame our own mothers, though. They only told us what they were taught themselves when they wore pink dotted swiss—to be, at all costs, "ladylike."

"The trouble with the Victorian word 'ladylike,' " an enlightened friend of mine observes, "is that it seems to imply 'without sex,' which is to say 'sexless,' with crossed legs, demure, coy, subservient, and ultimately deceitful. All that is changing, and it's about time. Now there isn't so much talk of 'settling'—'settling down,' 'settling for' this is that wretched compromise. What people really mean, when they ask why you don't settle down, is 'why don't you die a little, kill a part of yourself, and stop jumping around so much you make me feel lifeless by comparison?' "

It is surely promising that "femininity" no longer need mean lifeless or stunted or limited. "Feminine" now can mean continuing to grow, and tapping the potential of our wits as well as of our wombs. The trouble is that in trying to do so we slip into modes of behavior that may not come across as feminine. "If I'd lived my life the way I should have," said a businesswoman friend of mine who looks as feminine as a bouquet of lavender but apparently feels otherwise, "there'd never be any question of me opening my own doors. But I didn't, so there is."

Her trouble, and mine, is that it's hard to shift gears from the competent aggressiveness we're expected to display in our work to the demure parody of helplessness considered more seemly out of the office. We love feeling protected and taken care of, but, even so, we sometimes find ourselves starting to open our own doors, or light our own cigarettes, or do other things men might do for us. I don't like it when I catch myself picking up my own suitcase, or hailing taxis and catching waiters' eyes when a man I'm with forgets to do those things. I don't like it when a man lets me win a little social skirmish, either—if I want to hear the Doors and he wants to hear Saint-Saëns and he bows to my stubborn will. This, I must admit, is quite perverse. "You want to be ordered around, all right," a man who knows me well once said, "but you want to be ordered to do what you planned to do all along, with no argument."

I guess I wouldn't be suited for the "system" a friend of mine just back from a year in Europe says she so admired in Italy and Greece. "In those countries," she told me, "men are more contemplative and more dominating, and women are expected to take care of all the domestic details. It may sound servile, but in Mediterranean countries it's a pleasure to do those things, because there men make you feel taken care of, in a way American men don't know how to, or don't want to, or can't."

American men, indeed, perplex American women. Once a man was staying overnight in my apartment and had his car parked outside. I woke at 7:50 A.M. and remembered that if the car wasn't moved by 8:00 it would be towed away. Since he was still asleep, I threw a raincoat on over my nightgown and ran down to move it. He was mightily offended, on my return, that I hadn't waked him up to let him do it. I felt so unfeminine and misunderstood that I cried. He left, never to be heard from again. At a cocktail party several months ago I saw a man I had known slightly for years, and never especially cared for, nor had he for me. But this particular evening some new and promising chemistry developed between us. He said he'd never noticed before how soft and warm I was, and asked me to break the later date I had with someone else. I said I couldn't do that. He said he'd phone me soon. He didn't, though, not even two weeks later when I sent him a postcard to remind him of my existence. I wrote the postcard because I was afraid to do the bolder thing and call him up. "Girls don't phone boys," I remember learning in high school, "because that's too pushy and forward and unfeminine." But maybe I was dead wrong. Maybe phoning him, at the risk of seeming predatory, would have been the most feminine thing I could possibly have done.

"Sure you should have called him," a swashbuckling publisher friend told me later. "Feminine women don't hesitate; they know what they want and set out to get it. They're committed to something beyond their domestic circumstances. One thing I'll definitely expect of my wife, if I ever decide to get married, is to serve me ideas along with breakfast. I'll also expect her to have something women often lack: an elevated sense of mischief and play."

A professor I know told me a sad tale of a girl graduate student he used to like. "We'd go on walks through the woods together," he said, "and she'd delight me by pointing out mushrooms and wild flowers and little things I'd never have noticed otherwise. Women are very good at that sort of thing—picking up subtle little perceptions men miss. But this girl got all hung up with ideas of 'respect' and 'male chauvinism,' and after a while it got so that if I'd say something to her as innocent as 'Nice day, isn't it?' she'd answer, 'You have just made three incorrect assumptions.'

"A feminine woman," the professor went on, "is one who makes me feel like a man—one who makes me want to embrace and protect her no matter how bright and capable and sturdy I know she is. It doesn't matter a bit what her dress size is, or her tone of voice, or how much makeup she has on."

"The word 'feminine,' " said a 17-year-old whose maleness I no more doubt than a cat's felinity, "makes me think of self-assertiveness and striped bell-bottoms at the corner of 61st and Lexington. It isn't a question of who opens doors. Sometimes I start to think about opening doors 50 yards in advance, and then still go in first. As for coats, girls usually help me on with mine, because I have a surprising amount of technical ineptitude. Helplessness is the last thing I look for in girls. In fact, the more submissive and helpless they are, the less they turn me on."

Maybe we worry too much about coats and doors and taxis and chivalry. The important thing, I guess, is to realize that within us all are reserves of both strength and softness, and to know when to use which. "Softness," says a lady executive whose effectiveness is legendary, "is actually an asset in business. It can be disarming. If I go into a sales meeting where all the men are sitting around stiff and formal and cold, and tell one of them how nice he looks in his new suit, it can change the whole mood of the morning—for the better—for everybody.

"Some men think I'm tough when they first meet me," she goes on, "but later they often tell me they've changed their minds. They like to think, 'With the others she's tough, but with *me* she's feminine.' Real femininity is a way of being sure of yourself, and a feeling for all humanity. Not that men can't have that feeling, too. Real men, of course, *do* have it, and aren't afraid to show it. Any masculine male has softness and compassion in him, just as any really feminine female has strength." That, I think, must have been what Virginia Woolf was talking about in *A Room of One's Own,* when she alluded to "that curious sexuality which comes only when sex is unconscious of itself."

Another woman I know who has raised nine children, run a business, and written a book says that "I always feel most effective when I'm using my uniquely feminine qualities, finding importance in the little things men overlook. Sure, it's a man's world—I wouldn't want it not to be—but men couldn't get along without us, and wouldn't want to."

And so we grope our way out of this strange interregnum toward a new "system" of behavior between the genders, probably a better one than that which my friend admired in Greece and Italy. Perhaps, as a school principal thinks, "the thing that's great about now is that anything goes. You can dress as you like and be as you like—tough, gentle, moony, moody, managerial, whatever, without sacrificing anything. All the young kids who are concerned about feminism want equal rights, sure, but despite all the brouhaha about dressing alike and looking alike and unisex, they're very concerned about femininity and romance, too. The new breed wants everything—self-expression, work, and children—and they see no reason not to go after all those things. They should. I have. I'm 43, divorced, and a grandmother, with a whole lifetime behind me and I hope a whole new one ahead."

A friend who is in her sixties, and enviably monogamous, does me the honor of worrying about me. "Wouldn't it be nice," she once speculated, "if you could quit being concerned with the problems of the world—which let's face it, *you're* never going to solve—and just zero in instead on problems, and the happiness, of one man? Wouldn't it be nice if you could fine someone as right for you as Arthur is for me?" Sure it would. While I look for an Arthur, though, I'll still keep on making gestures, however ineffectual, about less immediate problems, I'll keep complaining about air pollution and protesting the war. I was immensely pleased and almost smug to be part of the November 15 multitude that converged in Washington to demonstrate for peace. The spirit of that day was far more impressive than the rhetoric, but one line touched me so much, on so many levels, that I wrote it down on the back of an envelope. It has quite a bit, come to think of it, to do with femininity.

"Teach us to be twice as tough and twice as tender," the voice said over the loudspeakers by the Washington Monument, "as only the truly tough can be tender."

Discussion

Available socialization studies show that parents, and especially fathers, try to foster completely different characteristics, abilities, and skills in boys and girls, in accordance with the traditional notions of masculinity and femininity.[1] "Masculine" toys are given to boys and "feminine" toys to girls. Boys are urged to become independent, competitive, aggressive; girls are rewarded when they are obedient, sweet, attractive, and delicate. Boys are given adventure stories, science fiction, and simplified scientific books to read, and girls are given insipid, romantic stories about little girls and their girl friends and ponies. These sex-differentiated socialization patterns are continuously reinforced by mass media, especially television, the great modern educator of children and adolescents. Thus, the continuous admonition of boys to become scientists, or as famous as their fathers, and of girls to become good wives and mothers ("like your mother") and, among more liberal parents, also to "help" other people is coupled with an outstanding national show for preschool children, "Sesame Street," permeated by traditional sex-segregated role models.[2] Finally, when the children reach school age, teachers, textbooks, and curricula complete the process by an even more "official" endorsement and reinforcement of the segregated masculine and feminine sex roles.

This differential socialization process transmits to boys and girls not only knowledge concerning sex-appropriate values, attitudes, characteristics, and behaviors, but also an evaluation of the relative worth of the two sexes. Thus, as adolescent girls grow older, their opinion of themselves grows progressively worse and their opinion of boys grows better. Adolescent boys, on the contrary, become gradually cognizant of the "superiority" of their sex and tend progressively to think better of themselves and worse of girls.[3] Other evidence of the adolescents' awareness of the differential prestige of the sexes is the fact that girls less often than boys judge girls' games and other activities and girls as playmates as being better than games, other activities, and playmates of the opposite sex.[4] In light, then, of these early results of socialization, Goldberg's findings presented in this part are hardly surprising.

Despite the basic hormonal differences between females and males and the entrance of sex hormones in the brain,[5] probably the best proof that such a physiological difference cannot by itself determine the particular felt emotional and outward behavior of people[6] is provided by the fact that the socially expected behaviors and characteristics cannot be observed in very young boys and girls. There is evidence that girls do better than boys throughout elementary school in many subjects, including mathematics, and it is only at high school that cultural expectations catch up with girls. It is only then that they often attempt to hide the fact that they might be brighter or more capable and talented than boys and that they suddenly cannot "understand" mathematics.[7] Also conforming with the desired image of women "as less smart" than men, girls, when they become aware of this "feminine" characteristic, willingly stop their further mental growth and their IQs suddenly drop below those of boys in the corresponding age.[8] This fear of appearing intelligent is coupled later on with a strong motivation to "avoid success,"[9] since such an achievement could make them appear superior to many men (or specifically, to their boyfriend or husband)[10] and gain for them the notoriety of being a "compensating, aggressive career woman." Along the same lines, it has been found that girls in junior high school have a career drive significantly more often than they do in senior high school, by which time they have internalized the inferior status of women and men's negative reactions to women who use their intelligence creatively and have adopted housework and motherhood as their unchallenged life sectors.[11]

Other interesting indirect evidence is the fact that despite a very intensive socialization aimed at making women dependent and "nurturant"[12] rather than independent and, therefore, analytic and creative (and "sweet" rather than intelligent), some American women become creative and successful scientists, businesswomen, writers, and artists. If it is remembered that this type of socialization can deeply affect the woman's conceptualization process, the way she thinks, perceives the world, writes, and speaks, the appearance of a considerable number of socially deviant women becomes even more significant. And it is no coincidence that those "deviant" unusual women have been most often socialized as boys because in some way they were playing the symbolic role of a son.[13]

Another type of evidence, similarly indicating that the intensive parental and social efforts toward sex-role segregation do not completely succeed, is represented by the results of the administration of femininity-masculinity scales to boys and girls, men and women. Despite the fact that psychologists have devised femininity-masculinity scales which are based upon and sensitive to the prevailing traditional sex-role segregated activities and characteristics, still the obtained results do not completely separate men and women with regard to these characteristics. For example, in one attempt to validate a femininity scale, 18.41 percent of the men received predominantly "feminine" scores and 22.24 percent of the women received predominantly "masculine" scores.[14] Furthermore, a factor-analytic study of items used in different femininity-masculinity tests showed that these tests tap "cultural sex-role differences in interests . . . not homogeneous or clear-cut."[15] Finally, a psychologist reviewing many relevant cross-cultural studies concluded "that there was little agreement on the meaning of the concepts of masculinity and femininity. . . . The meaning of sexual differences tends to depend upon cultural interpretation and the particular phase of history in which one lives."[16] Thus, despite the fact that masculinity-femininity tests are based upon the traditional sex-role segregation followed during the socialization process, the results are overlapping and ambiguous.

Similar sex-differentiated socialization trends are still true for many Western European countries, and are often much more accentuated for developing countries in Latin America, Asia, and Africa.[17] Some notable exceptions do exist, however, in some countries in which a conscious effort has been made to eliminate the traditional sex-role segregation or where some social changes have taken place that have made for a significant extension in the limits of the "feminine" role.[18]

In the Scandinavian countries, for example, and mostly in Sweden, a conscious and widespread movement for sex-role change gained the approval of the government and was implemented in part by the Swedish Ministry of Family and Youth (the ministers in recent years having been outstanding women), and thus some profound and radical social changes have come about. These changes touch upon the type of training received in school, so that boys can also learn sewing and cooking, and girls can learn woodworking and mechanics. They touch upon legislation, according to which when both work, they are taxed less than when only the husband works; upon the image of men and women presented by mass media; and upon the definitions of "masculinity" and "femininity" and of "masculine" and "feminine" tasks and occupations.[19]

However, even in Sweden, where some "radical' changes have taken place during the last ten years and continuous discussion about the abolition of sex roles has abounded in mass media, a study conducted in 1969 in Uppsala showed that boys and girls aged five, eight, eleven, and fifteen were still clearly aware of sex roles and sex-differentiated tasks and activities.[20] So it seems that when even conscious and significant efforts are made for the abolition of sex-role differentiations, the process is slow and it takes probably two generations before it can be achieved.

There are also some indications that among middle-class Athenians (and possibly among other middle-class urban Greeks), whose fertility is quite low, the average number of children being 1.2, there is a tendency where the only child is a girl to bring her up without any sex-role differentiation.[21] In these cases, the girl is never told that there are some things she is not able or not allowed to do, because she is a girl, and she is encouraged and aided to accomplish as much as she can in whatever field she wishes. Marriage and motherhood are taken for granted, as marriage and fatherhood would be taken for granted in the case of boys, but by no means do they become the central foci of the girl's life. Recent research data have shown that all Athenian men and women, even those with traditional values, believe that women can enter all professional and paraprofessional occupations.[22]

A different type of question raised in some of the articles in this section concerns the degree to which men may become motivated toward the elimination of the present sex roles. While it is true that traditional sex-role segregation provides men with superior status and many rights, it seems that men have been increasingly perceiving the obligations attached to these rights, the limitations placed upon their options in many life sectors, and the often undesirable nature of resulting man-woman relationships.[23] Men, for example, for the first time in any significant number are rejecting one of their unchallenged rights and obligations, that of serving their country by fighting (which, of course, entails the possibility of their being injured or killed while doing so). Bravery and the willingness to risk one's life, traditionally qualities basic to the masculine identity, are, thus, rejected by young American males. Men also, probably for the first time, feel unduly burdened by requirements to supply lifelong economic support not only to current wives and children but also to ex-wives and children, and they feel stifled by the fact that they have always to appear cool, rational, self-confident, never showing weakness or hesitation.[24] It seems also that as more men are living happily with working wives (their whole family enjoying a higher income) and are benefiting from the understanding and cooperation of an equally tired, preoccupied, and absorbed wife, the word has been going around that maybe it's easier, more pleasant, and more satisfactory to live with a working wife than with a bored housewife.

Men need liberation as much as women in all areas, but especially in the sexual and interpersonal realm as well as in their sex identity and sex-role–related behavior, activities, and characteristics. The abolition of sex roles and sex-segregated activities, behaviors, and characteristics can set both men and women free to be human beings who can explore interests, potentials, and relationships without artificially imposed restrictions by sex-appropriate behavior.

Summarizing the findings presented in all the articles in this section as well as the literature referred to in this discussion, we can state the following basic conclusions:

1. Boys and girls are not born with distinct sex roles (except for the distinct anatomically determined sexual tasks); they are taught the culturally approved sex roles. The socialization and indoctrination process is slow and is not usually complete till some time in adolescence.

2. Boys and girls learn that the female sex role is inferior to the male sex role, and girls (as well as boys) start from adolescence on to judge themselves and women in general accordingly, regardless of a particular woman's merit.

3. The acquired, culturally determined sex roles and sex-appropriate values and orientations lead to differential thinking, writing, and speaking patterns for men and women, reflecting the sex-appropriate behavior of action versus passivity, personal achievement versus vicarious identification with the achievement of significant others, etc.

4. Although the masculine role is considered by both men and women as having more advantages and fewer disadvantages than the female role, both men and women perceive at least some disadvantages in the male role and some advantages in the female role. Thus, although women have to gain considerably from "taking over" some of the rights and advantages of males, both men and women stand to gain from the elimination of the traditional segregation of sex roles and sex-linked behavior.

Notes

1. David F. Aberle and Kaspar D. Naegele, "Middle Class Fathers' Occupational Role and Attitudes Toward Children," in *A Modern Introduction to the Family*, eds. Norman W. Bell and Ezra F. Vogel (New York: Free Press, 1960), pp. 126–136; and Melvin Kohn, "Social Class and Parental Values," *American Journal of Sociology*, vol. 64 (January 1959), pp. 100–110.

2. Jo Ann Gardner, " 'Sesame Street' and Sex-Role Stereotypes," *Women*, vol. 1, no. 3 (Spring 1970), p. 42.

3. David B. Lynn, "A Note on Sex Differences in the Development of Masculine and Feminine Identification," *Psychological Review*, vol. 66, no. 2 (1959), pp. 126–135.

4. Lawrence Kohlberg, "A Cognitive-Developmental Analysis of Children's Sex-Role Concepts and Attitudes," in *The Development of Sex Differences*, ed. E. Maccoby (Stanford, Cal.: Stanford University Press, 1966), p. 120. For further supporting evidence, see Vytautas J. Bieliauskas, "Recent Advances in the Psychology of Masculinity and Femininity," *Journal of Psychology*, vol. 60, second half (July 1965), pp. 255–263.
5. D. A. Hamburg and D. T. Lunde, "Sex Hormones in the Development of Sex Differences in Human Behavior," in *The Development of Sex Differences*, ed. Maccoby, pp. 1–24.
6. S. Schacter and J. E. Singer, "Cognitive, Social and Psychological Determinants of Emotional State," *Psychological Review*, vol. 69 (1962), pp. 379–399.
7. Eleanor E. Maccoby, "Sex Differences in Intellectual Functioning," in *The Development of Sex Differences*, ed. Maccoby, pp. 25–55.
8. Betty Friedan, *The Feminine Mystique* (New York: Dell Publishing Co., 1963), pp. 165–166.
9. See the research findings of Matina Horner as reported in Jo Freeman, "Growing Up Girlish," *Trans-Action*, vol. 8, no. 1/2 (November–December 1970), pp. 36–43.
10. See Chapter 5.
11. Esther Matthews and David V. Tiedeman, "Attitudes Toward Career and Marriage and the Development of Life Style in Young Women," *Journal of Counseling Psychology*, vol. 11, no. 4 (1964), pp. 375–384.
12. For a discussion of research findings relating socialization for dependence or independence and analytic ability, see Jo Freeman, *op. cit.*
13. For more information on this topic, see Chapter 6.
14. Harrison G. Gough, "A Cross-Cultural Analysis of the CPI Femininity Scale," *Journal of Consulting Psychology*, vol. 30, no. 2 (1966), pp. 136–141.
15. Ilona M. Engel, "A Factor-Analytic Study of Items from Five Masculinity-Femininity Tests," *Journal of Consulting Psychology*, vol. 30, no. 6 (1966), p. 565.
16. Vytautas J. Bieliauskas, "Psychological Aspects of Femininity and Masculinity" (Paper given to the Catholic International Congress of Psychology, Toulouse, France, July, 1963).
17. See parts two and three in Georgene H. Seward and Robert C. Williamson, *Sex Roles in Changing Society* (New York: Random House, 1970).
18. In addition to the two cases discussed in the text, there are the outstanding examples of Russia, Communist China, and the Eastern European countries, but available information in the socialization area is rather sketchy.
19. *The Status of Women in Sweden*, Report to the United Nations (Stockholm: The Swedish Institute, 1968); Robert McKeown, "Is a Woman's Place in the Home?" *Weekend Magazine* (September 6, 1969); Edmund Dahlstrom, *The Changing Roles of Men and Women* (London: Gerald Duckworth and Co., Ltd., 1967); and Harriet Holter, *Sex Roles and Social Structure* (Oslo: Universitetsforlaget, 1970).
20. Gunvor Dahl, *Barns könsrollsuppfattning* [Children's comprehension of sex roles], Department of Sociology Research Report (Uppsala: University of Uppsala, 1969).
21. From unpublished data of the author, collected from clinical and survey studies in Athens, Greece, in 1964, 1966–67, 1968, and 1970–71.
22. From unpublished data of the author, collected from a study of family modernization conducted in Athens in 1970–71.
23. See also Andy Hawley, "A Man's View," *Motive*, vol. 29, no. 6/7 (March–April, 1969), pp. 72–75.
24. Mary Calderone, "It's Really the Men Who Need Liberating," *Life*, September 4, 1970, p. 24.

The Images of Women

MARGARET B. LEFKOWITZ

The Women's Magazine Short-Story Heroine in 1957 and 1967

In 1963 Betty Friedan charged in *The Feminine Mystique*[1] that educated women have been duped into believing that they could best fulfill themselves by living up to the "mystique" of the happy housewife. She pointed to women's magazine fiction heroines as prototypes of this "mystique" and names the women's magazines among the parties guilty for propagating the false image.

Mrs. Friedan included the results of a study of women's magazine heroines in her book to back up her accusation. This study found that in 1939 heroines in *Ladies' Home Journal, McCall's, Good Housekeeping,* and *Women's Home Companion* had been career women for the most part.[2] By 1949, however, Mrs. Friedan found only one out of three heroines in these magazines was a career woman, and she was shown preparing to renounce her career for her true calling as a housewife.[3]

In 1958 and 1959 Mrs. Friedan was unable to find a career-woman heroine in the magazines, and only one woman in a hundred even had a job. The happy housewife heroine was dominant—younger than her counterpart of ten years earlier and with no vision of the future except to have a baby.[4]

In 1949 another writer, Ann Griffith, was also deploring the change in the women's fiction heroine from career woman to housewife. In addition, Miss Griffith asserted that out of a hundred stories in women's magazines perhaps ten would be concerned with a genuine, recognizable problem and that most stories did not involve believable people or settings.[5]

In view of the changes in the American woman over the 1957–67 decade, including rising education and employment levels, the question was whether the women's magazine short-story heroines had changed also or were still pictured as the happy housewives of the postwar fifties. The following study was designed to test Mrs. Friedan's and Miss Griffith's findings for the 1957–67 decade.

Methodology

McCall's Ladies' Home Journal, and *Good Housekeeping* magazines were chosen for the study because of their appeal to American women in general. Preliminary interviews conducted with fiction editors of these magazines revealed several important factors. First, the editors admitted that they would have been happy to print more adventuresome fiction, but the risk was too great with their mass audiences.

Second, two of the three editors thought that more changes would be noted in the nonfiction of women's magazines over the 1957–67 decade than in fiction. Third, the fiction editors of *McCall's* and the *Journal* placed most responsibility for bringing change into women's magazine fiction with writers. They indicated that stories reflecting changes in the American woman would be printed if they were being written.

The sample for the study used all issues of each of these three magazines in 1957 and 1967. Only short stories and those short-short stories which had a well-defined female character were included.

Novels and novelettes were not included because of limited research time and also because the interest was in fiction written specifically for the women's magazines. The novels and novelettes which appeared often were not.

In addition, to be included in the study a short story had to have a well-defined female character who was an American woman at least 18 years old. If more than one such character appeared within a story, all were included in the sample. The final sample consisted of 161 short stories with a total of 167 female characters from these stories.

The traits of each character in the sample were recorded under the following categories:

Age—18–25, 26–35, 36–45, 46–60, 61 and over
Marital Status—single, married, separated, divorced, widowed
Appearance—ugly, average, attractive, beautiful
Economic Class—low, middle, high
Education—grade school, high school, college, above, vocational
Major Occupation—housekeeping, job, study, career, leisure
Number of Children—0, 1–2, 3–5, 6 and over
Residence—city, country, suburb, small town
Housing—house, apartment, hotel, room
Marital Status—happy, unhappy, happy to unhappy, unhappy to happy, happy-unhappy-happy
Goals—love, career, personal fulfillment, community betterment, material
Problem—marital, psychological, children, romantic, beauty, health, financial, danger, moral, interpersonal relations, community, no problem

If a trait of a character was not stated explicitly but implied, it was recorded as *I* rather than by a check. The *Is* were tabulated with the other statistics, however. The number of responses in each category for each magazine for each year was totaled, and percentages of the total for each division of a category were computed. These percentages were then compared to determine any changes within individual magazines in the ten-year period and any overall changes observed for all the magazines.

Results

The statistics of the study showed that in both 1957 and 1967 the typical heroine in one of these magazines' short stories was an attractive, married woman in the 26–35 age group. She lived in a house in a city, had one or two children, and though she had been to college, her main occupation was housekeeping. She was in the middle economic level and her goals were love-oriented.

The one change noted over the decade was in the type of problem she was most likely to have. In 1957 this would have been a romantic problem, while in 1967 it was a psychological one.

Betty Friedan's accusations about the trend to younger heroines and their spurning of careers were still largely true. The exception to this trend was in *McCall's*, which decreased its percentage of 18–25 year-olds from 45% in 1957 to only 13% in 1967 and spread the rest of its characters into the older age groups. The greatest gain was in the 36–45 age group, which went from 14% in 1957 to 30% in 1967. Since *McCall's* has proven a pacesetter in women's magazines over the past several years, its trend to older characters may be very significant.

As for characters with careers, there was an overall decrease, from 9% in 1957 to only 4% in 1967. Furthermore, each magazine in the study decreased the percentage over the period.

One fact not revealed in the statistics was that the career women who did appear were almost never sympathetic characters. They were usually pictured as "unwomanly" and were seen most often in the act of threatening some "true" woman's marriage.

The happy housewife proved to be more solidly the image in 1967 than in 1957. Marriages got even happier over the period. In 1957, 81% of the marriages were happy or ended happily, but this figure increased to 93% in 1967. Further, the number of marriages which ended unhappily went from 20% in 1957 to only 8% in 1967.

These happy wives were more likely to have children in 1967 also. In the total sample childless families decreased from 31% in 1957 to 18% in 1967, and the one-to-two-child family increased from 47% in 1957 to 66% in 1967.

As was mentioned earlier, the only major change in the characters over the decade was in their problems. The percentage of psychological problems increased from 12% in 1957 to 24% in 1967, and romantic problems decreased from 30% to 20% over the period. (Psychological problems did not imply mental illness but such problems as overcoming grief at a child's death.)

Marital problems constituted 16% of the sample in 1957 and 15% in 1967. But in 1957 marital problems were the second largest group, after romantic problems, while in 1967 they slipped to third place behind psychological and romantic problems.

The drop in romantic problems indicated a trend toward more realistic situations, though as a whole the problems were not of the deeply serious variety. Two notable exceptions appeared in *McCall's* in 1967—one story about a Negro family in Harlem by James Baldwin and another story about a woman's struggle with alcoholism.

Conclusion

It would seem as if these magazines had taken almost a reactionary stand against the career woman, which may have been intensified by Betty Friedan's criticisms. There is no doubt that women are going to work in increasing numbers, however, and with rising levels of education should come a rise in the number of career women in the American society. In an age when the demand for professional skills is growing, the question is raised as to whether a magazine can consistently present the professional woman in fiction as "unfeminine" and still claim to be responsible.

Whether the happy housewife is a "mystique" is debatable. However, she was still the heroine of the women's magazine short story in 1967 as in 1957. Her problems, though more realistic in 1967 than in 1957, were still not particularly serious. The basic conservatism of the mass circulative magazine seemed to dominate in 1967 as in 1957; and changes in real-life American women will probably have to be more definite before they are reflected in women's magazine short-story heroines.

Notes

1. New York: W. W. Norton & Co., 1963.
2. *Ibid.*, p. 30.
3. *Ibid.*, p. 33.
4. *Ibid.*, p. 37.
5. Ann Griffith, "The Magazines Women Read," *American Mercury*, vol. 68 (March 1949), p. 274.

The American Women in Mass Media: How Much Emancipation and What Does It Mean?

Tradition may decree that "women's place is in the home," but the trend, for better or worse, indicates increasing choice of roles open to milady—but not without social trauma. Whether labeled "Revolution of Women," "Women's Liberation," "New Feminism," or "Woman Power," the current women's movement with its attendant debate over the role of women is expected by many to be *the* problem of the seventies.

Women's Liberationist Betty Friedan accused the women's magazines of creating "the feminine mystique" and foisting the narrow one-role world on American women with their "happy housewife" image. When representatives from the various fields of mass media met with the President's Commission on the Status of Women to discuss the portrayal of women, it was suggested that the "weak spot in all mass magazines is fiction." Morton Hunt, male journalist, considered this to be of little concern and of minimal influence, since fiction is meant for escape and entertainment. Feminist writers Betty Friedan and Marya Mannes disagreed and felt that it was in precisely this area that the image had the greatest impact.[1] Numerous content analyses have been made of popular periodicals on the assumption that the medium reflects society and reinforces prevailing attitudes, but except for fiction surveys, little has been done. Fiction may be suffering from cultural lag not present in the nonfiction content. The present study was undertaken with this data gap in mind.[2]

McCall's, Ladies' Home Journal, Cosmopolitan, and *Playboy* were selected for a comprehensive analysis to determine the overall image of women in each (excluding the advertising, which is a field in itself). *McCall's* and the *Journal* have the leading circulation figures among the women's family-oriented magazines, *Cosmopolitan* seeks the "career girl" reader, and *Playboy* is the country's best-selling men's magazine. *Playboy* was also included because one media research company reported that it is the most widely read magazine among employed women readers,[3] and because many serious writers consider it a very influential magazine (although many deplore the kind of influence it exerts). One writer suggests that for the young, literate urban man it is playing "a role corresponding to the function of *McCall's* and American housewifery."[4] Recent attacks on the magazine have come from militant women; "*Playboy* is partly responsible for Women's Lib . . . It made women objects. . . . There are times when a woman reading *Playboy* feels a little like a Jew reading a Nazi manual," charges Gloria Steinem (*McCall's,* October 1970).

If the cultural ideal is that "woman's place is in the home," there is an increasing gap between the ideal and the real. The United States Census Bureau reported that in 1952 only about one out of five wives worked (8 million out of 35.2 million married women), but by 1969 one out of three of these had paid jobs (15.3 million out of 43.3 million married women). These figures do not include, of course, the single, the divorced, and those widows who work. Labor Secretary James D. Hodgson predicts that by 1980 the country's female labor force will have grown to 37 million. Of the 7 million additional women entering the work force, 4 million will be working mothers.[5]

However, despite the fact that today more women *are* getting higher educations, their job status does not necessarily reflect this. Mary Keyserling, director of the Women's Bureau of the United States Department of Labor, said that while in 1967 46 percent of American women between eighteen and sixty-four were in the labor market, they concentrated in the less skilled, less rewarded, and less rewarding occupations. She also noted that in the last fifteen years there had been a steady decline of women in the professions.[6]

In our society the role of wife and mother is still the expected—indeed, the only "true"—occupation for a female. A married woman may hold down a *job* under certain conditions: as an interim activity until she fulfills her biological destiny; as an activity in addition to child rearing if financial pressures make it necessary or if a part-time job does not interfere with family obligations in any way; and as a full-time or part-time activity after the children have grown up. Although she may work at a job, she dare not pursue a career. But if she does and is successful, then men and women alike tend to regard her suspiciously; she is not only "unfeminine" but "emasculating" as well. The "career woman" label is still a social stigma.

Women's Liberation groups focus on freeing women from the cultural pressures that push them into the limited roles of wife and mother on the basis of biology alone; they seek freedom of *choice,* which requires equal opportunity in the world of work. The distinction between a *job* and a *career* is based less on the type of occupation than on the type of attitude. A career implies more than a job—it involves commitment and becomes a vital part of one's life, with monetary considerations only a partial factor. Today, occupations, which have nothing to do with reproduction of the species, are categorized as "male" and "female." The myriad of routine, nonprestigious jobs in retail, clerical, and service areas are "women's jobs," and teaching, nursing, social work, and home economics are "women's professions."

Role Models—McCalls and the Journal

What kinds of role models do the magazines in our study present to their readers? How faithfully do these magazines represent the real world, and to what extent do they indicate a position in regard to the changing roles of women?

Despite the fact that there is an almost equal number of housewives and working women in the fiction in both *McCall's* and the *Journal,* this represents no break with tradition—most of the working girls are single and still looking for "Mr. Right." Out of the thirty-five working women in *McCall's*, only two were married. Of those, one was a young bride with no children and it was made explicit that her job would terminate when her husband finished medical school. The other, a minor character, was a remarried widow who was a medical doctor.

The *Journal's* fiction offered a wider range of role models. Of twenty-nine working women, eight were married. Of these eight, three became successful and a divorce resulted, two were still childless, one combined career and family, but suffered greatly due to role conflict. The remaining two were pictured as having successfully combined careers with the roles of wife and mother. The career-wife-mothers were an English architect and an American educator; the most significant thing, however, was the fact that the main characters were the children. In both stories they are pictured as happy, well-cared-for, sensitive youngsters who are thoughtful of others, and in both stories the housekeepers are doing an admirable job.

Occupations for women followed much the same pattern in *McCall's* and the *Journal* as they do in real life. In addition, certain types were regularly stereotyped: spinsters were office workers or librarians (color me drab), divorcées were usually actresses (color me scarlet), and widows were school teachers (color me respectable).

The nonfiction in *McCall's* and the *Journal* would appear to be nearly identical if one looked only at their respective tables of contents, with their comparable departments and regular columns on child psychology, pets, etc. However, when the content is carefully analyzed, the differences become apparent. Attitudes toward working women are quite different. *McCall's* is rather ambiguous about working wives and tends to ignore working mothers. Of the sixty-two issues examined, the one major article on working women referred only to young single girls in the big city (May 1967). Another debated the question, "Should Wives Work?" (February 1969) and concluded that the determining factor was not "Do the children suffer?" or "Is the marriage endangered?" but "Are husbands resentful?" and that "No man is really crazy about the idea of his wife's working."

McCall's encourages volunteer work as a culturally acceptable outlet for wives; part-time work is permitted. The need for these activities outside the home is recognized for "The Empty Days" (September 1965) when the children have gone. The article speaks of the "crisis no mother escapes," "a pain sharper than childbirth," the "crisis of identity when every women questions the whole meaning of existence, 'If I am no longer a mother, who am I?' *Now* it is acceptable for a woman to seek a job or return to the university for noncredit courses to fill the "vast wasteland stretching before her." This "empty-nest syndrome" is the theme of both short stories and the various articles on volunteer work and part-time employment opportunities. It looms as the largest flaw in the life of the otherwise "happy housewife."

In contrast, the *Journal* appears more concerned with preventing the problem in the first place. The regular columns on marital problems, psychological problems, and medicine all recognize the "tired housewife syndrome" caused by psychogenic fatigue (produced by boredom, monotony, and frustration).

The *Journal* takes a forthright stand in favor of not only working wives but working mothers as well! In June 1966 the *Journal* began a campaign for what it called a "new family birthright" with the first of six articles on day care for children. The birthright, "What Every Mother Owes Her Child and Herself," implied a "new vital freedom for mothers; the freedom to make the most of her professional resources, while at the same time gaining periods of respite from the often crushing responsibilities of her children" (June 1966).

All of the regular features support the idea that a woman is *more* than a wife and mother and should be allowed wider scope. "Can This Marriage Be Saved," a series of case histories taken from the files of the American Institute of Family Relations, analyzes the marital problems that are most typical of American marriages. Out of forty-seven cases in the sample, ten were in some way related to limitations placed on the wives by their assigned cultural role. Depending upon the individual situation, wives were encouraged to return to college for professional training, to develop their creative talents, or simply to get out of the house with a part-time job. The difficulties were not always due to unfeeling husbands; often parents' attitudes toward what was "proper for girls" was a basic cause of the subsequent women's conflicts with regard to their working.

A number of Dr. Bruno Bettelheim's "Dialogue with Mothers" columns challenge the cultural myths about working mothers. He is concerned about the needs of "Restless Mothers" (September 1968) and gives reasons "Why Working Mothers Have Happier Children" (June 1970). He deplores the fact that

> . . . our educational system, while preparing girls for equal occupa-
> tional life, advocates the value of a now antiquated form of marital
> life. What school reader ever shows mother working outside the
> home? Yet millions do. . . . Until she marries she studies the same
> subjects or works the same jobs as her male friend. Then she must
> switch from studying or working to being a wife and mother. After
> years of apparent equality, it is made clear to her that males are
> really "more equal" and she may well resent this.
>
> (*Ladies' Home Journal*, June 1970, p.24)

Walter O'Donnell, M.D., discussed the widespread ailment of "housewife fatigue" (April 1967) and blamed the syndrome on the frustration of living in a one-world rut. He sees an obvious lesson for women in a comparison of their lives to those of their husbands:

> *Men live in at least two worlds.* Usually they have 16 hours daily
> and two days weekly away from their jobs. They are in contact with
> the outside world as well as with home and family. The two worlds
> make for a nice balance. . . . The lesson is so obvious that I am
> sometimes reluctant to point it out to patients. Furthermore, it
> arouses hostility in some women. "Here I am without an extra
> minute," they say, "and you're suggesting that I get out more and
> develop outside interests!". . .
> *Men can—or at least think they can—change jobs if they want
> to.* . . . But women can indulge in no such fantasy. They are frozen
> in their jobs for the duration and they know it. They may recall
> Harry Truman's famous dictum, "If you can't stand the heat, get

out of the kitchen," but they know this alternative is not available to them.

A feature article on "The Bored Housewife" (November 1966) took a close look at the life of one typical American woman who had everything she ever wanted but not what she expected. She suffered from the "tired housewife syndrome" and was "exhausted from unstimulation." The comment preceding the article read, "Millions of women share her feelings. Read them, we dare you. Then tell us: what can we do for Lois . . . what can she do for herself?"

And the readers *did* tell the *Journal*. Over 500 housewives replied: *Bored? Ridiculous!* Less than 10 percent said they felt as Lois did, another 20 percent said that they had at one time felt as she did but had overcome it, while 70 percent responded that they had never felt bored like Lois. Six major patterns appeared in the responses: (1) Develop more interests *within* the home (i.e., reading); (2) Enjoy, Enjoy! Enjoy your children, enjoy being a homemaker; (3) Take a day off now and then; (4) Do volunteer work; (5) Take adult education or correspondence courses; and (6) Develop more religious faith. One woman wrote, "But we can't change society. So we have to change ourselves."

Which picture best describes the "typical American housewife"—the one presented by the doctors, psychologists, the marriage counselors, or the one presented by 500 readers? Probably both.

McCall's reflects no such concerns. Sure, a housewife has her little difficulties, but she laughs them off, aided by experts (in humor, that is) who console her with articles such as "Mrs. Parkinson's Law" (February 1966), which is useful for those days when everything goes wrong. This is not to say that the serious problems are ignored, but *McCall's* is more often concerned with the generation gap and with the new morals (or lack of same) in today's young.

Compare Dr. Bettelheim's encouragement of working mothers with this advice from Dr. Lendon H. Smith's "Pediatrician's Almanac" in *McCall's*:

> Mothers should teach their daughters to be clean, smart, attractive, friendly, and—most important—a little weaker and a little less knowledgeable (not less wise) than the male. I worry about any girl's becoming, for instance, a great athlete—especially a runner. She might run so fast she'd never get caught by a boy.
>
> (January 1969)

With the exception of Marya Mannes, a maverick in the *McCall's* stable, the writers reflect the doctor's traditional view of male and female. Clare Boothe Luce writes about the "female's nesting instinct . . . her homemaking proclivity . . . woman's natural function—her common destiny is wife and motherhood" (February 1966). This is echoed repeatedly in Bentz Plagemann's column, "The Good Life," which drips with saccharine observations such as this one about his neighbor hanging clothes out on the line: "For Sally all of this is merely one of the happy rites of a priestess, and I can see her out there, arms upraised to the clothesline, her profile classically beautiful and pregnant . . ." (June 1967).

McCall's featured a story of "America's Very Own Beautiful Couple—Tom and Nancy Seaver" in May 1970. They were described as "the silent majority's own couple." When Tom was asked, "What is the most inspiring thing that's ever happened in your life?" He replied, "My wife. She gives me reason for striving. Without her, I wouldn't have been as successful in baseball. . . . Two things make me happy: playing baseball and being with my wife."

As for Nancy, "Tom fulfills me. He's what I want, and he's all I want. . . . You know you have ways to charm your husband." When Tom is blue, Nancy charms him by taking the dog's paw and pointing it at Tom and forming the dog's mouth into a smile; "It makes Tom laugh."

Writers and readers alike emphasize this traditional role for girls. Education of females is not stressed. *McCall's* gathered a panel of readers to discuss "Growing Up? Why the Rush?" (March 1965). Few of the mothers desired careers for their daughters. Most agreed with the woman who said:

> I don't think women are truly happy unless they are happy in the home. This is what girls are for, to raise a family. My greatest desire for my three daughters is for them to get a suitable education, be able to make a wonderful home, and have intelligence and maturity to select a fine husband. I don't want them dissatisfied raising a family.

What *is* a suitable education for girls? If one were to ask, "What is a suitable education for boys?" it would raise a number of other questions: What type of boy? What is he interested in? What are his aptitudes? Is he good in math, languages? Does he like to work with people? How simple it is to advise girls. How nice that they are all alike. Blessed are little girls, for they shall become wives and mothers.

If the goal is getting a husband, and if men are not to be "liberated," girls would indeed be well advised to follow Dr. Smith's advice and conceal any taint of intellectuality, for he appears to know his sex well. Sam Blum, a frequent *McCall's* contributor, describes "The Perfect Wife" on the basis of conversations with a number of well-educated middle-class men (May 1968). He found that "with only one exception, every man thought that his wife should not be as intelligent as himself." There was no real objection to her working *if* it in no way interfered with her efficiency as a wife (his comfort and convenience). *However,* they did not want their wives to be brighter in the working world or to make more money than they did.

Blum's rather casual survey reflected the same results as an earlier, more methodical one conducted by social scientists who questioned more than 1000 people about attitudes toward potentially controversial situations involving working wives. They found that men will agree, "Yes, a woman should have an active mind. Yes, she should work if she wants to. Yes, she should have an equal say about sex, money, and the children." *But,* the test results showed that what they say is not what they feel. Intellectually, at least, they do not deny women these things, but are they emotionally able to grant them? The most sensitive area was the high-status job for women. Both men and women viewed such a situation as "threatening to marriage."[7] There is such a strong prejudice against a "brainy" girl that Robert Havighurst, educator and authority in human development, places "intellectuality" at the top of the list of forms of deviancy which high-school guidance counselors must help girls overcome.[8]

Although the *Journal* provides moral support for the "trapped housewife" who wants to expand her world with an additional role, it doesn't provide much in the way of stimulation for the daughter of the house who may share the magazine with mother. Any work information is directed toward the part-time job, which is seen as the "happy middle ground between a full-time job and doing nothing for extra income and psychic rewards" (March 1968). Incidental information does pop up often in the special columns; for example: "Yes, there is a place for women in the field of veterinary medicine." An occasional fashion article uses as models young women who lead "dual lives," but on the whole the *Journal's* "notables" came from the fairy-tale worlds of royalty and Hollywood and are not successful career women from the world of work.

McCall's is very similar to the *Journal* in terms of its paucity of specific vocational information but paradoxically provides a splendid array of models in its profiles of successful career women in a wide variety of fields ranging from medicine (Dr. Janet Travell, physician to President Kennedy) to shoe design (Beth Levine).

Cosmopolitan

But since neither the *Journal* nor *McCall's* professes to be work-oriented we had better turn to *Cosmopolitan* for advice to women who work, or want to. *Cosmopolitan* is not family-oriented and is for the "career girl reader who is hip, attractive, 18–34 years old, intelligent, [and a] good citizen girl who wants to have a more rewarding life."[9] Both fiction and nonfiction from twenty-seven issues were analyzed and categorized into types and topics. Although much more occupational information is given, *Cosmopolitan* cannot be considered "career-oriented," as defined earlier.

Cosmopolitan is for women but about men. The guiding philosophy is outlined by its editor, Helen Gurley Brown: "A woman can't have a really wonderful life if she doesn't have a man to go to bed with. We try to tell her how to find her man, how to attract him, to keep him interested, and how to get him back after he has wandered off the reservation."[10]

And that's what it's all about . . . .

In fiction, *Cosmopolitan* presents a bit more variety, since neither the characters nor the language has to be as "ladylike" as in its sister publications. In the sample of forty-seven short stories and twenty-five novels (mystery), only six women were limited to the role of housewife, and children were rarely mentioned. Most women were employed in typical "female" *jobs,* although there were more "glamour types" such as models and actresses and even a prostitute was mentioned. There were eight *career women:* five were entertainers, and although all were successful, none was happy. The remaining three were an executive secretary out to get her boss's job (she's murdered), an English archaeologist (she's murdered), and the head of a public relations firm (she's nearly murdered). But since *Cosmopolitan* regularly features a mystery novel, this is to be expected and should not necessarily be interpreted as a comment on career women.

In the twenty-seven issues of *Cosmopolitan* studied, fifty-eight articles related to the world of work. There was an obvious attempt to glamorize the mundane clerical jobs by presenting the opportunities in "romantic" fields, as in "Men, Martinis, Glamor: All in a T.V. Girl's Day" (about typists, etc., April 1969), or in a "romantic" location, as in "Getting a Job Overseas" ("We get lots of Ph.D.'s but never enough secretaries and stenographers," December 1965). Three articles specifically discouraged higher education and suggested acquiring secretarial skills: "Nightschool Isn't All Education" (men you'll meet, July 1966); "Why You Shouldn't Go to College" (September 1966); "Today's Secretary—Wow!" (and you may marry the boss, June 1969). Eight additional articles pointed out the attractive possibilities open to a girl with secretarial skills.

"*Cosmo*," as the editor affectionately calls the publication, helps you find the men, and this is an important consideration in employment. Go west, young woman, go west! "Brand New Girls in a Brand New City," an article about San Jose, California, reports that "this city not only has *jobs*—it has *men*." Ranchers, industrialists, salesmen, engineers, scientists . . . you name it . . . they're *there!*" The major concern is *men*, not careers (July 1968, p. 102).

Eight articles dealt with various aspects of modeling, three with the performing arts, and five with writing occupations such as journalism and advertising. Several dealt with problems of being successful (you are called a "castrating female" by men); eight described discrimination against women in particular fields (e.g., advertising). Prostitution, albeit of an elegant kind, was covered in an article about "The Park Avenue Call Girl" (is she happy —no, July 1968) and in "The Young Mistresses: Occupation: Sex; Duties: Making a Man Happy; Working conditions: Excellent; Future Prospects: ???" (December 1967). The young mistresses are in England, since "American women don't know how to be mistresses even when they *are*. We [American women] are conditioned to get married. . . ."

Some articles *did* provide explicit information concerning subfields, potential for advancement, and where to get additional information for professions such as librarian, teacher, home economist and for careers in the armed services. Two articles suggested a number of possibilities for owning your own business. Despite gushy enthusiasm ("Franchises are Fun!!!!") and cute titles ("The Fat's in the Fire," about home economists) which reflect the literary style set by the editor in an attempt to be "hip" and "groovy," sound advice can be found under this flippant veneer. Although four articles were about successful career women and listed some sixty of them, most over age thirty, the magazine is more for the "working girl" of any age.

Playboy

Time magazine (February 9, 1968) called *Cosmopolitan* a "sort of female *Playboy*." This presumed resemblance appears to be based upon the liberal attitudes toward sex which both share. Other than the editorial stamp of approval on premarital sex, I found little resemblance between them. *Playboy* is for men, by men, and about men. Women, of course, are prominently featured, but the male-female relationship is a sexual one and woman are not the main focus except in pictures. *Cosmopolitan*, on the other hand, is for women but is totally preoccupied with the opposite sex. The fiction in Playboy is generally the best that money can buy, and the women characters are as varied as the stories themselves—sometimes saints, sometimes sluts, but never the insipid, simpering stereotypes of "ladies'" magazines. Occupations of women in these stories are dictated by the plots: if the setting is an office, then there are the usual clerical types; if the plot deals with the stock market and high finance, a woman financier appears. There is a difference in *Playboy*'s fiction in the higher percentage of models, actresses, and prostitutes; these are not necessarily presented as shady ladies but are included because they exist and men know them.

The general disinterest in women outside of romantic involvements is reflected in the nonfiction content: women writers are rare and so are women as "featured personalities." In the sixty-six sample issues, only five women were interviewed: Madalyn Murray (atheist), Princess Grace (royalty by marriage), Virginia Johnson (sex researcher with Dr. Masters), Mary Calderone (sex educator), and Raquel Welch (sex symbol). Seven other women appeared briefly "On the Scene" but mainly as members of groups in the entertainment world. Three articles were concerned with the changing role and altering image of women, but they will be discussed later in relation to the Women's Liberation Movement.

Sexual Behavior and the Status of Women

It is when we leave the office and go home to the bedroom that all four magazines have a common interest. The relationships between the sexes are a major topic in all, but not in the same way, nor to the same extent. Sex is no longer a subcategory under "Love and Marriage." We are in the midst of both a sexual revolution and a women's revolution, and while related, they are not identical. The double standard has not yet fallen, but how much has it declined? To what extent do *McCall's*, the *Journal*, *Cosmopolitan*, and *Playboy* reflect the changing status of women and shifting values in sexual behavior?

Not too many years ago the lyrics of a popular song said it all:

> Love and marriage, love and marriage
> Go together, like a horse and carriage
> This I tell you, brother
> You can't have one,
> You can't have one without the other.

Although the days of the horse and carriage are gone, love and marriage are still linked in the minds of millions, especially in the minds of middle-class, middle-aged Americans. In our culture, marriage is a dominating life goal, and those who are single bear a social stigma despite the fact that there is an increasing number who endure this status. The traditional moral code states explicitly that sex outside of marriage is *sin*—for women. Although extramarital sex is not sanctioned for men, it is generally condoned because "boys will be boys." But that's all changed. Or has it?

McCall's and the *Journal* generally reflect the traditional values about occupational roles and sexual behavior of women, with *Cosmopolitan* and *Playboy* deviating in some areas. *Playboy* does not have a family orientation, but marriage is regarded as an eventual step. The magazine "is aimed at the premarital period, a time for play then he [the young man] can better appreciate marriage. . . . You can't reach the 'I love you' stage without dating" (February 1965, p. 44). Despite its reputation, *Playboy* has a romantic outlook; to a young man contemplating marriage the Advisor wrote: "You praise the girl in terms of her assets, which do sound admirable; you never say you love her. That's a pretty important ingredient in marriage" (March 1970, p. 47).

Numerous magazine articles in other publications tell us how *Playboy* feels about women. Most of them are critical and accuse the magazine of treating women as "sex objects," things to be used and cast aside. And to judge from such "gossip" or a superficial newsstand perusal, the sexual emphasis in the magazine does appear overwhelming. Admittedly there is a masculine preoccupation with sexual intercourse in most of the humor, but this emphasis on sex reflects the customary delight that most males in most cultures have taken in the "dirty joke." *Playboy* didn't invent sex, and elimination of the centerfold is not going to abolish it. The magazine's phenomenal success with men and women alike must rest on more than a prurient appeal; there are other "girlie" publications that are both "dirtier" and cheaper. Censoring *Playboy* for sex won't eliminate the problem; *if* the magazine assigns women their status and role on the basis of biology, it is not alone. What women really seek is an appreciation of the "whole" woman as an individual. What *Playboy says* may be more significant than what it *shows*. Let's let the magazine speak for itself.

Attitudes toward women were elaborated on in a number of installments of the "Playboy Philosophy" that appeared prior to 1965 (beginning date of this sample), and it is necessary to refer to these earlier installments, since they are frequently discussed in the "Playboy Forum" and the "Playboy Advisor." Although specific "love and marriage" articles are absent from *Playboy* there are symposiums dealing with premarital sex, infidelity, sex and religion, sex and the state, and many other topics. Comparisons between the editorial outlooks of *Cosmo* and *Playboy* reveal some surprising things. The *Cosmo* girl is far from being a liberated female; she stands for equality in sex but not equality between the sexes. The "Playboy Philosophy" stresses the importance of the individual and rejects *all* double standards: sexual, racial, and economic. *Cosmopolitan* presents almost a caricature of the traditional stress on marriage for a girl; *Cosmo* stresses a *man* for a girl. *McCall's* and our mothers have drilled it into us that "Papa is all"—we pet him, we pamper him, we persuade him, we pacify him, we praise him, and our purpose in life is to be a *good wife* to him.

Cosmo gives us the same advice but doesn't hold out until the legal knot is tied. Not that *Cosmo* doesn't stress marriage—it does. An interview with Helen Gurley Brown in 1969 screamed in large letters across the top of a newspaper page: "ARE 4 MILLION GIRLS DOOMED TO BE OLD MAIDS?"[11]

When asked about this disaster figure and the plight of the deprived girls, the editor of the "career-girl" magazine answered that with such a shortage of men, the competition is cutthroat and a girl has got to be aggressive. (And *Cosmopolitan* will show her how.) Although Mrs. Brown believes "being married is the only way a woman can be happy," marriage is represented in the magazine as not so much a total relationship as the maximization of sexual opportunity.[12] There is an overall impression of frantic action to get a man, any man, as soon as you can, because there aren't enough to go around.

Playboy is not antimarriage as such but doesn't believe in rushing into marriage because it is the "thing to do," and this applies to young girls as well as young men:

> Old maid is a state of mind, not a state of being, and the phrase stems from a period in history when it was disgraceful for a woman to remain unmarried. It is a put-down to the female sex, since it carries unpleasant connotations from which the word bachelor is free. We think a better definition of old maid would refer to members of either sex, of any age, who prefer to avoid life rather than participate in it. . . . By all means don't fall into the trap of an early marriage while trying to make up your mind about your life style.
>
> (June 1970, p. 45)

The advice is good, but the philosophy isn't very widespread. Singleness in our society is suspect, especially after the first blush of youth has passed. Even the formerly married—the divorced and the widowed—suffer subtle discriminations and are pressured into remarriage. Social life in America is much like Noah's ark: we can enter it only two by two. This social fact is the basis of *Cosmopolitan*.

Only recently have the women's magazines given much attention to the single adult. Morton Hunt, in "The World of the Formerly Married" (*McCall's* (September, October, November 1966), observed that someone without a partner is considered an "emotional defective." The *Journal* referred to the unmarried as "the most neglected segment of our family-oriented population" (July 1966). Obviously the brunt of society's disapproval and neglect falls on women, since there appear to be so many more of us. Marriage requires a man, but according to the 1960 census there were 11,884,000 single women over age fourteen and women of voting age outnumbered men by almost 5.2 million.[13] In the context of these statistics and our culture in general, *Cosmopolitan's* advice can be understood, if not condoned. The *Cosmopolitan* articles not geared to man hunting are few. Some are the tongue-in-cheek variety and others should be. Many are blatantly written to appeal to the sex-starved, man-hungry, frightened female, and a first reaction might be, "You've *got* to be kidding!" No matter how they are written, the fact that they are *taken* seriously is not funny . . . . In fact, *Cosmopolitan* is a sad commentary on the status of women in our culture. As it is now, life without a man *is* difficult and sex is the least of the single girl's problems. Regardless of her salary, many finance companies require a male cosignatory if an unmarried woman wants a loan to buy a car; imagine how difficult it is for her to get a mortgage if she wants to own her own home. Through the ages women have married and exchanged children and domestic services for their husbands'

provision of food, shelter, and financial security for their declining years. Young women waited to be "asked" and hoped the person who chose *them* would be an acceptable "choice."

Cosmopolitan has changed the mood from passive to active. *Cosmo* tells you "how to" get *your* man. Premarital sex is assumed, and if your knowledge of the facts of life is the kind collected haphazardly from "knowledgeable" friends, there are numerous articles on how to understand female physiology (and male), many on how not to get pregnant, and also on how to swing several affairs at the same time and "how not to be known as a sleep-around girl" (May 1970). There are *no* articles, however, on how to *not* get VD.

In the meantime, a girl must work, and *Cosmo*, as we have mentioned, tells you what kinds of jobs to get, and in what cities, in order *to meet men* (secretaries marry their bosses: statistics on major cities and the occupations of men apt to be there, June 1967), where to take your vacation *to meet men* (twenty-four articles), what sports to pursue *to meet men* (invest in a boat-handling course because "now the boys aren't on the beach, they're in the boats," July 1967; skydiving is recommended since "men outnumber girls 19 to 1 in that sport," April 1969).

Cosmo is with you every step of the way. Once the quarry is sighted, there are guides which tell you how to identify his type (thirty-one articles), especially how to tell if he's married, and how to move in for the kill. Then you need to know "How to Turn a Man On" (April 1968 and July 1969) and "How to Love Like a Real Woman" (June 1969). Apply "What They Teach You about Men in Airline School" (arts of man-coddling, July 1967). Try "Seductive Cooking" (March 1966), especially "Food for Lovers" (aphrodisiacs, October 1968). *Cosmo* includes lots of important beauty tips such as "how to keep your makeup on when showering with a man" and how to shop for the "Romantic Nightgown" (to make you more of a woman, March 1966). When the time comes, there is a "Living-Together Handbook—whether you are on-the-verge or already 'living in sin'" (April 1969). There's also an uncensored lowdown on "How Girls *Really* Get Husbands" (December 1965) and another version in June 1967. *But* if *Cosmo* didn't get to you in time, there's "How to Get Married if you're over 30" (May 1970), with some special advice from one woman who says, "I was an over-age Virgin" (March 1970).

Cosmo does not desert you at the altar either. It tells you "How Not to Get Dumped on His Way Up" (his ego must be fed forever and ever, don't ever forget it! October 1968). Read up on "How to Give Your Husband an Alcohol Rub" and all of the other "Things to Do with Your Hands That Men Like" (especially study all the nooks and crannies of his anatomy with your hands, April 1970). Each issue is literally packed with such bits of wisdom, along with stories about *fabulous* people such as "The World's Greatest Lover—Aly [Khan]" (July 1965).

We must remember that *Cosmopolitan* has a circulation of 1,100,680 and is still growing; the circulation has risen for every single issue since Helen Gurley Brown became editor in July 1965.[14] The women aren't reading it for laughs.

Men are a scarce commodity in the marriage market; the odds are all on *Playboy*'s side. Despite its reputation for encouraging Don Juans, the magazine turns out to be surprisingly "moral," especially when compared with its female counterpart. Premarital sex has generally been permitted to the young male who "sowed his wild oats" before he settled down and became a family man. Even then a man's transgressions were tolerated by society and by his wife, because biology supposedly had given the male a handy excuse in the form of a "stronger sex drive." *Playboy's* main break with the prevailing moral code is complete elimination of the sexual double standard plus open advocation of *premarital* sex.

Although *Playboy* has a liberal attitude toward *premarital* sex, it takes marriage very seriously: divorce is seen as the result of premature marriages. *Playboy* believes, along with *McCall's* and the *Journal,* that our society pressures youngsters into marrying before they are mature enough to cope with the attendant responsibilities and that "the maturing male courts disaster when he attempts to select a lifetime mate before he himself has become a complete man" ("Playboy Advisor," April 1964, p. 39).

Once the man is married, fidelity is valued. The traditional attitude toward *extramarital* sex is modified only to the extent that there might be extenuating circumstances such as rejection by the marriage partner, permanent separation, or mutual consent. Extramarital sex is viewed as a more complex moral issue than other kinds of sex: "Marital happiness is not easily achieved where vows of fidelity are taken lightly by either partner . . . . Adultery is most often a result, however, rather than a cause of marital maladjustment . . ." (February 1965, p. 140). The *Playboy* reader is told flatly, "Legal game is the only fair game for a bachelor" (December 1961, p. 47); the *Cosmo* reader is given a clear go-ahead in this every-girl-for-herself world:

> Frankly, he wouldn't be on your doorstep if his homelife was delicious. (And you might as well blame his wife for making it dreary. She's probably older than you and she may well be depressing in bed. She's not your problem, so stop worrying about her.)
> ("Pleasures of a Temporary Affair," March 1969)

Although unfaithful wives appear in *Cosmopolitan* fiction, they are strangely absent from the nonfiction content. In the entire sample, no mention was made of a wife committing adultery. Extramarital sex was presented only in terms of married men and single girls. Perhaps this seemingly odd omission from the "anything goes" philosophy is based on the marital maxim that "a bird in the bed is worth two in the bush."

Those who accuse *Playboy* of treating women as "objects," specifically "sex objects" to be exploited for male enjoyment, are disturbed by the idea that "sex and love are not the same thing *obviously;* and each can exist wholly apart from the other. But I [Hefner, *Playboy's* editor] think the best sex, the most meaningful sex, is that which expresses that strong emotional feeling we call love . . ." (February 1965, p. 44). Elsewhere, however, he does admit that "sex without love is better than no sex at all."

The traditional "biology as destiny" view of woman reflected in "The Good Life" by Bentz Plagemann in *McCall's* (April 1967) also suggests the woman-as-sex-object theme but perhaps in a more subtle manner:

> A girl is born with an identity. She is a woman. That is a function in itself, and she seems to have a serene knowledge of that

from the beginning. But a man has to find himself. His biological function is only a part of his life, and after that he is required to get out of the house and do something to support the results.

And not so subtle is the copy from an advertisement which appeared in the women's magazines (italics mine):

> This is a page that will tell you about an external vaginal deodorant spray. A product that would have made your grandmother faint and your mother blush.
>
> All it should do to you is make you happy. Very happy.
>
> Because now that the "The Pill" has freed you from worry, "The Spray" will help you make all that freedom worthwhile.
>
> "The Spray" is called Feminique.
>
> Feminique. The name is feminine, which is precisely what this product will make you. Feminine in every sense of the word. It has a fresh, clean fragrance that couldn't be captured in a thousand perfumed baths.
>
> So from now on when you bathe and when you perfume your body, don't neglect *the most important part of you.* And don't risk using your harsh underarm deodorant or your strong perfume on that most important part of you. . . .

Does *Playboy* encourage exploitation of women, as its critics charge? It assumes that women too enjoy sex and that both partners should be eager and willing. A young man with a fiancée "who wants to wait until we are married" is told to respect her wishes if he loves her and if she believes waiting is important. Another reader is advised to stop his "conquest and 'scoreboard' approach to partners . . . . Sex, after all, is more than the joining of genital parts, it's a process of giving and receiving and—like any gift—it is enjoyed most when shared with a friend or a loved one" (December 1969).

To the man worried about guiding his fourteen-year-old daughter, *Playboy* says:

> What your daughter needs, in addition to the physiological facts of life . . . is a set of moral values to give meaning . . . to [help her] realize the confusion [of] indiscriminate and irresponsible sex with sexual freedom, making it clear to her that freedom of any kind entails responsibility . . . [and that] sex that is indiscriminate and impersonal is neither love nor freedom, but only empty, pointless promiscuity.
>
> (February 1966, p. 40)

Adultery and the Double Standard

Playboy clearly denounces every aspect of the sexual double standard, in articles on premartial pregnancies (March 1969, p. 38), virginity for females only (December 1969, p. 64), and one-sided marital fidelity. To men who feel wives should be faithful but excuse themselves "because women have a more sacred obligation . . . whereas men find it harder to control emotions," *Playboy* says: "We can't justify infidelity for one any more than the other . . . woman does not have any more sacred obligation than a man. . . . Culture is responsible for the ideas of women being less sexual" (January 1966, p. 52). A soldier writes, "I'm stationed in a battle zone and don't think I should feel guilty about indulging in sex now and then. . . . My wife has all the amenities and pleasures of the United States and I feel that she should abstain"; but *Playboy* disagrees: "We think that your wife is the same distance from you as you are from her. The same standard of behavior, whatever it is, should apply to both of you" (February 1969, p. 42). Finally, to the wife who disassociates sex from love and would like to enjoy purely physical relationships with other men, the advice is: "There is no reason your husband can't become more than one person in the sense of developing a wider repertory of sexual practices. Seek satisfactions with your husband" (July 1969, p. 39).

Several articles in *Playboy* reported on the increasing number of groups who *do* separate love and sex in free-for-all, anything-goes parties. In "The Sexual League" (November 1966), for example, the activities of a "new breed of unabashed orgiasts and casual couplers" are described, and "The Swingers" (April 1969) reports on spouse-exchange clubs, but there is little in either article that could be construed as advocating such affairs.

Playboy emphasizes the distinction between its "liberal sexual philosophy" and promiscuity and has advocated reform of many archaic sex laws concerning such things as abortion, divorce, adultery, fornication, and cohabitation, "not as an endorsement of either premarital or extramarital sex but in the firm belief that such personal conduct should be left to the private determination of the individual and is not rightly the business of government in our democracy" (September 1963, p. 64).

Playboy accuses the women's magazines of being "sick, sick, sick where sex is concerned" and speaks of the "ladies' home jungle" (February 1965, p. 42), but oddly enough it is the *Journal* which comes closest to *Playboy* in many ways. The *Journal* doesn't "sell" premarital sex as a way of life in the manner of *Playboy* and *Cosmo* but recognizes it as a fact of life; articles point out the *need* to prescribe "the Pill" for unmarried girls, to reform sex laws, and to adopt varying attitudes toward adultery. Frequently an article of a controversial nature will be prefaced with an editorial comment supporting a position which the editors know is contrary to the majority opinion of their readers. It is in *McCall's* that the articles by or about well-known figures affirm all the "tried and true" beliefs on "decency and morality" (along with motherhood and apple pie).

Bishop Pike, in his book *You and the New Morality*, discussed types of adultery and defined three types of moral attitudes toward it: *code ethics*, the traditional "Thou shall not commit adultery"; *non-normative contemporary ethics*, do what you like as long as it doesn't hurt anyone; and *situation ethics*, the act viewed in the total context of a relationship and the effect upon all concerned. Following this framework, we might say the overall approach to adultery in *McCall's* is based on traditional code ethics and in the *Journal*, on situation ethics.

McCall's is concerned with opinions toward adultery as expressed by theologians, psychologists, and sex researchers (e.g., Niebuhr, Fromm, Masters and Johnson) and as determined by a survey of 1112 adults (May 1966). The survey sample included twice as many women as it did men; all were married, middle-class, and generally well-educated. Both readers and writers indicated that infidelity is seen as pathological and a clear sign of "sickness" both in individuals and in society.

The "experts" all presented defenses for love and morality but *not* for the double standard; readers, however, gave reasons for the continuance of differing expectations for wives and husbands. Eighty percent of the survey sample considered infidelity a grave moral wrong, a most serious sin. However, opinions were about equally divided as to whether it should be considered a crime and the proper concern of law (45 percent, yes; 46 percent, no). A few felt that "sin is sin," but most did recognize mitigating circumstances. On the whole, however, infidelity was considered far more serious for a woman; nearly one-third condemned the unfaithful wife more than the unfaithful husband. Thirty-five percent of those who condemned women more than men used biological explanations: "male lust," "men don't get deeply involved," "female sex drive is weaker so women should be able to resist temptation more." Other reasons involved the "woman as angel" image: "women have higher standards," "worse for women because they are mothers," "more trouble if a woman is unfaithful than if her husband is." One particular excuse for wayward males suggests a reason for their reluctance to have their wives work: offices are viewed as breeding grounds for extramarital affairs. Men are seen as being constantly subjected to temptations at work, whereas their wives, at home, are less tempted; to be unfaithful, according to this view, a woman really has to go out of her way. Love and infidelity were seen as incompatible; only 30 percent of the sample believed that someone who loved his spouse could be unfaithful. Divorce was seen to be morally preferable to infidelity.

Indications are that today's woman is rejecting the double standard somewhat more than did her mother; when dear old dad strayed, mother often had no choice so she "screamed, suffered, lived with it," while today's woman is more apt to divorce him. Since adultery is viewed as a serious transgression that requires some action on the part of the "innocent party," many wives wear blinders and adopt a "what I don't know won't hurt me" attitude to protect their marriage—or at least this is the case in a number of short stories.

That males tend to uphold the double standard is reflected not only in the survey on infidelity but also in Sam Blum's article, referred to earlier, on what would constitute "The Perfect Wife" (May 1968). In addition to not being as smart as her husband she also "would not be terribly thrown if her husband's foot now and then happened to slip. . . . Most of the men who wished that their wives would be tolerant of occasional short 'medicinal and rejuvenating' lapses from fidelity were uncertain how they'd feel if their wives had similar tendencies when alone out of town. Some thought they could live with it; more did not. And one said, 'The ideal wife doesn't create worries. She doesn't do anything to worry you, and she doesn't make you worry about anything you've done."

The *Journal* is more concerned with the phenomenon of adultery itself— frequency, type, causes, and consequences—although the "Voice of Women" polls have touched upon attitudes. In response to a poll on divorce, 1272 *Journal* readers considered the statement, "A single act of adultery by either partner should not be cause for divorce." Thirty-five percent said "often true"; 39 percent, "sometimes true"; and 22 percent, "rarely true." In another poll, 607 readers were asked about "What Women Want in a President"; 8 out of 10 felt that a known adulterous affair would cost a candidate the votes of women and that even a rumor would cause 4 out of 10 to vote against a candidate.

A report on infidelity was prepared by the Family Service Association (April 1965) based on data collected by 154 agencies across the country. Unlike most readers, who believe adultery is *the* cause for divorce, the marriage counselors polled felt that it should not even be considered as sufficient legal grounds and should be treated as a symptom rather than a cause of marital problems. They also observed, "The emancipation of women has made no appreciable inroads on the tradition of the double standard. . . . Wives . . . are more likely to put up with the situation because they want to preserve the family." Infidelity figured in nine out of forty-seven cases in "Can This Marriage Be Saved?" and a "situation ethics" approach was evident in the comments by advising counselors; in one case the blame was placed squarely upon the faithful, "innocent" husband who only had time for business.

The eternal triangle has long been a favorite theme of writers, and infidelity occurred in the fiction of all four magazines, but not to the same extent. *McCall's* sample included 127 fiction items but infidelity was the theme of only 6; of the *Journal's* 104 stories, 15 involved infidelity; 21 of *Playboy's* short stories concerned unfaithful spouses, but this number comes from a total of 220; *Cosmopolitan's* sample included only 76 fiction contributions but 25 of the 76 included adultery. In the women's magazines, including *Cosmopolitan*, the affair was not always that of the main character, and infidelity was usually pictured as leading to trouble. *Playboy* had more cases of casual sex on the part of men and also a number of jealous husbands. In the women's magazines, a story often revolved around the reaction of the wife to her husband's infidelity; wives never acted rashly, rarely made a scene, and generally handled the entire situation calmly. If a divorce followed, it was at the husband's request to marry the "other woman." Usually only one spouse was shown as being unfaithful, but in the few stories where both partners had affairs, three clearly implied a double standard. Approximately one-tenth of *Playboy's* short stories involved adultery, but there were interesting variations not found in the women's magazines: in 13 out of 21 stories there was an unfaithful wife, but 5 of the 13 were cases in which the wife's adultery had been engineered by the husband for his own gain. In general, there were more philandering men than promiscuous women, and fiction writers were not often inclined to provide the erring individual with the kind of excuse that readers might regard as "acceptable" in real life; love appeared less often as a motive than opportunity and boredom. *Cosmopolitan* had only six women who were housewives, and five of these became involved in affairs out of boredom. Although several stories concerned the problems of wives whose husbands traveled, only the traveling husbands were presented as seeking casual sex to pass the time; wives were shown at home with constant crises. A nonfiction assessment of "What a Husband's Business Trips Do to a Marriage" (*Journal*, May 1970) indicates that many of the wives concerned are bored and lonely, feel that their femininity is threatened, and thus become vulnerable to every man.

It appears, then, that men are reluctant to have their wives work because it increases their opportunities for infidelity, but on the other hand a bored housewife may be more susceptible to the temptation of an extramarital affair. Perhaps adultery and this concern with it is simply a question of some degree of "liberation" as a result of the Pill and the trend toward a franker treatment of sex.

Women's Liberation and the Image of Women

New contraceptive technology may have given women an increased feeling of freedom by decreasing the chances of an undesired pregnancy, but it takes a good deal more than the Pill to liberate women from many of the ideas that confine them both physically and mentally to their homes. Many have no wish to be "liberated," nor are they willing to accept any "unnatural" tendencies in other women. Even the amount of volunteer work and the kind of community activities must be within the culturally acceptable areas— the local PTA and the community hospital. The reactions of American women to the death of a white female civil rights worker reflected what the *Journal* called "isolationism of the heart." A leading research organization undertook a survey in which a representative national sample of women was asked, among other questions: "No matter what your opinions are on the question of voting rights, do you think that Mrs. Viola Liuzzo, the Detroit civil rights worker who was killed in the Alabama shooting incident, had a right to leave her five children to risk her life for a social cause, or not?" The answers varied regionally, with 61.2 percent of southern women and 45 percent of women in the West replying no. The overall total of women replying was 55.2 percent, with 18.4 percent giving no opinion. The *Journal* found this implied image of women very disturbing and followed the survey with a panel of suburban wives. From that meeting, the editors came away asking: "Can women really manage to make their homes tight, safe little islands in these days and the days to come?" (July 1965).

In a less comprehensive survey the *Journal* asked 500 readers about "Their Most Secret Fears" (March 1968). The women were given a list of 100 fears and asked to check those that affect them personally. The top two (39 percent and 38 percent) were "afraid of all the hate and killing in the world" and "afraid of getting fat." The complete list of fears was not given, but the remaining top five most mentioned were "thoughts of today's young people" (27 percent), "religion won't mean enough to my children" (25 percent), "lack of willpower" (25 percent), "never be able to stop smoking" (24 percent), and "inability to manage money." Can these really be typical of American women?

The *Journal*, always alert to the developments that critically affect the role of women, was concerned with Alabama Governor Wallace's defiance of the state law when he "ran for reelection" by placing the name of his wife Lurleen on the ballot. The wives of each of the nation's governors were asked if they felt that the candidacy would reflect on American women and on the dignity of government. Of the thirty-one responses, most approved Wallace's action or overlooked the relevant issues about how a woman achieves a place in public life.

Possibly women approve of women if they know that there's a "strong man" who's really running things, but of the 607 women who were asked about qualifications for President, 6 out of 10 said they would not vote for a women.

How are the Women's Liberationists going to overcome the prejudices held by their own sex? Does the *Cosmo* girl want to be liberated?

> Like many other women I've come to respect it [the Women's Liberation Movement] late in the day, thinking at first that it was just an attack by a few hostile nutburgers who were giving ALL women a bad name. . . . How does *Cosmo* fit in? The girl this magazine is edited for loves men . . . doesn't feel alive unless she's in love and *giving* to a man and because there is a shortage (5 million more single girls than men not counting the large homosexual population which stacks the statistics even further against her) she works, yes *works*, at being a living doll. And that is perhaps where we and Women's Lib part company. We are pleasing men not because they demand it or to get anything material from them but because we adore them, love to sleep with them, want one of our own, and there aren't enough to go around! The *Cosmo* girl doesn't live *through* men, however, or through children.
> (Helen Gurley Brown, editorial, June 1970)

McCall's has been the most consistently conservative of the magazines in our study and normally reflects the more traditional aspects of our culture in both writers and readers. Clare Boothe Luce finds it difficult to share the indignation about the overall "inferior" status of women in economic and social life and says, "Women who do bemoan the inferior status of their sex should occasionally remind themselves that there is no equality when it comes to the hardest and the dirtiest job—fighting a war" (April 1967). The October 1969 *McCall's* asked, "Is a Women's Revolution Possible?" A young "liberated woman" took the affirmative and attempted to give a progress report, but it relied more on optimism for progress in the future than on evidence of progress already achieved. She reported the mustering of "opposition" forces in the form of an organization called SEAM: Society for the Emancipation of the [American] Male. SEAM and its women's auxiliary want to put man back in his "rightful place as head of the family"; it esteems women who are submissive and obedient, and it believes that today's troubles are caused by the fact that men no longer rule the home and women no longer want to stay there.

The negative reply to "Is a Women's Revolution Possible?" was presented by sociologists John Gagnon and William Simon. They agree that women are the largest underprivileged class in America, but their demands center on a restructuring of "the very core of social relationships in the society . . . . Occupational change will influence the domain of sex and the family." In other words, to preserve the status quo, women must stay home, and the article implies that changes in the roles of women would affect "the very image of what men and women are and can be—and this image is sacred. How're you going to keep 'em home? The time-honored formula is "barefoot and pregnant."

Jeanne Sakol, a *Cosmo* contributor who is "still auditioning for a husband," appears in *McCall's* as the founder of "The Pussycat League" (February 1970), a new breed of women who believe in being extremely nice to men (scarce, you know). Why the name "Pussycat"?

> We chose it because it expresses our kind of woman. Like pussy-cats, we are essentially domestic animals, intelligent, sophisticated, affectionate, and loyal. Although Pussycats adore adulation, they remain their own woman. They neither grovel nor apologize. They have self-esteem combined with a desire to please. . . . The Pussy-cat League would be feminine rather than femin*ist*.

Pussycats advocate "doing your own thing" even if it's being a "love slave," and they also favor changing laws and providing greater opportunities for women who want them, *but* they prefer to gain these opportunities by "sweet persuasion." The philosophy of individuality is admirable and no one denies that love is better than hostility, *but* the article is pure *Cosmo* alley cat cleaned up for the Ladies' Aid Society:

> A few flat-heeled ladies accused us of being Victorian throwbacks. "You're playing into men's hands. All men want is your body," one warned.
> Where, where? I wanted to know, the shortage of lusty menfolk being a known concern to career girls in New York. . . .
> Several sterling men have volunteered to be Tom Cats and Cuddly Bears in the Men's Auxiliary. One of them might even turn out to be mine. Purr-purr.

Rudyard Kipling's observation about the Colonel's lady and Judy O'Grady (from "The Ladies") could well be paraphrased:

> When you get to man in the case,
>   They're alike as a row of pins—
> For *McCall's* lady and the *Cosmo* girl
>   Are sisters under their skins.

McCall's has not been under fire from the Women's Liberationists. Shana Alexander was appointed editor in April 1969 and became the first woman to hold the top position since 1921.[15] Perhaps the publisher recognized the political expediency of putting a woman at the helm before the shooting started. The first year brought very little change, and the new editor dealt cautiously with Women's Liberation groups and appeared to be watching which way the wind was blowing. The latest bulletin from the media front reports that Betty Friedan, of *The Feminine Mystique* and Women's Lib group NOW, has signed on as columnist for *McCall's*. Articles on day-care centers and other relevant issues are making a belated appearance, and Mrs. Alexander has apparently decided the direction in which forces are moving: "Now I feel a general function of women's magazines is to be not only a voice speaking to women but the voice of *women* speaking to women" (*Newsweek,* February 8, 1971).

Playboy and its editor are in a slightly different position in relation to the demands of Women's Liberationists. Hugh Hefner's not the scoundrel they accuse him of being. As with John Mack Carter of the *Journal,* one suspects his chief crime is being male. Respect for the individual has always been part of the "Philosophy," and as far back as 1966 *Playboy* published an article by Pearl Buck, "Women as Angels," in which she pointed out that men themselves had created "the vestal-virgin view of females" that they were now decrying and that when a man insists a woman be an angel, he loses her as a woman. "The New Girl," the postfeminist girl, was applauded in January 1968, but the most impressive thing about her in the eyes of writer John Holmes was her liberated attitude toward sex (Christmas everyday?). Red-blooded male Morton Hunt, as might have been expected, came to the defense of his sex in "Up against the Wall, Male Chauvinist Pig!" (May 1970). Many intelligent men do become defensive when confronted with the militant man-haters. At the present time, reactions are more against the anti-male faction than against the profemale agitators among the Women's Liberationists. Letters pro and con from male and female alike pour into the *Playboy* letterbox, but how much *should* the magazine change? Would the image be so drastically changed if some of the well-qualified women writers were published in *Playboy*'s pages? I'm not sure that Mr. Middle-class Middle-age Male is quite ready to accept it (unless, of course, he couldn't judge the sex of the author by the name).

Although the *Journal* has been edited by a man, John Mack Carter, for a number of years, it has been the most consistently concerned about women as individuals and it advocated day-care centers five years ago, not in one article but in a series of six. Individual contributors consistently supported the belief that women were persons and not just the "wife of so-and-so" and "so-and-so's mommy." Yet it was the *Journal* which was stormed by 200 militant feminists demanding that the editor turn the operation over to them and let them select an all-female staff. Carter's reaction was understandably defensive when he spoke of "extremist eccentricities" of the movement. Following their sit-in, he acknowledged that many of their demands were not unreasonable, but he maintained that "there is still a predominant block of intelligent women who enjoy centering their lives around a family and don't consider domesticity demeaning" (May 1970). The June issue appeared almost reactionary, with a group of short stories all moralizing on the sanctity of motherhood. Thousands of readers responded to the March sit-in and the tally of comments, though still incomplete in November, indicated that 46 percent were for the New Feminism, 34 percent against, and 20 percent mixed, in that they were for equal rights but against the "antics." One would almost wonder if the bra-burners were not on a secret payroll of the "enemy." However, by February 1971, Carter conceded, "Some of the complaints made about our magazines by the women's lib types were right. There has been a lot of silliness cranked out to sell products and life-styles to women, but it will never happen in this magazine again. The *Journal* will not be guilty of any sort of stereotyped formula or position concerning women" (*Newsweek*, February 8, 1971).

Now all we do have to do is convince Ms. America.[16]

Notes

1. Margaret Mead and Francis Kaplan, eds., *American Women*, Report of the President's Commission on the Status of Women (New York: Charles Scribner's Sons, 1965), app. III, pp. 214–219.
2. The study sample included issues beginning with January 1965 and ending with June 1970, but not all 66 issues of each publication were included, since all were not readily available in the limited time. *Playboy* was complete with 66 issues; *McCall's*, 62; *Ladies' Home Journal*, 52; *Cosmopolitan*, 27 issues, beginning with July 1965, when Mrs. Brown became editor.
3. Ellis Folke, "Working Women III: What They Watch, Read, Listen To, Their Relation to the Media," *Media-Scope*, vol. 12 (December 1968), p. 82.
4. Darell L. Guder, "Who Is Man and What Is Love?" in *Eternity*, as quoted in *Playboy*, vol. 12 (January 1965), p. 54.
5. Jude Wanniski, "More Women, Fewer Blue Collars Will Mark Work Force in 1980," *National Observer*, November 16, 1970.
6. Nancy Gittelson, "The Doctors Disagreed," "Needles and Pins" column, *Harper's Bazaar* (April 1967). This represents an interesting example of selective perception; *Ladies' Home Journal* and Kelly Girl Services, Inc., jointly sponsored a seminar titled "Quo Vadis, Today's Woman?" with ten distinguished panelists and "300 female opinion-makers." The *Journal's* report of the conference appeared in February 1967 under the heading, "The Battle of the Sexes Is Over. Who Won? We Did." According to the *Journal*, "American women now have the best of all possible worlds—almost. And in the future, they'll have it even better. That's what the experts said at the . . . Forum." According to Miss Gittelson, "The doctors disagreed" among themselves, and this opinion was not unanimous.
7. Ardis Whitman, "Why Husbands Don't Say What They Really Think," *McCall's* (September 1966). This article was based on research by psychologist-psychotherapist Dr. Anne Steinmann and by Dr. David Fox, associate professor in the School of Education, City College, New York.
8. Robert J. Havighurst, "Counseling Adolescent Girls in the 1960s," *Vocational Guidance Quarterly*, vol. 13, pp. 153–160.
9. Kirk Polking and Natalie Hagen, eds., "Women's Magazines," in *Writer's Market* (Cincinnati: Writer's Digest, 1970), p. 311.
10. As quoted in Peter T. Chew, "Women's Magazines Dig New Ground," *National Observer*, June 23, 1969, p. 1.
11. Jeanne Sakol, "Are 4 Million Girls Doomed to Be Old Maids?" *Detroit News*, November 16, 1969.
12. Chew, *op. cit.*, p. 12.
13. Phyllis I. Resenteur, *The Single Woman* (New York: 1962), p. 9.
14. "Liberating Magazines," *Newsweek*, February 8, 1971, p. 101.
15. "Lady at the Top," *Newsweek*, April 28, 1969, p. 88.
16. *Ms.* stands for a woman without differentiating for her married status; it is the equivalent of *Mr.* for men.

Instead of a Discussion: Companionate Marriages and Sexual Inequality: Are They Compatible?*

In all societies practically all individuals from a very early age start forming some idea concerning the meaning of marriage, the needs that may be reasonably well satisfied within it, and the nature of their future marital roles. The way one has been socialized, the types of marital relationship one's parents, relatives, and close friends are perceived as having developed serve, as "positive" or "negative" models in the formation of marital expectations. Whether these models will be "positive" or "negative" probably depends upon the degree to which they deviate from societal norms or upon the individual's overall socialization experiences as well as upon the nature of ongoing social changes in laws, structures, and familial values.

In contemporary societies, mass media are an equally important (if not more important) influence upon young people's conception of marital expectations than are socialization experiences. Furthermore, in some industrialized societies, formal education at the secondary as well as at the college level also includes education for marriage. Of course, the content purveyed by the mass media as well as that of the courses preparing the young for marriage varies widely from society to society, according to the respective stage of social modernization. In some societies, mass media as well as formal education may be used as tools in reaffirming traditional values and structures and in justifying them in terms of new, culturally congenial, and appealing grounds (as is the case in the United States). In other societies, mass media and formal education may be used in order to encourage or bring about social change and provide the members of that society with and psychologically prepare them for a greater variety of behavioral alternatives (as in the case in Scandinavian countries, especially Sweden and Finland).

Let us examine in some detail the example of one society, namely, the United States, about which there is considerable information. Probably it is the country where more than anywhere else the family has been "professionalized." Family specialists of all kinds abound, family textbooks at different levels of sophistication are written every day, marriage and family courses are

---

* A very early version of this paper was read at the ICOFA (International Scientific Committee on the Family) meetings in Rennes, France, April 3–7, 1969. Thanks are due to Jan Trost, whose comments and suggestions both on the version of the paper presented at the meetings and on some of the subsequently revised drafts have reoriented my thinking, by sensitizing me both to linguistic and to conceptual "biases" about the roles of men and women.

taught at the secondary and the university levels, and all mass media carry explicit and implicit messages as well as explicit models of married life and of "masculine" and "feminine" roles.

Reviews of family sociology and family-life textbooks have shown that the authors rely less on actual research studies than on secondary sources (mainly other textbooks, the authors of which have often expressed their opinions and values instead of reviewing research findings).[1] In this way, myths about the American family are born, perpetuated from textbook to textbook and from family course to family course, and further disseminated through the mass media. For example, the myth that the American family is equalitarian, reflecting an ideal congruent with major American values, has been perpetuated despite all research evidence to the contrary. Neither decision making nor the division of labor in the family (even among middle-class spouses) has been found to be equalitarian, nor has the conception of marital roles by married people been reported as companionate or equal in any sense.[2]

Furthermore, a content analysis of selected family-life textbooks used in high schools has shown that the family is usually presented as an ideally harmonious unit free from conflict in which everyone is very democratic, understands everyone else, discusses reasonably, and compromises.[3] This ideal, which does not exist in any country and probably not even in heaven, becomes confused with and colors the actual evidence—whenever such evidence is at all considered. As we have seen in this section, the family is presented in a similar spirit in the mass media, that is, as blissfully happy, unless "sick" families are portrayed, in which case conflict and hatred abound and lead to their eventual disintegration.

Furthermore, the two content analyses of women's magazines included in this part, one comparing the heroines of fiction published in *Ladies' Home Journal, McCall's, Good Housekeeping,* and *Woman's Home Companion* in 1957 and in 1967 (Lefkowitz) and the other analyzing fiction and nonfiction in the first two magazines (Ray), have come to the same conclusion. Working or career women are still very few (especially, in the case of wives and mothers) and are fewer now (in 1967) than in the past (1957). And the few career women are usually portrayed as "unwomanly," that is, as deviants.

Moreover, the importance of the two principal roles for women, *wife* and *mother,* is greatly stressed by articles advocating that young girls be properly socialized for these roles and that they avoid becoming intellectual or learning "too much." Furthermore, the same magazines tend to idealize the husband-wife relationship as a happy, close, companionate, and fulfilling relationship for both spouses.

It seems that, in general, in both family textbooks and mass media it is taken for granted not only that the wife's lesser development and nonworking status are compatible with a companionate marriage but even that they are conducive to such a marriage. But, in fact, can a marriage of two unequal people blossom into a companionate relationship? Does not the very notion of a companionate marriage presuppose the union of "equals"?

To begin with, we should examine the nature of a companionate marriage, the extent to which young people's expectations about marriage fall within the range of a companionate relationship, the extent to which married American men and women are "equals" and manage to be companions during marriage, and, when they fail, the reason for their inability to become marital companions.

A companionate or equalitarian marriage is one in which both spouses are primarily friends and companions to each other, joined in a mutually supportive and complementary relationship rather than a dominant-subservient one, and sharing about equally all the familial tasks, responsibilities, and privileges. We might note here that implied in this definition is the assumption that equalitarian or companionate marriages are the most fulfilling, if not the most happy and successful, ones.

With this definition in mind, let us now see what young people expect from marriage and how they define their respective marital roles. Reflecting to some extent the ideal of family life presented in mass media, family textbooks, and family courses (and despite the family model they report to have existed in their family of orientation), young men and women desire an equalitarian family in which decisions are made jointly and familial roles are shared between husband and wife.[4] But while this is the overall pattern, there are some quite interesting differences between boys' and girls' answers concerning division of labor. For example, boys tend more often than girls to think that traditionally "masculine" chores should remain a male province, while they are willing,[5] more than the girls are willing to let them, to share equally with their future wives in the performance of traditionally "feminine" tasks (such as "cooking and keeping house" and "staying at home with the children").[6] Also, in case both spouses work, boys are much more willing to assume family and household responsibilities than the girls are psychologically prepared to let them.[7]

Similarly, an investigation of the sex-role concepts among elementary school age boys and girls showed that boys tended to "desegregate" behaviors perceived by the girls and by an adult group as feminine. This tendency was particularly true in the case of child-care items.[8] It is also interesting to note that the decision concerning whether or not the wife will work is envisaged by college students as a joint decision, and there is some evidence that increasingly some boys would like their future wives to work or would tend to leave it up to them.[9] Young girls, however, are not inclined to consider a career, because, as they say, their fiancé or boyfriend "does not like them to work," but in actual fact in many cases they have never even contemplated the possibility of this option because of a "correct" sex-role socialization nor have they attempted to negotiate with their potential spouses.

Research evidence from newly married young people, on the other hand, has shown that the transition from the ideal equalitarian model to the traditional sex-segregated model tends to be gradual. For example, money management is much more of a joint activity during the first year of marriage than ever after.[10] Also young childless couples or couples with children under five tend to assume much more equally the responsibility for housekeeping tasks than couples with children over five years of age.[11] And some current evidence from my research in Detroit shows that newly wed husbands and wives (both black and white couples) significantly more often than spouses after five years of marriage tend to see their own and their spouse's role as "expressive" and "companionate."[12]

Research evidence from different surveys corroborates the fact that marriages increasingly become nonequalitarian and sex segregated. Since the earlier data on married and unmarried college students refer to a population drawn from a specific social class (middle and upper-middle), they can be compared only to the findings about middle- and upper-middle-class families. And data obtained from middle-class families show that the joint decision-making aspirations of the young people turn into father-dominated decision making (at least in the important decisions)[13] and that married women end by defining the "breadwinner" function as the most important element in the husband's role and the "mother" function as the most important element in the wife's.[14] What happens to companionship and equalitarianism? By what process do those who marry come to exchange their equalitarian ideals for the traditional mode of family life?

Probably the answer to these questions lies in the controversial issue of equality between men and women. From the very beginning not only are American boys and girls socialized into the traditional "masculine" and "feminine" roles[15] but the belief is instilled in them that the sexes are socially, psychologically, and biologically unequal, the female sex being the inferior one.[16] Furthermore, one particularly interesting feature of the socialization process of American women is the discouragement of the development of a distinct and strong personality, because it is feared that such a personality would become an obstacle in getting married, restricting the field of eligibles, although the narrowed field will then be made up of "desirable," "nontraditional" men.[17] It is believed that "maximum flexibility" facilitates not only mate selection but also marital adjustment, since the bride has no set preferences, habits, values, and attitudes and can easily adopt those of her husband. Thus, women sometimes fail altogether to develop an identity and a well-organized personality out of fear that they might displease someone or offer opposition. Identity questions posed to adolescent as well as young adult girls have shown that their conception of who they are and who will they be in the future is diffuse and hazy and bound to who their husband will be.[18] Characteristically, when girls in their junior and senior years of college were asked to project what they planned to be doing and how they planned to be living in ten years, most of them answered that they would be married, have two or three children, and be living in a middle- or upper-middle-class neighborhood.[19] Also the girls more often gave descriptions of their future husbands' occupations than of their own jobs, which were usually seen as part-time and of secondary importance to home and family. This discouragement from developing a distinct identity at an early stage often leads to an altogether incomplete and hazy development of identity even in adulthood, as Gass's findings about married women thirty to fifty years old show. Most of these women were not sure who they were, what they could be, and what they wanted to be, thus having typically adolescent questions and preoccupations.[20]

So it seems that the spouses are not socialized to be equals. Women tend to have generalized, broad expectations of fulfillment and self-actualization in marriage and motherhood. It is no wonder then that wives, in general, report a smaller degree of marital satisfaction than men, who have been socialized to expect fulfillment and self-actualization mainly from work and secondarily from marriage and fatherhood.[21] Furthermore, there is research evidence indicating that the marital relationship is much more important to wives who stay at home than it is to those who work.[22]

For wives, unless they are "deviants" and their major commitment is to their work, the roles of wife and mother are the only ones where they can find, if not fulfillment and self-actualization, at least justification for their existence. Thus, housekeeping and motherhood become the only sources of prestige and identification (besides the husband's occupational success), and, therefore, it is rather understandable that wives tend to keep exclusive rights to housework and children, including decisions concerning home and children. Such an exclusivity precludes the husbands' effective participation in housework and child-related tasks, since a more equalitarian division of labor would tend to diminish the wives' self-esteem[23] and the potential outlet for their time and energy.

Thus, wives more than husbands may encourage the early segregation of roles and tasks along traditional lines, according to which the husband must primarily be a successful breadwinner and the wife a "good" housekeeper and mother. Interestingly enough, Feldman has found that before the first child is born, married men desire and plan to share in parental duties much more than their wives anticipate or ever permit once the child is born.[24] Since the tasks relating to housework and children are not exactly very pleasant, the husbands, having often been discouraged from sharing in them, learn quickly that only tangible proofs of occupational success (especially, greater income) are appreciated and rewarded, and they lose the motivation to participate in household tasks. Children and home become the domain of women and the occupational world the domain of men.

It seems, then, that the traditional sex-segregated socialization of American boys and girls leads to nonequalitarian marriages. Furthermore, since husbands and wives tend to live in separate worlds, "real" communication, beyond the routine matters, becomes often strenuous and sometimes impossible. Under such conditions it is very difficult, perhaps impossible, to develop a "vital," "intrinsic" marital relationship that is truly a companionate one, fulfilling to both spouses.[25] But, of course, in some cases, marital satisfaction may be great from a "utilitarian" type of marriage that permits one or both spouses to develop all kinds of other parallel relationships that satisfy some emotional and/or intellectual needs. But increasingly more often these days, as recent statistics seem to indicate,[26] disillusionment from "empty shell" marriages leads to divorce, once the children are adolescents and guilt feelings over the potential negative effects on them can be more easily overcome.

One could, of course, ask the question, But would it be fair for husbands to share in household and child-related tasks or for wives to have a significant say in important decisions when the wives do not share a major responsibility, that of providing the economic support for the family? Available research evidence indicates that when the wife works full time and earns a substantial income, she then plays a more important role in decision making (including major decisions) and her husband tends to a varying degree to share with her the tasks *inside* the family.[27] But as long as her income is not substantial enough or is not used to cover some of the basic economic needs of the family, then, despite some equalitarian trends, the husband still retains breadwinning as his primary responsibility and the wife the traditional feminine tasks as her primary responsibility.

The available research findings from American dual-career families indicate that an equalitarian, companionate relationship really exists only when the wife has a career and not just a full-time job, when she has an income about equal to (or sometimes higher than) that of her husband which is used for family needs, and when her commitment to her work is similar to that of her husband.[28] It is only when the economic support of the family ceases being the primary responsibility of the man that housekeeping and child care cease being the primary responsibility of the woman.

We can conclude, then, that sexual inequality resulting from the traditional sex-segregated socialization of boys and girls and reinforced by a multitude of "pseudoscientific" myths about motherhood, the child's need for twenty-four hours per day of attention from his natural mother, etc., is incompatible with the formation and maintenance of an equalitarian and companionate marriage. Such a type of marriage presupposes the near equality of partners in all life sectors and their potential of being true companions in all of them.[29] So, contrary to what is asserted by mass media and family textbooks, career women are the ones who seem to enjoy more equalitarian and companionate marriages, and often happier and more fulfilling marriages.

Notes

1. Hyman Rodman, "The Textbook World of Family Sociology," *Social Problems,* vol. 12, no. 4 (Spring 1965), pp. 445–457; also, an unpublished review of family textbooks completed by the graduate students enrolled in my seminar on comparative family sociology (Winter 1969).
2. Actually, it would be more accurate to say that we do not really know very well what the familial power-structure patterns are in the United States because of the unsophisticated methodology used in the available studies. (See Constantina Safilios-Rothschild, "Family Sociology or Wives' Family Sociology? A Comparison of Husbands' and Wives' Answers About Decision Making in the Greek and American Culture," *The Journal of Marriage and the Family,* vol. 29, no. 2 [May 1969], pp. 345–352.) And if the data of the available studies are examined closely, it can be found that despite the authors' conclusion that the family is equalitarian, the findings indicate a strong tendency toward husband prevalence, at least among middle-class families. (See Robert O. Blood, Jr., and Donald M. Wolfe, *Husbands and Wives* [Glencoe, Ill.: The Free Press, 1960].) For the traditional definition of marital roles, see Helena Znaniecki Lopata, "The Secondary Features of a Primary Relationship," *Human Organization,* vol. 24, no. 2 (Summer 1965), pp. 116–123.
3. John W. Hudson, "A Content Analysis of Selected Family Life Education Textbooks Used at the Secondary Level" (Ph.D. diss., Ohio State University, 1956).
4. Debi D. Lovejoy, "College Student Conceptions of the Roles of the Husband and Wife in Family Decision-Making," *The Family Life Coordinator,* vol. 9, no. 3/4 (March–June 1961), pp. 43–46; Theodore B. Johannis, Jr., and James M. Rollins, "Teenager Perception of Family Decision-Making," *The Coordinator,* vol. 7 (June 1959), pp. 70–74; and Marie S. Dunn, "Marriage Role Expectations

of Adolescents," *Marriage and Family Living*, vol. 22, no. 2 (May 1960), pp. 99–111.

5. Jan Trost's comments made me aware of the traditional bias underlying such expressions as, the husband "helps with household chores," which implies a basic acceptance of the traditional segregation of roles (and to some extent helps maintain it). Therefore, I have replaced such expressions with more "equalitarian" terminology, such as, the husband "shares" the household chores with his wife.

6. Lovejoy, *op. cit.;* research data quoted by Paul H. Landis, *Making the Most of Marriage*, 3rd ed. (New York: Appleton-Century-Crofts, 1965), p. 125; and Dunn, *op. cit.*, pp. 101–102.

7. *Ibid.*

8. Ruth E. Hartley and Armin Klein, "Sex-Role Concepts Among Elementary School Age Girls," *Marriage and Family Living*, vol. 21, no. 1 (February 1959), pp. 59–64.

9. Lovejoy, *op. cit.;* Constantina Safilios-Rothschild, "College Students' Marital Role Expectations" (unpublished paper).

10. Karen F. Geiken, "Expectations Concerning Husband-Wife Responsibilities in the Home," *Journal of Marriage and the Family*, vol. 26, no. 3 (August 1964), pp. 349–352.

11. *Ibid.* Similar data have been reported among married college students: Victor A. Christopherson and Joseph S. Vandiver with Marie N. Krueger, "The Married College Student, 1959," *Marriage and Family Living*, vol. 22, no. 2 (May 1960), pp. 122–128.

12. From unpublished data of the author, collected from a study of 406 black and white middle- and lower-class spouses conducted in Detroit in 1969–1970.

13. Blood and Wolfe, *op. cit.*

14. Lopata, *op. cit.*

15. David F. Aberle and Kaspar D. Naegele, "Middle Class Fathers' Occupational Role and Attitudes Toward Children," in *A Modern Introduction to the Family*, eds. Norman W. Bell and Ezra F. Vogel (New York: Free Press, 1960), pp. 126–136; and Melvin Kohn, "Social Class and Parental Values," *American Journal of Sociology*, vol. 64 (January 1959), pp. 337–351.

16. For a more detailed discussion and relevant articles, see Chapter 1.

17. Alice Rossi's discussion as quoted in John Lear, "Will Science Change Marriage?" *Saturday Review*, December 5, 1964, pp. 75–77.

18. Elizabeth A. Douvan and Joseph Adelson, *The Adolescent Experience* (New York: John Wiley & Sons, 1966), pp. xii, 471.

19. Gertrude Z. Gass, "Identity: A Contemporary Problem for Women," in *The University in Motion: The Status of Women*, Bevier Lecture Series (Urbana: University of Illinois Press, 1967), pp. 14–32.

20. *Ibid.*, pp. 23–28. We might note that in the American culture a woman's identity is also symbolically (and to a large extent legally) surrendered to her husband at the time of marriage: not only does she lose her last name, but she also loses her first name, to become Mrs. John Doe. For an interesting discussion of this issue, see Alice E. Palmer, "Color Me Female," *Graduate Comment* [Wayne State University], vol. 12, no. 1 (1969), pp. 20–24.

21. Elina Haavio-Mannila, "Sex Differences in Satisfaction" (Paper delivered at the Eleventh International Family Research Seminar, London, September 4–10, 1970); Constantina Safilios-Rothschild, "Deviance and Mental Illness in the Greek Family," *Family Process*, vol. 7, no. 1 (March 1968), pp. 100–111.

22. Haavio-Mannila, *op. cit.*

23. The same point has been made by Alice S. Rossi in "Equality Between the Sexes: An Immodest Proposal," *Daedalus*, vol. 93, no. 2 (Spring 1964), pp. 641–642.

24. Harold Feldman, "The First Child" (Paper delivered at the Groves Conference, San Juan, Puerto Rico, April 1967).

25. Interesting data concerning the different types of familial adjustments can be found in Cuber and Harroff's revealing study of family dynamics among upper-

middle-class Americans: John F. Cuber and Peggy B. Harroff, *The Significant Americans* (New York: Appleton-Century, 1965).

26. Paul C. Glick, "Marital Stability as a Social Indicator" (Paper delivered at the annual meeting of the Population Association of America, Boston, April 19–20, 1968); "Marriages and Divorces," *Vital Statistics of the United States* (1965), vol. 3, sect. 2, Tables 2-4, 2-5 (Washington, D.C.: National Center for Health Statistics), pp. 2–8.

27. Louis Wladis Hoffman, "Parental Power Relations and the Division of Household Tasks," in *The Employed Mother in America*, eds. F. I. Nye and L. W. Hoffman (Chicago: Rand McNally, 1963) pp. 215–230; Blood and Wolfe, *op. cit.*; Deborah H. Kligler, "The Effects of the Employment of Married Women on Husband and Wife Roles" (Ph.D. diss., Yale University, 1954); Geiken, *op. cit.* However, this trend is not conclusive; it may be that there is more sharing of decisions and tasks but not a net change in power structure. See Robert O. Blood, Jr., "The Husband-Wife Relationship," in *The Employed Mother in America*, eds. Nye and Hoffman, pp. 282–305; and Hoffman, *op. cit.*

28. For more details, see the discussion and relevant articles in Chapter 5.

29. Rossi, "Equality Between the Sexes," *op. cit.*

CHAPTER 3

Money, Sex, and Women

Dowry in Modern Greece: An Institution at the Crossroads Between Persistence and Decline*

Introduction

In reviewing current sociological literature on family and marriage, the position of women, and related themes, one cannot help wondering why so little attention has been paid to the institution of the dowry, an institution which still is, after all, part of the social web of a good number of contemporary societies (Ireland, southern Italy, Spain, Portugal, Malta, Greece, Tunisia, Lebanon, etc.).[1]

This neglect is very probably due to the fact that in those countries where sociology and related disciplines are most developed, the institution of the dowry is either altogether unknown (as, for example, in the United States) or has only a limited historical interest, as, for example, in England, Germany, Belgium, and France (where, although it has not been legally abolished, *de facto* French people tend on the whole to regulate property relations between husband and wife on the basis of another legal institution, that of the *communauté de biens*). On the other hand, it is in precisely those countries where the institution of the dowry is still alive with manifold economic and social consequences, and where it could become the object of detailed research, that the study of the native social institutions is not favored, because of the underdevelopment of the social sciences.

The purpose of this article is in some small way to help fill this gap in our knowledge of the function and structure of the institution of the dowry in contemporary societies that this article seeks to fill, even if only in small part and for only the Greek society.

The material for this study has been drawn mainly from three sources: Greek legal sources (mainly the Greek Civil Code of 1946); the relatively few studies carried out, mainly by American and English social anthropologists, on Greek village life; and personal observation and research data collected in

* I wish to acknowledge my indebtedness to the Ford Foundation, whose financial assistance enabled me to study in some detail this aspect of Greek social life. To Professor John Peristiany I would like to express my deep gratitude for recommending me for this grant. Finally, my thanks are also due to Mr. James Warner of the United States Educational Foundation in Greece for the unfailing interest he showed during the completion of this small study, and to my friend and colleague Professor Constantina Safilios-Rothschild, who helped toward its publication.

the course of two sociological projects I conducted, one on a Greek provincial town and the other on university students.

Structure, Function, and Effects of the Institution of the Dowry in Modern Greece

The Legal Rules

The dowry is primarily a legal institution, and therefore the examination of its modern structure must take as its starting point the legal rules which govern it. These are contained in the Greek Civil Code, which has applied in this country since 1946.[2] The Greek Civil Code includes a special chapter on dowry (articles 1406–1437); a number of additional articles referring to the dowry are found mainly in the chapters dealing with the relations between parents and children and the rights to inheritance.

The Legal Definition of the Dowry

The following definition of the dowry is given in the Greek Civil Gode (article 1406): "Dowry is the property which the wife or somebody else on her behalf gives to the husband in order to alleviate the burdens of marriage." In this definition the main purpose of the dowry is very clearly stated. We note that the modern legislator considers, as has been the case throughout the centuries in this country, that the main function of the dowry is to provide a contribution on the part of the woman to the expenses of marital life.

The Rights of the Husband and of the Wife over the Dowry

According to article 1412, the husband, unless stated otherwise in the marriage contract (which is always drawn up before a notary), acquires the right of owning the movable dower property and the right of managing and enjoying the use and advantages (i.e., the usufruct) of the real estate which is part of the dower property. According to article 1414, in case the wife (or whoever acts on her behalf) does not transmit to the husband the right of ownership of the dower property, then he is entitled, as long as the marriage lasts, only to the management and the usufruct of the dower property, while the wife is its real legal owner.

According to articles 1416–1417, the husband is not entitled to alienate either the movable or the real dower property without his wife's consent; when the marriage is dissolved by divorce, the dower property is returned to the wife (or to her heirs), the husband having no more rights over its management (article 1426). In view of these restrictions, it is only too obvious that the dowry is not a gift to the husband.

The Obligations of Parents vis-à-vis Their Daughter's Endowment

According to article 1495, the father is "obliged to provide his daughter who is about to get married with a dowry proportionate to his wealth, to the number of his children, to his social position, as well as to the social position of the future husband." He can be exempted from this obligation only if it can be proved that by giving a dowry he will become impoverished or that the daughter has some other source of revenue which can provide her with a dowry. In case the father has died or is incapable of providing his daughter with a dowry, this obligation is transferred to the mother (article 1497). Parents have the right to refuse to fulfill this obligation in case their daughter has married without their consent or there are valid reasons for disinheriting her.

It should be noted that the dower property is not given to the daughter as a gift: what is given to her (and through her to her husband) is in fact a part or the whole of what she is legally entitled to inherit one day from her parents. Dowry-giving is indeed a transference of property from the girl's family of origin to her and to her husband, by another means than inheritance. It should also be added that according to Greek law all children have equal rights to their parents' property. The sons acquire their share mainly through the system of inheritance, whereas the daughters acquire it sooner by getting their dowry.

The Social Rules

> So, all these parents, all these families, all these widows are under the obligation of marrying off all these daughters—five, six, seven of them: and to provide them all with a dowry. . . . And what a dowry according to the customs of the islands: a house at Cotronia, a vineyard at Ammoudia, an olive grove at Lechouni and a field at Stroflia! But recently, in the middle of the century, another disease has started to spread. The "counting." Each [parent] was obliged to give also dowry in cash. Two thousand, thousand, five hundred, whatever. Otherwise he had better keep his daughters and admire them. He had better place them on the shelf, lock them up in the wardrobe, send them to the museum.[3]

This is how the well-known Greek novelist Papadiamantis described the social pressure for dowry provision which prevailed in Greece in the 1900s. Two-thirds of a century later these comments have lost nothing of their pertinence. For even today, the penalty that many a poor girl pays for not having a dowry is to remain unmarried, that is, to remain "an old maid" (*a gerontokori*), something which is still considered by the majority of Greeks as one of the worse fates that can befall a woman.

In contemporary Greece two tendencies coexist: on the one hand the tendency to judge a woman's worth as a bride primarily on the basis of the size of her dowry, and on the other, the tendency to judge her primarily on the basis of her educational achievements and, more generally, her whole personality. The first, "traditional" tendency is still more common than the second, more "progressive" one, which has started only recently to gain ground, especially among the better educated and the more "Europeanized" Greek families; their attitude is reflected in the motto one hears especially among students, that "A woman's dowry is her education."[4]

The majority of those Greeks, however, who belong to the farmer class, or the working class, or the lower-middle class, continue to regulate the property relations between parents and daughters and between husband and wife on the basis of the rules which emanate from the institution of the dowry. From a purely rational point of view this seems indeed extraordinary, for in most cases their economic interests would be better served if instead of clinging to the tradition of the dowry they broke away, as has happened, for example, in France. Once the parties concerned were in agreement, they could either ignore altogether any legal arrangement to settle the property relations between husband and wife (in this case the couple would decide how each partner should contribute to the household expenses) or choose the legal alternative to the dowry arrangement that the Greek Civil Code provides, the "common pooling of resources" (i.e., *koinoktimosini*; see article 1402 of the Greek Civil Code).

The fact that the institution of the dowry continues to regulate, to a great extent, the property relations between Greek men and women cannot then be explained in terms of the power of its legal norms; the explanation must lie in the power of its social norms, which render this institution a highly valued good that each family must at all costs offer to the daughter, and each woman to her husband. Otherwise, the status of the family and of the woman, as well as her chances of marrying or of marrying well, becomes endangered.

Innumerable instances point to the fact that today the dowry is still a powerful status symbol. For example, in Megara, a provincial town near Athens where I did some research a few years ago, the inhabitants are given the opportunity of assessing a girl's trousseau and dowry during the three days preceding the wedding and on the wedding day itself. "It is then that the linen (named the *youko*), the furniture and the cutlery are exhibited in her [the girl's] house and that neighbors and friends are invited to throw flowers and rice on them [the trousseau items]. One of the aspirations of the Megarian girl is to have a *youko* so voluminous that its pile reaches the ceiling."[5] The origins of this custom may be traced to a time in the past when the society had few status symbols, as was the case with Greek society under the Turkish occupation; thus, the size of the dowry became an important criterion of status and power. Indeed the roots of the modern phenomenon reach far back into the past, whence they draw their strength and their persistence.

The elements which usually compose a dowry—besides the necessary minimum of the trousseau, the household goods, and the furniture—are agricultural property (land, animals, olive trees, etc.), money (usually in gold sovereigns; one gold soverign equals approximately ten dollars), and residential property (a house or an apartment). Any one of these three elements or a combination of all of them may compose a dowry.[6] Under the existing social pressure for the woman to get as large a dowry as possible, a considerable number of Greek families are faced with an economic problem, which becomes more acute the more daughters they have. Discussions and decisions relating to the question of how to meet the often excessive demands for a large dowry on the part of the daughter's future husband form an inextricable part of the life experience of many a Greek family, and obsessive thoughts on the necessity of acquiring a dowry at all costs still embitter the lives of the Greek young women who come from propertyless families.

The Legal and the Social Reality

On the purely formal, legal level the institution of the dowry has been conceived of as economic assistance by the parents to their daughter and their daughter's family of marriage, the underlying assumption being, of course, that the young woman is not by herself capable of contributing to the expenses of family life (i.e., she cannot share with her husband the role of breadwinner) and that she is not able to look after her own property (hence the husband is to be responsible for its management).

Provided that these assumptions are rooted in reality, as they were in ancient Greece and even in Greek society at the turn of the century, the institution of the dowry has a real and useful purpose: to protect and strengthen the basically weak position of the woman. Once, however, the woman is no more in need of such protection, as is the case today in the most technologically advanced societies and as is becoming increasingly the case in Greece, the institution of the dowry ceases to fulfill any socially useful function. Moreover, in case, for a number of reasons, a woman's chances of marriage come to depend on her ability to provide herself with a dowry, the institution of the dowry defeats its own original purpose, for instead of strengthening the position of the woman, it weakens it considerably, especially in the lower ranks of the socioeconomic hierarchy, which means for the majority of women. This "lag" between the legal conception of the institution of the dowry and the social situation which it generates in practice is encountered undoubtedly in contemporary Greece.

The Institution of the Dowry and Its Main Effects

In discussing the effects of the institution of the dowry under two separate headings, the economic and the social, I am of course aware that this distinction is somewhat artificial, since the economic effects are in the last analysis also social. For purely classificatory purposes, however, this distinction seems useful.

Some Economic Effects

The existence of the institution of the dowry creates strong incentives, especially among the poorer Greek families, to save money over a long period of time, to emigrate, and to work.

Saving. Saving money for the daughter's dowry starts quite often, together with the preparation of her trousseau, at the time of her birth. According to Sanders the process of saving for the dowry starts when the girl is ten years of age and often represents the savings of two generations.[7]

A number of Greek economists have criticized, for obvious reasons, the tendency of Greeks to invest their savings in residential property rather than in industry. There is no doubt that the institution of the dowry, which places demands upon even the poorer families to provide their daughter with a house (be it only a one-room dwelling), is up to a point responsible for this trend.

Emigration. One of the basic reasons why a number of Greek fathers and brothers emigrate from Greece is to get higher wages in order to be able to help the younger females in the family back home with formation of their dowries.

A study conducted a few years ago at the Social Sciences Center of Athens[8] among the families of Greeks who had emigrated to Germany, Belgium, etc., concluded that the great majority of single girls who had emigrated had left Greece in order to earn more and be able to build up a dowry. It must be added, however, that when Greek young women emigrate, they are in search of not only higher wages but also a non-dowry-oriented society, such as the Australian or the German one, where they may get married to someone who does not demand a dowry.

Female work. In Greece, the wish to form a dowry is very often the decisive factor in a young girl's decision to work. In case the family (that is, the parents or the brothers) is unable to meet the obligation of providing their daughter with a dowry, this burden is shifted automatically onto the girl's shoulders, who now has to work in order to provide herself with a dowry. What in fact happens is that the girl substitutes her earnings for her share in the family property, which she is in no position to get, since there is no such property. This situation could be described as a parody of the institution of the dowry, which actually presupposes the existence of family property. But the influence of this institution has been so far-reaching in this country that it has affected even the propertyless classes. Furthermore, it should be kept in mind that "self-endowment" has a long history in this country.

In Megara, the hope of acquiring a dowry and thus contracting a "successful" marriage proved stronger than all other considerations and provided a powerful incentive for the young women to go to work in the newly built textile factory of Piraiki-Patraiki, and for their mothers to allow them to work there, in spite of the other inhabitants' reactions against the "immorality" of factory work.[9]

It is of interest to note that, ironically enough, it is the existence of a traditional institution—that of the dowry—which encourages female emancipation, for it is very often in order to meet the demands made by tradition that Greek women have to follow a nontraditional way of living, that is, to work outside their own homes either in this country or abroad. At the same time, however, the very fact that such emancipation is used to reinforce traditional norms—i.e., the wages earned are used to form a dowry—leads to a more rapid acceptance of social change than would have been the case in the opposite instance.[10]

Some Social Effects

The institution of the dowry has an impact also on intra- and interfamilial relations, on the age at which young people marry in Greece, as well as on the mechanism of social mobility through marriage.

Intra- and interfamilial relations and the institution of the dowry. Relations first within a girl's family of origin (between, that is, herself, her parents, and her brothers) and later within her family of marriage (between, that is, herself, her husband, and her in-laws) are affected in various ways and in varying degrees by the institution of the dowry.

Campbell, in his thorough study of the inhabitants of a shepherd community of continental Greece, the Sarakatsani, mentions that he encountered among them "women who harbour resentment against their fathers, because, as they allege, they were given to indifferent husbands in order to avoid the payment of a substantial dowry."[11] It is reasonable to assume that such family conflict is not confined only to the Sarakatsani for a number of Greek parents very probably adopt the "lowering of the standard" solution in order to marry off a daughter in case they are either unwilling or unable to give her a sufficiently large dowry; in this case, she will have to restrict her expectations and marry someone who is her inferior in a number of ways and whose demands, for this very reason, are humble.

In a society like that of modern Greece, where, in the countryside, parents are mainly responsible for arranging the marriages of their children and where the kind of marriage a girl makes depends to a large extent on the size of her dowry, which in turn depends on her parents' wealth and goodwill, the daughter may easily come to blame them for her unsuccessful marriage or for her not marrying at all.

In case the parents are unable to shoulder all by themselves the burden of providing their daughter with a dowry, they transfer part of this onto their sons, who, though not legally obliged to help their sister with her dowry, have definitely, however, a moral responsibility in this regard. To those familiar with the history of the institution of the dowry in Greece, it is well known that the brother's responsibility toward his sister's marriage has a very long tradition in this country. Campbell found that among the Sarakatsani the brothers do not claim their legal share in the family property unless all their sisters have gotten married.[12] There are times when the brother gives over to his sister part of what he is legally entitled to inherit from his parents, in order to enable her to marry. This is also mentioned by Friedl in her well-known study of a Boeotian village, Vasilika, where, in case the prospective husband made excessive demands, the girl's brother would add from his own inheritance to her dowry, so that the marriage arrangements would not have to be broken off. According to Friedl, it is in the brother's interest that his sister marry well, because in this way the prestige of the whole family increases, and as a result he is now able in his turn to marry a girl with a substantial dowry.[13]

Naturally, brotherly sacrifice, which leads to closer brother-sister relations, is not always the case. There must be brothers who refuse to help their sister with her dowry, thus giving rise to feelings of resentment against them not only on the part of their sister but very probably also on that of their parents.

In conclusion, it is suggested that in case parents and brothers do not offer the girl the dowry she expects or feels she is entitled to get, conflict occurs and intrafamilial relations suffer accordingly.

Relations within the girl's family of marriage are affected by whether she has brought with her a dowry, and if she has, by its size. A woman who brings with her no dower property, which represents additional land and cash for her husband to control and additional property to transmit one day to her children, is from the very start of her marriage at a disadvantage vis-à-vis not only her husband but also her in-laws, becoming a ready target for their criticism and even their contempt; her independence and authority within her own family is thus undermined. By working and contributing through her earnings to the family expenses, she might be able to raise her position, but only somewhat, since from the very start she failed to live up to the expectations long-sanctified by law and custom in regard to the Greek woman.

On the other hand, when her dowry is equal to or even smaller than her husband's property, by the very fact that she has conformed to the expected pattern and has some economic independence, her authority within her home is enhanced. When, however, her dowry markedly exceeds her husband's property, her economic superiority renders her position very powerful indeed, and in this case the authority of her husband might become endangered.[14] As for the usual friction between parents-in-law and daughter-in-law, this is probably mitigated by, as Friedl aptly points out, "the independent dignity a girl acquires by having brought her husband a dowry and by the pride her husband's family takes in their own skill at having helped arrange a good marriage for their son."[15]

The institution of the dowry and the age at marriage. The effect of the institution of the dowry upon the age at which young people marry varies, as logic and a few research findings suggest, according to social class. Among the very poor and the very rich, the institution of the dowry, for very different reasons, favors early marriage: The very poor landless families who can provide their daughters with only a small trousseau and dowry have only one way of increasing their daughter's worth in the marriage market and that is by her chastity; they therefore try their best to marry off their daughters as early as possible, so as to avoid the possibility of their "running wild" and thus forfeiting altogether their already slim marriage chances. This pattern has been observed also by Friedl among the poorer strata of Vasilika.[16] At the other extreme of the social ladder, among the rich and the very rich families, the girl, if she so wishes, can get her dowry at a very young age, and the young man, knowing that he will get a substantial dowry, need not wait a number of years before getting married. At this high socioeconomic level the institution of the dowry on the whole favors early marriage.

However, in the middle ranges of the social hierarchy, where the majority of Greek men and women are found, the institution of the dowry is, in all probability, an obstacle to early marriage. The average farmer's family often needs time to accumulate a dowry which will satisfy the prospective groom's demands. Friedl, for example, found that in Vasilika the age of the girls who marry men from the city (that is, men of higher prestige than their own) is usually twenty-five to thirty.[17] In the urban middle classes marriage tends also to be delayed so that young girls are able to finish the university and get a decent job that will help them increase not only their prestige but also their dowry. Moreover, the majority of Greek young men have to work for a number of years before they are able to shoulder even in part the responsibilities of marriage.

These considerations explain, in part, why Greece (together with Ireland, Italy, Spain, Portugal, and Malta, all countries where the institution of the dowry still functions), when compared with the other European countries, stands out by the relatively late age at which men and women tend to marry.[18]

The institution of the dowry and social mobility through marriage. In the most technologically advanced societies of the West, it seems that "homogamy" (marriage between people of equal wealth and prestige) is becoming the general rule, and "hypergamy" (marriage to someone of higher social and economic status than oneself), whether by the man or the woman, is tending to become the exception.[19] In order to state with any degree of certainty what the trend in this respect is in contemporary Greece, we would need much more empirical evidence, both from rural and from urban areas, than is available at present. In the absence of adequate data, the following hypothesis has to be considered as only tentative: *It is suggested that, in contemporary Greece, upward social mobility through marriage, in other words "hypergamy," tends to take place more often than "homogamy" and is encountered especially among men; this, of course, means that "hypogamy" is more common among women.* The following are some arguments to support this view.

Whereas in the European societies of the past the institution of the dowry tended to encourage the tendency of "homogamy,"[20] in Greece this institution had and has dissimilar effects and seems to encourage mainly "hypergamy" (that is, upward social mobility through marriage) among men. This is largely due to the fact that in Greek society men have been able to create a kind of "dowry inflation" by demanding disproportionately large dowries, disproportionate, that is, to their own means; at the same time, the prospective bride's families have played up to these demands by trying to meet them "at any cost," partly out of a strong sense of responsibility toward the girl, partly out of fear of losing the prospective groom, and last, but not least, out of a sense of honor (*philotimo*) which closely associates dowry provision with family prestige. It should be noted that the interplay of these social forces has its roots in the Greek tradition.

In Greece, marriage is still the main means through which a woman can acquire full status in the society. On the part, then, of the women within a certain age group (and of their families), there is a strong *demand* for a husband, and, of course, preferably for a socially and economically successful one. On the part, however, of the young men in the corresponding or slightly older age group, there is not an equally strong demand for a wife. This is so because the Greek culture exerts a much weaker pressure on the man to get married, especially when he is relatively young, and also because the structure of job opportunity and remuneration in Greek society is still such that a young man has to work for a number of years before he is in a position to cover even the essential expenses of a new household. Under such conditions it is only natural that, within the marriage market and within a given age group, men are valued more highly as husbands than women as wives. As a consequence, women (and their families) are obliged, so to speak, to use strong bait in order to lure men into marriage; conversely, men (and their families) can wait for suitable enticement, thus dictating their own terms for marriage. Given the tremendous force and endurance of the social norms which emanate from the institution of the dowry, playing the game on "their own terms" means asking for as large a dowry as possible; in exchange, the man offers the girl the much sought-after status of being a married woman, and in addition whatever other social assets he may possess. For example, many a rural family values highly the prospective husband who lives in the city,[21] and many a lower-middle-class family, the man with a college degree. The price paid for catching such a husband is a dowry which often exceeds not only the girl's legal share in the family property but also the actual earnings and property of the prospective groom.

Thus, in line with Greek tradition, the institution of the dowry becomes, in practice, abused on both sides, leading to economic hypergamy among the men and to economic hypogamy among the women. Since, however, the acquisition of wealth is also a way to social advancement, hypergamy among men is not just economic but also social. It should be noted, however, that by some criteria, such as education, urban status, etc., Greek men tend to be superior to their wives.

Economic and social considerations are not, of course, always the leading criteria in the choice of a marriage partner. A girl's beauty and personal charm are always strong weapons in the husband-seeking game, and love may override all other considerations. Anyone, however, who lives in Greece today and who is in touch with its countryside and its uneducated classes, realizes that the factors discussed in the preceding paragraphs are still more powerful than the forces of personal feeling in the choice of a marriage partner.

Dowry, An Institution at the Crossroads Between Persistence and Decline

Greek society is, of course, not dominated only by those traditional forces we have described at some length in this article. New trends, such as the increasing participation of women in higher education and in the labor force, and the decreasing influence of the family in the arrangement of marriages, are already at work, especially in Athens and the other large cities. Such trends have already started to undermine the institution of the dowry and in time, as they gradually become stronger and more widespread, will lead to its extinction.

In most European societies the advent of the Industrial Revolution marked a turning point in the history of the institution of the dowry. In brief, the basic changes which followed industrialization and which negatively affected this institution were these: the rise in the educational standard of the population, the increasing participation of women in the labor force, the weakening of the role of the family as matchmaker, and the wide acceptance of a new social ethos which placed greater value upon individual achievement than upon inherited wealth and which recognized the woman's right to play other roles in addition to the strictly biological ones of wife and mother. Today, in the technologically advanced societies, a woman's dowry is her education and her work.

Greece has still quite a long way to go in order to reach this level: in Greek society the institution of the dowry still draws its strength from its economic function within the institution of marriage and from its social function as a powerful status symbol. According to the supporters of the institution of the dowry, it also helps to strengthen the position of the Greek woman by increasing her marriage chances and by enhancing her power within her own family. Greeks, however, are becoming increasingly aware that this institution, and the ways in which it has been abused in practice, has the effect much more often of destroying the marriage chances of the woman, restricting her freedom of choice of a marriage partner, and undermining her position inside the home. This destructive social situation created in Greece by the institution of the dowry cannot but gradually undermine the power of its associated social norms and thus render powerless its legal norms, too. Economic, and especially educational, progress will do the rest.

Notes

1. A case in point is that the definition of the term *dowry* is not given in the recently published *Dictionary of the Social Sciences*, eds. J. Gould and W. L. Kolb (London: Tavistock Publications, 1964); the reader is asked to look up instead *bride-price,* a different, even if related, term.
2. The Civil Code of 1946, on the whole, followed the principles of earlier Byzantine-Roman law, according to which husband and wife were not under any legal obligation to regulate their property relations according to the rules of the institution of the dowry; by mutual agreement, each could retain his/her economic independence.
3. A. Papadiamantis, *I Fonissa* [The Murderess], in *Collected Works* (Athens: Estia, 1954), vol. 1, pp. 26–27.
4. Jane Lambiri-Dimaki, "Greek Students: An Analysis of Their Demographic, Social, and Cultural Characteristics," 1969 (Unpublished manuscript).
5. Ioanna Lambiri, *Social Change in a Greek Country Town* (Athens: Center of Planning and Economic Research, 1965), pp. 34–35.
6. See also I. Sanders, *Rainbow in the Rock* (Cambridge, Mass.: Harvard University Press, 1952), pp. 163–165.
7. *Ibid.,* pp. 165–166.
8. The center's name is now National Center of Social Research. For more detailed reference to this research, see Ioanna Lambiri Dimaki, "Dowry in Contemporary Greek Society," *Nea Oikonomia,* no. 11/12 (November–December 1966), p. 886.
9. See Lambiri, *op. cit.,* pp. 59–70.
10. *Ibid.,* pp. 94–107.
11. See J. K. Campbell, *Honor, Family, and Patronage* (Oxford: Clarendon Press, 1964), p. 172.
12. *Ibid.,* p. 44.
13. See E. Friedl, *Vasilika, A Village in Modern Greece* (New York: Holt, Rinehart & Winston, 1962), p. 66.
14. This point is discussed by E. Friedl in her paper, "The Position of Women: Appearance and Reality," *Anthropological Quarterly,* vol. 40, no. 3 (July 1967), pp. 97–108.
15. Friedl, *Vasilika,* p. 55.
16. *Ibid.,* p. 69.
17. Friedl, "The Position of Women," p. 66.
18. See *European Population Conference* (Strasbourg: Council of Europe, 1966), pp. 9–10.
19. See W. Goode, *World Revolution and Family Patterns,* (Glencoe, Ill.: The Free Press, 1963).
20. See M. Radin, "The Dowry," *The Encyclopaedia of the Social Sciences* (New York: The Macmillan Company, 1931), and W. J. Thomas and F. Znaniecki, *The Polish Peasant in Europe and America* (New York: Dover Publications, 1958), pp. 87–128.
21. In Vasilika, for example, Friedl found that a girl is considered to have contracted a successful marriage if she marries a man of urban origin. (Friedl, *Vasilika,* pp. 65–66.)

"Honor" Crimes in Contemporary Greece

Honor, as the core of one's essence, representing one's masculine or feminine integrity, is the prevalent value in the traditional culture of Mediterranean countries.[1] Unless one is a member of the upper class or the power echelons of the society, social acceptance is not possible in the absence of unspoiled honor.[2] Closely connected with honor is the concept of shame: an individual usually feels ashamed when he is dishonored in the eyes of his friends and the community at large. The Greek concept of *philotimo* clarifies the connection between honor and shame and determines whether or not any action will be taken in order to restore the damaged honor. Etymologically *philotimo* means "love of honor" and is used to identify the character of a Greek who is concerned with his honor and his good name above all and who is willing to safeguard it at any price. *Philotimo* acts as the sensitizing catalyst which makes the individual feel shame when one of his own or his family's dishonorable actions is exposed and which drives him (her) to the culturally appropriate action. The following diagram offers a brief description of the process:

$$\text{Event or situation socially defined as dishonorable} \rightarrow \frac{+ \; philotimo}{- \; philotimo \quad \text{Shamelessness}} \rightarrow \frac{\text{Suicide or violence}}{\text{No action taken}}$$

Since it is the possession of *philotimo* that sensitizes a Greek to public opinion and obliges him (her) to conform to the transitional norms of conduct, only a *philotimos* Greek (one who has *philotimo*) is respectable and thought to be well socialized. There is, of course, a minority of people, the *aphilotimoi*, who are not adequately socialized and do not experience shame; they therefore are less concerned with "what others say" and may do nothing to "wash away" the stain upon their honor.[3]

Dishonor may come about for different reasons in the case of men and women: men are dishonored either when they do not behave in an appropriate masculine manner or when their female relatives or their wife is dishonored.[4] As Kenny writes, "A man's honor finally and irrevocably lies in the hands of his women,"[5] since men are considered to be masculine and honorable only when they can control their wives and all female relatives in such a strict manner that the women behave appropriately and never acquire a dishonorable reputation in the community. A woman becomes dishonored when she behaves like a man, enjoying freedom, especially sexual freedom.[6]

Traditional values prescribe different actions for the restoration of honor in the case of women and men. Women who feel ashamed because their unchastity or unfaithfulness is known can only resort to suicide if they have *philotimo*;[7] they must not commit acts of violence.[8] Male members of the family, on the contrary, must defend their honor and the family honor in an aggressive, violent manner by assaulting or killing the dishonored woman and/

or those responsible for the dishonor—that is, by committing an "honor" crime.[9] Dishonor can be "washed away" only with blood, and only the men in the family carry the responsibility for the restoration of family name and honor.

In the light of traditional values, killing in defense of family honor was not considered to be a crime; it was, on the contrary, a socially expected and approved behavior. Because of the complete social acceptance of such violent behavior, sometimes community members and even the local police would cover up the circumstances of the death so that the offender would not be arrested or tried. There are no statistics or specific data available about the incidence of "honor" crimes in earlier years, but folkloric and anthropological evidence points out their occurrence and their social acceptability.[10]

After World War II a number of social changes took place in Greece; some of these changes affected directly and weakened considerably the hold of traditional moral and family values. Such changes were the gradual urbanization of the country and the appearance of an educated, urban middle class. By 1961, Greece was predominantly urban,[11] and survey studies indicate that urban upper and middle class prefer "Western" moral norms to the traditional Greek norms, the more so the higher their education and occupational standing.[12] Only the rural Greeks and the urban working and lower classes remain tradition-oriented probably because of their very recent rural origin.[13] But even the traditional segments of the Greek population are affected to some extent by larger societal changes. For example, in the cities women cannot always be closely watched because they often work away from home; in this way, women of all ages do in fact gain more freedom. Also, not all marriages are arranged by parents, so that girls have a choice as to whom they wish to marry.[14] Similar changes are taking place on a smaller scale in villages as industries employing women move in[15] and as transportation to the cities becomes increasingly easier and permits frequent visits with urban friends and relatives.

Most changes entail greater freedom and choice for women. Such changes, threatening as they are to traditional men, can potentially create new situations in which a man could be made to feel inadequate and possibly dishonored. Thus, the newly acquired right of the woman to exercise self-determination may sometimes result in men's experiencing failures in love. Such failures could make them feel ashamed lest other people judge them to be inadequate, since they could not get or hold the woman they desired. The question then arises as to whether or not these new sources of personal failure would necessarily be defined as dishonorable and as requiring the punishment of the dishonoring agent as a proof of unquestionable masculinity. Such a definition of honor would be quite new. Anthropological evidence suggests that traditionally a man would consider his personal honor insulted only if he were publicly accused of lacking masculinity, loyalty, cleverness, or competence.[16]

Since the different social changes which have taken place have not equally affected the entire Greek population but on the contrary differentials seem to exist with age, place of origin, occupational category, and social class, it should be instructive to examine the "honor" crimes committed in the 1960s, since such crimes might reflect the effect of social changes upon the definitions as to kinds of situations which are considered to be dishonoring as well as upon the appropriate reaction to dishonor.

Methodology

Information concerning the honor crimes were derived from newspaper reports in the daily Athenian newspaper *Kathimerini*;[17] this newspaper was chosen because it is a serious journal which reports factual information without the sensational treatment often given to crimes by other papers.

All arrests for honor crimes reported in *Kathimerini* from May 1, 1960, to October 30, 1963, were analyzed; there were 197 cases. In all cases the report of the arrest included most of the following information: the offender's and the victim's age, sex, origin, occupation; the weapon used, the alleged motive; the setting of the crime; the relationship of the offender to the victim; and the circumstances of the crime. In some cases, further reports at a later time gave a more detailed account of the offender's and victim's life and personality along with excerpts from court proceedings and an examination of other possible motives besides the alleged honor motives.

For our purpose an "honor" crime was defined as any crime in which the offender claimed his motive to be an insult brought to (or a molestation of) his personal or family honor (*thia logous timis*).

The social class of the offender and victims was determined on the basis of their occupation, according to a modified version of Hollingshead's occupational scale and Lambiri-Dimaki's classification of Greek occupations.[18]

Findings

Sex and Age Differences

The 197 honor crimes examined were committed predominantly by men (168 of them, or 72 percent), as the traditional honor norms prescribe; here the man-to-woman ratio is 2.6:1. This sex differential becomes more pronounced when the honor crimes resulting in the victim's death are examined separately; in this case, the ratio is 3:1. It seems that women are not so concerned with killing their victims as they are with punishing them or threatening them. This is also reflected in the kind of weapon most often used by women: throwing sulfuric acid at the victim's face.[19] Sulfuric acid never kills the victim; it only punishes him through a long, painful torture, since it either disfigures him or blinds him. The satisfaction these women seem to derive from thus taking revenge upon an estranged lover most probably lies in the fact that the disfigured or blinded man will no longer be attractive to other women.

In the case of victims, the man-to-woman ratio is not as great as it is for the offenders, since the dishonored woman is often killed along with the dishonoring male (or only the dishonored woman) if the family honor is to be restored.

Table 1 indicates that male offenders were older than female offenders, a difference which is statistically significant (median test $= 5.3017$, $p < .05$). This finding suggests that there is a sex and age differential among those who commit honor crimes. This difference could be a reflection of the fact that the older family member, that is, the father or the older son, was responsible for defending family honor. However, the inspection of each offender's age proved that among the 25 male offenders who were 50 years old or older, only 9 were fathers or older brothers; the other 16 were husbands or men who were defending their personal honor. Among women offenders, however, the 4 who were 50 or older were all mothers defending their daughters' honor in collaboration with other family members. When a new chi-square was computed, excluding male and female offenders who were older family members defending family honor, the same sex differential held true (chi-square $= 5.502$, $p < .05$). That is, men were significantly older than women.

Table 1 Characteristics of Offenders and Victims

	OFFENDERS		VICTIMS	
	Males	Females	Males	Females
Median age	32	28	32	28
*Occupational Status**				
Professionals and high administrators	—	—	2	—
Lower professionals and administrators	—	—	5	—
Small-business owners, businessmen, and clerical workers	2	—	8	—
Skilled workers	11	—	10	5
Semiskilled workers	18	—	9	—
Unskilled workers and unemployed	34	8	5	4
Small-farm owners	16	2	9	—
Housewives	—	15	—	41
High school students	—	—	2	1
College students	—	—	1	1
Place of Residence†				
Rural	75	29	66	25
Urban	56	17	45	37
Semiurban	12	8	14	10

* In the remaining cases the offenders' occupation was not mentioned in the newpaper reports.
† In both the case of offenders and victims, the main offender or victim was recorded.

Therefore, it seems that the older a man, the greater the probability that he will adhere to traditional moral norms which define dishonor in terms of sexually inappropriate behavior of female relatives and which prescribe honor crime as the appropriate restorative measure for a damaged reputation. On the contrary, the younger a man, the greater the probability that he will come in contact with modern moral norms and notions concerning women's right to self-determination, so that he may feel hurt or sad but not necessarily dishonored when his girl friend abandons him, a girl rejects his proposals, or his sister has a lover who does not eventually marry her.

While the relationship between age and adherence to traditional moral norms seems to be as true for Greek women as for Greek men, such adherence affects differently the criminal behavior of women than of men. Thus, the older a Greek woman, the smaller the probability that she will engage in potentially dishonoring behavior, but also the smaller the probability that she will commit an honor crime even if she is dishonored, since the traditional conduct norms do not allow her to defend her honor in any other manner—but passively through suicide.[20] The younger Greek women, however, may be caught in a moral dilemma between conflicting traditional and modern moral norms. The latter are usually maldefined but nevertheless quite attractive to them since they allow a relatively free sexual expression. However, young women may be tempted to enjoy sexual freedom but because they definitely expect marriage, they may feel quite hurt or even ashamed when a liaison known to others is terminated. They may vacillate between traditional and modern moral norms according to what they judge more appropriate from situation to situation. In attempting to persuade their lovers to marry them, they may like to play the old role of the weak and passive woman in need of masculine protection. When, however, they have been rejected by their lovers, they may not be able to suffer passively but instead feel tempted to punish them. By taking the vengeance of their honor in their own hands, they are transgressing twice the traditional conduct norms for women: once by enjoying a freer sexual expression, and once by exhibiting aggressive behavior.

In the case of victims, the apparent sex differential in the median age of males and females is not statistically significant (median test).[21] It seems that the age-sex differential plays no role in the selection of victims; probably other factors play a more crucial role as to whether or not they will transgress punishable traditonal moral norms.

Rural-Urban Differences

The available data indicate that about the same number of crimes are committed in villages (91 crimes, or 46 percent) or big cities (82 crimes, or 42 percent), while only a few are committed in small towns (24 or 12 percent).[22] However, many of the honor crimes taking place in cities are committed by rural people who come to the city where the victim lives with the specific intention to defend their honor. Table 1 indicates the distribution of the offenders' places of residence; these data show that 53 percent of the offenders live in villages and only 37 percent of them live in urban areas. Even in this table, however, the rural origin of offenders and victims may be seriously underrepresented, since the place of present residence rather than the birthplace is usually reported in the newspapers. In all instances in which the address of the offenders in the Greater Athens Metropolitan Area and Salonica was reported they were found to be clustered in working- and lower-class neighborhoods which are largely made up of recent rural migrants.[23]

It seems then that the honor crimes examined tend to be more frequent among people of rural origin who usually adhere to traditional values and norms concerning family roles and behavior.

In comparing the honor crimes committed by rural people with those committed by urban people, some clear patterns of differences become evident:

1. While the majority of honor crimes (75.8 percent) were committed by an unabetted man or woman, this was practically the rule for urban honor crimes but not for rural ones. A collaborating group of relatives, either all men, all women, or men and women, committed 12 percent of the rural honor crimes. Some of these rural honor crimes committed by an entire family had several elements of a vendetta type of crime, since there was retaliation, criminal involvement of the entire family, and a nonspecific direction of the criminal attack (not just against the "guilty" person but rather toward some "significant other," especially the most vulnerable one, e.g., his child). No similar elements of vendetta could be discerned in any of the honor crimes committed by urban offenders.

2. A difference in the definition of honor can be noticed in the motives claimed by urban and rural offenders. While in rural areas honor and dishonor have family-wide dimensions, in the cities it becomes more restricted and individualized. A rural man may feel dishonored by the improper behavior of any of his close female relatives, since he feels responsible for the honor of the entire family. Thus, he may kill his sister or her lover or both because this lover abandoned the sister after having promised to marry her (and/or after having had sexual relations with her) or because the sister is pregnant. And he may behave in a similar manner if the dishonored female is not a sister but a niece or a cousin.

Urban men, on the contrary, tend to restrict the number of women whose behavior reflects upon their masculinity and honor. They may feel that their personal adequacy as men is seriously and directly challenged only when their wife is unfaithful or wishes to divorce them, when a mistress wishes to end their relationship, or a girl finally refuses their amorous proposals;[24] the moral misconduct of female relatives, including sisters, does not seem to lead them to violence in order to restore family honor.[25] While this finding does not necessarily mean that a sister's moral integrity is unimportant for the urban man's definition of honor, it does seem to indicate that the ties with the family of orientation tend to lose the all-pervading and lifelong psychological importance they still have for rural Greek men. In urban areas, personal ties (within and outside marriage) are no more subordinate to ties with parents and siblings and tend to become more crucial for a man's identity. Even in the most traditional segment of the urban Greek population, some changes seem to be taking place which permeate the entire family organization.

3. No females appear among rural offenders except as accomplices of other male and female family members. Dishonored rural women either take no action, and they are then killed by a father, brother, or other male relative, or prove their high degree of *philotimo* and shame by committing suicide. On the contrary, when urban women feel dishonored (and their male relatives, as previously indicated, will not defend their molested honor), they themselves may undertake violent acts in defense of their honor.

In the urban setting, working- and lower-class women seem to be able to choose whether or not they will use their sexual freedom, whether or not they will define themselves as dishonored when an affair does not lead to marriage (despite promises), and whether or not they will resort to violent acts in order to punish the dishonoring man and restore their challenged feminine self-image. In some respects, then, the patterns of sexual and criminal behavior of lower-class urban women becomes very similar to that of urban lower-class men; both cannot tolerate failures in their love life, and they often define such failures as dishonoring events.

4. Divorce or separation was never involved in a rural honor crime. In urban honor crimes, on the contrary, divorce or desertion was often mentioned as the main reason or one of the reasons leading to the crime. These findings reflect the different attitudes toward divorce in rural and urban Greece. In the former, divorce is hardly ever considered as a possible alternative for unsatisfactory marriages. The wife is supposed to love, cherish, and support her husband forever, regardless of what he is or what he does. The husband, on the other hand, in the case of dissatisfaction may rely on beating or on the interference of her parents in order to make her obey him and perform the household tasks, the two main expectations he has from his wife. In the cities, however, even among the most traditional people, that is, the working- and lower-class people, divorce, desertion, or separation seem to have become possible alternatives for both men and women.[26] There are, however, indications that despite the fact that divorces do occur in the urban working and lower class, it is still very difficult for a traditional man to accept that divorce frees his ex-wife of his domination and that she can then act as she pleases. Thus, some urban honor crimes were committed by indignant ex-husbands or estranged husbands who discovered that their ex-wives had lovers, for ex-husbands and estranged husbands seem to feel that the moral "misconduct" of their ex-wives still reflects upon their masculinity and indicates to others their failure as men and lovers.

Occupational Patterns

Since it is known that the higher the educational achievement required for one's occupation, the more modern will tend to be his values, we could expect that honor crimes would be mostly committed by those having semiskilled or unskilled occupations. And in fact, Table 1 indicates that the majority of men offenders whose occupation was reported in the newspaper accounts were unskilled workers or unemployed (44 percent), or semiskilled workers (34 percent); the remaining were either skilled workers (14 percent) or small-farm owners (20 percent). And the majority of the offenders whose occupation was not specifically reported in the newspaper accounts resided in villages and were described as peasants (71 percent). Although only a small percentage (15 percent) of women offenders were reported as working, their occupations follow the same pattern as in the case of men (Table 1). It seems, then, that honor crimes are committed only by those who still adhere to traditional values, that is, rural people and working lower-class Greeks residing in small towns or big cities.

The occupational distribution of victims, however, differs markedly from that of the offenders in that very few victims belong to the lower class (only 10 percent were unskilled or unemployed) and there is a considerable concentration of them in the middle class (35 percent). Similarly, of the female victims reported in the labor force, more than half of them (56 percent) were holding skilled occupations. This finding tends to indicate that the closer one adheres to traditional moral values, the greater the probability that he may commit an honor crime if dishonoring events are forced upon him; the less one adheres to traditional moral values, the less probable that he will commit an honor crime even in the presence of dishonoring events but the greater the probability to become a victim of an honor crime if he has dishonored a traditional man or woman.

Urban middle-class men who no longer adhere to traditional moral values may not think that a girl is necessarily dishonored by premarital sexual relations (to which she consented), and they may believe that they have the right to change their minds about a marriage proposal. Their "modern" views will not be shared, however, by their partners (or the rural brothers of their partners) in case the latter still adhere to traditional moral values; the "modern" behavior of these men may be judged as immoral and dishonoring, and some kind of punishment may ensue. Similarly, urban middle-class women usually feel free to consent or not to the initiation of a relationship or to bring about the dissolution of an unsatisfactory marriage or a no longer desirable affair. In doing so they may seriously threaten the masculinity and honor of their partners, if they happen to be traditional men, thus inviting violence.

Real and Alleged Motives

Although in all cases examined, some kind of molestation to personal or family honor was claimed by the offender, in some cases the reports of the trial indicated that a different motive might underlie honor. For example, a father killed his daughter and her fiancé because this fiancé was asking that the dowry be doubled after learning that his future wife was pregnant from a previous affair. The father claimed "honor" as motive, stating that the man had refused to marry his daughter after having promised to do so, thereby dishonoring her and her entire family. Similar economic reasons, most often connected with dowry, may underlie honor crimes in which a sister or a daughter is killed because she has dishonored her family by granting sexual license to a lover without a promise of marriage or by being abandoned by a prospective groom after having had sexual relations.

The traditional moral norms require that a girl be completely chaste at the time of marriage; otherwise, she cannot be considered as a potential marital partner.[27] However, there is evidence that the rich girls have usually been exempted from this strict moral requirement; they could marry even when they were known to have had premarital relations.[28] Pitt-Rivers has explained the upper-class women's immunity to the honor norms in terms of their high social status, which lends them uncontestable honor.[29] It seems, then, that feminine honor and the possession of money and "uncontestable" social status become interchangeable assets of women in the marriage marketplace. Thus, a poor but chaste girl may marry with very little or no dowry; a girl of a questionable reputation may also marry, provided she can offer a large enough dowry—the worse the reputation, the larger the required dowry.[30]

According to the traditional family norms, the male members of a family must provide unmarried female members with a dowry. Because of this requirement it may well be that when a father or a brother kills the dishonored daughter or sister, he is not so much concerned with honor per se but rather with the practical consequences of her behavior. He will now have to provide the ill-reputed girl with an extravagantly large dowry in order to marry her off, and he may be unwilling to shoulder this additional and unreasonable family burden, which may very seriously compromise his own life (especially true in the case of married or unmarried brothers).[31]

In a few other cases in which a husband had killed his wife because, as he claimed, she had dishonored him by being unfaithful, the trial uncovered that his claims were completely unfounded and that instead he had a mistress whom he wanted to marry. These cases were almost identical to the theme of the Italian movie *Divorce Italian-Style*. Despite the fact that divorce is permitted by the Greek Orthodox Church, divorce proceedings are extremely costly, lengthy, and involved, and an honor crime may be an easier solution.

The main reason an honor motive is often claimed instead of a variety of other motives is the fact that even today the idea of honor persists in Greece among those who would not consider an honor crime appropriate when faced with dishonor. Honor as an ideal in the Greek culture still seems to have the high degree of societal desirability that equality has in the American culture. Most Greeks, including some judges, still feel quite sympathetic toward those who commit honor crimes. The favorable public opinion may be responsible for the frequent lighter sentences for honor crimes than for similar offenses with different motives, and for the fact that once the sentence is over, no social stigma is attached to the ex-convicts by their friends and the community in which they live.[32] An examination of the reported sentences reveals that sometimes perpetrators of honor crimes are acquitted despite the fact that they have killed their victim.

Although data on sentences are only sporadically available in newspaper reports, some patterns are evident. It seems that a woman killing her lover because he broke his marriage promise and abandoned her after having sexual relations (and sometimes after extracting money from her) is usually acquitted.[33] This acquittal seems to reflect the sympathy of public opinion toward women who were abandoned after having lost their virginity; the idea still seems to persist that women are weak, helpless creatures who cannot take care of themselves and that, under the circumstances, they have irrevocably compromised their chance to marry and live a normal life. Also, husbands killing their wives (but not their wives' lover) because they were unfaithful are usually acquitted unless during the trial other motives become evident. Brothers who kill their dishonored sister tend to get a lighter sentence than those who kill their sister's lover or both the sister and her lover. Finally, the only severely punished type of honor crime is the one in which a man kills a woman because his masculine honor was insulted by her refusal of his amorous proposals. Life imprisonment and the death penalty was the punishment in two of the cases. It seems that public opinion is least favorably inclined toward this type of honor crime, probably because it is motivated mostly by hurt pride and masculine ego and very little by any conception of honor.

The fact that the perpetrators of some honor crimes are acquitted or punished by only a few years of prison[34] seems to have led to the creation of a social problem in contemporary Greece. Some individuals use the traditional honor values and norms, which still seem to be highly respected (even by those who do not follow them), as a shield in order to justify self-serving criminal behavior. For this reason, Greek journalists have been calling honor crimes "the camouflage of the criminals."[35]

Conclusion

We have seen how the social changes which took place in Greece in recent years brought about some changes in the definition of what constitutes a dishonoring event as well as in what is an appropriate action in case of dishonor. The ideal of honor, however, seems to persist despite these changes and despite the ever-decreasing number of people who adhere to traditional moral norms. This persistence of the ideal of honor makes possible its use as a cover for criminal behavior not necessarily resulting from strict moral standards or feelings of shame.

It is possible that as the modern moral values influence to a greater extent the younger people in the traditional segments of the Greek population, honor may be redefined in such a manner that fewer situations bring about intolerable feelings of shame and that no violent acts are required for the restoration of molested honor. The elements of such a change already seem to be present in the urban redefinition of honor as based only upon one's own situation rather than the behavior of other members of the family.

Notes

1. This is the theme of an entire book: J. G. Peristiany, ed., *Honour and Shame: The Values of Mediterranean Society* (London: Weidenfeld and Nicolson 1965).
2. *Ibid.*, pp. 12–13; Julian Pitt-Rivers, "Honour and Social Status," in *Honor and Shame*, ed. Peristiany, pp. 50–73.
3. An excellent discussion of *philotimo* can be found in J. G. Peristiany, "Honor and Shame in a Cypriot Highland Village," in *Honour and Shame*, ed. Peristiany, pp. 179–185.
4. Pitt-Rivers, *op. cit.*, pp. 42–45.
5. Michael Kenny, "Social Values and Health in Spain," *Human Organization* vol. 21 (Winter 1962–63), p. 281. A similar point is made by John F. Campbell, *Honour, Family and Patronage* (Oxford: Clarendon Press, 1964), pp. 269–271.
6. Pitt-Rivers, *op. cit.*, p. 42.
7. Because the Greek culture is a typical shame culture it does not socialize its members to feel guilt when committing or after having committed a socially disapproved act. Only when his own or his family's shortcomings or socially disapproved acts become known to others does a Greek feel ashamed, that is, feel inadequate and weak. It is a feeling of inferiority which causes shame, but an inferiority which results from not having measured up to the expectations of others rather than from not having lived up to internal standards. A feeling of shame cannot be experienced as long as one's behavior is not defined as dishonorable by others. See Helen Merrell Lynd, *On Shame and the Search for Identity* (London: Routledge and Kegan Paul, 1958), esp. pp. 22, 50.
8. In Greek folklore and literature we find that a dishonored girl feels so ashamed

that she no longer wishes to live, and she therefore commits suicide. See Constantina Safilios-Rothschild, "Morality, Courtship, and Love in Greek Folklore," *Southern Folklore Quarterly,* vol. 29 (December 1965), pp. 301–302.

9. *Ibid.,* pp. 297–298, 300–301; John F. Campbell, "Honour and the Devil," in *Honour and Shame,* ed. Peristiany, pp. 147–149.

10. Safilios-Rothschild, *op. cit.,* pp. 300–301; Campbell, *Honour, Family and Patronage,* pp. 199–203.

11. While, in 1951, 37 percent of the Greek population lived in cities of over 10,000 inhabitants and 16 percent in towns of 2000 to 9999 inhabitants, by 1961, 43 percent of the Greek population lived in big cities and 13 percent in towns. Meanwhile, the clearly rural population (living in villages of less than 2000 inhabitants) declined from 48 percent in 1951 (and 53 percent in 1940) to 43 percent in 1961. Since, according to the American definition, many of the towns with more than 2500 people would be classified as "urban," Greece can be considered by now as being predominantly urban.

12. Constantina Safilios-Rothschild, "Comparison of Power Structure and Marital Satisfaction in Urban Greek and French Families," *The Journal of Marriage and the Family,* vol. 29 (May 1967), pp. 347–350; Constantina Safilios-Rothschild, "Marital Role Definitions of Urban Greek Spouses" (Paper delivered at the National Council for Family Relations Conference, Toronto, Canada, October 22, 1965).

13. *Ibid.*

14. Mary Gutenschwager and Constantina Safilios-Rothschild, "Attitudes of Greek Refugee Women Towards Marriage: A Comparative Study" (Paper delivered at the Mediterranean Conference, Athens, December 12–17, 1966).

15. Ioanna Lambiri, *Social Change in a Greek Country Town* (Athens: Center of Planning and Economic Research, 1965).

16. Campbell, *Honour, Family and Patronage,* pp. 280–286.

17. Up to now no statistics have been available on "honor" crimes. It seems that the Greek Census lumps together the large majority of "honor" crimes with a variety of others under the category of "family crimes."

18. For details, see Constantina Safilios-Rothschild, "Class Position and Success Stereotypes in Greek and American Cultures," *Social Forces,* vol. 45 (March 1967), pp. 377–378.

19. The throwing of sulfuric acid was recorded in the beginning of the twentieth century in Russia (Emil Hey, "Die Vitriolseuche in Russland," *Archiv fur Kriminal-Anthropologie,* vol. 57 (1914), pp. 311–315), but in these cases the victims were not only ex-lovers but also rival mistresses. Men were also recorded as throwing sulfuric acid at ex-mistresses. Jassny reported similar assaults in central Europe: "Zur Psychologie der Verbrecherin," *Archiv fur Kriminal-Anthropologie,* vol. 42 (1911), p. 101; similar reports appear in Adeline M. Bedford, "Fifteen Years' Work in a Female Convict Prison," *The Nineteenth Century and After,* vol. 68 (July–December 1910), p. 619; and Louis Puibaraud, "La Femme Criminelle," *La Grande Revue,* vol. 12 (1899), p. 415. Puibaraud writes that the sulfuric acid was used only against a rival woman but never against an estranged lover whom the assaulting woman still loved. The Greek findings show different patterns, since women offenders assaulted with sulfuric acid their ex-lovers rather than their rivals.

20. The only time that a woman was permitted by traditional norms to use trickery or, in extreme cases, some type of violence was when somebody was attempting to rape her and she had no other way to escape from the dishonorable situation. See Safilios-Rothschild, "Morality, Courtship, and Love," p. 302; and Spyros Mourelatos, *She Killed for Her Honor* (Athens: 1957), pp. 46–48. In the latter case, the killing of her assailant was morally justifiable also because he was an Italian (during the Italian occupation) and, therefore, an enemy.

21. Despite the fact that the median ages of male and female offenders and male and female victims are the same, the median test is significant only for the former because of markedly different age distributions.

22. See note 11 for definitions of villages, towns, and cities.

23. The author's survey studies in Athens in 1964 and 1966 have shown that the working and the lower class are largely composed of recent rural migrants who have arrived in Athens during the last fifteen years.

24. In order to cope with this situation, Greek girls have devised a useful routine for getting rid of unwanted boyfriends and lovers without running the danger of possible retaliation; they say that they have to end the relationship because they really love them and they do not wish to burden them since they are seriously ill (tuberculosis and anemia being the most popular alleged illnesses).

25. This, of course, does not mean that urban lower-class brothers approve of their sisters' flirtations or affairs before their marriage. However, since practically all girls in urban lower-class families are gainfully employed, often earning as much as the brothers, and accumulate money themselves in order to build their dowry, this relative economic independence tends to somewhat strengthen their position in the family and to weaken to some degree the traditional, almost absolute power of brothers over sisters. The brother's disapproval of a sister's moral misconduct may be limited to quarrels and an occasional beating but does not lead to an honor crime.

26. For example, a wife wanted a divorce when she found out that her husband was a racketeer; the husband's masculine self-image was hurt and he attacked her in order to publicly restore his honor and masculine reputation.

27. Safilios-Rothschild, "Morality, Courtship, and Love," pp. 298–299; Constantina Safilios-Rothschild, " 'Good' and 'Bad' Girls in Modern Greek Movies," *Journal of Marriage and the Family.*

28. *Ibid.*

29. Pitt-Rivers, *op. cit.,* p. 71.

30. Lambiri found that village girls who worked as factory workers are thought to be of questionable morality because of their contacts with men and their potentially increased freedom. However, because their industrial wages helped them acquire a considerable dowry, they were easily married off and their marriages were upwardly mobile (Lambiri, *op. cit.,* pp. 106–107).

31. Another alternative is to chase the dishonored girl away from home and disown her. Although this solution is not infrequent in rural Greece, it is looked upon unfavorably; in traditional communities, an honor crime would be a much more acceptable alternative. When Greek movies portray such a theme, it is to show the cruelty of parents and the unfortunate effects such cruelty may have upon the unprotected and rejected daughter.

32. During the trial of an offender of a triple honor crime (he had killed his sister, her lover, and the mother of her lover because the lover and his mother did not consent to a marriage), the mayor of the island said that people back on the island (the offender's birthplace) justified the crime morally because it was committed with a noble purpose: the defense of the family honor. Also, the defense attorney said, "If you will ask the eight million Greeks why did the offender kill, they will tell you: for his honor. For their honor people live and die."

33. Only one woman, who killed her uncle because he abandoned her after having been her lover, was sentenced to nine years of imprisonment. In this case, the jury did not acquit her because of her incestual relationship with the uncle.

34. A sentence of eight or nine years of imprisonment in case of honor crimes is a very light sentence, because after the offender has served two or three, he is granted all sort of "graces," such as counting every two days he serves as three days, and after he has served two-thirds of his sentence, he can be released on parole. The result of this very lenient treatment is that prisoners convicted of honor crimes often serve only half of the original sentence. See Th. Papakonstantinou, "The Government and the Crime," *Eikones* (1963).

35. See Th. Papakonstantinou, " 'Family Honor,' The Camouflage of Murderers," *Eikones* (September 1963).

On the Temptation to Be a Beautiful Object

We are constantly bombarded in this society by the images of feminine beauty. There is almost an obsession with it.

It is used extensively in advertising, particularly in advertising directed at women: be like this, they are saying, use our product.

The image sells everything, not just beauty products, but the beauty products reap the benefits of the image having sunk so well into everyone's consciousness.

And oh! those beauty products. Shimmering, magical, just waiting to turn the plainest girl into a heartbreakingly beautiful, transfixing graven image.

Or so they claim and imply, over and over, with extravagent hypnotizing advertising copy and photograph after photograph of dewy-fresh perfect faces.

Inevitably it penetrates the subconscious in an insidious and permanent way.

We may be sophisticated enough (or bitter enough) to reject specific advertising claims, but we cannot purge the image from us: if only we *could* get that look with a few sweeps of a lambsdown buffer dusting on translucent powder, making our faces glow like satin, accented with shimmery slicked-on lip glow, a brush of glittery transparent blusher, eyes soft-fringed and luminous, lash-shaded and mysteriously shadowed . . . suppose we *could* get the look they promise from their products and the look they all sell in their advertising? Ah, how few could resist!

Many of us are scarred by attempts as teen-agers to win the promised glamor from cosmetics. Somehow it always just looked painted, harsh, worse than ever, and yet real life fell so far short of the ideals already burned into our consciousness that the defeat was bitter too and neither the plain nor the painted solution was satisfactory.

How often the date sat impatiently below while the girl in anguish and despair tinged with self-loathing applied and wiped away the magical products that despite their magic were helpless against her horrifying plainness. She would never be a woman, mysteriously beautiful.

Then, as we grew older and better looking, our faces more mature, and our handling of cosmetics more expert, there were times when nature and artifice combined to make us unquestionably beautiful, for a moment, an hour, or an evening.

The incredible elation of looking in a mirror (the lighting just right . . .) and seeing, not the familiar, plain, troublesome self, but a beautiful object, not ourself, but a thing outside, a beautiful thing, worthy of worship . . . no one could resist falling in love with such a face.

The lighting changes, or the evening wears on, and the face slips imperceptibly back into plainness, harshness. Happy gaiety becomes forced gaiety, we laugh louder because we must make up for the ugliness we suddenly found, must distract attention from it.

Or we crawl back into ourselves in an agony of humiliated self-consciousness. We had thought ourselves beautiful, and carried on, attracting attention to what we thought was irresistible beauty but had somehow shifted into plainness again. How they must be laughing at us.

[When] we do succeed we make ourselves objects, outside ourselves, something we expect others to admire because we admire, and which we admire through others' admiration.

But it's not us really. Narcissism is not really love of the self, because self is the soul, the personality, and that is always something quite different, something complex and complicated, something strange and human and very familiar and of this earth.

That beautiful object we stand in awe before has nothing to do with the person we know so well, it is altogether outside, separate, object, a beautiful image, not a person at all. A feast for the eyes.

A feast for the eyes, and not for the mind. That beautiful object is just an object, a work of art, to look at, not to know, total appearance, bearing no personality or will. To the extent that one is caught up in the beauty of it, one perceives object and not person.

This goes for others as well as for ourselves. The more beautiful we are, the more admired our appearance, the closer we approach the dream of the incredible beauty, the less reality our personality or intellect or will have.

It is unthinkable that this work of art has a will, especially one which is not as totally soft and agreeable as the face it presents. You cannot be taken seriously, people will not even hear what you say. (If they did they would be shocked and displeased—but since they do not take it seriously they say "You are too pretty to be so smart"—by which they mean, you are an object, do not presume to complicate the image with intellect, for intellect is complex and not always pleasing and beautiful. Do not dare to spoil my pleasure in your beauty by showing it to be only the facade of a real person; I will not believe that, you will only succeed in marring your beauty.)

How can anyone take a manikin seriously? How, even, can one take a heartbreakingly beautiful face seriously? One is far too caught up in admiration of the object presented. It is merely beautiful, but it becomes an object when it is presented to the world.

This only goes for women, of course; men's character and personality and will always shine through their appearance, both men and women look at them that way. But one is taught in society by the emphasis on the images of feminine beauty to view women differently. The important thing is not the mind, the will, but the appearance. You *are* your appearance.

And if your appearance is pleasing, you are sunk, for no one will ever look beyond. You have fulfilled all that is expected of you and you may rest (this all assumes you have the feminine womanly virtues of noncharacter such as kindness, gentleness, and the "pleasing personality").

In fact, if you are beautiful, or if you have made yourself beautiful, you had *better* leave it at that, because you have no chance of compelling people to look beyond. They are so enchanted with what they see.

They adore you for your appearance. If you are "brainy" it will be taken as quaint, a charming affectation. If you are disagreeable it is offensive, a particularly stinging affront, disrespect for your beauty, the sacrilege of a work of art. (This does not detract from the mystique of the beautiful bitch. That is just another form of flirtation, tantalizing the man by simultaneously alluring with the beauty and playing hard to get by putting up a verbal fence—a fence, by the way, which the man sees himself ultimately surmounting in triumph.)

It is true that this is part of the burden of being a woman. We are expected to be beautiful, and not being beautiful does not make us automatically accepted as people. To some extent and for some people we are never more than our appearance.

If we are ugly and plain, men demand angrily (at least in their own minds) why don't we *do* something with ourselves; surely a more becoming hairdo, better makeup, or even (if the situation is bad enough) a new nose. . . .

Women react the same way to women. All are victimized by the image of woman as object, appearance. "Why doesn't she *do* something with herself?"

A man who is neat and clean may get away with being ugly; if he is intelligent and personable he may even be immensely popular, but for a woman, being neat and clean is never enough if she is still plain, if she doesn't at least *try* to improve on nature with the most flattering hairdo (however limp or unruly her hair is, however many hours of effort and frustration she must put into the endeavor), the newest makeups artfully and painstakingly applied, every new exercise and diet fad, the newest and chicquest clothes. The ugly woman who does her best in this way will still be a "dog" but she won't be a threat and may even be popular if she has the other qualifications, popular as a "sister."

If you are truly ugly it is always an offense against your role as woman. You can never be truly feminine, womanly. Always an affront to men and women both, trapped as they are in the myth of feminine beauty.

How dare you be ugly? You are a woman, an object, you exist to please the eye, and yet you fail so utterly. They will be obsessed with your appearance, only this time they are affronted rather than admiring.

They will still have difficulty listening to what you are saying, this time because they are so busy wondering why on earth you don't get a nose job or something.

Still, being ugly has its advantages. At least they will not be lulled into hypnotic admiration with you as a beautiful object.

You will be a constant gadfly, shattering their preconceived notions. At least they cannot say "You're too pretty to be so smart." They will have to say "You had better be smart because you're certainly not pretty." This is certainly a healthier situation for an individual who wishes to be more than a passive object.

The most fortuitous situation for a woman might be to be inoffensively plain, thoroughly nondescript. It would be very difficult for her to win initial attention, for with a woman one notices only the beautiful (admirable) and the ugly (repulsive); one does not offer a woman a chance to show by words or actions what her personality or character is in the way one automatically does to a man.

But when one does command attention there would be least distraction from the person by the appearance, least temptation for the woman to be made an object in the minds of the beholders.

And yet this thoroughly nondescript-looking woman is the one cosmetics advertisements aim at. They want to take the mice and with their magic powders and creams transform them into princesses.

And for many mice they can succeed. Even men, as we have seen in the case of drag queens, can often make themselves into beautiful women with enough of the magic powders and creams.

But to the extent that we keep our self-image as persons as we manipulate our appearance in this way, it will seem artificial and unnatural, and look strange and perhaps even frightening.

Only as we slip into the schizophrenic world of play-acting and narcissism will we be able to enjoy the beauty we create. And then we will be imprisoned within the walls of the object we created in the minds of others and in our own minds—we will no longer be able to function as persons, or only fitfully, self-consciously, and puzzling others by our strange behavior.

Discussion

Since historically women have been (and probably the majority of them around the world still are) economically dependent upon men, be they their fathers, brothers, husbands, or sons, females have been bought and sold and bargained for as objects by the transacting males. For example, in the Muslim countries the father sells his daughter to the highest bidder, while the non-Arab Mediterranean father has to transfer the economic and moral responsibility of his daughter to another man, her husband, by attaching enough dowry to her to make her a desirable "good."

The price at which she is bought by a man or the price that the father has to pay in order to get rid of her becomes the object of hard bargaining during which each one of the interested parties tries to get the best deal by pointing out "blemishes" and shortcomings or virtues and advantages in the woman, according to his respective viewpoint. Sometimes the bargaining reaches a dead end and the prospective husband makes it clear that unless the dowry is raised to the desired level, he will not marry the girl. In such cases, few parents have had the heart to avoid ruining themselves at the cost of letting their daughter stay a spinster or of marrying her to a man of lesser social status who might require less dowry.

In addition to beauty and youth, two visible and important characteristics of the woman in the transaction, her domestic skills, but mainly her chastity, docility, and obedience, play a crucial role in the determination of the price.[1] The husband is usually interested in acquiring a faithful and obedient wife whom he can order around and whose lifelong fidelity he can feel assured of. Therefore, the more the husband suspects any blemish on her chastity, the less money he is willing to pay or the more money he requests in order to permit his strict conscience to relax enough so as to accept a woman of such questioned virtue as his wife (" 'Honor' Crimes in Contemporary Greece"). At this point it is interesting to note that it has been reported from Brazil, Iran, Greece, Morocco, and other Mediterranean countries that city women who have had premarital sexual experiences undergo a special kind of plastic surgery that renders them technically virgins for their wedding night.[2] Thus, although the actual sexual behavior of women has changed, values have not changed so as to permit men and women to be sexually liberated.[3]

Since brothers have the responsibility to help the father (or in the latter's absence, the total responsibility) to provide sisters with adequate dowries so that they can be "sold" at the marriage market, they have as much vested interest as fathers in safeguarding their sisters' virginity and reputation in order not to have to raise unreasonably high dowries to cover up the shame of dishonorable behavior. In the past, of course, the dishonor brought upon the family by the girl who went astray was so great that only blood (the girl's death and/or that of her lover through an honor crime) and not money could restore order and the family's esteem in the community ("'Honor' Crimes in Contemporary Greece"). This extreme reaction to dishonor may be also explained on the basis of its consequences for the rest of the family, especially for brothers, who, if a sister did not marry, were expected, according to traditional norms, to remain single themselves and support their unmarried sister throughout life.

In modern times, however, even among very traditional segments of societies, women's virginity could be replaced by a large dowry from the parents or by the woman's economic independence through work and a stable salary, which might or might not lead to her amassing a substantial dowry on her own. Only when women's working became defined as an actvity to be continued throughout marriage were women rid of the slavery of dowry and all its many connotations.

But the connection between a woman's sexual activities and money does not end here. Prostitution has always been the most obvious example of sex used as a commodity, but other subtler forms of using sex as a commodity abound, probably the most typical and widespread one being, at least in many cases, marriage. The husband is bound by the marriage contract to provide economic support (but not to make love to his wife), while the wife in exchange must be willing to have sexual relations with her husband and do the housework. Thus, again many married women exchange sex and housework for economic security in a socially acceptable way, but they have no legal right to refuse to have sexual relations with their husbands, since such a refusal on their part (but not on the part of the husbands) constitutes a ground for divorce.[4] Again here the economic independence of women through their own work is very important, since it guarantees them a greater degree of sexual freedom and self-determination.

The economic subjugation of women to men through sex has always been accentuated (and still is in large segments of the population around the world) through pregnancy and the birth of children.[5] The discovery of "safe" contraceptives and the possibility of abortion has freed some women (most often middle- and upper-class women) from this type of often "forced" subjugation, but still the great masses of women have not been touched by this new, "liberating" technology.

But what constitutes sexual freedom or sexual liberation for women? The meanings and behavior attached to this concept vary, especially with the sex of the definer. Thus, according to the so-called "liberal" men, sexual liberation means that women will have sexual relations with a variety of men and will enjoy them without any "hang-ups" about the necessity of being in love, without the fear of pregnancy, and without the restrictions of traditional double-standard morality. Or, as described in *Playboy*, this new type of girl is ". . . self-emancipated, unabashedly sexy, charmingly individualistic and a joy to the men in her life."[6]

But women have found out through bitter experience that this conception of sexual liberation hides a new type of subjugation for them. Women must agree to have sexual relations with any man who desires them in order to prove that they are psychologically "normal," "well adjusted," and feminine and must show that they have greatly enjoyed the experience. Failure to accept the sexual overtures of any man gains a woman the epithets of "neurotic" and "frigid." Women's sexual liberation includes the right to refuse to make love with any man and for a variety of reasons other than fear of pregnancy or belief in double-standard morality.[7] But it seems that few men are liberated enough to grant this right to a woman they desire. The injury to their self-esteem, which in other times and still now in some societies has led or leads to honor or "passion" crimes, makes them search for something wrong in the woman who rejects them.

Furthermore, in the case of young single girls, being a virgin or not having had interesting sexual experiences is often treated by liberal men (and also women) as a sign of naïveté, social inferiority, and inability to enjoy life.[8] Seldom is such a state thought to be the result of a mature and rational decision.

The sexual liberation of women does not imply that each woman must sexually please as many men as find her sexually desirable or that she must dramatize her sexual satisfaction and orgasm (whether she experiences one or not) in order to please the man. Sexual liberation means rather that the woman can determine with whom, when, how often, and in which way to have sexual relations in order to derive maximum gratification and, therefore, be able truly to satisfy her partner. For by now, sex research has shown that women have sexual urges equally as strong as those of men and a somewhat greater capacity for sexuality as measured by the frequency of coitus and the frequency of orgasm in coition.[9] But strong repression for centuries has somewhat damped these sexual urges and capacities at least in some women.

Some women, such as the *hetaerae*, the prostitutes of all times and societies, the "bad" women and the libertine widows of traditional societies, have always found ways to express their sexuality through deviant and stigmatized options. Lately, in instances where "respectable" women have been given a chance by their husbands to express their sexuality more fully, as is the case with "swinging" couples, usually after their initial resistance, they seem to enjoy the experience greatly and to want to continue with this licensed and somewhat controlled promiscuity.[10] This evidence from "swinging" couples disproves the myths that women are by nature (and in contrast to men) monogamous and that they must be in love in order to enjoy sex, since any sentimental attachment beyond sex is taboo in "swinging." Similarly in a survey of college students in five countries, it was found that in England, where both boys and girls adhered the least to double-standard morality and were the most liberated (more so than even Norwegian students), coeds admitted having "one-night stands" with someone they liked but did not love or want to love.[11]

Sexual liberation for women does not mean obligatory promiscuity to please all the men in their lives, but instead, an open-minded exploration of their sexuality, free of myths, stereotypes, fears, and double-standard morality proscriptions, in order to discover the sexual model that best suits their temperament and personality, be it monogamous or polygamous. But of course such sexually liberated women need sexually liberated men in order to achieve their liberation and find sexual as well as sentimental satisfaction.[12] They need men who do not have to prove their masculinity through sexual acrobatics and the sexual conquest of their partner, men who are not afraid to show tenderness, weakness, and even an occasional lack of interest in sex.

Since, however, the sexual liberation of men and women requires the effective control of births on the part of women (through the use of contraceptives and easy access to abortion) and the economic independence of women, it will probably remain a dream for the majority of women in developing countries and, elsewhere, a luxury reserved for the middle and upper classes for a long time to come.

Notes

1. In the case of some farm marriages in which the wife is required to work hard in the fields, good health and physical strength are also greatly valued.
2. Emilio Wilhems, "The Structure of the Brazilian Family," *Social Forces,* vol. 31, no. 4 (May 1953), pp. 339–345; Constantina Safilios-Rothschild, "Morality, Courtship and Love in Greek Folklore," *Southern Folklore Quarterly,* vol. 29 (December 1965), pp. 301–302; Nadia Bradley, "Le Scandale de la Virginité," *Lamatif* [Morocco], no. 25 (December 1968), pp. 15–17.
3. Constantina Safilios-Rothschild, *Myths and Realities About the Family: A Cross-cultural Perspective* (New York: Random House, forthcoming in 1972).
4. Kate Millett, *Sexual Politics* (New York: Doubleday & Co., 1970); also Claudia Dreifus, "The Great Femancipator" [interview with Kate Millett], *Penthouse* (November 1970), pp. 79–82.
5. Andrew Hacker, "The Pill and Morality," *New York Times Magazine,* November 21, 1965, pp. 32–34, 138–140; Gloria Steinem, "The Moral Disarmament of Betty Coed," *Esquire,* vol. 58, no. 346 (September 1962), pp. 97, 153–157; John Clellon Holmes, "Opinion," *Playboy,* vol. 15, no. 1 (January 1968), pp. 181–186, 214–216; and Dana Densmore, "Against Liberals," *No More Fun and Games,* vol. 1, no. 2 (February 1969), pp. 60–63.
6. Holmes, *op. cit.,* p. 181.
7. Millett, *op. cit.*
8. Steinem, *op. cit.;* "Postscript on the Single Woman: Report from Brazil," *Grail Review,* vol. 6, no. 4 (1964), pp. 32–35.
9. W. H. Masters and Virginia Johnson, *Human Sexual Response* (Boston: Little, Brown & Co., 1966).
10. L. James Gold, "The Desire for Sexual Variety," *American Journal of Psychiatry,* vol. 127 (1970), pp. 521–523; and Robert R. Bell and Lillian Silvan, " 'Swinging'—the Sexual Exchange of Married Partners," mimeographed (Philadelphia: Temple University, 1969).
11. Eleanor B. Luckey and Gilbert D. Nass, "A Comparison of Sexual Attitudes and Behavior in an International Sample," *Journal of Marriage and the Family,* vol. 31, no. 2 (May 1969), pp. 364–379.
12. Mary Calderone, "It's Really the Men Who Need Liberating," *Life,* September 4, 1970, p. 24.

The Options of Women

How Come a Nice Girl Like You Isn't Married?

Since the single female American is numerically becoming rare as the whooping crane, I'll answer that tiresome question myself.

My qualifications as an expert: some 40-odd years of quixotic Singlehood, though I also checked out 19 other lady loners, age 27 through 47, a breed hard to find. For statistics prove that 94 percent of American females by age 40 have been hitched at least *once*.

My sampling is limited to "nice" girls, meaning personable, respectable, no more neurotic than run-of-the-mill Americans, and still pursued by men. I exclude divorcées and widows, who live alone by the millions, since theirs is presumably a life of involuntary solitude.

Now, when I was growing up as a parson's daughter in the thirties, ladies without husbands were known as "old maids." They weren't glamorized then as "bachelor girls," and tended to be schoolteachers, deans at colleges, missionaries to Africa, or nice Swedish girls who had never hooked a good breadwinner and thereafter became meticulous secretaries and lived with their mothers. Useful citizens all, but would you want to be one? Perish forbid. One read of legendary females like Jane Addams, who had sacrificed Wifemanship for Humanity, but who could identify with *them?*

Like most nice girls—Swedish, Jewish, or Chinese—I assumed I'd marry —preferably, someone who looked like Joel McCrea. At 5, my favorite game was playing bride, draped in a window curtain. At 13, my ultimate life's ambition, like Luci Johnson's, was to be a nurse. In college, where I wound up editing the school paper, I hankered to be the beauty queen. Mine, in short, was a fairly "normal" American girlhood, whatever that is. But, by 27, when I was still wild goosing it without a wedding band, parish ladies began to ask: "Well, dear, aren't you being too *choosy?*"

As any lady loner over age 27 can tell you, polite people who would never dream of prying into one's age, weight, or size of bank account can't resist asking That Question. There you are, at: the cocktail party, the alumni reunion, having a high old time solo on some vacation beach, or maybe tooting off on business. Someone, usually male, uncovers the astounding! incredible! fact that never, not once, have you married. "Nice" is the key word again. Meaning that though clearly pushing 30 (or 40 or 50), you are not overly eroded by the years, apparently not psychotic, not repellent to men, and not famous.

Content married ladies ask That Question with curiosity and compassion. The discontent often do it with malice. They are apt to be the bright girls who opted early for the washer and dryer and the suburbs, and found that Wifemanship hasn't solved all life's problems. They don't see the Single

Female as a sexual threat, I decided, but can't bear the thought that she seems to be having an "interesting" time and isn't miserable. OK, my girl, they say, you're having a fine time racketing around now and changing jobs and men like musical chairs, *but what about your lonely old age?*

It is also assumed, by people expert in Freudian jargon, that any lady loner is "neurotic," natch, "unable to assume the 'female' role," or "relate" to men. Worse yet, if you work, as everyone short of Doris Duke must, especially at anything absorbing, you are that beast, "a career woman." That's the new fate worse than death. It means you are riddled by "masculine" drives or "unfeminine" ambition. It's acceptable for a young alumna with spark to dabble a few years as a Girl Friday, researching on a magazine, writing bright advertising copy, helping out a senator, as long as she gets her hair done regularly and has a throw-it-away attitude about the deal. The problem of the educated girl, says Margaret Mead, is to be successful, but not *too* much so. If she takes a passionate, life-time interest in work, travel, or butterfly collecting, she risks dealing herself out of the marriage market.

I have recently plowed through most of the current fiction or sociology on the belabored subject of Women (*The Feminine Mystique, Women Who Died in the Chair, The Second Sex, Sex and the Single Girl, The Woman Executive*), and I have yet to find a spinster with whom I could identify. That includes the Playgirls of Helen Gurley Brown, who live in a world I never knew. To follow her advice and spend 24-hour days polishing oneself as a mantrap seems far more exhausting than being a Trapped Housewife. (Clean hair is sexy, says Helen, so are apartments with books. To intrigue men at a party, wear a pin labeled "Fight That Will Power." Is she kidding?)

Take even a perceptive . . . book, *Leah,* by Seymour Epstein, billed as a "brilliant and revealing novel about a single woman alone in New York." Leah is intelligent, Jewish, 37, has a father complex, a boss on the make, her own apartment, a history of shattered romances, and is miserable: especially on Sunday, a "gray, grinding predator from whom one must hide, in restaurants, in movies, or in one's own apartment, drugged with coffee and boredom." (Personally, I always found the solitude of Sunday, with all that sleep, perusing of the New York *Times,* and retreating from the maddening world, delicious.)

My title question pops up on page 3, put to Leah by old Irving, an ex-beau newly divorced and therefore a "retread." (As all lady loners know, the divorce rate being what it lamentably is, men you passed up in [their] 20s are quite apt to come on the market again in the 30s and the 40s.)

> IRVING: "Why didn't you ever marry?"
> LEAH: "Please, Irving."
> IRVING: "No seriously. A girl like you doesn't stay unmarried . . . you're what? 33? 4? . . . Do you mean to tell me that you're happier living the way you are living than you would be married to me? Etc., etc.

By page 249, having endured another traumatic go-round with an "eligible" bachelor of 40, who turns out to be impotent, Leah opts for old Irving. She'd just lost her job anyway, so why not?

Any Leah would settle for Irving, if she'd read *A Woman Doctor Looks at Love and Life,* by one Dr. Marion Hilliard, a big seller of 1956. For the single-woman patient who asks (unlikely question), "But what do I do when I am in real distress because of desire?" the good doctor has this advice: "Read a mystery story. Visit a friend with five children under age 10. Take a very hot bath and plan your next vacation." Avoid listening to New Orleans jazz records, for they have a "primitive tom-tom rhythm that does a single woman's peace of mind no good." When lonely, join a badminton club, where "an unescorted girl doesn't feel out of place." But, there's hope by the 40s. Tranquility awaits because sexual desire and all that disturbing jazz lie down, and you can, presumably, settle into some serious badminton.

What strikes me about all this coy or archaic advice is that in this great U.S. of A., land of free choice, opportunity, etc., girls today seem to have so *little* choice. To quote writer Marya Mannes: "Security is the goal, and as soon as possible. Marry the boy right away, get the house right away, have the brood right away. No time for search of self, no time for experiments in love and life, no time for interior growth, no time for the great world outside."

There's the nub of it, for most lady loners—*freedom.* Its rewards can be illusory. But for a special breed of cat, it is essential for a few years or even the long haul.

Take my own sampling of 19 loners. As a type, they are inquisitive, educated, restless, exploratory, and at age 20 had no Grand Design for life. Here are some of their reasons for Singlehood:

> When you marry, especially very young, you're not just marrying a man, but a whole way of life. You are limited and defined by what your husband is, essentially, by his income and his friends and the geography of where he works. Perhaps I'm egocentric, but I didn't know, even at 25, who I was yet or what I wanted to be. I like the freedom of being my own mistress. If I choose to adventure off to California or splurge on clothes, I'm not taking food out of babies' mouths.

Or:

> Getting out in the world on your own can't help changing you. It's sink or swim. You're forced to grow, stretch, and become some-body. My sister married at 22, and that was right for her. But if I had, I'd have been one of those "married martyrs." They're the girls I knew at Smith, whose professors told them they had some ability, for acting or writing or science or whatever, but who never tried. So they have illusions about what-might-have-been. Getting out in the world and up against the pros would have at least made them realistic. Maybe they had it, maybe they hadn't. I know, the hard way, that New York glamour isn't what it's cracked up to be. But they don't. Some of them, by 30, though they have perfectly sound husbands get "adventure" out of their systems by having affairs. I think I prize the homely virtues more than they do, because at least I've chosen them and not had them thrust upon me.

The hazards of Singlehood?

> Sometimes, I think if I died in my bed on Friday night, no one would know until Monday. One has greater emotional highs and lows, and swings of mood, without the ballast of another person. Everyone, the female particularly, needs to be needed, and I'm not, essentially. It makes you feel guilty, selfish. . . . It's said that working involves as much drudgery, in its own way, as housekeeping, and that's so, but I prefer it. For one thing, I've met dozens of people I never would have, had I married. You also learn, with experience, to be discriminating—about clothes, ideas, jobs, men.

My own background, though antiquated and atypical, is the kind apt to produce the modern lady loner. I was a PK (preacher's kid), growing up in a world that put high store on education, character, and good works— virtues more highly prized than good looks or being the belle of the ball. Perhaps that mix produced a rebel or a great barbaric wish to explore the great world outside. Four years at the freewheeling University of Chicago did nothing to damp the urge.

Earn a living—I had to. My parents, I'm sure, hoped I would evolve into somebody "useful," like a teacher, or doctor or social worker. Instead, I blundered off, to work a night shift on a New Jersey newspaper, a cold-bath experience for any parsonage-bred female—an eye-opening world of cops, hard-drinking reporters, gangsters.

The most gruesome birthday of my whole Singlehood, as I recall, was No. 21. I had neither married, like most of my sensible friends, nor saved the world, an activity then in vogue. I recall pouring out my woes to one Beardsley Ruml, a famously sophisticated professor-economist, later turned chairman of the board of Macy's. When I complained that *nothing was ever going to happen to me,* he couldn't have been more cruelly amused. I was a bright enough girl, he said, but half-baked, and I wouldn't be worth talking to until age 35. He was right.

In two decades of solitary exploring, some of it traumatic, since that's the way life is, I kept on blundering and learning. I did social work in the Negro slums of Chicago, rang doorbells for politicians, saw Hollywood in its heyday, then headed for Mexico for three weeks and wound up there for nearly four years. Friends diagnosed this exit as "escapism," and perhaps it was. But there's nothing quite like exposure to a culture polar opposite of your own. Working with Mexicans was like living perpetually in the third act of *Carmen.* Suddenly, all the good Anglo-Saxon Protestant values were turned upside down. Here was a life that valued the emotional intuitional, personal and erratic. Was it worth it, including explosive go-rounds with Latin males? Of course.

I know a few (very few) wise, lucky women who, early in life, found the right man and lived relatively happy ever after. (More often than not, second marriages seem to turn out better and are more final.) But I wasn't born that way, and I've known other rewards. I have, thanks to Singlehood, like most lady loners, known an infinite variety of men—as friends, more-than-friends, and working colleagues: movie stars, Mexican revolutionaries, advertising tycoons, bankers, writers, fishermen, jazz musicians, Russian spies. Was it worth it to give up domesticity to see Castro's Cuba, Khrushchev's Moscow, Kennedy's White House, Trujillo's Dominican Republic? For me, yes.

And so, what happened a few months ago, when everyone, including my Aunt Clara, had given up asking the title question? I got married.

The young never believe their elders. I know that I never did. So what restive 20-year-old female, stampeding off to the altar, will believe that romance can be just as blazing, available, and satisfying for a woman in her 40s? (Or 50s?) Moral of this story, if any: All things come to her who waits, including the wild goose.

A Vote Against Motherhood: A Wife Challenges the Importance of Childbearing

I don't want to have any children. Motherhood is only a part of marriage, and I am unwilling to sacrifice the other equally important feminine roles upon the overexalted altar of parenthood. Instead of condemning myself to the common syndrome of the unhappy creature who is mother first, wife second, woman third, and human being last, I champion the wondrously satisfying love of a woman and her husband, two adults enjoying the knowledge and mystery of each other, tasting dependence, accepting responsibility, yet individual and free.

Femininity is the acceptance, appreciation, and enjoyment of being a woman. Motherhood is only a part of it. The complete woman is also devoted wife, lover, playmate, buffer, a man's stimulant and tranquilizer, a creator (in the kitchen if not at the easel or typewriter), an active mind, an unfettered human being involved in activities and causes and battles beyond the boundaries of a particular plot of crabgrass.

The idea that a couple would deliberately choose to remain childless seems to strike sparks of uncontrollable indignation. The decision is not one we have been able to discuss calmly with friends. Occasionally visitors to our apartment—so obviously designed for two adults with no thoughts of family expansion—will ask, "But where do you plan to put a nursery?"

"We're not planning for babies, so we don't need a nursery," I answer.

The shock and disbelief could not be greater if my husband announced he had just accepted a job spying for the Russians and I was busy running a Communist party cell in the basement boiler room.

Our decision not to have children was neither simple nor sudden. Both my husband and I come from families where children are a major *raison d'être* for marriage and each new grandchild is looked upon as a divine blessing. Under these circumstances it certainly never occurred to me that one might consider married life without children. Children were taken for granted as a part of marriage. Indeed, as a teen-ager I had rather ambitious plans for a huge brood, mostly boys. (I felt I had been greatly deprived as a child by not having an older brother and was determined no daughter of mine would be so underprivileged.) These were the dreams of an adolescent who had been captivated by the adventures of the Bobbsey twins and the Gilbreth youngsters of *Cheaper by the Dozen* fame. I wasn't thinking what it might mean to be a Bobbsey's mother. I was thinking what fun it would be to be a Bobbsey twin. "Mother," beyond the warm, loving, gentle creature who was my own, was a vague, inconceivable concept.

Parenthood's Real Price

Then I began to have doubts. When I looked about at our friends—young couples with children—I was shocked and appalled at what I saw. Men and women floundered under awesome responsibilities, suffered total loss of independence and privacy. Frustration, tension, and bitterness strained love. Most frightening of all, women appeared shredded, pulled apart by the demands of a dozen conflicting roles.

In the homes of my friends I received my first intimate and disillusioning insight into the meaning of motherhood. Too many of these mothers had made the supreme sacrifice to motherhood. They felt trapped. They simmered with resentment. For others it was a passive surrender, an automatic, often unthinking, response to a thousand pressures.

I refuse to be pressured into this state of parenthood just because society or some advice columnist tells me it is a noble, joyous state and my sacred duty. Everywhere I turn, there are the voices assuring me that a woman can only know fulfillment through motherhood. My experience tells me differently.

Recently my husband, leafing through one of the ladies' magazines, came across a paragraph in a column of marriage counseling that infuriated him. "In the early months of marriage," it read, *"when love is at its height,* each spouse is most generous and tolerant. . . ." The suggestion that love reaches a peak with the honeymoon and then begins to taper off as romance fades and reality intrudes is shocking. Implicit in the following paragraphs was the "reassurance" that when the glow goes, various other roles (parenthood) would take up the slack.

From this must follow that line, so often uttered in supposed jest, "Well the honeymoon is over." Ours is not. Love only seemed "at its height" in the early months of our marriage. We keep discovering new peaks. We enjoy our life and the things we do singly and together. We appreciate the time and freedom to pursue potential talents (even if they should prove to be nothing more than minor skills). We treasure the freedom to pick up and disappear for a weekend or a month or even a year, to sleep odd hours, to breakfast at three A.M. or three P.M., to hang out the DO NOT DISTURB sign, to slam a door and be alone, or alone together, to indulge in foolish extravagances, to get out of bed at seven A.M. on a sudden whim and go horseback riding in the park before work, to become embroiled in a political campaign or a fund-raising drive, to devote endless hours to intensive research for a project that might lead somewhere or nowhere, to have champagne with dinner for no special reason at all, to tease and love anywhere, any hour, anytime we please without a nagging guilt that a child is being neglected. We take so small a privilege as privacy for granted; yet, to our friends with children, privacy is a luxury for which they envy us.

I have read too many articles by young mothers and heard too many of my own friends complaining that motherhood is a prison. It is plain that the creation of a child, its care, and tending a home are not enough for many women. Some turn to a job or back to a career or lock the door of a spare room to make it a studio, trying to serve on three or four fronts at once and serving on none well. Money and a reliable baby-sitter free a mother to spend afternoons haunting museums or studying ballet or serving as a Gray Lady, but money apparently does not buy away a conscience that talks of child neglect.

Many women thrive on motherhood and never stop growing. I am thinking of a college dorm-mate who took her degree in archaeology and was hailed in the class yearbook as "the girl most likely to find the ruins of lost Atlantis." Well, the only digging she's done since has been in backyard sandboxes. She has a passel of kids—four, and one on the way, at last count. She obviously loves her life, wades happily through what others might consider sheer drudgery, and approaches such tasks as brewing an infant's formula or umpiring a brood of toddlers with all the zest she once devoted to geology expeditions. She's a fine mother, a great wife, and an exciting woman to be with.

Yet I see so many of our friends, some of them with children they hadn't necessarily planned on—bitter, frustrated, vacillating between devotion and despair, screaming at their youngsters, tearing into each other. The child is there. Never for a moment would they wish it away, but they seem to be fighting a furious battle as they watch themselves becoming people they never meant to be.

"All I want is just an hour a day to be me," I overheard a woman complain to her husband. "Not to be a chauffeur or a bandage dispenser or a screaming harpy in a torn muumuu. Me, glamorous, calm, funny, in lingerie that isn't held together with safety pins—remember?"

"I don't know why you even call me anymore," a former classmate said to me recently. "I haven't had an original thought in two years, and the only multisyllabic word that's come out of me all week was 'Toidy-seat.' And that's hyphenated, so I don't even know if it counts."

Envy of the Childless

Cara left her job as an interior decorator three years ago—reluctantly, in her eighth month of pregnancy. "You don't know how lucky you are," she said gazing about our living room. "To have a stairway without a kiddy gate and a velvet sofa without stain-resistant slipcovers. If you'd told me three years ago I'd have slipcovers or plastic-laminated anything, I'd have laughed myself silly."

Betty reads medical journals whenever she can sneak the time—while the kids nap or at the Laundromat. "It took me eleven years to become a pediatrician, and I've never even practiced," she says. "I want to go back as soon as all three of the boys are in school, but it frightens me to think I'll be ten years behind."

The more we watch our contemporaries trying to cope with child-rearing, the more we see them bowing to its conflicting demands and surrendering their individualities and dreams, the stronger our decision to remain childless becomes.

Our resolve has been strengthened by the prevailing philosophy of child-rearing. They call it "permissiveness." But it emerges as total child autocracy. All decisions revolve around the child. Vacations are planned to suit the children. A mother who would not sacrifice a new winter coat to buy her son an English racing bike is looked upon as an unnatural animal. Never mind that mother's idea of a relaxing holiday does not happen to include camping out and cooking three meals a day on a portable barbecue—it suits the youngsters. Girls I met when I first came to New York, who vowed they would never leave the city, have moved to the suburbs: "It's so wonderful for the children." Papa becomes a commuter, and a man and a woman who once shared the world now occupy two separate and distant islands, meeting for a few hours each night.

Parents Become Children

To be less than the complete mother the community expects one to be leaves a woman racked with guilt. She becomes so much the mother that she may one day find herself treating that tweedy, commuting chap who was once her husband and lover as just another one of the brood—another runny nose to wipe, another mouth to pop a vitamin pill into, another finicky appetite to cater to—an overgrown and petulant child. He even calls her "mom." She calls him "dad," and that sums up their relationship.

"No you may not have another Martini before dinner," she will say in exactly the same tone in which she would forbid the six-year-old another slice of chocolate cake.

I have heard some women say they refuse to bring children into a nuclear-panicked world or into a civilization that has lost all morals. These are not the only legitimate reasons for remaining childless, and I suspect some couples have reached conclusions similar to those of myself and my husband, yet hesitate to express them for fear of being accused of subversion, immaturity, or selfishness.

Why then do people have children? They should not be so quick to condemn us for selfishness without first examining their own motives. People have children because they want them. Fine—go to it. But what of those who use their children as pawns or as instruments of revenge or as amusing little pets or as glue to patch a foundering marriage? What of those who don't really like children but have them anyway? And there are such people—just as there are those who don't like cats or jazz or abstract painting. What of those who produce progeny and regard them as a sort of status symbol? What about couples who procreate because they're afraid of being criticized for not having children? And what of those who haven't the courage or interest to face squarely what parenthood will mean or what kind of parents they will make?

Too many men and women who don't really want children, who are selfish, immature, ill-prepared, hostile, and baffled, are spawning youngsters with less thought than they would give to the purchase of a new car. These children must suffer.

Whom do I harm by not having children? The nonexistent child? The world—which already has too many? Surely having children for the wrong reasons or for no reason at all or bringing them into an atmosphere of resentment and neglect is the greater selfishness.

There is a choice. Couples should be permitted to make a decision, whether to have children or not, without social pressures. There is no reason why their choice should be regarded as shocking, evil, or an affront to humanity.

Is College Compatible with Marriage?

All over the United States, undergraduate marriages are increasing, not only in the municipal colleges and technical schools, which take for granted a workaday world in which learning is mostly training to make a living, but also on the green campuses once sacred to a more leisurely pursuit of knowledge.

Before we become too heavily committed to this trend, it may be wise to pause and question why it has developed, what it means, and whether it endangers the value of undergraduate education as we have known it.

The full-time college, in which a student is free for four years to continue the education begun in earlier years, is only one form of higher education. Technical schools, nonresidence municipal colleges, junior colleges, extension schools which offer preparation for professional work on a part-time and indefinitely extended basis, institutions which welcome adults for a single course at any age: all of these are "higher," or at least "later," education. Their proliferation has tended to obscure our view of the college itself and what it means.

But the university, as it is called in Europe—the college, as it is often called here—is essentially quite different from "higher education" that is only later, or more, education. It is, in many ways, a prolongation of the freedom of childhood; it can come only once in a lifetime and at a definite stage of development, after the immediate trials of puberty and before the responsibilities of full adulthood.

The university student is a unique development of our kind of civilization, and a special pattern is set for those who have the ability and the will to devote four years of exploring the civilization of which they are a part. This self-selected group (and any other method than self-selection is doomed to failure) does not include all of the most able, the most skilled, or the most gifted in our society. It includes, rather, those who are willing to accept four more years of an intellectual and psychological moratorium, in which they explore, test, meditate, discuss, passionately espouse, and passionately repudiate ideas about the past and the future. The true undergraduate university is still an "as-if" world in which the student need not commit himself yet. For this is a period in which it is possible not only to specialize but to taste, if only for a semester, all the possibilities of scholarship and science, of great commitment, and the special delights to which civilized man has access today.

One of the requirements of such a life has been freedom from responsibility. Founders and administrators of universities have struggled through the years to provide places where young men, and more recently young women, and young men and women together, would be free—in a way they can never be free again—to explore before they settle on the way their lives are to be lived.

This freedom once, as a matter of course, included freedom from domestic responsibilities—from the obligation to wife and children or to husband and children. True, it was often confused by notions of propriety: married women and unmarried girls were believed to be improper dormitory companions, and a trace of the monastic tradition that once forbade dons to marry lingered on in our men's colleges. But essentially the prohibition of undergraduate marriage was part and parcel of our belief that marriage entails responsibility.

A student may live on a crust in a garret and sell his clothes to buy books; a father who does the same thing is a very different matter. An unmarried girl may prefer scholarship to clerking in an office; as the wife of a future nuclear physicist or judge of the Supreme Court—or possibly of the research worker who will find a cure for cancer—she acquires a duty to give up her own delighted search for knowledge and to help put her husband through professional school. If, additionally, they have a child or so, both sacrifice— she her whole intellectual interest, he all but the absolutely essential professional grind to "get through" and "get established." As the undergraduate years come to be primarily not a search for knowledge and individual growth, but a suitable setting for the search for a mate, the proportion of full-time students who are free to give themselves the four irreplaceable years is being steadily whittled down.

Should we move so far away from the past that all young people, whether in college, in technical school, or as apprentices, expect to be married and, partially or wholly, to be supported by parents and society while they complete their training for this complex world? Should undergraduates be considered young adults, and should the privileges and responsibilities of mature young adults be theirs, whether they are learning welding or Greek, bookkeeping or physics, dressmaking or calculus? Whether they are rich or poor? Whether they come from educated homes or from homes without such interests? Whether they look forward to the immediate gratifications of private life or to a wider and deeper role in society?

As one enumerates the possibilities, the familiar cry, "But this is democracy," interpreted as treating all alike no matter how different they may be, assaults the ear. Is it in fact a privilege to be given full adult responsibilities at eighteen or at twenty, to be forced to choose someone as a lifetime mate before one has found out who one is, oneself—to be forced somehow to combine learning with earning? Not only the question of who is adult, and when, but of the extent to which a society forces adulthood on its young people arises here.

Civilization, as we know it, was preceded by a prolongation of the learning period—first biologically, by slowing down the process of physical maturation and by giving to children many long, long years for many long, long thoughts; then socially, by developing special institutions in which young people, still protected and supported, were free to explore the past and dream of the future. May it not be a new barbarism to force them to marry so soon?

"Force" is the right word. The mothers who worry about boys and girls who don't begin dating in high school start the process. By the time young people reach college, pressuring parents are joined by college administrators, by advisers and counselors and deans, by student-made rules about exclusive possession of a girl twice dated by the same boy, by the preference of employers for a boy who has demonstrated a tenacious intention of becoming a settled married man. Students who wish to marry may feel they are making magnificent, revolutionary bids for adulthood and responsibility; yet, if one listens to their pleas, one hears only the recited roster of the "others"—schoolmates, classmates, and friends—who are "already married."

The picture of embattled academic institutions valiantly but vainly attempting to stem a flood of undergraduate marriages is ceasing to be true. College presidents have joined the matchmakers. Those who head our one-sex colleges worry about transportation or experiment gingerly with ways in which girls or boys can be integrated into academic life so that they'll stay on the campus on weekends. Recently the president of one of our good, small, liberal arts colleges explained to me, apologetically, "We still have to have rules because, you see, we don't have enough married-student housing." The implication was obvious: the ideal would be a completely married undergraduate body, hopefully at a time not far distant.

With this trend in mind, we should examine some of the premises involved. The lower-class mother hopes her daughter will marry before she is pregnant. The parents of a boy who is a shade gentler or more interested in art than his peers hope their son will marry as soon as possible and be "normal." Those who taught GIs after the last two wars and enjoyed their maturity join the chorus to insist that marriage is steadying: married students study harder and get better grades. The worried leaders of one-sex colleges note how their undergraduates seem younger, "less mature," or "more underdeveloped" than those at the big coeducational universities. They worry also about the tendency of girls to leave at the end of their sophomore year for "wider experience"— a simple euphemism for "men to marry."

And parents, who are asked to contribute what they would have contributed anyway so that the young people may marry, fear—sometimes consciously and sometimes unconsciously—that the present uneasy peacetime will not last, that depression or war will overtake their children as it overtook them. They push their children at ever younger ages, in Little Leagues and eighth-grade proms, to act out—quickly, before it is too late—the adult dreams that may be interrupted. Thus they too consent, connive, and plan toward the earliest possible marriages for both daughters and sons.

Undergraduate marriages have not been part of American life long enough for us to be certain what the effect will be.

But two ominous trends can be noted.

One is the "successful" student marriage, often based on a high school choice which both sets of parents have applauded because it assured an appropriate mate with the right background, and because it made the young people settle down. If not a high school choice, then the high school pattern is repeated: finding a girl who will go steady, dating her exclusively, and letting the girl propel the boy toward a career choice which will make early marriage possible.

These young people have no chance to find themselves in college because they have clung to each other so exclusively. They can take little advantage of college as a broadening experience, and they often show less breadth of vision as seniors than they did as freshmen. They marry, either as undergrad-uates or immediately upon graduation, have children in quick succession, and retire to the suburbs to have more children—bulwarking a choice made before either was differentiated as a human being. Help from both sets of parents, begun in the undergraduate marriage or after commencement day, perpetuates their immaturity. At thirty they are still immature and dependent, their future mortgaged for twenty or thirty years ahead, neither husband nor wife realizing the promise that a different kind of undergraduate life might have enabled each to fulfill.

Such marriages are not failures, in the ordinary sense. They are simply wasteful of young, intelligent people who might have developed into differ-entiated and conscious human beings. But with four or five children, the husband firmly tied to a job which he would not dare to leave, any move toward further individual development in either husband or wife is a threat to the whole family. It is safer to read what both agree with (or even not to read at all and simply look at TV together), attend the same clubs, listen to the same jokes—never for a minute relaxing their possession of each other, just as when they were teen-agers.

Such a marriage is a premature imprisonment of young people, before they have had a chance to explore their own minds and the minds of others, in a kind of desperate, devoted symbiosis. Both had college education, but the college served only as a place in which to get a degree and find a mate from the right family background, a background which subsequently swallows them up.

The second kind of undergraduate marriage is more tragic. Here, the mar-riage is based on the boy's promise and the expendability of the girl. She, at once or at least as soon as she gets her bachelor's degree, will go to work at some secondary job to support her husband while he finishes his degree. She supports him faithfully and becomes identified in his mind with the family that has previously supported him, thus underlining his immature status. As soon as he becomes independent, he leaves her. That this pattern occurs be-tween young people who seem ideally suited to each other suggests that it was the period of economic dependency that damaged the marriage relationship, rather than any intrinsic incompatibility in the original choice.

Both types of marriage, the "successful" and the "unsuccessful," emphasize the key issue: the tie between economic responsibility and marriage in our culture. A man who does not support himself is not yet a man, and a man who is supported by his wife or lets his parents support his wife is also only too likely to feel he is not a man. The GI students' success actually supports this position: they had earned their GI stipend, as men, in their country's service. With a basic economic independence they could study, accept extra help from their families, do extra work, and still be good students and happy husbands and fathers.

There are, then, two basic conclusions. One is that under any circumstances a full student life is incompatible with early commitment and domesticity. The other is that it is incompatible only under conditions of immaturity. Where the choice has been made maturely, and where each member of the pair is doing academic work which deserves full support, complete economic independence should be provided. For other types of student marriage, economic help should be refused.

This kind of discrimination would remove the usual dangers of parent-supported, wife-supported, and too-much-work-supported student marriages. Married students, male and female, making full use of their opportunities as undergraduates would have the right to accept from society this extra time to become more intellectually competent people. Neither partner would be so tied to a part-time job that relationships with other students would be impaired. By the demands of high scholarship, both would be assured of continued growth that comes from association with other high-caliber students as well as with each other.

But even this solution should be approached with caution. Recent psychological studies, especially those of Piaget, have shown how essential and precious is the intellectual development of the early postpubertal years. It may be that any domesticity takes the edge off the eager, flaming curiosity on which we must depend for the great steps that Man must take, and take quickly, if he and all living things are to continue on this earth.

PAMELA ROBY*

Structural and Internalized Barriers to Women in Higher Education

Looking at educational statistics in a national perspective, we find.

50.6 percent of the nation's high school diplomas are granted to women

75.0 percent of all intellectually qualified youngsters who do not enter college are girls

40.4 percent of bachelor's or first professional degrees are awarded to women

33.8 percent of master's degrees go to women

11.6 percent of the nation's doctoral degrees are awarded to females[1]

8.3 percent of the medical students in the United States are women

5.9 percent of the nation's law students are women.[2]

When these statistics are viewed in a historical perspective, we find that the picture for women has worsened rather than improved. In 1930, women were granted 40 rather than 34 percent of the master's degrees and 15 rather than 12 percent of the doctorates.[3]

Turning to the nonacademic side of undergraduate life, Ruth Oltman, in a survey based on a random sample of 200 coeducational colleges and universities, found that in

85 percent of the institutions, *men* held the position of student-body president *all three academic years* from 1967–68 through 1969–70

81 percent of the schools, men were class presidents all three years

70 percent of the schools, men were chairmen of the campus judicial board all three years

61 percent of the institutions, men were chairmen of the union, senate, or board of governors all three years

75 percent of the (sixty-six reporting) institutions, men held the top SDS post all three years.[4]

The above illustrative figures give a good idea of the nature of barriers women are confronted with in higher education today. In this article we will first analyze the structural or institutional barriers which confront women in higher education. Secondly, we will examine the social attitudes and norms

---

* I wish to thank Jo-Ann Gardner, Kay Cassell, Daphne Joslin, and Ruth Oltman for assisting me in gathering material for this article.

121

which, once internalized by women, further bar women from obtaining education and from utilizing the education they have obtained. In the last section, we will suggest steps which must be taken to provide women with equal educational opportunities.

Structural Barriers to Women in Higher Education

Structural barriers refers to those organizational patterns and practices in higher education which hinder or halt female students in their efforts to obtain college or university educations. These organizational barriers include practices pertaining to student admission and the granting of financial aid, to rules governing life on campus, to residency and full-time-study requirements, to the sexist character of much subject matter taught within universities today, to the composition of faculties, and to maternity and paternity leaves and married students' domestic responsibilities.

Admission

The first hurdle which confronts all students seeking higher education is that of admission. Regardless of intelligence or past academic performance, female applicants frequently find themselves confronted by barriers never experienced by men during the admission process. Discriminatory admission policies are disguised in various garb. One is the concern that men enjoy parity with women in those departments or colleges where, on the basis of their qualifications for admission, women "threaten" to outnumber men. The concern leads to a policy in which admission is refused to women who have higher qualifications than men who are granted admission. Such a practice at first appears equitable: "We don't, after all, want to discriminate *against* men," it is said. Then one notices that in other colleges or departments of the same university where men far outnumber women (the medical and engineering schools are always good examples), the concern with sexual parity is strikingly absent.[5]

A second type of discriminatory admissions policy simply gives special attention to women's applications. In the *American Bar Association Journal* Beatrice Dinerman notes, for example:

> Although no law school uses either a formal or informal quota system to limit the number of females enrolled, they do admit to scrutinizing female applicants more closely for ability and motivation. Some schools give close consideration to the marital status of women before granting admission, and other schools take into account the possibility that a female student might not graduate and continue to practice. It follows that a male applicant is often chosen over an equally qualified female.[6]

Other traditional admissions policies, the entrance examination and the requirement that entering students provide recent recommendations from teachers and professors, discriminate against older college applicants. Because women are more likely than men to delay their college education, they are disproportionately affected by the policy. College Entrance Examinations, Graduate Record Examinations, and the SATs are all based on knowledge taught in high school or lower-division college courses. These exams, which are relatively easy for students who have recently completed their high school or college course work, are extremely difficult for even the brightest students who have been away from the classroom for ten or twenty years.

Another prevalent discriminatory admissions policy is that which restricts the student population to men or sets a lower quota for female than male students.[7] Quotas and selective admissions policies are often supported on the ground that men are more likely than women to complete their course of study. Time and again, however, in the very universities where this argument is given, a visit to the recorder's office reveals that not only do women students have higher grade averages than men, but a higher portion of the entering women than the entering men have obtained their degrees.[8]

Financial Aid

Following admission, students must face the question of how they are to pay for their education. The height of this hurdle varies both by economic class and by sex. Upper-middle-income parents generally consider the under-graduate education of both sons and daughters to be part of their parental responsibilities. These parents generally feel that their responsibility in the case of sons extends through law or medical school, but that in the case of daughters, it has been fulfilled after four or five years of college. Many also believe that they would be doing their daughters a disservice by helping them obtain education beyond the B.A. or M.A. level, for doing so might make catching the right man difficult.

While the financing of undergraduate education is virtually guaranteed for upper-middle-class men and women, such is not the case for working-class students. At this income level, parents, who cannot afford to send all of their children to college, generally make considerable sacrifices in order to put their sons through four years of college but do not offer to finance their daughters' college educations. The daughters may take two-year nursing courses, three-month courses to qualify as beauticians, or one-year secretarial courses. Others, immediately following high school, apply for jobs typing, waitressing, selling, or working in factories. Some help their parents pay for their brothers' educations.

Within the university, women are frequently discriminated against in the distribution of fellowship aid. As in the case of admission, many departments subtly discriminate against women, who on the average have higher mean grades than men, by ruling that fellowship aid be distributed to men and women students in proportion to the ratio of men and women students in the department. The general consequence of such a rule is that men who have lower qualifications than women are given aid.[9] Many of the best scholarships, as Bernice Sandler has pointed out before the Senate Judiciary Committee, are limited to men only.[10] Only under considerable pressure from Women's Liber-ation did New York University Law School agree to consider women, who make up one-third of its student body, for some of the highly coveted $10,000 law scholarships. Married women who must combine schooling with some responsibilities are excluded from competing for practically all federal scholarship and loan aid as well as many university scholarships by the limitation of these prizes to students engaging in full-time study, an impossibility for a woman who is managing a household. Unmarried female students, unlike their male counterparts, are also discouraged from borrowing heavily to pay for their education because doing so may overly burden their future husbands.

Married females not only face difficulties in obtaining financial resources for themselves but are expected, no matter what their own educational desires, to help their husbands through college and the first years of their careers. "Putting hubby through" usually means the assumption of a full-time job as well as household chores. The advent of better means of birth control has not lightened the burdens of young wives: now their graduate-student husbands can pursue their studies, often taking the time to switch from one area to another, without the pressure of knowing that they may soon have to assume the family's financial responsibilities. Meanwhile, the child-bearing and -rearing stage of the wives' lives is postponed, delaying the time when they may eventually return to school. Many universities' hardened view and actual support of these women's plight is illustrated by an account from Yale University. The *Yale-Break* reported: "The wives of graduating medical students at Yale were 'dishonored' this spring by a 'PHT' degree. In fancy lettering, on creamy parchment, signed by Dean Redlich's wife, the diploma read 'Congratulations for PUTTING HUBBY THROUGH.'" One of the "PHT" recipients, angered that Yale obviously defined herself and others only in terms of the men they were attached to, sent her "degree" back.[11]

Campus Rules and Counseling

After they have surmounted the hurdles of admission and financial aid and have arrived on the university campus, women face not only the "normal" trials of university life which constitute the common complaints of all students, but a whole new set of obstacles to their education which are peculiar to their sex.

Both freshmen and graduate students are also greeted by a "college counselor." This advisor, whom they will meet with intermittently throughout their college careers, frequently counsels women students away from rigorous, traditionally masculine courses of study or away from the university altogether. At the University of Maryland, Bernice Sandler reports, a male member of her own department "feels strongly that women should not be professionals and tells this to his women students."[12] At New York University women students in the School of Education report that one of their professors teaches that "the fact that women have produced less than men professionally and artistically is an indicator of women's lesser ability."[13] At Princeton, in a proposed memo to the university's first female undergraduate students, a well-meaning career services officer suggested that "although it sounded old-fashioned, it really was a good idea for women to have secretarial skills to fall back on."[14] My first-day experience at Columbia University's graduate school included a meeting with a professor who, rather than counseling me as to which courses I might take, proceeded for a quarter of an hour to tell me that *"since I was a woman* [my emphasis], I had better be very serious about the business of pursuing a graduate career." Friends from nearly every school and department outside of education and social work in major universities throughout the nation have told of similar or worse experiences they have had.

The serious effects which such experiences can have on women's academic and career decisions are shown by the findings of a four-year longitudinal study involving interviews and psychological tests of female undergraduate students at Stanford. The data reported from the study show that "women students need special encouragement to develop intellectual, artistic and professional ambitions." Repeatedly, their college histories "indicated the effect of encouragement or lack of such encouragement as a catalytic agent." The study revealed further that "an interested male has the power to communicate to the maturing young woman that she is not damaging her femininity by developing her mind and skills. Sometimes even a subtle form of consent or disapproval from a male served as a stimulus for a young woman to advance or retreat."[15]

Degree Requirements

Those women who have the fortune to be encouraged by counselors and professors and those who persevere in spite of discouraging counselors next face the multiple obstacles of university residency, full-time study, and course-credit requirements. Because wives traditionally follow their husbands, female students must move from campus to campus more often than men. Undergraduate and graduate degree course-credit requirements, which vary from college to college, as well as residency requirements obviously deter mobile students. These barriers should be among the easiest to remove from the paths of women, for, as Cless has observed, most students attend colleges and universities which are members of one of the six regional accreditation commissions of higher education. Since all these institutions belong to the National Federation of Accreditation Commissions, "it would be expected that credit for similar courses at different institutions would be automatically interchangeable among accredited colleges or universities; that requirements for the field of concentration would be similar; and that residency requirements would be nonexistent."[16]

Many colleges and universities are now loosening some of their degree requirements by granting credit for Peace Corps, VISTA, teacher-aid, and ghetto tutoring experience. Equity suggests that institutions of higher education should grant female students who have returned to college after raising a family similar credit for the experiences they have had managing families, raising and tutoring their children, budgeting expenses, and serving the community. Demonstration programs in women's continuing education suggest that schools might be well rewarded for assisting the older student. They have shown that no matter how well women had performed in college when eighteen to twenty-one years of age, they did better when they returned to formal study after the age of thirty.[17]

The final obstacle which peers out of many college catalogs at women is the full-time study requirement. Not only does the requirement that students enroll for a full-time course of study prevent the woman who must devote part of her time to familial responsibilities from studying, but it coercively shapes the marital patterns of all couples in which one partner is a student. An increasing number of young husbands and wives are attempting to share family and household responsibilities equally.[18] The requirement that one partner must study or work full time makes the achievement of an equal division of familial responsibilities more difficult, if not impossible.

Subject Matter: Or, Where Have All Our Women Gone?

Once in the classroom, women soon discover that instructors and textbook writers in every field have, consciously or unconsciously, joined hands to keep "women in their place." Introductory sociology texts, which are required reading for over a hundred thousand students a year, mention women only in chapters on the family. In these chapters women are described in their "traditional" roles as full-time homemakers and mothers unlinked to the economic and political world—roles which in fact only upper, or in some societies also the upper-middle, classes can afford.[19] Most "Marriage and the Family" courses leave problems of the modern family as an institution unexamined and reinforce the rapidly disappearing social belief that brides must be virgins for a marriage to be "happy."[20] In sociological theory courses, Betty Friedan has noted, structural-functionalists, "by giving an absolute meaning and a sanctimonious value to the generic term 'woman's role' . . . put American women into a kind of deep freeze."[21] As in the case of Talcott Parsons's widely read essay on social stratification, these theorists' discussions of "what is" quickly become interpreted as "what should be." Perhaps a million college women have been instructed to read the following passage by Parsons:

> Absolute equality of opportunity is clearly incompatible with any positive solidarity of the family. . . . Where married women are employed outside the home, it is, for the great majority, in occupations which are not in direct competition for status with those of men of their own class. Women's interests, and the standard of judgment applied to them, run, in our society, far more in the direction of personal adornment. . . . It is suggested that this difference is functionally related to maintaining family solidarity in our class structure.[22]

Neither Parsons himself nor most professors who discuss his article go on to question the desirability of the class structure he describes or the need for such family solidarity.

Female aggression, initiative, and creativity are not ignored solely by sociologists. History courses skip over feminist movements and overlook the contributions (except for that of Betsy Ross), achievements, and oppression of women. Literature students are fed a constant diet of male writers—Ernest Hemingway, James Joyce, Norman Mailer, etc.—while the notable accomplishments of female writers go unanalyzed. In schools of medicine, engineering, and architecture, where the subject matter itself cannot be used to reinforce male and depress female egos, women students are continuously, informally pressed into "feminine" areas such as pediatrics, gynecology, or interior design. In the engineering school of a midwestern university, a female student found that all the lockers assigned to students for their laboratory equipment and clothes were in the men's lavatory.[23] Women who persevere in such areas as surgery despite the negative sanctions of male students and male professors find themselves eventually blocked when no hospital will allow them to fulfill their surgical internship requirements.

The continual emphasis which college and university professors have placed on the culture and achievements of white males has naturally served to motivate white male students, who feel comfortable with the culture and with the models who are like themselves. For blacks and women it has done the opposite. It has clearly carried the message, "You do not belong among those who make important decisions for or significant contributions to society." And for women, additionally, "If you try to become something other than a housewives or low-income workers, you will be unsuccessful." Rather than degrade themselves by memorizing and regurgitating such "facts" as "women's place is in the home," many able women have dropped out of college or have discontinued their education after completing their B.A.; others have capitulated to their male colleagues and professors by becoming interior designers rather than architects or contractors, pediatricians rather than surgeons, kindergarten teachers rather than university professors.

Today, women, like blacks a half decade ago, are discovering that they have a history and that there are alternatives to a male-dominated sexist society. Around the nation new courses are being developed and offered on the sociology and history of women. Textbooks (like this one) are beginning to be written and published on the subject of women. At least one literature instructor, Elaine Showalter of Douglass College, has switched to teaching about Mary McCarthy and other female writers. She reports, "The whole quality of the classroom and quality of term papers has changed since we switched to McCarthy!" Now she knows why her all-female class had difficulty identifying with the adolescent times of Hemingway and Joyce![24] The new developments are exciting, but to date, a female student is lucky if she gets one course out of ten which is not characterized by male chauvinism and sexist bias. In January 1971, fifty-five out of 2600 colleges and universities offered one or more courses in women's studies.[25] All should offer them. Large numbers of additional female faculty are needed to teach courses on women, to help male faculty recognize and overcome their sexist practices, and to serve as role models and confidantes for female students.

Role Models: Faculty Women

The statistics cited at the beginning of this article show that although half the students in America's prestigious institutions of higher education are women, less than one-tenth of their faculty is female and that most of these female faculty members are to be found on the lower rungs of the professorial ladder.[26] Even seventy out of seventy-four directors of the largest college and university libraries are men.[27] The absence of women in faculty and administrative positions serves as a silent but potent message to female students that "aiming high" would be foolish indeed. Outright sexist discrimination in hiring and promotion, nepotism rules, full-time work requirements, lack of child-care facilities and maternity-paternity leaves, as well as barriers to women's attaining higher education account for females' low representation in high-ranking university positions.

Outright discrimination in university hiring and promotion of women has been frequently revealed. The Women's Equity Action League and the National Organization for Women in the spring of 1970 charged forty-three colleges and universities with discriminatory employment practices against women under Executive Orders 11246 and 11375, which forbid discrimination by federal contractors on the basis of race, color, religion, national origin, or sex. The colleges charged with discrimination were from every part of the nation, and their number included large and small, rich and poor institutions.[28]

The depth of sexist discrimination in university hiring practices was discovered by Lawrence Simpson in 1968. For his Ph.D. dissertation, Simpson distributed mock resumes of "men" and "women" to 234 representative deans, departmental chairmen, and faculty members who were involved in faculty hiring. The responses to the resumes showed that "where qualifications of men and women were equal, substantially more men were chosen, although the selection should have been almost equal, based on the previously determined choices of the faculty panel when no sex identification was given. In a choice between a superior woman and a less qualified man, the employers selected a significant number of women."[29] The nature of these hiring agents' sexist attitudes is illustrated by a conversation Jo Freeman had with Professor Arthur Mann of Chicago University's history department:

> [Mann] said his department would be happy to hire more women, but that there were only three good women historians in the country and none of them were available. He may be right in his assessment of the top historians, but he is wrong if he meant that only the best people in any field ever teach at the University of Chicago. . . . Judging the status of women by that of the most successful is not only a sham, but a dangerous one because it perpetuates tokenism and clothes it in a self-righteous mythology. It cannot be said that women are judged equally with men until ordinary men are judged by the same standards.[30]

The common arguments given by institutions for discrimination against academic women have been explained and refuted by Martha Griffiths on the floor of the United States Congress:

> For years there has been a shortage of college teachers, yet there has been little serious effort to recruit women for college faculties. The excuse often given that there is a shortage of qualified women is ridiculous. For example, at Columbia University women receive about 25 percent of its doctoral degrees, but comprise only 2 percent of the tenured faculty in its graduate schools. Furthermore, contrary to academic mythology, a higher percentage of women with doctorates go into college teaching than do men with doctorates. The argument that women are lost to the academic world when they marry is also a myth, since over 90 percent of the women with doctorates are in the labor force.[31]

Universities' closest sources of women qualified to fill faculty positions and to serve as role models for female students are faculty wives, the very women against whom colleges have erected the highest barriers. Antinepotism rules which hold that husbands and wives cannot teach within either the same department or the same university are the most obvious form of discrimination against faculty wives. Supporters of the rules, who maintain that granting positions to both husbands and wives would constitute a form of departmental patronage, overlook the facts that universities and colleges annually lure scholars to their campuses by guaranteeing their protégés positions as assistant or associate professors, and that since persons with similar educational backgrounds frequently marry, both husbands and wives are likely to be qualified for university positions. Other supporters of the nepotism rules argue that the task of faculty selection would be more difficult if the nepotism rules were dropped. They maintain that in the cases of couples where the husband and wife do all their writing together (and, therefore, the acceptance of the second spouse, that is, the wife could not bring "new" ideas into the department) and where one has considerably higher qualifications than the other, the department would have to face the prospect of accepting one and rejecting the other. Women, on the other hand, are responding that although no one likes the job of having to reject students or prospective faculty, such rejections are obviously made every day. Therefore why should a selection committee's task be made easier solely in the case of married couples? Specifically, why should it be made easier by a policy which deprives universities of much talent and leads to blanket discrimination against women? These women point out that underlying these questions is a basic issue of power: Are the lives of selection committees or the lives of women to be made difficult?

Women are beginning to refuse to carry such burdens continually. In Arizona, faculty wives have begun, successfully, to contest the state university system's antinepotism rule.[32] Meanwhile, most other universities, rather than use qualified and talented faculty wives as a resource, isolate them and thereby create an entire community of negative role models for female students—role models which daily say: No matter how much education you have, you may expect to forget your career if you marry.

One Yale faculty wife has described her position as follows:

> Today was a rather typical day. The morning and afternoon were spent at home alone with the baby. I'm not free to study or pursue a career and I haven't even the satisfaction of developing close friendships with other faculty wives. We are isolated from one another and, by the nature of our husbands' careers, we are transient, in fact, maddeningly so. This evening I wanted to go to a political meeting; my husband felt he should go back to the lab. And so, of course, I'm still at home babysitting. . . .
>
> I am not so naive as to think that I could have an interesting and challenging job in my field if only I had more time and more freedom. Three years ago I took a job at Yale which required a B.A. in English and some knowledge of Latin. I was optimistic that I would be doing work which utilized my knowledge and would allow me to follow through with my interest in English. I soon

learned that a knowledge of Latin was deemed necessary for proof-reading Latin texts and a degree in English considered essential for writing routine business letters.[33]

Once women are hired for faculty positions, they face discrimination in regard to promotion, salaries, and day-to-day matters of university life. At the University of Michigan when a world-renowned scientist retired as the director of the Gerontology Institute, it was learned that her salary was equivalent to that of many assistant professors. Men with markedly lesser reputations who were considered to replace her were all offered well over twice her retiring salary.[34] At that university, the University of Chicago, and numerous other prestigious institutions most female Ph.D.'s are placed in neither directorships nor faculty positions and are given instead temporary positions as research associates.[35] As such, they are "allowed" to teach at low salaries and without a faculty vote; the years of teaching they accumulate do not lead to associate and full professorships, for these higher positions require that one begin her career with the title "assistant professor." Since many assistant professors primarily do research and teach a course or two on the side, the distinction between "assistant professor" and "research associate" is a matter of title only, but it is a matter of important consequence for one's later career.

Maternity and Paternity Leaves, Child Care, Meal Service, Part-Time Work and Study

Working women spend an average of twenty-eight hours a week on household tasks and child care.[36] The burden of household tasks and child care must be shared equally between men and women if women are to be considered to have an "equal opportunity" to study or work in institutions of higher education. If colleges and universities are to provide young married women with equal educational opportunities and attract sizable numbers of women to serve as faculty role models for all female students, they must not only destroy discriminatory rules and practices but also provide married students and faculty with maternity and paternity leaves, twenty-four-hour child-care facilities, meal service, and part-time work and study arrangements. Present university regulations which exclude maternity and paternity leaves and forbid part-time work or study for men and women not only force women to withdraw from academic life for longer than they would like but also prevent men from assuming parental responsibilities during their children's early years.[37]

The availability of excellent child-care facilities is, as shown by a longitudinal study of students graduating from college in 1961, the most important condition affecting women's decisions to attend graduate school.[38] Despite this critical finding, universities have continued to ignore female students' and faculty members' cries for nurseries and child care. After months of confrontation with university officials, Princeton's chapter of the National Organization for Women in the autumn of 1970 was able to get the university to provide space and funds for a nursery which is expected to meet the child-care needs of one-third of its faculty and students. At least Princeton has made a start. Hundreds of colleges and universities have yet to follow its lead. Until they do, the necessity of child care will continue to bar many women from pursuing or using their higher education.

Not only child care, but household tasks and meal preparation hamper wives who wish to develop or utilize their talents. Unless other women are to be enslaved as domestics, husbands are academic women's only source of household help. University policies must be reshaped to encourage rather than discourage faculty and student men from sharing domestic responsibilities. Universities might also construct communal dining rooms for families such as those in American dormitories or Swedish "service apartment houses" which would relieve faculty and student *couples* of the task of preparing meals.

Internalized Barriers to Women in Higher Education

> . . . prejudices and outmoded customs act as barriers to the full realization of women's basic rights which should be respected and fostered as part of our Nation's commitment to human dignity, freedom, and democracy. . . . (John F. Kennedy, in establishing the President's Commission on the Status of Women in 1961)

The structural barriers to women in higher education which we have reviewed above are buttressed by the social attitudes and norms taught both men and women concerning "feminine" behavior.[39] Today's American college women received their first bit of socialization concerning sex roles when, as newborn infants, they were carefully wrapped in pretty pink blankets. Later as young children, they were encouraged by their families to play house, take care of their baby dolls, and act like "ladies." "Masculine" traits such as physical and intellectual aggression, problem-solving ability, and overt hostility, while encouraged in their brothers, were severely discouraged in them. Their grade-school teachers continued to socialize them to "their roles." Despite the increasing proportion of mothers in the national labor force, their grade-school readers seldom, if ever, portrayed mothers at work. Their own mothers were expected to be available to assist teachers on field trips and to bake cookies for class parties.

In high school their activities and career plans were viewed in relationship to traditional "women's roles." Teachers and guidance counselors gently persuaded them that it was not proper to run for class president, that they would be better off not pursuing physics and third-year algebra, and that despite the nation's desperate need for physicians and innovative leaders, they would be happier as nurses than as doctors, as secretaries than as politicians. They were taught that while women can only be truly fulfilled as mothers and wives, it is compatible with the "feminine nature" and perhaps necessary that they also seek to bring "peace and comfort into the world" as social workers, nurses, sympathetic assistants, and primary-school teachers.[40] This form of socialization is perhaps best described by the following reflection of an MIT student:

> For years I have had to fight to retain my interest in aeronautics. My high school teacher thought I was crazy to even think of going

into aeronautical engineering. My mother said I'd never find a man willing to marry a woman who likes to "tinker with motors," as she put it. My professors say I won't get a job in industry and should switch to another engineering specialty.[41]

In addition to being socialized away from "unfeminine" careers and from positions which might challenge the status of their future mates, young women were taught to compete with other women for the admiration and attention of men and ultimately for a husband.[42] Other women were to be distrusted; women were to place their faith in men. They saw that, in the minds of their parents and teachers, having a date (however dull) for the junior prom took precedence over writing a creative essay, tutoring a poor child, and myriad other things. Life was defined for them in terms of being the "other half" of some man, a subordinate, submissive, dependent, unequal position.

Such wisdom imparted by parents and teachers was reinforced by the mass media. Whenever they flicked on the television they either saw themselves portrayed by liquor, cigarette, and auto advertisements as sexual objects whose goal was to give men pleasure, or were induced by the doting-wife-mother image portrayed in household ads to feel that indeed their only desire was to please a husband and his children.[43] Many came to feel that they had little of worth to say, that what they had to say could probably be said better by someone else (most likely a boy), and that they really were silly, emotional creatures. Those who, despite this consistent socialization to "feminine roles," continued to question their own roles in life usually found themselves talking with psychiatrists who treated their "problems" as requiring personal rather than societal change and urged them to find self-fulfillment through devotion to marriage and parenthood.[44]

Philip Goldberg's study of women's prejudice against women[45] proved quite clearly the tremendous effects of current sex-role socialization upon the self-images of women. In the same vein, in a study of students at six California high schools, Don McNeily III found that girls as young as thirteen or fourteen years old had already been socialized to believe that powerful social roles are not for them. When asked whether they "could be" President, only 13 percent of them, as compared with 31 percent of the boys, said yes, and when asked about the possibility of becoming governor, 17 percent of the girls and 44 percent of the boys replied that they could see themselves as someday holding that office.[46]

During the early fifties David McClelland and his colleagues isolated a psychological characteristic which they termed the "need to achieve." Subsequently, McClelland's students studied many aspects of this internalized motivation to excel. In each of the studies, however, women were conspicuously absent, for early in the studies the female subjects had produced inconsistent, confusing results and the investigators had decided to leave them out. Ten years later, Matina Horner decided to investigate the success needs of women. Her first consistent finding on women was that they had much higher text-anxiety scores than men. With the use of the TAT (Thematic Apperception Test) and a story completion test concerning a successful male and a successful female medical student, Honer went on to isolate in women a fear of success. Horner concluded that the motive to avoid success was born in her female subjects when they learned the truth of Samuel Johnson's comment, "A man is in general better pleased when he has a good dinner upon his table, than when his wife talks Greek."[47]

What about the women who do "succeed" in academia? Jessie Bernard reports that a study of 706 college teachers in Minnesota, 27 percent of whom were women, found that the women had been much more tentative, much more modest, and much more influenced by others in their career choices than the men. On the basis of the study's findings, Bernard noted that an academic career appeared to be something almost thrust upon these women, something which they would not of themselves have aspired to.[48] Thus, these "successful women" had also learned not to seek success aggressively, as this would not have been considered "ladylike," but to deny their aspirations and to allow their career paths to be shaped by whether or not someone happened to offer them a college teaching position.

Women's lack of confidence in other women, their "need to fail," their fear of acting aggressively are societally taught norms which, once internalized, become formidable psychological barriers buttressing the structural barriers to the higher education of women. These norms as well as organizational features of universities which deter women must be transformed if women are to enjoy the basic rights which Kennedy declared "should be respected and fostered as part of our Nation's commitment to human dignity, freedom, and democracy. . . ."

Women Unite! Education's a Right!

How can persons who seek educational opportunities for women abolish the structural and psychological barriers which confront women in higher education today? Glancing backward, we see that for generations women have been advised to seek change by working harder individually or by being "twice as good as men." Women have tried this strategy and have found that it doesn't work. The individual woman who struggles and finally becomes an outstanding scholar may be hired by a top-notch university, but her appointment guarantees neither that ordinary women, like ordinary men, will be hired by that university nor that she will not at some future time be discriminated against purely on the basis of her sex.

Feminists must work together and become politically organized if they are to destroy the barriers which confront women in higher education and other areas of life. Ours is a politically organized society which, as Richard Quinney notes, is based on an interest structure characterized by an unequal distribution of power and by conflict. Various segments of any society have different interests. The distribution of power, which is determined by conflict, determines the laws, policies, and practices of societies.[49] The conflict may involve violence or social conditioning.[50] When members of an interest group are split by geographical barriers or political conditioning, they are more vulnerable to socialization which supports norms and ideologies counter to their own interests. Marx, for example, noted that in his day Irish and English workers were separated by political conditioning to ideologies which misrepresented their interests, and that in feudal times peasants had been geographically separated.[51] Now in the 1970s, women are coming to realize, as blacks did some ten years ago, that through their socialization to individual and class competition, they too have been politically separated from one another. This separation has made them vulnerable to discrimination and sexist socialization in all spheres of life.[52] The effects of this separation may be countered only if women analyze the means by which they have been separated and exploited, resocialize themselves to their own interests, and act politically on the basis of these interests.

The discussion in the first two sections of this paper suggests many steps which feminists, as a politically organized segment of society, must take to provide women with equal educational opportunities. As a first step, overt and covert sexist discrimination in university admissions and financial aid practices must be halted. The addition of women to admissions and financial aid staffs will not guarantee fair practices but would be a step in the right direction. Admissions and financial aid staffs must work toward evaluating applications without regard to or information concerning sex, as they have done in the case of race. The practice whereby one sector of a university discriminates against women so as to maintain an even ratio of men to women while other sectors with a high ratio of men do nothing to obtain an even sexual balance must be stopped. Entrance examinations which discriminate against older applicants, most of whom are women, should be abolished. The limitation of many scholarships and fellowships to men must be contested. Until such time as sexist discrimination is abolished in elementary and high schools, admissions and financial aid policies should be designed, as they have been in the case of blacks, to favor women, particularly women from families which cannot afford to send all their children to college. Institutions of higher education which are found to have sexist admissions and financial aid practices must be sanctioned. Toward this end, the Civil Rights Act of 1964 should be amended to authorize the Attorney General of the United States both to aid women and, in the case of girls under twenty-one, parents in suits seeking equal access to public education (Title V), and to make a survey concerning the lack of equal educational opportunities for individuals by reason of sex (Title IX).

Second, college counseling should be made to broaden rather than restrict women's views of career possibilities. College counseling is one point at which women may be helped to reexamine their attitudes, taught by the media and other socializing agents, concerning their roles and status. College counselors should discuss with female students the significant changes which have occurred in the life-patterns of American women since 1900 and their grand-mothers' day. These changes include the twenty-five-year extension of the average American woman's life; a continually decreasing housework load; birth control, which has resulted in smaller families and, in the last nine years, in an increasing proportion of twenty- to twenty-four-year-old wives who have no children and therefore have greater freedom to work or continue their schooling; and changing attitudes concerning the wisdom of mothers' full-time presence with their young children.[53] Counselors should next help women evaluate their educational and career choices in the context of these changes.

Women's Liberation groups on college campuses might help counselors reexamine their attitudes concerning women and might work with the counselors in advising groups of female students. Many women have already found that small "Women's Lib" group discussions provide a valuable basis for reexamining their personal goals and values.

Not only must counselors stop discouraging and begin encouraging women to develop their full potential, but universities must remove the degree requirements which bar many women from completing their education. In 1963 the President's Commission on the Status of Women stated that changes in degree requirements were among the basic essentials for the provision of adequate education for women. The commission recommended the provision of ready transfer of credits from college to college, increased uses of testing for credit, the substitution of life experience for course work, the facilitation of part-time study, the lifting of age limits, and the reassessment of time requirements.[54]

Women now realize that, in addition to the "essentials" outlined by the 1963 commission, courses on women should be added to college curricula, large numbers of female faculty should be added to college staffs at all levels of the professorial and administrative hierarchies, and child-care facilities plus maternity and paternity leaves must be provided. Recently the American Federation of Teachers has begun to construct lesson plans on women's history and to conduct a major investigation of how high school history books portray the struggle for women's rights.[55] Similar efforts need to be made at the college level. In addition, the works of women writers plus texts analyzing them and examining the images of women in literature should be introduced in English classes. Social science instructors across the nation might follow the lead of Leni Weitzman, who at Yale University uses a collection of advertisements as a teaching aid to alert both men and women to the oppressive, manipulative nature of advertising and the role that it plays in shaping the population's image of women. Excellent courses specifically on the role of women in society have been instituted in some colleges and high schools, and similar courses should be made available at all American colleges and universities.

Large numbers of female faculty should be added to college staffs at all levels of the professorial and administrative hierarchies so that female like male students may have faculty role models and representatives of their own sex. In order to hire adequate numbers of female faculty, universities will have to recruit women actively and abolish written and de facto nepotism rules and sexist hiring practices. Executive Orders 11246 and 11375, which, as mentioned earlier, forbid discrimination by federal contractors, including universities, on the basis of race, color, religion, national origin, or sex, must be enforced. The United States Office of Education's Higher Education General Information Surveys should include questions on the sex of teaching personnel.

So that male members of the academic community will not be forced to lead lopsided lives with little or no domestic activity and their wives will not be forced into unending isolation within the home, more flexible part-time employment arrangements should be made available to all university person-nel, and part-time study arrangements should be offered to students. All institutions of higher education should also provide maternity and paternity leaves and child-development centers to all members of their communities. Until good preschool child-care centers and after-school centers are available for all children in the society and until husbands come to share domestic responsibilities equitably with their wives—or until the family institution is totally transformed—all should recognize that *in the United States women do not enjoy equal rights.*

As feminists strive to destroy the structural and attitudinal barriers con-fronting women in higher education and other spheres of life, they see more clearly the political and exploitative base which underlies the barriers. De-stroying institutional barriers to women and changing traditional patterns of socialization will be difficult. The present barriers and forms of sexist socialization are not accidental: the inculcation of values and goals through the socialization process is universally the strongest means where dominators can exert social control over those they dominate. That sexism is an integral part of the present social structure and that those in power benefit from it is illustrated by the quick appearance of vengeful hostility when women seek freedom, power, or status greater than that given to or defined for them in their "feminine role." Like the label of "black racist" pinned on blacks struggling for freedom, the labels "man-hater," "castrating bitch," "lesbian," and "tough" are hurled at women who wish to define their destinies and goals for themselves. To have the strength to ignore such labels and to eradicate sexism in society, feminists must unite and treat the question of sex politically, as those who discriminate against women have done.

Notes

1. Elizabeth Cless, "A Modest Proposal for the Educating of Women," *American Scholar,* vol. 38, no. 4 (Autumn 1969), p. 620; U.S. Department of Labor, Women's Bureau, *Handbook on Women Workers* (Washington, D.C.: Govern-ment Printing Office, 1969).
2. *Report of the Presidential Task Force on Women's Rights and Responsibilities* (Washington, D.C.: Government Printing Office, 1969), sec. 3C.
3. "Discrimination," *Parade* (*Sunday Magazine of the Washington Post*), June 15, 1969.
4. Ruth M. Oltman, "Status of Women on Campus," stenciled (Washington, D.C.: American Association of University Women, April 9, 1970), p. 1.; cf. Marge Piercy, "The Movement: For Men Only?" *Guardian,* January 31, February 7, 14, 1970.
5. Cf. Kathleen Shortridge, "Women as University Nigger: How the 'U' Keeps Females in Their Place," *The Daily Magazine,* April 12, 1970; Jean D. Grambs, "Editorial," *Women's Education,* vol. 7, no. 1 (March 1968); Eric Wentworth, "Women Seek College Equality," *The Washington Post,* June 22, 1970.
6. "Sex Discrimination in the Legal Profession," *American Bar Association Journal,* vol. 55 (October 1969), p. 951.
7. Only recently, legal action forced the state of Virginia to admit women to the University College of Arts and Sciences at Charlottesville (*Kirstein et al.* v. *University of Virginia,* F.C. Va. Civil Action No. 220–69 R). The suit, which charged the university with the violation of women's rights under the First and

Fourteenth amendments, was dropped because the university changed its policy to admit women (*The Washington Post*, June 26, 1969).

8. Jo Freeman, "Women on the Social Science Faculties of the University of Chicago Since 1892," stenciled (Chicago: University of Chicago, Department of Political Science, Winter 1969).

9. Cf. Anne Row, "Women in Science," *Personnel and Guidance Journal*, vol. 44, no. 8 (April 1966).

10. Bernice Sandler, "Statement Regarding the Equal Rights for Women," in U.S. Congress, Senate, Judiciary Committee, Subcommittee on Constitutional Amendments [Re S.J. Res. 61], May 6, 1970.

11. Editors, "Atrocity of the Month," *Yale-Break*, vol. 1, no. 4 (June 1, 1970).

12. Sandler, *op. cit.*

13. Personal communications with women students at the School of Education of New York University.

14. Elaine Showalter, "Women and the University," *Princeton Alumni Weekly* (February 24, 1970), p. 8. Harold I. Kaplan, M.D., who conducted a seven-year study under a National Institute of Mental Health grant of medical schools' attitudes toward women students, recently said that "some replies to [my] questions were so 'scandalous' that [I] did not include them in [my] final report," which concluded that "widespread prejudice is depriving the nation of urgently needed physicians." See: "Women Seek Bigger Medical Role," *American Medical News*, November 23, 1970, p. 1.

15. Marjorie M. Lozoff, "Abstract of *College Influences on the Role Development of Female Undergraduates*," stenciled (Palo Alto, Cal.: Stanford Institute for the Study of Human Problems, 1969), p. 3.

16. Cless, *op. cit.*, p. 624.

17. *Ibid.*, p. 623.

18. "Women's Lib Movement Inspires More Couples to Strive for Equality," *The Wall Street Journal*, August 4, 1970; Pat Mainardi, "The Politics of Housework," in *Sisterhood Is Powerful*, ed. Robin Morgan (New York: Random House, 1970), pp. 447–455; Alix Shulman, "A Marriage Agreement," in *Women's Liberation: Blueprint for the Future*, ed. Sookie Stambler (New York: Ace Books, 1970), pp. 211–216.

19. Marlene Dixon has noted that "in Mexico, with its modified purdah and machismo . . . it is the middle-class women who are inferior, irrelevant, held in contempt—peasant women contribute too much to the support of the household, farm, and industry to be placed in the totally subservient position of middle-class Mexican women. Women have it bad everywhere, but with the loss of necessary economic functions, the position seems less psychologically bearable, not to mention the loss of all power except manipulation" (Marlene D. Dixon, "A Position Paper on Radical Women in the Professions," stenciled (Chicago: University of Chicago, Department of Sociology, 1967). Cf. Thorstein Veblen, *The Theory of the Leisure Class: An Economic Study of Institutions* (New York: The Macmillan Company, 1899).

20. Among the most blatantly sexist texts is Henry A. Bowman, *Marriage for Moderns* (New York: McGraw-Hill Book Co., 1942). In recent years a small number of articles and texts have appeared which have questioned the traditional writings of American family sociologists. Most of these have been by non-Americans or by sociologists who do not consider themselves "family sociologists." Cf. Barrington Moore, "Thoughts on the Future of the Family," in *Radical Perspectives on Social Problems*, ed. Frank Lindenfeld, (New York: The Macmillan Company, 1968); Constantina Safilios-Rothschild, "Toward a Cross-Cultural Conceptualization of Family Modernity," *Journal of Comparative Family Studies*, vol. 1, no. 1 (Fall 1970), pp. 17–25; Safilios-Rothschild, "A Cross-Cultural Examination of Women's Familial Educational and Occupational Options," *Acta Sociologica* vol. 14 (Winter 1971); Safilios-Rothschild, "Marital Expectations: Discrepancies Between Ideals and Realities," in *Images and Counter-Images of*

Young Families, eds. C. Presvellou and Pierre de Bie (Louvain: International Scientific Commission on the Family, 1970), pp. 169–174; and Safilios-Roths-child, "The Influence of Wives' Work Commitment upon Some Aspects of Family Organization and Dynamics," *Journal of Marriage and the Family,* vol. 32, no. 4 (November 1970), pp. 681–691.

21. *The Feminine Mystique* (New York: Dell Publishing Co., 1963), p. 118.
22. "An Analytical Approach to the Theory of Social Stratification," *Essays in Sociological Theory,* rev. ed. (New York: Free Press, 1965), pp. 79–80.
23. Esther Westervelt (Paper delivered at the Midwest Regional Pilot Conference, cosponsored by the Women's Bureau of the U.S. Department of Labor and the U.S. Office of Education on "New Approaches to Counseling Girls in the 1960s," University of Chicago, February 26–27, 1965).
24. S. Dianne Dublier, "What Makes A Feminist?" *Trenton* (May 1970), p. 18.
25. Women at San Diego (Cal.) State College organized the first complete women's studies program, with courses including women in comparative cultures, the socialization process of women, contemporary issues in the liberation of women, women in history, women in literature, the status of women under various economic systems, and women and education, among other subjects. According to the *Guardian,* the women have encountered considerable faculty and administrative resistance. Visiting Professor Roberta Salper reported that many faculty members "make comments like, 'This is absurd. Women come to college to get husbands and we all know that'" (see "Women Win Courses at 55 Schools," *Guardian* [January 2, 1971], p. 7).
26. Caroline Bynum and Janet Martin, "The Sad Status of Women Teaching at Harvard or 'From what you said I would never have known you were a woman,'" *The Radcliffe Quarterly* (June 1970), pp. 12–14; Women's Caucus, The Western Political Science Association, "Report on Women on the UCLA and Stanford Faculty," *The Spokeswoman,* vol. 1, no. 3 (July 30, 1970), p. 2; Jo Freeman, *op. cit.;* Kathleen Shortridge, *op. cit.*
27. Women's Liberation meeting announcement (American Library Association Conference, Detroit, June 29, 1970).
28. Nancy Gruchow, "Discrimination: Women Charge Universities, Colleges with Bias," *Science,* vol. 168 (May 1, 1970), p. 559.
29. Lawrence A. Simpson, "A Study of Employing Agents' Attitudes Toward Academic Women in Higher Education" (Ph.D. diss., Pennsylvania State University, 1968).
30. Freeman, *op. cit.*
31. U.S. Congress, House of Representatives, *Congressional Record,* 91st Cong. 2d sess., 1970, vol. 116; cf. Helen S. Astin, *The Woman Doctorate in America* (New York: Russell Sage Foundation, 1969); Patricia Graham, "Women in Academe," *Science,* vol. 169 (September 26, 1970), pp. 1284–1289.
32. The *Spokeswoman* reported, "An anti-nepotism rule that operated to exclude faculty wives from faculty positions in the Arizona state university system has been rescinded. The Board of Regents abolished its long-standing policy while a class declaratory judgment action attacking the rule was pending in the state courts. Brought by five faculty wives who had been affected by the rule, the complaint asked the court to declare it invalid under state law and the federal constitution. The case remains before the court, as of July 1970, while the plaintiffs watch what action the administration takes to implement the policy change" (*Spokeswoman,* vol. 1, no. 3 [July 30, 1970], p. 4).
33. Anonymous, "Status Woe," *Yale-Break,* vol. 1, no. 4 (June 1, 1970), p. 3.
34. Discussion between the author and Louis A. Ferman, Professor, The Institute of Labor and Industrial Relations, University of Michigan, September 1969.
35. *Ibid.*
36. Astin, *op. cit.,* p. 95.
37. Cf. Lynda Lytle Holmstrom, "Career Patterns of Married Couples" (Paper delivered at the Seventh World Congress of the International Sociological Associa-

tion, Varna, Bulgaria, September 19, 1970). In Sweden, Prime Minister Olof Palme has noted, the large trade unions "have prepared their own programmes which will make it possible for men to share the child care with the women" (Olof Palme, "The Emancipation of Man" [Address to the Women's National Democratic Club, Washington, D.C., June 8, 1970], p. 9).

38. U.S., Department of Health, Education, and Welfare, National Institutes of Health, *Women and Graduate Study* (Washington, D.C.: Government Printing Office, 1968), p. 9.

39. See Sandra L. Bems and Daryl J. Bems, "Training the Woman to Know Her Place," Kathleen Barry, "A View from the Doll Corner," Leah Heyn, "Children's Books," Jamie K. Frisof, "Textbooks and Conditioning," and Donna Keek, "The Art of Maiming Women" (an analysis of television commercials), all in *Women*, vol. 1, no. 1 (Fall 1969); and Jennifer Gardner, "Woman as Child: Notes from a Meeting," stenciled (The Radical Women of New York, 1968), p. 2; Elizabeth Fisher, "Children's Books: The Second Sex, Junior Division," *New York Times Book Review* (1970) pp. 89–94, rpt. in *Women's Liberation: Blueprint for the Future*, ed. Sookie Stambler; Cynthis Fuchs Epstein, *Woman's Place Options and Limits in Professional Careers* (Berkeley: University of California Press, 1970), pp. 50–86; Ruth Hartley and A. Klein, "Sex Role Concepts among Elementary School-Age Girls," *Marriage and Family Living*, vol. 21 (February 1959), pp. 59–64; and Ann Eliasberg, "Are You Hurting Your Daughter Without Knowing It?" *Family Circle* (February 1971).

40. An extreme example of sexist attitudes and of a belief in the "feminine nature" became a national controversy during the summer of 1970, when in response to Congresswoman Patsy Mink's request that the Democratic party's Committee on National Priorities "give the cause of women's rights the highest priority it deserves," Dr. Edgar F. Berman, a retired surgeon and a member of the committee, declared that physical factors, particularly the menstrual cycle and menopause, disqualified women for key executive positions. Subsequently, psychiatrists and endocrinologists noted that menopause is "usually most upsetting to women who stay home and think about it rather than do a good day's work" and that, even when women have menstrual dysfunctions, they don't "usually stay off the job or go off at noon and drink too much liquor as so many men do" (Christopher Lydon, "Role of Women Sparks Debate by Congresswoman and Doctor," *New York Times*, July 26, 1970; Marilyn Bender, "Doctors Deny Woman's Hormones Affect Her as an Executive," *New York Times*, July 31, 1970, p. 33).

41. Alice Rossi, "Job Discrimination and What Women Can Do about It," *Atlantic*, vol. 225, no. 3 (March 1970), p. 99.

42. Redstockings Collective, "How Women Are Kept Apart," in *Women's Liberation: Blueprint for the Future*, ed. Stambler, pp. 23–39.

43. Cf. Sue Munaker, Evelyn Goldfield, and Naomi Weisstein, "A Woman Is a Sometime Thing," in *The New Left: A Collection of Essays*, ed. Priscilla Long (Boston: Porter Sargent, 1969), pp. 236–271; Alice Embree, "Media Images: Madison Avenue Brainwashing" and Florika, "Media Images 2: Body Odor and Social Order," in *Sisterhood Is Powerful*, ed. Morgan, pp. 175–197.

44. Cf. Alice Rossi, "Equality Between the Sexes: An Immodest Proposal," *Daedalus*, vol. 93 (Spring 1964), pp. 607–652; and Rossi, "Sex Equality: The Beginnings of Ideology," *The Humanist* vol. 28–29 (September–October 1969), pp. 3–6.

45. Philip Goldberg's article is contained in Chapter 1 of this volume.

46. Editors, "Research Round-Up," *Trans-Action*, vol. 8, no. 4 (February 1971), pp. 4, 6, 10.

47. Matina Horner, "A Bright Woman Is Caught in a Double Bind," *Psychology Today*, vol. 3, no. 6 (November 1969), pp. 36–38, 62.

48. Jesse Bernard, *Academic Women* (University Park, Pa.: The Pennsylvania State University Press, 1964), p. 65.

49. Richard Quinney, ed., *Crime and Justice in Society* (Boston: Little, Brown & Co., 1969), pp. 25–29.

50. Cf. Kate Millett, *Sexual Politics* (Garden City, N.Y.: Doubleday & Co., 1970), pp. 23–58; and Hannah Arendt, "Speculations on Violence," *New York Review of Books,* vol. 12, no. 4 (February 27, 1969), p. 24.
51. Karl Marx, *The Eighteenth Brumaire of Louis Bonaparte* (New York: International Publishers, 1926).
52. Cf. Bems and Bems, *op. cit.*
53. U.S., Department of Labor, Bureau of Labor Statistics, "Marital and Family Characteristics of Workers, March 1969," Advance Summary: *Special Labor Force Report* (Washington, D.C.: Government Printing Office, 1970), pp. 2–7.
54. The President's Commission on the Status of Women, *American Women* (Washington, D.C.: Government Printing Office, 1963).
55. *Spokeswoman,* vol. 1, no. 5 (September 30, 1970), p. 7.

ALICE S. ROSSI

Women in Science: Why So Few?

Where women are concerned, the late 1940s and the 1950s were marked by a national mood of domesticity demonstrated by the rapid rise in the birth rate and the flight of families to the suburbs. It was a period of high praise for woman's domestic role. That mood has shifted in the 1960s. Educators, employers, government officials, and manpower specialists are urging women to enter more fully into the occupational life of the nation. A President's Commission on the Status of Women has recently issued a set of wide-ranging recommendations to this end.[1] Particular stress has been put on the need for women in fields in which there is a critical shortage of manpower—teaching, science, and engineering—and conferences on women in science have been held under federal auspices, at Marymount College in 1963 and at the Massachusetts Institute of Technology in 1964. [Of course, with the current rate of unemployment in many of these fields, one cannot claim that women are "needed" as one could have argued in the past.]

What can we expect as a result of this campaign? Working women in the industrial, service, and clerical occupations will probably experience an improvement in status. The implementation of the Equal Pay Act and the retraining possible under the Manpower Development and Training Act will be of help to such women, as will all attempts to improve community child-care and housekeeping facilities [provide] increased tax deductions for families including a working mother, and the like. A steady supply of older, married women secretaries, clerks, machine tenders, and technicians seems assured.

A second group directly benefiting from the campaign consists of women residents of the national and state capitals. There is a renewal of optimism among women in government employment, and some indications that in Washington itself their opportunities for advancement may be increasing. But a very large proportion of women in all grades of the Civil Service are unmarried, and a very large proportion of those who are married have no children.[2]

Most college-educated women in this country are married and living with their husbands and children. Whether we are interested in the status of women or in the needs of science or both, I do not think we can expect any appreciable increase in the representation of women in the top professions unless that fact is taken into account. As long as it is mostly spinsters or widows who are appointed or elected or promoted to a college presidency, a national commission, a senatorship, or a high post in a government agency or scientific institute, we cannot consider that a solution has been found to the problem of women's status in American society. Marriage, parenthood, and meaningful work are major experiences in the adventure of life. No society can consider that the disadvantages of women have been overcome so long as the pursuit of a career exacts a personal deprivation of marriage and parent-hood, or the pursuit of happiness in marriage and family life robs a woman of fulfillment in meaningful work.

The Present Situation

How many women are there in the fields of science and engineering in the United States, and what are their characteristics? The latest figures available are from the 1960 Census. In 1960,[3] only 9 percent of the employed natural scientists and less than 1 percent of the engineers were women (see Table 1). Within these broad fields, there was considerable variation: from 2 percent in

*Table 1 Employment of Women in Sciences and Engineering, 1950 and 1960, as Percentage of Total Personnel, and Rate of Increase of Each Sex**

	FEMALE (%)		INCREASE (%)	
Occupation	1950	1960	Female	Male
Biologists	28	27	38.2	56.2
Chemists	10	9	− 3.6	13.5
Geologists, geophysicists	6	2	−27.3	81.1
Mathematicians	38	26	209.8	428.1
Physicists	6	4	20.2	92.5
All natural scientists	11	9	10.4	30.0
All engineers	1.2	0.8	11.0	64.3

* Figures from *1960 Census of Population*, vol. 1, pt. 1, Table 202.

the earth sciences and 4 percent in physics to 26 percent in mathematics and 27 percent in the biological sciences.[4] Women lost rather than gained ground in the sciences between 1950 and 1960, for although they appeared in greater absolute number in 1960, the rate of increase was much lower than that of men. Thus while there was a 209 percent increase in the number of women mathematicians, the number of male mathematicians increased 428 percent, so that the proportion of women actually declined from 38 percent to 26 percent in that decade. Hiestand[5] has shown that this is a characteristic of all occupations undergoing an accelerated rate of growth. The majority group in the labor force is white men, and it is their growth pattern which defines the rapidly growing fields. Since women constitute a far smaller proportion of the total labor force, they can usually provide only a small proportion of the added manpower in rapidly growing fields. That this is not the whole story, however, is suggested by the fact that in fields like medicine and law, which have not had the same accelerated rates of growth, women were no better represented in 1960 than in 1950.

Women employed in the scientific and engineering fields in 1960 were less likely than men to have advanced degrees, particularly the Ph.D., less likely to be employed in industry, considerably less likely to be married; they earned less money and worked fewer hours per week. At each level of educational attainment the median salary of men was markedly higher than that of women. Half the women scientists but only one-fourth of the men worked in educational institutions, and men were four times as likely as women to be in industrial management.[6] Among those who were teaching science, women were more likely than men to work less than 35 hours a week; significantly larger proportions of men reported work weeks in excess of 40 hours. As of 1960, the chances were rather slim that a woman in engineering or science would find part-time employment other than in teaching. For example, the proportion reporting fewer than 35 hours a week was 41 percent among women teaching chemistry above the secondary school level, but only 9 percent among women identifying themselves as "chemists."[7]

Four out of five men scientists but only two out of five women scientists were married and living with their spouses.[8] Since these figures represent employed women only, they exaggerate the proportion of unmarried women among those trained as scientists. Significant numbers of women have been trained in the professions but withdraw for varying periods of time to home and child-rearing. Table 2 shows what proportions of experienced professional men and women in 1960 were in the labor reserve (defined as those not employed and not seeking employment but who worked in a given field within the previous ten years).[9] Among men, there is little withdrawal from the active

Table 2 *Voluntary Withdrawal from Labor Force** in Selected Professions, by Age and Sex† (Expressed in Percentages)*

Profession and Sex	AGE		
	25 to 44	45 to 64	65 or Older
Natural scientists			
Women	51	13	61
Men	2	1	57
Engineers			
Women	31	13	42
Men	1	4	58
Secondary schoolteachers			
Women	34	13	65
Men	2	2	54
Physicians-surgeons			
Women	19	10	31
Men	2	2	25

* The labor force is defined as all persons, whether currently employed or not, who have worked in the stated capacity during the last 10 years. The figures are as of 1960.
† Figures from *1960 Census of Population: Characteristics of Professional Workers*, Table 4.

labor force before age 65; among young men the proportion is typically under 5 percent. Among women, sizable proportions withdraw, particularly in the 25 to 44 age group, when family responsibilities are at their peak.

There are considerable differences among the professions, however, in this regard. Women doctors have very low withdrawal rates, whereas the rates for women secondary school teachers and engineers are moderately high. It is rather surprising to find that women scientists have an even higher rate of voluntary withdrawal than the teachers—51 percent as against 34 percent. One might expect that having undertaken careers in science, still a pioneer field for women, these women would have motivation high enough to offset the easier accommodation of work and family responsibilities to school teaching. Apparently this is not so.

What about the future supply of women in science? An examination of the career plans of younger women, in a study of college seniors of the class of 1961 by the National Opinion Research Center,[10] indicates no new trend toward more women physicists and engineers, although there is an increase of women headed for the biological sciences. Among college seniors planning graduate work in physics 8 percent were female, in engineering 1 percent, in chemistry 20 percent, in mathematics 28 percent, in all biological sciences 43 percent. Furthermore, some of these women will become secondary school science teachers rather than practicing scientists. A follow-up study one year after graduation showed that among those actually enrolled in graduate school, the percent female in the physical sciences was 16, in the biological sciences 34.[11] If the pattern shown in Table 2 holds for this younger group of women, by 1965 about half of them will have voluntarily withdrawn at least temporarily from advanced training or jobs in science.

Several questions emerge from the foregoing review. Why are there so few women in science? Why are they less apt to get advanced degrees than men? Why are they less apt to marry? Why do they withdraw from their fields?

The Priority of Marriage

What a man "does" defines his status, but whom she marries defines a woman's. In meeting strangers, one can "place" a man socially by asking what he does, a woman by asking what her husband does. This is particularly true for the top professional and technical strata of American society. Only small proportions of the wives of doctors, scientists, engineers, and lawyers are employed, ranging (in 1960) from a low of 16 percent of doctors' wives to a high of 25 percent of scientists' wives.[12] In contrast, 44 to 47 percent of the wives of librarians, social workers, and schoolteachers are employed.

This has decided implications for the paths young women see as open to them for success in American life. A man must express his intelligence and ambition in the occupational sphere. A women's ambition can find an outlet in marriage or in work, seldom in both. If a woman has a successful husband, there are no cultural pressures upon her to use her intelligence or training in the work of the world. In fact, her husband may resist a desire on her part for such a separate career, for a wife with leisure is one symbol of his success, and a wife's career might require him to carry some of the parental responsibilities his wife has carried for him.

I think it is the awareness that marriage and careers are not now compatible for women in the upper middle class (despite protestations to the contrary in recent years) that lies behind the often pathetic vacillations of high school and college girls between the pursuit of social popularity (a route to successful marriage) and excellence in scholarship (a route to successful careers). Surely it plays a role in the different concerns parents have for their adolescent boys and girls—the educational goals of their sons and the dating patterns of their daughters.

A sample of women college graduates three years beyond graduation were asked the following question:[13] "An American woman can be very successful in a variety of ways. Which of the following would you most like to be yourself?" The most frequent answers were: to be the mother of several accomplished children and to be the wife of a prominent man. Yet some echoes of earlier aspirations and the imprint of their college education are found in their responses to the further question, "Which of the following do you personally admire very much?" Four out of five chose winners of scientific, scholarly, or artistic awards. They admire the minority within their sex who have careers, but choose themselves to live in the shadows of their husbands' and children's accomplishments.

Unless there are changes in the organization of professional and technical work or in the attitudes of men toward women's roles, it seems likely that fewer rather than more college-trained women will pursue serious careers in the future, for there has been a steady increase in the proportion of the male labor force found in the top occupations. This is not to say that wives of such men will not work. They will, particularly early in the marriage when their earnings supplement university stipends to support the graduate training of their husbands. And we shall hear from these women again when they reach their forties. As long as their husbands are not "too" successful, they may become social workers, teachers, computer programmers, professional or technical aides in laboratories or offices. Only rarely will they become doctors, lawyers, scientists, or engineers. Harriet Martineau's observation in 1834 that the "prosperity of America is a circumstance unfavorable to its women," meaning women are not "put to the proof as to what they are capable of thinking and doing,"[14] is as true for the upper middle class in 1964 as it was when she compared America with England on her first visit to the young nation.

It is ironic that with a life span now long enough to experience many and varied adventures of the mind, the spirit, and the senses, the major life experiences of marriage and parenthood and the intellectual excitement of advanced study are compressed into the same narrow few years of early adulthood. Instead of savoring each to the full and in their turn, we feast upon all three simultaneously as on a triple-decker sandwich. This quickened pace of life and the earlier age at which marriage, parenthood, and occupational success take place play an important role in lowering the career aspirations of women and in deflecting them from the pursuit of such goals as they have. There is not enough time in late adolescence for young women to evolve a value system of their own and a sense of direction toward an individual goal, for they are committing themselves prematurely to marriage and adapting to the goals of their husbands at the expense of their own emotional and intellectual growth.

Men are more conservative than women concerning the role of careers in the lives of women. Much larger proportions of college-trained men than women in the NORC [National Opinion Research Center][15] believed women should not choose a career difficult to combine with child-rearing, and disapproved of women's working when they have preschool children. The same men were between two and three times more likely than the women to say there was "no need at all" for the major recommendations made by the President's Commission on the Status of Women—increased child-care facilities, equal opportunity in hiring and promotion, and [the encouragement of] more women to enter the professions and national political office.

Women see the sharp differences between their own views and those of "most men." Women in the NORC sample were given a brief account of a hypothetical family conflict and asked how they themselves would resolve it and how they thought "most wives" and "most husbands" would resolve it. In the story, a woman graduated from college with honors in biology, married, and held a teaching job while her husband completed law school. Now he has a degree and a good job. Both wish to have children, but she would like to take an advanced degree in biology and eventually pursue a career in biological research. The respondents were asked what decision the couple would make: to start a family and have the wife get the degree later; to start a family and give up the wife's career goal; to postpone childbearing and let the wife get the degree now; or carry out both wishes simultaneously. Only one-fourth of the women thought the couple should start the family now, with the wife either giving up or postponing her training and career plans; but half of them believed these two decisions would be favored by "most wives," and three-fourths that it would be favored by "most husbands."

In actual fact, most women do as they say most husbands would prefer: they are less apt to complete any advanced training, highly likely to work after marriage and then withdraw for the childbearing and -rearing years. The typical pattern of work for American women shows two peaks of employment, the first in their early twenties, the second in the 40 to 55 age group. As seen in Table 2, this withdrawal in the 25 to 44 age group is particularly high for women in the sciences. Thus, in their expressed attitudes, women are less conservative than men, but their actual behavior reflects an adaptation to the views of men.

Effect of Interruption of Career

During the last five years there has been a mushrooming of centers for counseling and retraining older women who wish to return to professional employment. I think there is a danger that by thus institutionalizing the withdrawal-and-return pattern of college-educated women, we may reduce even further the likelihood that women will enter the top professions. Older women who have not worked for many years may be retrained and contribute significantly to personnel shortages at the lower professional levels as laboratory assistants, technical writers, nurses, and schoolteachers, but only rarely as doctors, full-fledged scientists, and engineers. Not only is training for such fields a long and difficult process, but the pace of technological and scientific knowledge has been so rapid that even those who remain in these fields have difficulty keeping up, let alone those who return to advanced training after a ten-year break.

Even more fundamental, however, is the effect on potential creativity of withdrawal precisely during early adulthood. Lehman's researches into the relation between age and achievement[16] have shown that the quality of intellectual output in strongly related to age, and that in the sciences the peak of creative work is reached in the late twenties and early thirties. The small number of women included in his samples showed their most creative years to be no different from those of the men. They were making their major contributions during the very years when most American women withdraw and devote a decade or more to home and family.

If more women are to choose science and remain active in science, it must be possible for them to do so without lengthy interruption of their careers during their potentially most creative years. There has to be a better balance between marital, parental, and career obligations and pleasures for both sexes: work must be less dominant than it is in the lives of men in order for it to be more dominant in the lives of women.

New View of the Maternal Role

Women will not be strongly motivated to remain active professionally during the early years of child-rearing simply out of concern for the effect of withdrawal upon their intellectual creativity. The development of their children is a concern equal to if not greater than their own work. Until very recently, there was a widely held belief that any separation of the mother and the child would have dire consequences for the emotional development of the child, and many women who worked throughout their children's early years did so with considerable anxiety about the effect of their daily absence upon their children. It is only very recently that this myth has been laid to rest. A current volume of some twenty-two empirical studies on the employed mother[17] has shown that maternal employment has no unfavorable effects upon children. Of much greater importance than employment per se are the mother's reasons for working, the quality of the care the child receives in her absence, and the attitudes of her husband. In the last few years, social scientists have begun to stress the desirable rather than the unfavorable consequences of maternal employment.[18]

There is a second body of research on child development that reflects a further shift in the concept of the maternal role. For years psychologists focused rather exclusively on the mother's feelings toward and physical care and training of the child. Now there is increasing emphasis on the role of mothers in their children's cognitive development. It has been found that how well the child takes to his early school experiences is strongly related to whether he has had stimulating experience with language and ideas during his preschool years. The better educated the mother, the greater will this stimulation of the child tend to be. There is research currently under way testing the hypothesis that it is the lack of cognitive stimulation that contributes most heavily to poor school performance among lower-working-class children.[19]

The implications for social action in behalf of children in culturally deprived homes are clear: enrich the environment of the very young child by means of child-care facilities designed to provide such cognitive stimulation.[20] The implications as regards children of college-educated parents are less clearcut. Some child specialists may say that the mother is more necessary at home than ever, not only to love and care for the child but to stimulate the growing mind of the child. This is to stress the role of the mother as a *teacher*. She may be even more effective, however, as an *example* to the child. If she is utilizing her education in a professional job which keeps her alert and involved with things of the mind, she may transmit far more zest for learning than the educated mother who shelves her books along with her diploma. With the view that maternal employment will harm the child now shown to be unfounded, younger women are potentially free of one source of anxiety if they choose to pursue a profession.

Women and Science: Incompatible?

What is there about women on the one hand, and science on the other, that leads to such a very low affinity between them in American society? What are the major characteristics of the scientist, and why are women in our society less apt to have these characteristics than men?

The following thumbnail sketch of the scientist is based largely on the intensive research of Roe[21] on eminent physicists and biologists. Two caveats must be noted. First, there have been no detailed psychological studies of women scientists in any way comparable to those of men scientists. Some studies suggest that differences in students' interests and values are more closely related to their fields of study than to sex differences, but in drawing a portrait of the characteristics of the scientist it is an assumption rather than an empirically established fact that women scientists do not differ from men scientists in the major characteristics relevant to their occupational role. Secondly, Roe's studies of scientists were conducted in the 1940s with men largely in their fifties at that time. Whether younger men entering the considerably changed world of science in the 1960s and 1970s will differ we do not know, though a comparison of physics students with the physics faculty at a major university in the 1950s show such striking similarity in personality and social traits as to suggest little change from generation to generation.[22]

The four characteristics Roe found most typical of outstanding natural scientists are the following:

1. *High intellectual ability,* particularly spatial and mathematical.

2. *Persistence in work;* intense channeling of energy in work such that the greatest personal satisfaction was experienced when working.

3. *Extreme independence,* showing itself in childhood as a preference for a few close friends rather than extensive or organized social groups, and preference for working alone; in adulthood as a marked independence of intense relations with others, and a preference for being free of all supervision.

4. *Apartness from others;* low interest in social activities, with neither preference for an active social life nor guilt concerning such tendencies toward social withdrawal.

All four characteristics manifest themselves early in life; hence a predisposition toward science as a career goal is established long before the college student makes a formal commitment to a "major." Furthermore, these are all characteristics girls in American society are considerably less apt to have than boys. Both at home and at school, girls are socialized in directions least likely to predispose them toward science as a career. What are these sex differences during the formative years?

Intellectual Ability

For many years it was assumed that there were practically no sex differences in intelligence, for studies relying on the Stanford-Binet intelligence test showed almost no differences between boys and girls. It had somehow been forgotten that, in standardizing this test, items which revealed consistent sex differences were discarded so that the scores of boys and girls could be evaluated against the same norms. During more recent years, as specific tests were constructed to measure different dimensions of intellectual and creative ability, consistent sex differences began to emerge.

These differences may be summarized as follows:[23] Girls talk at younger ages, put words together into sentences somewhat sooner, and learn to read more easily than boys. After the fifth or sixth grade, however, boys do as well as girls in reading comprehension, though girls show somewhat greater verbal fluency. In mathematical skills there are no sex differences during the early school years, but during high school boys begin to excel, and by the time they take the Scholastic Aptitude Tests the boys score an average of 50 points higher on the mathematical portion, while girls score only 8 or 10 points higher on the verbal portion. Throughout school boys do better on spatial tests (for example, detecting a simple figure embedded in a more complex one), which suggests that "boys perceive more analytically, while the girls are more global, more influenced by all the elements of the field together."[24]

Thus girls develop cognitive abilities along somewhat different lines than boys, and enter adolescence with a style of thinking less appropriate to scientific work. Any final interpretation of this sex difference awaits further research, but what is known to date is that one key lies in the kind and degree of training in independence the child receives. Bing[25] found that high verbal ability is fostered by a close relationship with a demanding and somewhat intrusive mother, while high mathematical abilities were enhanced by allowing a child a considerable degree of freedom to experiment on his own. Children whose scores on standard intelligence tests rise between their sixth and tenth years are highly likely to have been six-year-olds who were "competitive, self-assertive, independent and dominant in interaction with other children," while those who showed declining scores were "passive, shy and dependent" youngsters at six.[26]

Early Family Influences

If we look more closely at the family environment of the young child, we can guess at some of the sources of this difference in cognitive style between boys and girls. The scientist's characteristics of independence, persistence in work, and social isolation are mirrored in significant differences between the father and the mother as seen through the eyes of the child. No matter what the father works at, the child sees him leave the family to pursue it; it is a normal part of every day's expectation that father will not be present. Mother, in contrast, is usually at home and and instantly available, someone who takes care of the thousand details of home and family life, none of them so important that she cannot be easily interrupted. Even when he is at home, father may be far less "available" than mother.

It is easy for the child to conclude from daily observation that men work for long stretches of time at something important, and that men are less involved with people than women are. There is a consistency between these observations of the parents and the characteristics of young children. Very young girls have a greater interest in other people than boys have and are influenced to a greater extent by what other people think of them. Coleman[27] has found that in adolescence, girls are far more often involved in same-sex cliques than boys, who are more often independent loners. Girls comply with the demands of social situations more than boys do, whether at home in doing what parents ask of them or at school in doing what teachers ask. In short, by the example of their parents boys receive encouragement to stand on their own, to be alone, to aim high, and girls are encouraged to be cooperative and responsive to people and to minister to their needs.

The result of these early influences is a marked contrast between men and women in the values that underlie their career choices. Rosenberg[28] and more recently Davis[29] have indicated that the occupational value which most sharply differentiates the career choices of women from those of men has to do with the orientation toward people. Women strongly prefer fields in which they work with people rather than things, and hence we find college-trained women most heavily represented in the humanities, the applied aspects of the social sciences, education, and the health professions. Some of these differences persist even among men and women who have chosen the same occupational field. Women are often found teaching science than doing science. Women college teachers mention as most satisfying about their campus jobs "good students" and "desirable colleagues," whereas men teachers stress "opportunity to do research" and "freedom and independence."[30]

For most American women, growing up has meant shifting from being taken care of in a well-peopled social environment to taking care of others. If we want more women to enter science, not only as teachers of science but as scientists, some quite basic changes must take place in the ways girls are reared. If girls are to develop the analytic and mathematical abilities science requires, parents and teachers must encourage them in independence and self-reliance instead of pleasing feminine submission; stimulate and reward girls' efforts to satisfy their curiosity about the world as they do those of boys; encourage in girls not unthinking conformity but alert intelligence that asks why and rejects the easy answers. A childhood model of the quiet, good, sweet girl will not produce many women scientists or scholars, doctors or engineers. It will produce the competent, loyal laboratory assistant "who will not operate so readily on her own," as Pollard wrote recently in describing his preference for a female rather than a male laboratory assistant.[31]

Summary and Conclusions

American society has prided itself on itself on its concern for the fullest development of each individual's creative potential. As a nation, we have become sensitive to the social handicaps of race and class but have remained quite insensitive to those imposed because of sex. Those women who have entered the top professional fields have had to have extraordinary motivation, thick skins, exceptional ability, and some unusual pattern of socialization in order to reach their occupational destinations. In their backgrounds one is likely to find a professional mother, an unusually supportive father, or dedicated and stimulating teachers.

If we want more women scientists, there are several big tasks ahead:

1. We must educate boys and girls for all their major adult roles—as parents, spouses, workers, and creatures of leisure. This means giving more stress in education, at home and at school, to the future family roles of boys and the future occupational roles of girls. Women will not stop viewing work as a stopgap until meaningful work is taken for granted in the lives of women as it is in the lives of men.

2. We must stop restricting and lowering the occupational goals of girls on the pretext of counseling them to be "realistic." If women have difficulty handling the triple roles of member of a profession, wife, and mother, their difficulties should be recognized as a social problem to be dealt with by social engineering rather than [to] be left to each individual woman to solve as best she can. Conflicts and difficulties are not necessarily a social evil to be avoided; they can be a spur to creative social change.

3. We must apply our technological skill to a rationalization of home maintenance.[32] The domestic responsibilities of employed women and their husbands would be considerably lightened if there were house-care service firms, for example, with teams of trained male and female workers making the rounds of client households, accomplishing in a few hours per home and with more thoroughness what the single domestic servant does poorly in two days of work at a barely living wage.

4. We must encourage men to be more articulate about themselves as males and about women. Three out of five married women doctors and engineers have husbands in their own or related fields. The views of young and able women concerning marriage and careers could be changed far more effectively by the men who have found marriage to professional women a satisfying experience than by exhortations of professional women, or of manpower specialists and family-living instructors whose own wives are homemakers.

The physiological differences between male and female are sufficiently clear and so fundamental to self-definition that no change in the direction of greater similarity between male and female social roles is going to disturb the sex identity of child or adults. No one would be confused if men were more tender and expressive and women more aggressive and intellectual. If anything, greater similarity in family and occupational roles would add zest and vitality to the relations between men and women and minimize the social segregation of the sexes. An increase in the number of women scientists would be only one of many desirable outcomes of the socal changes that I have here urged.

Notes

1. The President's Commission on the Status of Women, *American Women* (Washington, D.C.: Government Printing Office, 1963).
2. *Report of the Committee on Federal Employment to the President's Commission on the Status of Women* (Washington, D.C.: Government Printing Office, 1963), pp. 104–105.
3. U.S., Department of Commerce, Bureau of the Census, *1960 Census of Population* (Washington, D.C.: Government Printing Office, 1961), vol. 1, pt. 1, Table 202.
4. Scientific personnel in government employment do not show so high a proportion of women in the biological sciences: the proportion female by major scientific field among those federally employed is 8 percent for physical sciences, 4 percent for biological sciences, 1 percent for engineering (Report of the Committee on Federal Employment, app. D).
5. D. Hiestand, *Economic Growth and Employment Opportunities for Minorities* (New York: Columbia University Press, 1964).
6. 1962 National Register data, reported in *Physics: Education, Employment, Financial Support, A Statistical Handbook* (New York: American Institute of Physics, 1964).
7. U.S., Department of Commerce, Bureau of the Census, *U.S. Census of Population: 1960, Subjects Reports: Characteristics of Professional Workers*, Final Report PC(2)-7E (Washington, D.C.: Government Printing Office, 1964), Table 4.
8. *Ibid.*, Table 3.
9. *Ibid.*, rates calculated from data in Tables 3 and 6.
10. J. Davis, *Great Aspirations: The Graduate School Plans of America's College Seniors* (Chicago: Aldine Publishing Co., 1964), pp. 154–155.
11. N. Miller, *One Year After Commencement*, Report No. 92 (Chicago: National Opinion Research Center, 1963), pp. 125–126.
12. U.S. Department of Commerce, Bureau of the Census, *U.S. Census of Population: 1960, Subjects Reports: Characteristics of Professional Workers*, Final Report PC(2)-7E (Washington, D.C.: Government Printing Office, 1964), Table 12.
13. Preliminary results of a recent questionnaire sent to the same sample as in Davis (see note 10).
14. H. Martineau, *Society in America*, ed. S. M. Lipset, abr. ed. (Garden City, N.Y.: Doubleday & Co., 1962), p. 295.
15. Miller, *op. cit.*
16. H. Lehman, *Age and Achievement* (Princeton: Princeton University Press, 1953).
17. A. Rossi, "Equality Between the Sexes: An Immodest Proposal," *Daedalus*, vol. 93 (Spring 1964), p. 615.
18. F. I. Nye and L. W. Hoffman, *The Employed Mother in America* (Chicago: Rand McNally & Co., 1963), p. 615.
19. R. Hess, "Educability and Rehabilitation: The Future of the Welfare Class," *Journal of Marriage and the Family*, vol. 26, no. 4 (November 1964), pp. 422–429.
20. One experimental day-care center in Syracuse, New York, will test the effect of an optimal environment for 6-month-to-3-year-old children on learning readiness at school age (B. M. Caldwell and J. ט. Richmond, "Programmed Day Care for the Very Young Child—A Preliminary Report," *Journal of Marriage and the Family*, vol. 26 [1964], p. 481).
21. A. Roe, "A Psychological Study of Eminent Biologists," *Psychological Monographs*, vol. 65 (1951), no. 331, pp. 1–67; Roe, "A Psychological Study of

Physical Scientists," *Genetic Psychology Monographs*, no. 43 (1951), pp. 121–129; Roe, "Psychological Monographs. Study of Research Scientists," *Psychological Monographs*, vol. 67 (1953), p. 2; Roe, "Crucial Life Experiences in the Development of Scientists," in *Talent and Education*, ed. E. Torrance (Minneapolis: University of Minnesota Press, 1960); Roe, *The Making of a Scientist* (New York: Dodd, Mead, 1963).

22. G. Stern, M. Stein, and B. Bloom, *Methods in Personality Assessment* (Glencoe, Ill.: The Free Press, 1956).
23. E. Maccoby, "Woman's Intellect," in *The Potential of Women*, eds. S. Farber and R. Wilson (New York: McGraw-Hill, 1963), gives a more detailed summary of sex differences in intellectual ability.
24. *Ibid.*, p. 29.
25. E. Bing, "Effect of Childrearing Practices on Development of Differential Cognitive Abilities," *Child Development*, vol. 34 (1963), p. 631.
26. Maccoby, *op. cit.*, p. 33.
27. J. Coleman, *The Adolescent Society* (Glencoe, Ill.: The Free Press, 1961).
28. M. Rosenberg, *Occupations and Values* (Glencoe, Ill.: The Free Press, 1957).
29. J. Davis, *Undergraduate Career Decisions: Correlates of Optional Choice* (Chicago: Aldine Publishing Co., 1970).
30. R. E. Eckert and J. E. Stecklein, *Job Motivations and Satisfactions of College Teachers: A Study of Faculty Members in Minnesota Colleges*, in U.S. Office of Education Cooperative Research Monographs, no. 7 (Washington, D.C.: Government Printing Office, 1961).
31. E. Pollard, "How to Remain in the Laboratory Though Head of a Department," *Science*, vol. 145, no. 3636 (1964), p. 1018.
32. Nye and Hoffman, *op. cit.*

Sex Roles in Politics

Introduction

"The finding that men are more likely to participate in politics than women is one of the most thoroughly substantiated in social science. . . . Economic and social modernization is slowly eroding this sex difference, however," writes Lester Milbrath (1965, pp. 135–136). According to Maurice Duverger, the last generalization applies mainly to voting participation, in certain countries, not to women's participation in political leadership: "The percentage of women members of parliament, for instance, is hardly increasing. On the contrary, it tends to fall after the first elections in which women have had the suffrage, and to become stabilized at a very low level" (Duverger 1955, p. 123).

Seymour M. Lipset et al. have classified explanatory factors related to original statistical regularities in rates of voting turnout (1954, pp. 1128–1135). According to this classification, men are an example of groups which tend to have a high voting turnout for several reasons, women of groups with a low voting turnout. Three out of four of their main propositions can be tied to sex roles. The second proposition concerns *access to information* about the relevance of government policies. This includes among others occupational training and experience making for general insight. "The housewife is at a great disadvantage in this respect, a fact that may help to account for the lower voting rate of women in general," Lipset et al. write (p. 1131). The amount of leisure is also related to political activity. "The group most affected by lack of leisure is probably the woman. The role of housewife and mother is particularly demanding. 'Man works from sun to sun, but woman's work is never done.' In every country women have a lower turnout than men. This sex differential increases as one goes down the income scale. This suggests its relation to the number of children and the absence of laborsaving devices or servants" (p. 1132).

The third proposition by Lipset et al. is related to *group pressures to vote:* Group pressures to vote are stronger in the case of men than of women. "There are some cases in which group pressures are directed in exactly the opposite way—against voting. The universally lower vote of *women* may be due in part to norms of a 'woman's place,' which disapprove of political participation of women. In the United States these do not seem to prevent voting among women who are interested; however, women with little interest feel free not to vote, while men with little interest still feel called on to go to the polls" (p. 1133).

The fourth proposition refers to *cross-pressures*, which have been found in Finnish studies also to affect women's voting more than that of men (Allardt 1956, pp. 125–130). Lipset et al. state (p. 1134) that "in European countries particularly, the working-class women are more concerned with religious values and more exposed to church influences than are their husbands, who tend to belong to leftist unions. The conflict between the pressure of their class position and of their husbands, in favor of leftist voting, and the opposition of the churches to the antireligious left parties may lead to a withdrawal from political choice and contribute to the lower turnout of women, which is particularly marked in the working class."

Apart from studying the influence of these kinds of explanatory factors, sex roles in politics, their change with time, and their variation in different circumstances can also be understood and explained in terms of *ideologies* concerning the roles of men and women.

According to the *traditional and romantic* sex role ideologies, politics belong to the man's role (Dahlström 1963, pp. 18–19). These ideologies are deeply rooted in Scandinavia. Even today in Finland only about a third of the people in both urban and rural areas consider it important for a woman to be interested in politics, whereas two-thirds of urban and more than 50 percent of rural people consider it important for a man. The Marxian sex role ideology is based on the principle of total equality of men and women in society, including the spheres of work life and politics. In practice women in the socialist countries have attained a fairly large representation on the lower political levels, but in the important positions men heavily dominate. The early women's emancipation movement in the late 1800s and early 1900s—which is still represented by many women's organizations, nowadays dominated by elderly women—has two successors. The *radical* sex role ideology in Scandinavia is, like the Marxian ideology, based on the principle of total equality of the sexes. It proceeds further than the Marxians and the early suffragettes in trying to bring about changes in the man's role, too. It encourages men to accept some traditionally feminine responsibilities like child care and housework. This would make it easier for women to be active in work life and politics. There are also men actively engaged in work for this movement. The goal is total integration of sexes. The woman power or liberation movement in the United States is based on the notion of the conflict of interests of men and women. It compares the fight for women's power with the class struggle and race struggle. It uses methods of direct action to achieve its goal, woman power. It assumes that integration is not possible but revolt and fight are necessary to bring women into power. In some ways it resembles the fight of the early suffragettes, but it is also tied in with the Marxian ideology.

We may assume that sex roles in politics are more traditional in those times and groups in which traditional ideologies concerning the roles of men and women prevail. Groups influenced by the Marxian or modern radical sex role ideologies should show less traditionalism in the political roles of the sexes.

In this article sex roles in Finnish politics will be examined on the basis of hypotheses based on the generalizations by Lipset and on assumptions about the possible influence of different ideologies.

The study is composed of two main parts, in which both behavior and attitudes are examined. In the first part *political participation* of men and women as voters, political discussers, and party workers [and] their political interest and expectations concerning [political participation] are studied. The second part describes men and women as *political representatives:* how candidates are nominated in the elections, how many votes they get, how many of them get into the decision-making representative bodies. In this section attitudes toward equality of the sexes in political leadership are also studied. In the final [section] the results of both parts are combined.

The study is based on official statistics and interview data. The official statistics of Finnish parliamentary and municipal elections in 1907–68 are fairly extensively used. Sex differences in voting activity are also analyzed in relation to other characteristics of Finnish society. This was possible on the basis of data collected by Erik Allardt, who kindly placed the original, partly unpublished results of his correlation and factor analyses of Finnish communes around 1950 at my disposal. Some comparisons to other Scandinavian countries are made, but they are quite fragmentary. The interviews referred to were made in 1966 in Helsinki, two small towns, and five rural communes. A representative sample of men and women aged 15–64 were interviewed in Helsinki and the rural communes. In the small towns only women were questioned. The communities studied do not represent Finnish communes in general. It is, however, possible to draw comparisons between western and eastern Finland.

Political Participation

Scandinavian Comparisons

Full enfranchisement of all adult men and women took place in Finland in 1906. Finnish women were the first in Europe to get the vote in parliamentary elections. Of the Scandinavian countries, Norway came next, with a partial right to vote in 1907; in 1913 women were enfranchised on the same conditions as the men. In Denmark and Iceland political franchise was granted to women in 1915. Universal suffrage for men and women was introduced in Sweden at elections to the lower chamber of the parliament in 1921.

The difference between men's and women's voting turnout at the beginning of this century was lower in Finland than in the rest of Scandinavia. . . . The rate of voting in parliamentary and municipal elections during the first half of the century was lower in Finland than in Norway. However, sex differences in the voting rates up to the 1940s were smaller in Finland. It has generally been found that the difference between men and women nonvoters seems to be smaller when the total vote is higher (Duverger, op. cit., p. 24). The cases of Finland and Norway are exceptions to this rule. The sex difference in Finland compared with that in Norway is especially noticeable in rural communes: in Finland the women's voting rate in 1908–50 was only about 10 percent, in Norway about 20 percent lower than the men's. The small difference is mainly due to the men's laziness in voting. The low rate of voting among Finnish men may be partly explained by deficiencies in the registration of eligible voters; in some parts of Finland . . . persons who had emigrated were kept in the voting register for a long time, and since the majority of emigrants in the beginning of the century were men, this in a way artificially lowered the voting rate of men.

In the 1950s and the 1960s the national differences have disappeared and the voting percentages of both sexes in all Scandinavian countries are high and very close to each other:

Table 1

| | | PERCENTAGE POLL | | | | |
| | | PARLIAMENTARY ELECTIONS | | | MUNICIPAL ELECTIONS | |
Country	Year	Men	Women	Year	Men	Women
Denmark		—	—	1966	79.2	74.9
Finland	1966	86.1	83.9	1968	78.4	75.3
Norway	1965	86.8	84.1	1967	77.7	74.9
Sweden	1964	86.9	84.8		—	—

Voting in parliamentary elections is in general more common than in municipal elections, and the sex difference is smaller.

Rural-Urban Differences in Voting Rates

Sex differences in political participation are diminishing with time. New ideas and behavior patterns are usually adopted first in the center of the society and later transmitted to the periphery (Galtung 1964, pp. 206–216). Urban areas belong to the center of society, rural areas to the periphery. We may thus expect that voting activity will be higher and sex differences in political behavior and attitudes smaller in towns and cities than in rural areas. This assumption is also based on Lipset et al.'s formulations one and two:

"A group will have a higher rate of voting if its interests are more strongly affected by government policies," and

"A group will have a higher rate of voting if it has more access to information about the relevance of government policies to its interests."

Voting turnout of men and women in Finland in parliamentary and municipal elections in urban and rural communes before and after the Second World War [can be analyzed as follows]:* during the latter time period, rural-urban residence had no influence on the voting rates of men, but according to the hypothesis, rural women voted less than urban women, and thus the sex difference was smaller in towns than in the country. In the earlier time period voting rates in parliamentary elections were about the same in urban and rural areas—contrary to the hypothesis, the voting rate of urban men was

---

* The table giving statistics on this point has been deleted in the interest of brevity. [Ed.]

even a little lower than that of rural men. Harriet Holter reports a similar finding from Norway (1970, pp. 101–102). The small sex difference in urban communes is thus due to the low voting rate of men. In municipal elections, place of residence had earlier a great influence on voting activity. Townspeople seemed to be more concerned about local community matters than country people; they went more often to the polls in municipal elections.

Sex differences are more significant in the countryside than in the towns also as regards other types of political behavior. In personal interviews about *interest in politics* the following results were achieved:

Table 2

Is Interested in Politics	HELSINKI		SMALL TOWNS	RURAL COMMUNES	
	Men	Women	Women	Men	Women
	%	%	%	%	%
Very much	24	10	6	10	2
Somewhat	46	41	31	41	25
Not very much	18	30	41	30	33
Not at all	12	19	22	19	40
	100	100	100	100	100
N	228	215	100	250	251

Political interest of women both in Helsinki and in the rural communes is weaker than that of men. Women in Helsinki are as interested as rural men.

Urban people are politically more active than rural people, and this applies especially to women. This may be due to their central position in society, the greater relevance of government politics to their lives and their easier access to political information, as was earlier assumed. Lipset et al.'s third condition for a high voting turnout might be appropriate here, too:

"A group will have a higher rate of voting if it is exposed to social pressures demanding voting."

On the basis of the interview data it is possible to study pressures toward political activity in town and country. Expectations concerning men's and women's political interest were, in the interview study, measured by asking how important the respondents considered certain activities to be for men and women. The items were: temperance, faithfulness in marriage, interest in culture, going to church, interest in politics, membership in associations, speaking at meetings, holding elected offices, getting a good education, and getting ahead in one's career. The first four were considered to be more important for women than for men, the last six more important for men than for women. The item concerning interest in politics differentiated the sexes more than any of the others. The following percentages give the distributions of answers:

Table 3

Importance of an Inter-est in Politics for Men	HELSINKI		SMALL TOWNS	RURAL COMMUNES	
	Men	Women	Women	Men	Women
	%	%	%	%	%
Very important	19	18	17	12	7
Fairly important	48	47	49	44	49
Not very important	23	27	26	34	37
Not at all important	10	8	8	10	7
	100	100	100	100	100

Table 4

Importance of an Inter-est in Politics for Women	HELSINKI		SMALL TOWNS	RURAL COMMUNES	
	Men	Women	Women	Men	Women
	%	%	%	%	%
Very important	8	9	7	3	3
Fairly important	28	30	27	33	35
Not very important	39	40	42	45	41
Not at all important	25	21	24	19	21
	100	100	100	100	100
N	225	211	98	243	246

An interest in politics is more often expected from men than from women. This is agreed upon by men and women in urban and rural communes. For a man to be interested in politics is considered more important in the city and towns than in the country. Role expectations concerning women are quite unanimous in different groups of respondents. When we compare actual and expected interest in politics, we find that the behavior of women in Helsinki has changed more rapidly than role expectations.

Coming back to the proposition of Lipset et al. [we may say that] men are clearly exposed to more social pressures demanding political activity than women. Expectations concerning men's political interest are more demanding in urban than in rural districts. This may partly explain the higher political interest of urban men, which is reflected in their higher voting activity (except in the general elections in 1907–39). In the case of women this explanation cannot be used: urban norms do not demand women to be politically more interested than rural norms. A change in the reference group of urban women might serve as an explanation. Urban women may be concerned with what is expected from people in general, rather then merely from women, when they act politically. Their reference group may be the whole society or the group of men, not that of women. Here I am grateful for a discussion with Rita Liljeström. Urban women are willing to interact with men more than rural women (Haavio-Mannila 1968, p. 235). They want to identify themselves with the men's, not with the women's, group.

We may conclude by saying that modernization and urbanization increase as expected the political activity of both sexes and decrease the difference between men and women. This may be due to the greater involvement of government politics in the interests of modern urban people and to their easier access to information about government policies relevant to their interests. Urban men were found to be more exposed to social pressures demanding voting than rural men, but no difference in the expectations concerning women's political interest could be seen between urban and rural areas. The urban norms do not demand women to be more active than rural norms, but urban women are so anyway. Other factors than social pressures demanding political interest from women may account for their higher voting turnout.

This conclusion as to the importance of urbanization in leveling off the sex differences in political behavior has support from, among others, Harriet Holter's study in Norway. She found that "the degree of industrialization of residence is the attribute that most discriminates between men's and women's rates of political activity" (Holter, op. cit., p. 103). She studied simultaneously the effect of occupation, education, and place of residence on the political activity of men and women.

☼　☼　☼

Political Representation

Comparison of Men and Women as Nominated and as Successful Candidates

A high voting turnout of women does not automatically mean that women become elected to political offices. [According to] Maurice Duverger . . . women's influence progressively declines as the higher levels of leadership are reached. "The political role of women grows smaller as we approach the 'centre' of political leadership. There are few women candidates at elections, fewer women members of parliament, still fewer women ministers, and no women heads of government," he wrote in 1955 (Duverger, op. cit., p. 123). Nowadays the situation in the world has somewhat changed: there are women acting even as prime ministers. But that is not the case in Finland. There is usually one or at most two female members of the Cabinet.°

. . . The proportional representation system in Finland does not function against women to as great an extent as in countries with other kinds of electoral systems, such as majority representation systems. . . . In the parliamentary elections of 1958–66 women got 15.4 percent of the votes and in the municipal elections of 1968, 16.3 percent. In the parliamentary elections women were elected in the same proportion as they received votes, but in the

---

° Duverger's figure illustrating this point has been deleted in the interest of brevity. [Ed.]

municipal elections the proportion of votes cast for women exceeded the proportion of women elected (10.7 percent).

The proportion of women elected to parliament has not increased with time quite as steadily in Finland as it has in Sweden. The proportion of women among the candidates is presented here on the basis of Tuula Kaurinkoski's careful investigation for the years 1907–54. Official statistics give the data for subsequent years.

Table 5

		FINLAND	SWEDEN
		Percentage of Women among	
		Those elected	Those elected to the Lower
Year	Candidates°	Those elected to Parliament	Chamber of Parliament
1907–09	8.0	10.8	—
1910–19	8.6	9.2	—
1920–29	8.1	8.5	1.3
1930–39	8.1	7.1	3.3
1940–49	10.2	10.2	8.4
1950–59	14.9	14.5	12.7
1960–66	15.2	15.0	13.7

° Kaurinkoski 1958, p. 31.

At the beginning of the century, in 1907–24, the proportion of women elected to parliament was greater than that of women candidates. Since then men candidates have had a slightly better chance of being elected. Tuula Kaurinkoski found that during 1907–54 female candidates represented 9.3 percent of all candidates and 9.5 percent of those elected. There were on the average 3.8 female and 3.9 male candidates per each representative elected.

Table 6

	PROPORTION OF SUCCESSFUL CANDIDATES, PERCENT					
	1948	1951	1954	1958	1962	1966
Men	24.2	21.4	22.0	19.5	16.2	19.5
Women	24.0	21.8	21.7	17.8	14.8	20.2

Women were thus elected to parliament in the same proportion as they stood as candidates. Since the war the proportion of those elected among all candidates, according to sex has been the following:

Sex differences have also recently been very small. Women are somewhat handicapped in the elections when they stand as candidates for small parties in small electoral districts. For example, in the Swedish People's party the proportion of women receiving more votes than the minimum necessary for election in the country as a whole has been larger than in other parties. In 1958–66 there were 23.5 percent women in this group in the Swedish People's party, but only 13.7 percent in the country as a whole. At the same time 14.7 percent of the members elected to parliament were women. Women thus do not belong to the group of "nearly elected" more often than men, except in some small parties. The proportional representation system with single person lists does not discriminate against women. Data from countries with other electoral systems show that women are elected to a lesser degree than they are nominated as candidates (Duverger, *op. cit.*, pp. 87–88; Kaurin-koski, *op. cit.*, pp. 33–34; Valen 1966, p. 131).

Table 7

PERCENTAGE OF WOMEN AMONG THOSE ELECTED

| Country | Parliamentary Elections | | Municipal Elections |
	Around 1930*	Around 1965	
Denmark	4.0 (1929)	11.2 (1967)	9.7 (1966)
Sweden	1.1 (1928)	13.5 (1966)	12.1 (1966)
Norway	1.3 (1930)	9.3 (1965)	9.6 (1967)
Finland	7.5 (1929)	16.5 (1966)	10.7 (1968)

* Source for 1930: Braunias 1932, p. 105.

In Scandinavia, Finland has the highest proportion of women in parliament. In the municipal councils there are more women in Sweden. The proportion of women in both bodies is lowest in Norway. This corresponds to the low rate of economically active women in Norway and to the low percentage of girls at universities there. In Finland there are more women in the labor force and at the universities than elsewhere in Scandinavia, especially than in Norway (Holter, *op. cit.*, pp. 9–11; Haavio-Mannila 1969, pp. 340–341).

Rural-Urban Differences in Voting for Men and Women

The election of women to parliament is an increasing trend. We may thus expect that women are more often elected as political representatives in the more modernized urban than in the rural areas.

The proportion of women among members elected according to their place of residence and the percentage of votes given to women in urban and rural communes in the parliamentary elections of 1958–66 were as follows:

Table 8

	PERCENTAGE OF WOMEN	
	Urban Communes	Rural Communes
Women among representatives elected by place of residence	15.9	13.1
Votes cast for women by place of residence of the voter	20.5	12.2

More women receive votes and are elected in urban than in rural communes. In general, urban residents are overrepresented in the parliament (Noponen 1964, pp. 223, 317). This seems to apply especially to women. As many as 61.4 percent of the female representatives were of urban origin in the parliamentary elections of 1958–66. Among the men the percentage was 55.4. Tuula Kaurinkoski found that female candidates from urban communes had better chances of being elected than those from rural communes. In 1907–54 only 57.9 percent of women candidates but 67.2 percent of women elected lived in towns or cities (Kaurinkoski, *op. cit.*, p. 52).

The rural-urban difference can be seen in the proportion of women elected to the municipal councils since 1945:

Table 9

	WOMEN AMONG THE MEMBERS OF MUNICIPAL COUNCILS			
	Towns and Cities	Towns* Market	Rural Communes	Whole Country
	%	%	%	%
1945	12.5		3.7	4.7
1947	13.8		4.1	5.1
1950	19.3	16.9	4.8	6.8
1953	18.0	18.0	5.5	7.4
1956	17.4	17.0	5.4	7.3
1960	17.1		5.6	7.6
1964	15.8		6.1	7.9
1968	17.5		8.9	10.7

* Market towns were in 1945 and 1947 combined with rural communes; in 1960, 1964, and 1968, with towns and cities.

The proportion of women in rural municipal councils has been growing more steadily than in the urban ones. The percentage of women in urban councils was highest in 1950 and 1953. In 1968 a sharp increase can be seen. This may be due to the active, radical sex role discussion in the mass media since 1965.

It is also mostly urban women who in practice give women the possibility of being political leaders. Women in Helsinki vote for women more than members of the other groups interviewed.

Table 10

Voting in 1966 Parliamentary Election	HELSINKI		SMALL TOWNS	RURAL COMMUNES	
	Men	Women	Women	Men	Women
	%	%	%	%	%
Voted for a man	89	48	78	90	72
Voted for a woman	5	42	15	5	22
Did not vote	6	10	7	5	6
	100	100	100	100	100
N (those entitled to vote)	206	184	85	184	203

However, a majority of women everywhere vote for men. Only a very tiny proportion of men, 5 percent, cast votes for women candidates. If sex roles were totally abolished from political life, half of the voters of both sexes would vote for men, half for women. As a matter of fact, women in Helsinki almost represent this "ideal."

Attitudes toward equality of the sexes in political leadership and toward women as leaders in general are more positive among urban than rural women. The rural-urban difference among men is minimal. As an example the distribution of answers to one item measuring this dimension will be presented:

Table 11

Women in General Ought Not to Have Managing or Leading Positions	HELSINKI		SMALL TOWNS	RURAL COMMUNES	
	Men	Women	Women	Men	Women
	%	%	%	%	%
Agree	17	12	12	25	21
Uncertain	28	28	12	15	18
Disagree	55	70	76	60	61
	100	100	100	100	100
N	228	215	94	220	216

Men in the capital are most hesitant in their opinions. Rural men have the most negative opinions, urban [that is, city and small-town] women, the most positive.

An attitude scale was constructed on the basis of answers to four items measuring women's participation in politics and leadership. The items were intercorrelated for Helsinki on the average by .26. The items were: "Women ought to participate as much as men in the affairs of politics and government," "Women ought to keep themselves in the background when politics and public problems are discussed," "Women ought to get as many chances for leading positions in occupational life as men," and the above-mentioned, "Women in general ought not to have managing or leading positions." The scale means for different groups of men and women were:

Table 12

ATTITUDES TOWARD WOMEN'S POLITICAL PARTICIPATION
AND LEADERSHIP (MEANS, + = FAVORABLE)

	Men	Women
Helsinki	5.5	6.2
Small towns	—	6.2
Rural communes	5.5	5.5

The radicals in the sex role discussion seem to be urban [city and small-town] women. In this case men have not adopted new ideas before women, as they generally do.

In the first part of this article it was found that sex differences in voting were smallest in urban communes. Now we have shown that the proportions of men and women among political representatives are more even in towns and cities than in rural areas. This is mainly due to the fact that urban women vote for women candidates. Men are as traditional in Helsinki as in the rural communes. To eliminate sex roles in politics, both men and women should vote both for men and women. If we only urge women to vote for women, we in a way create a "Women's party." But to achieve a more even representation of the sexes in parliament and other political bodies, women probably have to fight for themselves, as the "woman power" movement believes. At present men seem to favor candidates of their own sex, even in the most urbanized city in Finland.

Differences Between Parties in Voting for Men and Women

The proportion of women among candidates, among those receiving votes, and among those elected to the parliament is and has traditionally been highest in the socialist parties, especially among the Communists (see tables 13 and 14), lowest in the Agrarian party (recently renamed as the Center party) and

*Table 13 Percentages of Women Candidates, Votes Cast for Women, and
Women Elected in Parliamentary Elections during 1907–54 and
1958–66, by Party*

Party* (Size of Party: See the Following Table)	1907–54		1958–66		
	Women Candidates	Women Elected	Women Candidates	Votes Cast for Women	Women Elected
			(As Percentages of Total)		
Communist party Democratic League of the People of Finland (1945–)	16.0	15.6	18.2	21.0	18.1
Socialist Worker's party (1922–30)	9.3	10.2			
Social Democratic Social Democratic Union of Workers and Small Farmers (1958–)			16.0	35.6	50.0
Social Democratic party (1907–)	11.7	13.7	13.2	16.7	17.0
Agrarian Agrarian (Center) party (1913–)	5.0	3.1	11.2	9.6	10.0
Liberal party Finnish People's (Liberal) party (1951–)	16.5	13.0	13.9	18.3	16.7
Progressive party (1919–48)	11.0	8.9			
Young Finnish party (1907–17)	8.7	6.5			
Conservative party National Coalition party (1919–)	10.5	10.2	20.6	17.0	15.0
Finnish party (1907–17)	6.7	7.7			
National People's party (1933–39)	9.3	5.5			
Swedish People's party Swedish People's party in Finland (1907–)	7.7	7.0	7.9	5.7	—
All parties	9.3	9.5	15.4	15.8	14.7

* Some minor parties have been omitted. They are, however, included in the total.

in the Swedish People's party. Recently the National Coalition party (Conservatives) has had many women candidates, but the proportion of women among those elected is not as high. The proportion of women among candidates has been lower than among the elected notably in the Social Democratic party and in the small Social Democratic Union of Workers and Small Farmers.

The proportion of votes cast for women in 1948–66 has decreased in both socialist parties, among Communists as well as Social Democrats. In the Agrarian party, on the contrary, a steady increase has taken place since 1954. In the Conservative, Liberal, and Swedish People's parties the proportion of votes for women decreased from 1954 to 1962, but in the election of 1966 a small increase took place. This was most noticeable in the Swedish People's party.

Table 14   Votes Cast for Women Candidates as Percentages of All Votes Cast in Parliamentary Elections during 1948–66, by Party

Party	1948°	1951°	1954	1958	1962	1966	Mean Number of Votes Cast for the Party in 1958–66
Communist party	36.2	39.0	23.3	23.1	22.0	18.2	(487,000)
Social Democratic Union of Workers and Small Farmers	—	—	—	49.7	26.8	37.4	(65,000)
Social Democratic party	16.1	16.9	19.3	17.6	16.7	14.9	(511,000)
Small Holders party	3.1	0.0	—	—	5.3	5.9	(37,000)
Agrarian party	7.8	7.5	8.4	8.8	8.9	10.9	(493,000)
Liberal party	12.6	14.7	21.0	20.5	18.2	18.6	(141,000)
Conservative party	16.5	20.5	19.7	18.4	16.2	16.6	(323,000)
Swedish People's party	8.5	11.1	9.8	4.8	4.2	8.2	(140,000)
Other parties	6.6	12.1	16.1	3.9	4.6	0.8	(16,000)
All parties	17.4 (11.4)†	19.3 (13.2)†	17.1	16.7	15.5	15.3	(2,205,000)
Percentage of women elected	12.0	14.5	15.0	14.0	13.5	16.5	
Percentage of women candidates	12.0	14.0	15.7	15.1	14.5	16.0	

° In 1948 and 1951 the percentages also included votes given for lists consisting of names of both men and women. These types of lists were used mainly by the Communist party; lists of women only in this party got only 10.4% and 10.9% of the votes in 1948 and 1951. In other parties the percentages are almost the same as the proportion of votes cast for women only.
† The figure in parentheses show the percentage of votes cast for women only.

This increase in the number of votes cast for women in 1966 in the bourgeois parties may be related to the beginning of the radical sex role debate in Finland in autumn 1965. It was especially lively in the Swedish press but also in some other bourgeois newspapers and journals. Since then the other mass media have also joined in the discussion. The effects of this discussion could be seen in 1970 when as many as 21.5 percent of those elected to the parliament were women. Unfortunately the detailed results of the last election were not available for this article.

Table 15   Votes Cast for Women Candidates in Percent of Total Votes in Parliamentary Elections in 1958, 1962, and 1966, by Party and Type of Commune

	URBAN COMMUNES			RURAL COMMUNES		
Party	1958	1962	1966	1958	1962	1966
Communist party	30.5	28.7	23.6	17.5	16.6	13.1
Social Democratic Union of Workers and Small Farmers	46.7	36.4	39.0	55.2	23.5	35.5
Social Democratic party	20.9	20.0	17.4	14.7	13.1	11.7
Small Holders party	—	8.3	10.7	—	5.1	5.5
Agrarian party	9.7	9.5	12.1	8.7	8.8	10.7
Liberal party	21.5	19.7	21.0	18.2	15.8	13.7
Conservative party	19.9	17.8	17.8	15.2	13.8	14.3
Swedish People's party	7.5	6.2	9.5	2.1	2.5	6.7
Other parties	4.9	4.1	0.5	3.1	4.8	1.1
All parties	22.6	20.8	19.0	12.9	11.9	12.0

Table 15 shows that this increase of votes cast for women in the bourgeois parties has mainly taken place in urban communes. The overall decline in the proportion of votes for women has, however, also occurred mostly in urban communes. This is mainly due to the decrease of votes cast for socialist women.

Women are elected to municipal councils most frequently in the Social Democratic party. Then follow the nonsocialist parties, and finally the Communists. The increase in the proportion of women elected to municipal councils has been most noticeable in the nonsocialist parties (Haavio-Mannila 1966, p. 115). This may be due to the increase of women working in "white collar" occupations. Women represent typical "middle-class" groups in other ways also: there are more men at the top and at the bottom of almost any social rank or other dimension. Voting for nonsocialist parties is typical middle-class behavior. Because many women vote for middle-class parties, and women vote for women, women there get many votes. This assumption receives support from the larger number of votes cast for women in the Liberal party [than in] the Conservative party. However, the old socialist tradition of the equality of the sexes in political participation still keeps the proportion of votes cast for women high in the Social Democratic party in municipal elections and in both the Social Democratic and the Communist party in parliamentary elections. In parliamentary elections, the Communist party has had some very successful candidates, for example, Hertta Kuusinen, the daughter of the great Communist leader, Otto Wille Kuusinen, who herself has a very high position in the party.

Regional Differences in Voting for Men and Women

Sex differences in voting turnout are largest in eastern Finland. If voting for women follows the same rules as women's voting, as it does in the case of rural-urban differences, we would expect a low proportion of votes given for women candidates in eastern Finland.

The results are, however, quite contradictory to this hypothesis. Women have been elected to parliament, to municipal councils, and to the elementary school boards in the nineteenth century (which are taken as an example of traditional practices) more in eastern than in western Finland (. . . Haavio-Mannila 1970, pp. 34–36). This applies to urban as well as to rural communes. But when we redefine this result according to party . . . , an interesting phenomenon can be seen. In parliamentary elections it is only in the Agrarian and Conservative parties and in municipal elections in the nonsocialist parties that this "eastern Finland rule" holds true. In the socialist parties women candidates get most votes in those areas where socialism is deeply rooted

Table 16

ATTITUDES TOWARD WOMEN'S POLITICAL PARTICIPATION AND LEADERSHIP (MEANS, + = FAVORABLE)		
	Men	Women
Rural communes		
Eastern Finland		
Miehikkälä	6.6	6.4
Valtimo	5.9	5.4
Western Finland		
Finnish-speaking		
Kokemäki	5.0	6.0
Lehtimäki	5.6	5.7
Swedish-speaking		
Teerijärvi	4.6	5.2
Urban communes		
Eastern Finland		
Lappeenranta	—	6.0
Western Finland		
Seinäjoki	—	6.2
Southern Finland		
Helsinki	5.5	6.2

and traditional. In traditionally socialist areas the principle of the equality of the sexes seems to be followed better than in the areas of "emerging radicalism."

But why do the Agrarians and the Conservatives vote for women in eastern Finland? Interviews give some indication of the reasons or background for this.

The attitudes of men toward women's participation in public life are most favorable in eastern Finland. Among women it would seem that the south-north dimension or that of industrialization counts more. Thus it looks as though the *attitudes of men* toward women as leaders would "explain" the emergence of women political leaders. This result is, however, based on a very small number of communes and must be treated only as a hypothetical one. Some indications pointing in the same direction have been found in the results of a national survey by the Finnish Broadcasting Company in which one item about the equality of the sexes was included (Haavio-Mannila 1969, pp. 345–346).

We may also refer to the different social and political climate in eastern and western Finland. In western Finland the pressure toward conformity includes traditionalism in the division of labor between the sexes. Women can and must vote, but cast their votes for men. In eastern Finland, people, especially women, need not vote, but when they do, they have a greater choice [in] whom to vote for. There is a more variable distribution of parties and more possibilities of voting for a "deviant" candidate. The parties are aware of this tendency to vote for women, and put forth plenty of women candidates. These are elected in greater proportions than elsewhere.

A change is apparently on the way. Regional differences are diminishing. Levels of industrialization and urbanization are beginning to count more. The southern and central areas of Finland are more developed than northern and peripheral Finland. The dividing line is more that between center and periphery than [that] between east and west. Considering the traditional importance of the difference between eastern and western Finland, it seems permissible to say that a change is occurring in the social structure, and that the change in sex differentiation is an indicator of this more general change.

Summary

The results of this study on the voting activity of men and women in Finland, on the election of men and women, and on the attitudes and expectations related to this activity are, in general, consistent with those of previous studies and with the propositions set forth in the beginning. Some additions to the facts known earlier can, however, be reported.

Apart from the obvious effects of urbanization, of a rise in the socioeconomical level, and of a decrease in religious and conservative traditionalism, some other factors also help to explain small differences in the voting turnout of men and women. For example, in some areas, notably in the Swedish-speaking rural communes, economic development increases sex differences by bringing with it social disorganization and cross-pressures. An important result of the ecological analysis was that all over the country past class conflicts, traditions of inequality of social classes are reflected in present inequality or difference in sex roles in voting participation. Socialist traditions, which according to Marxian ideology stress the equality of the sexes in political life, and which are strong in the same communes where class conflict and inequality of the sexes prevail, are unable to decrease sex differences when the social structure is characterized by class conflicts.

The social and political climates in eastern and western Finland differ remarkably from each other. In eastern Finland women's voting activity is low but a high proportion of women are elected to parliament and municipal councils, notably in the bourgeois parties. This is due to a lack of uniform norms as to whether and for whom to vote. Pressure toward conformity in western Finland brings women to the polls but to vote for men. This shows that women's voting and voting for women are not one-dimensional phenomena in all social circumstances. On the other hand, it was found that urbanization increases both women's voting and voting for women. The liberal attitude of men in eastern Finland toward women's participation in politics and leadership reflects lack of homogeneous conservatism and provides a good foundation for those women who want to be politically active. Women in eastern Finland are not, however, as already mentioned, active as voters, but when they are, they often vote for women candidates. The east-west cultural difference seems to be losing importance at present, and the south-north or center-periphery difference, which is related to economic development, is gaining in importance.

The influence of sex role ideologies could be seen primarily in voting *for* women, not [in the voting] *of* women. The Marxian principle of the equality of the sexes is reflected in the larger proportion of women among candidates and [among] those elected in the socialist parties. This proportion has for some reason been declining since 1954. On the other hand, voting for women candidates in bourgeois parties has increased. This may be due to the growing number of women working in middle-class occupations. Women get votes almost always from other women—only a tiny proportion of men vote for women—and these educated middle-class women increasingly cast their votes for women candidates. Another reason for the increase in the proportion of votes cast for women in bourgeois parties, particularly in towns and cities, may be the radical sex role discussion which began in 1965 and which may have influenced the voting in the elections of 1968 and 1970. This assumption receives support from the sharp increase already in 1966 in votes cast for women in the Swedish People's party, whose supporters included the initiators of this discussion, imported from Sweden.

Socioeconomic development, conservative conformity, traditions of equality in the social structure, and ideologies concerning equality of the sexes are, on the basis of this study, some of the factors influencing sex roles in Finnish politics. There is, however, considerable variation in their importance in different social groups and geographical areas. They also have different effects on the voting turnout *of* men and women and on the voting *for* men and women.

References

ALLARDT, ERIK. Social struktur och politisk aktivitet. Borgå: Söderströms, 1956.
————. "Patterns of Class Conflict and Working Class Consciousness in Finnish Politics." In Cleavages, Ideologies and Party Systems, edited by Erik Allardt and Yrjö Littunen. Transactions of the Westermarck Society, vol. 10. Turku: Westermarck Society, 1964.

ALLARDT, ERIK, and PESONEN, PERTTI, "Cleavages in Finnish Politics." In Party Systems and Voter Alignments, edited by Seymour M. Lipset and Stein Rokkan. New York: Free Press, 1967.

BRAUNIAS, KARL. Das Parlamentarische Wahlrecht, 11. Berlin: Walter de Ghuyter & Co., 1932.

DAHLSTRÖM, EDMUND. "Analys av könsrolldebatten." In Kvinnors liv och arbete. Stockholm: Studieförbundet Näringsliv och Samhälle, 1963.

DUVERGER, MAURICE. The Political Role of Women. Paris: Unesco, 1955.

GALTUNG, JOHAN. "Foreign Policy as a Function of Social Position." Journal of Peace Research, nos. 3/4 (1964), pp. 206–231.

HAAVIO-MANNILA, ELINA. "Aktivitet och passivitet bland kvinnor i Finland." In Kynne eller kön? Om könsrollerna i det moderna samhället, pp. 105–131. Stockholm: Raben & Sjögren, 1966.

————. Suomalainen nainen ja mies. Porvoo: Werner Söderström Osakeyhtiö, 1968.

————. "The Position of Finnish Women, Regional and Cross-National Comparisons." Journal of Marriage and the Family, no. 2 (May 1969), pp. 339–347.

————. Sex Roles in Politics. Institute of Sociology Research Reports, no. 139. Helsinki: University of Helsinki, 1970.

HOLTER, HARRIET. "Women's Occupational Situation. in Scandinavia." International Labour Review, no. 4 (1966), pp. 383–400.

————. Sex Roles and Social Structure. Oslo: Universitetsforlaget, 1970.

JUTIKKALA, EINO. Suomen talonpojan historia [History of the Finnish farmer]. Helsinki: Suomalaisen Kirjallisuuden Seura, 1958.

KAURINKOSKI, TUULA. "Naisehdokkaat Suomen eduskuntavaaleissa." Master's thesis, University of Helsinki, 1958.

LIPSET, SEYMOUR M.; LAZARSFELD, PAUL F.; BARTON, ALLEN H.; and LINZ, JUAN. "The Psychology of Voting: An Analysis of Political Behavior." In Handbook of Social Psychology, vol. 2, pp. 1124–1175. Cambridge, Mass.: Addison-Wesley Publishing Co., 1954.

MARTIKAINEN, TUOMO, and SÄNKIAHO, RISTO. Äänestysaktiivisuus v. 1968 kunnallisvaaleissa. Institute of Political Science, Research Reports, no. 16 Helsinki: University of Helsinki, 1969.

MILBRATH, LESTER W. Political Participation. Chicago: Rand McNally & Co., 1965.

NAPONEN, MARTTI. Kansanedustajien sosiaalinen tausta Suomessa [Social background of the members of the Finnish parliament]. Porvoo: Werner Söderström Osakeyhtiö, 1964.

Official Statistics of Finland, vols. 6, 29. Helsinki: Central Statistical Office.

RIIHINEN, OLAVI. Teollistuvan yhteiskunnan elueellinen ertlaistuneisuus. Porvoo: Werner Söderström Osakeyhtiö, 1965.

Statistical Yearbooks. Finland, Denmark, Norway, and Sweden: Central Statistical Offices.

TINGSTEN, HERBERT. Political Behavior. Stockholm Economic Studies, no. 7. Stockholm: P. A. Norstedt & Söner, 1937.

VALEN, HENRY. "The Recruitment of Parliamentary Nominees in Norway." Scandinavian Political Studies, vol. 1 (1966), pp. 121–166.

Let's Draft Women Too!

Is the draft unfair? A number of critics have charged that it discriminates against Negroes, the poor, the uneducated, and particularly the high-school graduate who is through school in a neighborhood where the other boys are going on to college. Even if these charges are true, there is a greater inequity in the draft, one so big that nobody sees it. The draft is unfair to the whole male sex. Women are not drafted, and they should be.

When we talk about the obligation of men to bear arms in defense of their country, we have in the back of our minds a picture of a farmer leaving his plow in the field to shoulder a gun. Once it really was this way. In the Civil War, for instance, only one out of every 10 men did anything comparable to civilian work. But during World War II, the Pentagon is embarrassed to admit, military-manpower specialists figured that half the men in uniform had jobs that women could have done just as well as men. By 1960, a study showed, almost nine out of 10 servicemen were doing something that could have been a civilian job.

The citizen-soldier seldom has the rifle anymore, let alone the farm. In World War II, only one out of four in uniform served in what Pentagon manpower expert Harold Wool calls a "man-with-gun" job. Now only one in eight is in this category. One serviceman in eight is also needed just to keep the electronic hardware of the armed forces going.

The obligation to bear arms, in other words, is often not that at all. Instead, in the name of patriotism, most draftees are conscripted to do exactly what they did or might have done for a living back home—drive a truck, punch a Teletype, keep records, file letters, run a store, interpret foreign languages, do bookkeeping work, or swab floors. The draft has become detached from battle and transformed into a means of shifting manpower from the civilian work force to the military work force. Since women are now a major part of the civilian work force, it is only common sense to declare that women should be called into service.

Even Pentagon traditionalists concede that a modern army moves on paper-work, and this involves abilities and experience on which women have a near-monopoly. In particular, women in civilian life dominate such jobs as computer programmer and data processor, which are vital to military operations. There are important military jobs men simply cannot do. For some reason, men cannot run a telephone switchboard. In World War I, General "Black Jack" Pershing broke down and cabled Washington to send 100 French-speaking women telephone operators to save the sanity of the American Expeditionary Force in France. In World War II, at least one Air Force general publicly grumbled that his men would be a lot safer if he were allowed to take his women phone operators into battle areas. Mata Hari to the contrary notwithstanding, women make lousy spies, but for some reason they are extraordinarily good at making sense out of pictures taken from U-2 planes.

In spite of all the rich folklore which labels almost all jobs "his" or "hers," psychologists know pitifully little about what difference, if any, sex makes in aptitude for the work most people do today. But public policy is not clear. For nearly a year now Title VII of the Civil Rights Act of 1964 has forbidden employers to discriminate among their workers on the basis of sex (as well as race or religion) except where a bona fide sex qualification exists. There are unusual jobs, such as working in washrooms. Consistency demands that the armed forces abandon sex-typing of work [a practice] that is now proscribed for private employers.

Equity demands that women be drafted for jobs they can do as well as men. Draftees often suffer simply because they must accept soldiers' pay while postponing a career. It does not make sense to demand this sacrifice of men while women are left free to demand whatever they can command in a shrinking labor market.

Drastic as it may sound, the idea of drafting women is not really so unusual. The crack Israeli army, for example, drafts all boys and single girls at 18 and gives them both basic training with weapons. Girls who marry during the draft terms—and three out of 10 do—go into the reserves. Pregnant women and mothers are excused, but women officers in the regular army get four months of fully paid leave beginning with the ninth month of pregnancy, much as some women in United States civilian employment now do. Israeli women no longer serve with men in fire fights as they did—and gallantly—during the height of the Arab war, because Arab soldiers would literally rather die than surrender to a woman. Now women are assigned work in administration, communications, the medical corps, and the education of newcomers to Israel. Commanders report higher morale where men and women soldiers work together.

The British drafted women along with men in World War II. Our forces, meanwhile, had so much trouble competing with war industry for workers that two of our most celebrated military leaders, Generals Dwight D. Eisenhower and Mark Clark, warned Congress that women would have to be drafted in future wars. The Women's Army Corps grew so desperate it spent an average of $125 to recruit each woman. Pentagon staffers proposed a proclamation stating that military service is an obligation that "rests upon women as well as men."

During the Korean War, a women's draft nearly happened here. Women were so afraid of ridicule and humiliation that they would not come to recruiting offices and had to be interviewed in their homes. But women were needed, and Washington planners debated tactics for getting them with as little public outcry as possible. In 1950 President Truman hinted that he was thinking of registering women as a first step in the event of an "emergency."

"All the social forces which make women hesitate to volunteer for military duty would vanish if women were drafted," World War II Wave Director Mildred McAfee pointed out in urging conscription for women. To this day, the reluctance of women to volunteer is cited in the Pentagon as proof that women should not be drafted because "they don't want to serve." The reasoning is parallel to the notion that racial integration was unnecessary because "Negroes don't want to go to school with white folks."

Today, all the Pentagon manpower specialists agree that we will *have* to draft women if we get into a major ground war—for instance, with the Communist Chinese. It is a hoary tradition at the Pentagon that public opinion is against drafting women except in the direst straits. Actually, public-opinion polls have rolled up respectable and sometimes majority votes for drafting women, depending on the military outlook of the moment and the way the question is worded.

Almost anyone you ask in Washington tells you that it's someone else who stands in the way. Daniel Flood, Pennsylvania Democrat on the House sub-committee that handles the armed forces' appropriations, chimes in that "Congress won't stand for a draft of women now." The [former] Selective Service Director, Lieutenant General Lewis B. Hershey, [said] that "the public is still just not ready to see women as draftees, rained on, out in the cold, and getting killed. We might get to drafting women if we were near complete mobilization—say more than 12 million in the armed forces." What Hershey is reluctant to talk about is that he already *has* plans—classified, of course—for drafting women. Hershey goes on: "If Congress were to call me up and say, 'We're going to draft women,' I'm not going to just say, 'Huh . . . women?' as though it had never occurred to me."

If eventually, why not now? We now need three million in uniform and a lot of people think we're going to need more. Draft calls currently running over 25,000 a month pinch our tight labor market. Waiting to draft women until we run out of men is like waiting to hire Negroes until all the white men have jobs. Discrimination is easier but just as objectionable when there are more qualified people than there are jobs or more young men of draft age than the armed forces really need, or more qualified applicants for college than the colleges can take. What we do with the young people heading toward college and the draft today is just what we did with the young who queued up at the employment office during the depression. Rather than let the power possibilities of this choice go to waste, we invent qualifications which protect the status quo. In an "easy labor market" you can, if you wish, insist on hiring a blue-eyed white male Protestant clerk who plays the cello you need to complete your string quartet. Under full employment, you find that the office work proceeds swimmingly with a brown-eyed Catholic Negro woman who has no musical talent of any kind. So long as we need no more than half of the boys coming of draft age every year, we prefer to take those who might otherwise be unemployed and defer those who manage to get good grades in college. We can, in other words, afford the luxury of discriminating on rather tenuous grounds. I submit that if we are willing to accept such gross inequity, it would make better sense to spread it as thin as possible.

As I've discovered, you can sometimes get a policymaker to admit that women could serve and women should serve. Then he leans back with a smile and says, "Of course, but it's not practical." If you ask him why, he laughs. Plato had the same experience when he advocated military service for women as well as men in *The Republic,* and he did not let the laughers get away with it. "In his laughter," Plato wrote sternly, "he himself is plucking the fruit of unripe wisdom, and he himself is ignorant of what he is laughing at."

The "practical" reason that seems most obvious to Pentagon manpower researchers is cost. Women simply must cost more than men to maintain. You have to put doors on the toilets, and women need bathrobes and lounge chairs. And if you have them on a military post, you've got to maintain guard of men soldiers to keep off-duty GIs from breaking into the female quarters. In fact, however, a staff study of 1948 showed that a Wac cost the Army $77 *less* a year than the man she replaced. Her clothes did cost more, but her food cost less, she smashed up less furniture, and saved the government the money that might have been spent on moving the man's dependents. What is truly impractical is the military folklore which says that all servicemen, even the I.B.M. operators, must spend a lot of time marching up and down dusty fields and wasting ammunition on rifle ranges, and I trust that most female draftees could be spared foolishness of that kind.

For some reason, the idea of women in uniform produces highly emotional reactions and even fear. There were allegations that our women soldiers in World War II were issued contraceptives so that they could more readily bolster the morale of male soldiers. Some fear, in all sincerity, that military life will somehow "damage" women. To these objectors General Eisenhower had a notable remark:

> Like most old soldiers, I was violently against women soldiers, [he testified at hearings on the bill to integrate the women's services in 1948]. I thought a tremendous number of difficulties would occur, not only of an administrative nature . . . but others of a more personal type that would get us into trouble. None of that occurred. In tasks for which they were particularly suited, Wacs are more valuable than men and fewer of them are required to perform a given amount of work. . . . In the disciplinary field, they were . . . a model for the Army. More than this, their influence throughout the whole command was good. I am convinced that in another war they have got to be drafted just like men.

Unfortunately the bill that emerged from those hearings put a quota of 2 percent on women in military service.

In our military, the notion persists that women are nothing but defective men. "There is no question but that women could do a lot of things in the military service," General Hershey admits. "So could men in wheelchairs. But you couldn't expect the services to want a whole company of people in wheelchairs." The analogy is revealing—about the Selective Service experts. Confronted with a proposal that women be drafted, one of the manpower specialists wailed, "Think of the humiliation! What has become of the manhood of America?" I doubt that working alongside a woman draftee in a Pentagon office would do any more damage to American manhood than working beside a woman civilian on Madison Avenue or Michigan Boulevard. For that matter, I doubt that the American man is in such a precarious state of manhood that a woman's draft would destroy him.

Discussion

Each article presented in this chapter refers to some crucial option(s) in one life sector which is not "open" to women: options like singlehood, voluntary childlessness, late marriage, higher education in most fields (such as physics, chemistry, law, medicine, dentistry, pharmacy, engineering, architecture, mathematics, economics, biology) and advanced graduate work in all fields, holding political office, and the controversial option involving drafting women for active duty. Of course, there are many more related options negatively sanctioned in the case of women and not explicitly touched upon in any of the articles; among those are the possibility for a woman to marry a much younger man (though men have married much younger women for centuries), to have a career involving such high commitment that family comes second, or to become one of the top ten people in one's field *and be loved and admired* for this achievement.

All these options are not in reality open to women. Theoretically everybody, man or women, is free to do, short of criminal considerations, whatever he (she) wishes without bringing upon himself or herself a severe punishment, and without being actively prevented from exercising any particular option. But even this is not true. Very recently in France a thirty-five-year-old woman college professor was dismissed from her post, ostracized, and finally driven to suicide, not for having had sexual relations with a young student (as she did for a period of one to two years), but for having reached, together with her lover, the decision to marry.[1] Also, in the United States, women are actively kept out of medical, law, dental, and engineering schools[2] and science departments by means of a variety of formal and informal mechanisms described in detail in Pamela Roby's article in this chapter. Similarly, American women do not ever have a chance to become college presidents, chief administrators of large medical units or hospitals, or high-ranking members of the clergy (or in most churches even low-ranking members),[3] and they are rarely nominated for or elected to significant political posts.

But the greatest degree of social control exerted upon women is informal and indirect and, in general, quite effective. Women are socialized into a very restrictive world of choices, and the "right" choices in each life sector are the only ones which are consistently rewarded and reinforced throughout their lives. Most of these "right" choices are based upon and justified by the "fact" that the "nature" of women is such that their fulfillment can be found only in marriage and motherhood (and, it seems, even more specifically in early marriage to at least slightly older men and in "multiple" motherhood). Another crucial consequence of the women's "nature" theory is the belief that women would not feel comfortable and "feminine" in high positions, since they can follow but not lead and do not excel in undertakings that require hardships or abstract conceptualization. Some other "right" choices are based upon the pseudoscientific folklore, propagated by books on child development, courses on the family, and mass media, which states that children cannot develop normally unless tended to by their natural mothers twenty-four hours a day and that reliance upon mother substitutes can harm their "normal" development.

Also it must be noted that, very often, exercising one option can greatly limit the number of options available in several other life sectors. Choosing marriage, for example, as one "right" choice seriously limits the work options of women in the United States as well as many other countries, in some of which married women are automatically fired or are pressured to resign.[4] In Japan most large companies which employ a large number of single women often ask new women employees to sign a memorandum that they will resign upon marriage.[5] In the United States, only since 1967 have airline stewardesses been permitted to work after marriage. Furthermore, the decision to have children can even further limit the work options of married women,[6] while conversely the option of divorce for American women at least, even when they are mothers, is well documented as frequently opening a variety of educational and employment options for them.[7] And finally, the option to have a second, third, or fourth child (and so on) has been found to increasingly preclude the option of full-time employment for Canadian and French mothers.[8] This type of gradual option restriction with increasing numbers of children seems to hold true even in societies in which the majority of married women work, such as Poland, where 69 percent of married women work.[9]

This definite restriction of women's options in the United States does, of course, necessarily involve the restriction of men's options; however, the net result for men is not as serious a restriction of freedom and development as is experienced by women. Thus, men do not have the option to abstain from work even when they are severely disabled; they cannot study nursing or home economics, they cannot become nursery school teachers or domestics, and it is tolerated but not encouraged for them to become dancers, painters, etc. (and even then, they are under pressure to excel). They also have to marry while they are young, they must not marry a much older woman, they must become fathers, and they must support their wives and children for life, whether married, separated, or divorced from them. These "right" options do tend to curtail significantly the freedom and development of men in the following ways: they often must choose occupations that can provide them with high incomes rather than the occupations they would most be inclined to follow; they have little opportunity to "look around," grow up, and find out who they are and what they want before they are married; they do not have the chance to enjoy a stimulating and loving wife with a career and/or passionate interests and instead often must endure a psychologically tired, bored, and boring housewife and mother; and they are also never given the chance to develop, through socially approved channels, the "feminine" aspects of their minds and personalities.

Still their option restriction is much less severe than that experienced by American women, for whom the corresponding restrictions have much more devastating effects upon their freedom of choice and their chance for self-fulfillment and growth. The occupational options for women are restricted to only the four "feminine" occupations (nursing, home economics, elementary education, and social work) while most rewarding, stimulating, high-prestige and high-paying occupations are inaccessible regardless of the women's talent or ability that would qualify them for such occupations. Women as well as men have little opportunity to "look around," grow up, and find out who they are and what they want before marriage. But this restriction is much more acute in the case of women because their behavior is generally more regulated, they tend to marry earlier than boys, and they are not encouraged to develop a distinct personality or to have definite ideas and opinions in order not to restrict their field of eligibles. Their personalities must stay flexible to accommodate the man they will marry to the maximum, following his wishes and preferences as to the nature of options they should choose.[10] Therefore, women often fail altogether to develop their identities and personalities throughout their adult lives.

On the other hand, women in contrast to men do have spouses with stimulating careers and interests but these husbands are often totally absorbed in their work and unable as well as unwilling to enjoy life with them; also these women cannot share experiences with their husbands since they usually live in two separate worlds—the women's world devoid of intellectual stimulation or growth potential. And women suffer from an option restriction corresponding to one suffered by men in that they are socialized so as to stifle any "masculine" aspect of their mind and personality. Here again, however, the consequences for women are quite serious since all intellectual thinking tends to be labeled as "masculine." Finally, the fact that all couples must have children (preferably three) and must have them as early as possible places some restrictions upon men (in terms of economic support and the stability of the familial bond) but tends to restrict quite seriously the women's options in several life sectors and particularly the occupational one. Mothers must not work or if they do they must work part-time in jobs rather than in careers in that clearly their occupational role is secondary to their familial roles and particularly to the mother role.[11]

But if one is to consider women's options cross-culturally, the status of women in some African and Asian countries is such that it is impossible to talk about women's options even at a theoretical level. Probably Moslem women in many countries represent the most dramatic case of oppressed women, since even their clothing and their physical mobility are severely regulated, held under the strict control of their father and/or brothers, their husband and/or sons. In these cases, women and young girls must first secure some very elementary freedoms and privileges, such as being allowed to leave the house to walk alone in the streets, being given enough nutritious food to eat when young (the best food is usually given to their brothers), being permitted to attend elementary and secondary school, and not being physically mistreated if they happen to have indulged (or even to have aspired to) these activities. They have to struggle to obtain some degree of control and self-determination over their bodies and their lives in general, but evidence from some countries shows that they have been only moderately successful.[12] Thus, in Algiers, 175 attempted suicides were reported in 1964 by girls who had resisted arranged marriages and, therefore, had to face the serious disapproval of their families.[13] In their case, since some of the most basic options—physical mobility, literacy (or secondary education), and any kind of self-determination—are forbidden, all the other options are completely out of reach. Continuous childbearing makes them old women at thirty-five, and shortens their life expectancy; they live and die in the dark margin of life.

But besides this rather extreme example of an almost total restriction of women's options, there are other instances, in many developing countries, where the choices of women are quite restricted. For example, in most developing nations of Asia and Africa women are not given the alternative of vocational training in salable skills, being practically always excluded from all training except in the areas of cooking, embroidery, and child care.[14] Of course, it must be noted that upper- and upper-middle-class urban women in all developing countries have usually a great number of choices in all life sectors and can be considered as being much more emancipated than middle- or upper-class girls in developed countries.[15] The ordinary societal rules and constraints do not apply in their case, and they therefore enjoy an extraordinary degree of freedom of choice and action.[16]

However, it must be made clear that there is no linear relationship between a country's level of industrial and economic development and the range of options actually open to women. That is, the most developed countries, like the United States, Sweden, Japan, Australia, Canada, West Germany, France, England, do not provide women with more options than the less developed countries.[17] Existing evidence indicates that industrialization tends to narrow the range of work opportunities for women in those countries where women were traditionally employed outside the home.[18] And international comparisons of statistical data show that, in general, countries at an intermediate stage of development (with a gross national product of $1000 to $1500 per capita) provide women more choices with respect to women's participation in the labor force, married women's employment, and women's college enrollment than countries with a high GNP (over $1500 per capita) or a low GNP (below $1000 per capita). Furthermore, the number of women enrolled in pharmacy, dentistry, education, law, and medicine is much higher in countries with a GNP of $500 to $1500 per capita than it is in those with a higher or lower GNP. For example, Finland, Hungary, Poland, Argentina, and Greece generally provide women with more options than most highly developed or under-developed countries. But the USSR is an exception among highly developed countries, since it provides women with options to the same extent as Hungary or Finland. But the option of singlehood is generally much more open to men and women in countries whose development is low or moderate than it is in highly developed ones, and it tends to become less of an option the more "advanced" a country is. Thus, the United States provides the best illustration of a highly developed and almost entirely "married" society, while Austria, West Germany, Greece, Finland, Sweden, Norway, and France are examples of countries with high proportions of single men and women (over two-fifths of the men and one-third of women).[19] In all these last-named societies it is socially acceptable for a man or a woman to remain single, and he (she) is not pitied or labeled "deviant" (homosexual, mentally ill, etc.). And because a large percentage of men and women are single, these societies are geared not solely for married people and families (as is the American society par excellence) but at least equally for single people. Thus, single people can enjoy most of the rights and privileges of married people as well as socially, emotionally, and sexually satisfying lives.

Countries at a medium level of development may provide women with more options than highly developed countries by means of a variety of societal mechanisms mobilized in the presence or absence of ideologies concerning women's equality with men. Thus, in Hungary and Poland, this came about by means of an all-pervasive political ideology that included a belief in the equality of the sexes; in Finland, it came about through a social ideology concerning sex roles; and in developing countries like Greece, it has come about in the absence of any distinct ideology. As we shall see in the next chapter the degree of accompanying societal adjustments and facilitating mechanisms, and the degree of sex-role redefinition, varies greatly from society to society.

In a country like Pakistan, a Muslim society in which the seclusion of women is still practiced and enforced, it is the very need for women's avoidance of men that not only opens educational and work options but makes it necessary for women to take these options. For example, the fact that high school girls must be taught by women teachers, women must be examined by women physicians, and women must transact business in banks and other offices with women employees leads to a greater number of educational and employment options for women than is found in many highly developed countries where women are more "emancipated."[20]

Thus, it seems that the presence of many options in one life sector (e.g., education) does not guarantee that women will have many options in all life sectors (e.g., work, political life, marriage and family life, etc.). And the restriction of all options in some areas (as is the case in Pakistan) may bring about the creation of many important options in other areas of women's lives. Some interesting correlations, however, seem to exist between some options. For example, when the women's option to participate actively in the labor force was examined cross-culturally, it was found to be correlated with the proportion of women who marry younger men. Thus, exercising the option to work tends to "liberate" women and to give them the necessary confidence and freedom to exercise the option of marrying a man younger than themselves. Also whenever the option to become a dentist is open to women in a particular country, the probability is quite high that the options to become a lawyer or a physician are equally open to them.[21]

Since the restriction of options in most life sectors seems to be the core problem of women in most societies, an appropriate theoretical framework for the sociological analysis of women may be that of modernity at the societal, familial and individual level. A most appropriate conceptualization of modernity may be that based on the range of options actually open to both men and women in different life sectors, this range not being determined or affected by the sex status of the individual.[22] Societies could be studied and typed according to the social and structural conditions that make it possible for women (and men) to choose from among a wide range of marital, familial, educational, occupational, social, and political options. These social and structural conditions may include the availability of sufficient child-care facilities, financially accessible to all women, for children of all ages and for all hours of the day; three to six months' paid maternity leave; tax benefits for dual-career work families; alternate occupational models with respect to hours of work and level and type of achievement; social policies encouraging and promoting the education and employment of women in traditionally masculine fields and that of men in traditionally feminine fields.

Families, on the other hand, could be studied and typed according to the socialization models they follow with respect to the degree to which they encourage their children's potentials and inclinations without restrictions based upon sex-appropriate behavior, and the degree to which they psychologically enable their children to choose, from among a wide range of options, not necessarily the "right" option, but the option that best corresponds to their needs, abilities, and interests. Families could also be classified according to whether or not spouses have a considerable range of behavioral options— concerning childbearing, style of child care, performance of familial roles and tasks, and style of familial interaction—which permits them to realize the familial model best suited to their personalities, without regard to sex-typed behavior.

Keeping this theoretical framework in mind and the fact that both societal and familial modernity are multidimensional concepts, we may conclude, on the basis of cross-cultural examinations of the status of women, that the "emancipation" of women can be achieved at different levels and under varying degrees and types of societal or familial modernity. Thus, for example, in Poland, Czechoslovakia, Hungary, and Russia, where women have a wide range of educational, occupational, and to a lesser extent political options, this is a reflection of a certain level of societal modernity, at least along some societal dimensions.[23] However, in these countries familial modernity seems to be rather low, since spouses are still following sex-typed behaviors in performing familial roles and tasks. In Norway, Sweden, Denmark, and Finland, however, both societal and familial modernity seems to be high, although unevenly so in each of the four countries. Thus, in Finland, familial modernity seems to exist with respect to socialization models but not with respect to familial models and the spouses' familial behavior,[24] while in Sweden, familial modernity is rather high along all dimensions and the redefinition of sex roles as social roles is the most advanced.[25]

It seems, then, that women can gain access to a wide range of educational, occupational, and political options without, as a concomitant, the liberation of themselves, their husbands, or their children from sex-typed roles and behaviors, though the increased range of options may eventually facilitate a redefinition of sex roles. But real "liberation" or "emancipation" cannot come about before one's sex does not determine his thinking, feeling, and behaving.

Notes

1. Michelle del Castillo, *Les Escrous de la Haine* (Paris: Julliard, 1970).
2. It is interesting to note that the Polytechnic School of Paris (where all engineering specialties are taught) accepted women as students for the first time in 1970.
3. See George Dugan, "Episcopal Church Rejects Move to Allow Ordination of Women," *New York Times,* October 18, 1970.
4. "Discrimination in Employment or Occupation on the Basis of Marital Status," *International Labour Review,* vol. 85, nos. 3/4 (March–April 1962), pp. 1–44.
5. Elisabeth B. Dufourcq, *Les Femmes Japonaises* (Paris: Editions DeNoel, 1969), pp. 235–249.
6. "Discrimination in Employment or Occupation," pp. 36–38.
7. Most women in outstanding business positions are either single or divorced. See, for example, those women who made news in: "Women Gain Top Bank Jobs in Some Reserve Districts," *New York Times,* October 5, 1969; and "Feminine Hand Guides Texas Retail Store," *New York Times,* June 14, 1970. Also, about half the career psychologists are either single or divorced: see David P. Campbell and A. M. Soliman, "The Vocational Interests of Women in Psychology" (Paper delivered at the Middlewestern Psychological Association meetings, Chicago, May 1967).
8. Stanislaw Judek, *Women in the Public Service* (Ottawa: Canada Department of Labour, Economic and Research Branch, 1968), pp. 74–80; Françoise Gueland-Leridon, *Recherches sur la condition feminine dans la société d'aujourd'hui* (Paris, Presses Universitaires de France, 1967), pp. 81–84.
9. Jerzy Piotrowski, *Family Needs Resulting from an Increased Employment of Married Women: Adequacy of Existing Resources to Meet These Needs* (Warsaw: Chair of Sociology of Work, Institute of Social Economy, 1969), pp. 31–47.
10. For example, 86 percent of Stanford University's senior women were willing to have their husbands' wishes have priority over theirs with regard to their occupational choices (see Joseph Katz et al., eds., *Class, Character, and Career* [Stanford: Institute for the Study of Human Problems, Stanford University, 1969], p. 114). Also for more details on this issue, see Discussion in Chapter 1.
11. Constantina Safilios-Rothschild, "Quelques Aspects de Modernization Sociale aux Etats-Unis et en Grèce," *Sociologie et Société,* vol. 1 (May 1969), pp. 23–37.
12. See David C. Gordon, *Women of Algeria: An Essay on Change,* Harvard Middle Eastern Monograph no. 19 (Cambridge, Mass.: Harvard University Press, 1968); Germaine Tillion, *Le Harem et les Cousins* (Paris: Editions de Seuil, 1966); and Fadela m'Rabet, *La Femme Algérienne et les Algériennes* (Paris: François Maspero, 1969).
13. m'Rabet, *op. cit.,* pp. 149–154.
14. Costantina Safilios-Rothschild and UNICEF Secretariat, *Children and Adolescents in Slums and Shanty-Towns in Developing Countries* (E/ICEF/L.1277/Add.1), 1971, pp. 68–69.
15. Khushwant Singh, "India Is Led by a Women, but Emancipation Is Still Not Complete for the Women of India," *New York Times Magazine,* March 13, 1966, sect. 6, pt. 1, pp. 24–25, 37, 39–40, 42, 44–45, 47, 49.
16. Constantina Safilios-Rothschild, "Toward a Cross-cultural Conceptualization of Family Modernity." *Journal of Comparative Family Studies,* vol. 1. no. 1 (Autumn 1970), p. 24.
17. Constantina Safilios-Rothschild, "A Cross-Cultural Examination of Women's Familial, Educational and Occupational Options," *Acta Sociologica,* vol. 14, no. 1/2 (Spring 1971).
18. Elise Boulding, "Women as Role Models in Industrializing Societies: A Macro-System Model of Socialization for Civic Competence" (Paper delivered at the Seventh World Congress of Sociology, Varna, Bulgaria, September 14–19, 1970).
19. Safilios-Rothschild, "A Cross-Cultural Examination of Women's Familial, Educational and Occupational Options."

20. J. Henry Korson, "Career Constraints Among Women Graduate Students in a Developing Society: West Pakistan. A study in the Changing Status of Women," *Journal of Comparative Family Studies,* vol. 1, no. 1 (Autumn 1970), pp. 82–100.
21. Safilios-Rothschild, "A Cross-Cultural Examination of Women's Familial, Educational and Occupational Options."
22. Safilios-Rothschild, "Toward a Cross-cultural Conceptualization of Family Modernity."
23. Veronica Stolte-Heiskanen and Elina Haavio-Mannila, "The Position of Women in Society: Formal Ideology versus Everyday Ethic," *Social Science Information,* vol. 6, no. 6 (December 1967), pp. 169–188; Safilios-Rothschild, "A Cross-cultural Examination of Women's Familial, Educational and Occupational options."
24. *Ibid.*
25. Edmund Dahlstrom, *The Changing Roles of Men and Women* (London: Duckworth, 1967); *The Status of Women in Sweden* (Stockholm: The Swedish Institute, 1968).

On Combining a "Deviant" and a
Conventional Option

Role Conflict and the Married Professional Woman*

Role conflict in the American college-educated woman has been subject to much debate ever since the appearance in 1946 of Komarovsky's oft-read and oft-cited article, "Cultural Contradictions and Sex Roles." While it has been the topic of much discussion,[1] role conflict in such women has been the object of only limited empirical analysis, with findings that are far from consistent. Angrist (1966, 1969) observed that much of this confusion has resulted from imprecise definition and use of the concept of role conflict. Among the conceptualizations often subsumed by the term are (1) divergent role conceptions held by the same individual, (2) inconsistencies between role conceptions and actual behavior, (3) incompatible role behaviors, and (4) role strain.

When broadly viewed from a structural perspective, the "role conflict" we are concerned with is seen to be (by definition) a logical outcome of a certain status inconsistency in the position of a highly educated married woman in a male-dominated society. Once transposed to experiences in the behavioral realm, however, the actual existence of widespread role conflict among highly educated women becomes open to debate. Much of the actual research done on the topic is of limited scope. Since such studies deal primarily with young college women facing the stresses, pressures, and demands of embarking on adulthood,[2] inferences from these subjects can be made only with extreme caution (Podell 1966).

It appears possible that what may be asserted on one level of analysis has but limited applicability when reduced to another level. Role conflict may be viewed on the intragroup level and may provide a framework for analyzing the role constellations resulting from the meshing of family and career demands. But marginality may also be seen from an individual and situational perspective, and it is this last dimension that we will attempt to develop in this paper. While by definition "role conflict" exists on the intergroup level, it will be demonstrated that such conflict is not seriously problematic on the individual level. Conflict can arise only in a situational context, and there it is usually "managed" by the married professional woman without becoming internalized.

---

* Paper delivered at the annual meeting of the Ohio Valley Sociological Society, Akron, Ohio, April 30–May 2, 1970. The study was carried out with the assistance of the Lena Lake Forrest Fellowship, granted by the Business and Professional Women's Foundation, Washington, D.C.

Research Design

The sample consisted of fifty-three presently married couples in which the wife was actively engaged in the practice of either law, medicine, or college teaching. The reasons for choosing these three professions were the following:

1. Each field requires an extended period of training and the investment of considerable time, money, and effort on the part of the woman who attains this status. It was hoped thereby to attain a sample of women who were committed to their careers more than minimally and who would accordingly be most likely to pose a threat to their husbands' position as chief bread-winner of the family.

2. Law, medicine, and academia make different types of demands upon those who would be successful in them. It was thought that success in the medical field, for example, requires that the physician remain in one locality over an extended period of time in order to build up a large practice. Success in academic circles, on the other hand, may require a high degree of geographic mobility, for the aspiring academic person must be ready and willing to move to a higher-status university when the "right" job offer comes along. The author thus hoped to gain a more complete view of the ways in which career demands interrelate with family life when both spouses are engaged in the occupational world.

3. All three are predominantly "male" professions.

Both spouses were interviewed separately and simultaneously by the author. The interviews lasted on the average from one and three-fourths to over three hours and were tape recorded. The interview schedule was open-ended, patterned after that used by Rapoport and Rapoport in their 1959 study of the dual-career family in London° and focuses upon six major areas: (1) the husband's occupation or profession and career; (2) the wife's profession and career; (3) husband-wife career interrelationships; (4) handling of children; (5) relations with relatives; and (6) relations with friends.

This paper will attempt to answer two basic questions: (1) How does the married professional woman manage the seemingly conflicting demands of home and profession, and (2) How does the professional woman in the sample who revealed no signs of unresolved role conflict differ from the small minority in which some role strain was visible?

Role Conflict and Its Resolution

Role conflict must be seen as being not continuous but discontinuous and should be viewed in situational terms. In a given situation a professionally employed married woman may experience strain, but she usually resolves it, and then she drifts out of the uncomfortable position. She may manage the conflict consciously or the situations may change, thus allowing an automatic

---

° See Rapoport and Rapoport article, "The Dual-Career Family," in Chapter 5 of this volume.

resolution. Role conflict must then also be considered in terms of the stage of the family life cycle as well as the stage of the career (Angrist 1966).

Role Conflict and Role Sequence

In discussing the difficulties of their particular role constellations in terms of role sequence (Merton 1957), the respondents who had completed their professional training after their marriage recalled the duration of professional preparation as being very tension producing. The period of dissertation writing for women in academia and the internship for women in medicine were frequently cited as difficult times. These women (in retrospect) reported that there was some feeling of guilt, with their supportive husbands being indispensable in alleviating their strain and helping them maintain professional aspirations.

A young college professor and mother expressed it in the following way:

> I, like any woman with small children, felt guilty about going off to the library. You need someone to encourage you, to say you should get it [the dissertation] done, and to say that what you are doing is important. If you have someone who is reinforcing your guilt [a disapproving husband], then indeed you shouldn't go to that library. It is very hard to write a thesis under optimum circumstances, and his lack of encouragement would have been enough to make the difference—my husband's encouragement made the difference for me anyway. [04-W][3]

Once training or the degree is completed, however, the pressures reportedly can be better controlled. This appears to be due to the fact that women, for the most part, *work* in the professions but do not have *careers* in the same sense as their male counterparts. This enables the married professional woman to pace her work and professional progress to fit in with family demands. Such pacing is not always possible during the highly structured training program.

The data also suggest that resolution of role conflict may occur gradually over time. One respondent expressed it in the following way:

> When I entered my first marriage, I was young enough to think that this had to be an either-or thing. My [first] husband swore up and down that my education and career orientation wasn't any problem, but it was. Because I did feel that marriage and a career was an either-or thing, I overinvested in my child. Her present problems are probably at least partly a result. I sought satisfactions in marriage that no marriage can give anyone. Eventually I worked it out by making mistakes and learning what these mistakes were. . . . Once I realized that the demands of the situation were something other than the world of work, I began to loosen up a bit. But I still had all this energy and wanted to do something. That's when I started to work and took the teaching job—and that's when it dawned on me that you really can combine work and marriage. You can live one life as a wife and mother and another as a professor, and both your needs are met and you can be satisfied. [05-W]

In this particular case, personal conflict existed prior to actually engaging in professional employment but was resolved *when* profession and home were combined. The author's data indicate that similar cases of strain may be observed when the wife and mother is pursuing professional involvement. When this strain becomes too great, she may resign from her position, at least temporarily (as respondent #08-W did just a week before the author interviewed her), to alleviate the tension.

It is apparent that not all stages of professional involvement are as demanding, or as permitted by the woman to be as demanding, as the rigid training programs (particularly in the field of medicine). Once the requirements are met for the profession, the wife and mother is likely to regulate her involvement to allow the most comfortable position at *both* home and work. Twenty-eight of the 45 mothers in the sample chose not to work prior to their children's entering school: of those 17 who continued to work, over 10 limited their employment to part-time positions. Of the 37 mothers who worked while the children were in elementary school, 14 acknowledged taking only those positions which allowed them to be home when their children returned from school. In this sample, the woman with small children was likely either to stop working temporarily or to cut down on her professional involvement to minimize role strain.

Management of Role Strain Through Compromise and Compartmentalization

In all except four cases in the sample, any necessary compromise between home and profession was made in favor of home role demands. While the cooperative and obliging husband of the professionally employed woman may demand little in terms of personal service from his wife, she is careful not to make any unnecessary demands upon him. A woman physician's comment was typical:

> I bend over backwards not to have to make demands on him. He does not like to shop, for example, so I do not ask him to do so. Sometimes I forego doing things professionally that I might enjoy (such as attending a lecture) to keep from inconveniencing him. [50-W]

In order to solve the problem of management of both home and career, professional involvement was cut back as deemed necessary. One female physician (respondent 08-W) made it a practice to work intermittently in a clinic to allow herself to refuel when completely drained by full-time employment and the demands of four small children. When interviewed, she had just resigned as codirector of a clinic, but she pointed out that she had done this once before and probably would return to work within several months.

A highly successful attorney and mother of five resolves potential conflict by compartmentalizing her full-time professional involvement and her family role demands:[4]

> I can honestly tell you that before I leave this house, I try to prepare for everyone here. When I leave, I don't give them a thought—not a

thought. If my mother (who takes care of the children) would call the office and ask me to call her, I might not even remember to call her back. I don't give them a thought because I have done everything I thought was necessary before I left. And when I leave—on trips or anything—I don't even think about them [family members]. [09-W]

Thirty-six of the forty-five respondents with children interrupted their professions through either part-time employment or a complete cessation of work while the children were young. Professional involvement was increased (or planned to be increased) only as the children were deemed to be less in need of constant mothering. But even in those nine cases where professional involvement was continuous, the woman did not necessarily have *career* aspirations. One example of this is a nationally known academic woman (respondent 40-W) who divided her professional activities into the "job" stage when family demands were greater and the "career" stage once the children were launched.

Most women in the sample faced little, if any, unresolved conflict even when the children were younger. If a child objects to his mother's leaving the house to go to work, the mother reports some feelings of guilt but neutralizes them with the assertion that she is a better mother because she *does* work. Comments such as this one were typical:

> Obviously I have become used to a life that is very stimulating to me, to be able to go outside of the home, to get satisfaction from my work. Whether I would find being home too dull and whether this would affect my children, I don't know. I do find that being cooped up in the house with children who are demanding on your every single minute [is] fairly irritating to me. I shouldn't say "irritating," but "disruptive." So the chance to get out and "do my own thing" for a while does give me a sense of personal privacy which I can fall back on when I feel like everything else is closing in. [17-W]

While there is no evidence from existing literature that working mothers as a group are better mothers than those who do not work, the author's data suggest that professionally employed women perceive their employment as making *them* better mothers than they otherwise would have been. Those women in the second career group (those who began their training only after the children were older) were often able to compare perceptions of their performance in their wife and mother roles before and after they began to work. A lawyer (respondent 22-W) recalled how before she started working she used to sit home "waiting for the children to come from school so I could improve their characters." A psychology professor (respondent 05-W) who embarked on her career only after the birth of her first child and her subsequent divorce and remarriage commented: "I find that I enjoy the children a lot more because I am working. I don't feel confined with them like I did with the first child." A college professor who was "very dissatisfied with the club activities and the piano lessons" that she had engaged in when her children were preschool age began working on a Ph.D. once they entered elementary school. She noted:

> I told myself—and still tell myself—that if I had stayed home and not [done] what I did, I would have been one of those bloody awful

> martyred mothers who sat around all the rest of her life seeing her children as the cross to which she had been nailed. There is nothing more awful than that, and that is the way I would have felt. [28-W]

A physician and mother of three children (respondent 10-W) spoke for the majority of the women in the sample with her statement: "If I felt the children were being harmed, this would be the one thing that would keep me from working. I do feel, however, that my being away from the children part of the time makes me enjoy being with them all the more."

Many of these same mothers expressed the feeling that they were spending as much time with their children as their nonworking neighbors. A young physician reported:

> When I look around, I think I spend as much time with my children as most people do—you know, time actually with them. I seem to know my children as well. I have talked it over with the boy and he does not always like it that I work. These are the times that I feel most unhappy about it. I always tell him that you have to live with things the way they are and that you have to accept things the way they are. [18-W]

As the reader may have already observed, guilt feelings did occur in most mothers, but they were occasional and situational rather than overriding.[5] Very few mothers revealed any signs of being guilt-ridden (i.e., in a nearly perpetual state of feeling that they ought not be employed because of the possible harm their professional involvement was inflicting on their children), and all such cases in the author's sample were employed on a full-time basis and because of the family's economic need. Almost all of the other mothers whose children had not yet been launched occasionally felt pangs of guilt in tension-producing family situations. One mother of three commented:

> The only time that I have felt guilty about working is if my daughter would call me and sound upset about something. But this would be at 4 o'clock in the afternoon when she got home from school. I would be upset until I got home. But I have never felt guilty about going out working. [33-W]

Another mother of two (respondent 28-W) noted: "I would feel guilty whenever something went wrong—but not guilty enough to give up working."

Most mothers tried to organize things so that their families' needs would be met and so that there would be fewer opportunities for guilt-producing situations to arise. Some mothers did report guilt pangs when a child would come home asking, "Why don't you bake cookies like Mrs. So-and-so?" or "Why won't you be a den mother like Johnny's mother is?" The reaction of the mother is frequently to yield to the child's request. It may well be that the children of some working mothers may be able to evaluate their family situation and use it to their advantage. When denied something they want, they use the mother's employment as a lever. One mother (respondent 48-W) admitted that she is probably doing more running around for her children than her neighbors who are not employed precisely because she does not want to run the risk of neglecting her children. A few mothers apparently have not fallen prey to yielding to most such demands. One mother emphatically stated:

I don't feel guilty about working. For example, if the boy says on Monday morning that he needed gym shoes, I will say "You know we do the shopping on Saturdays. Why didn't you tell me? Now you will just have to wait until next Saturday." I make no apologies—no nothing. I explain that they know if it is on the shopping list, we get it; if it is not on my Saturday shopping list, I take no responsibility for it. I think the children will grow up a bit better too. They realize that things will have to get done in an organized way. [32-W]

Guilt feelings appear to be alleviated by the woman's performing all of the tasks that she subjectively feels are important as part of the mother role. As indicated earlier, a number of women were extremely anxious to be home from work when their children arrived from school. These respondents accepted only those positions which allowed them to meet this need. For example, one physician (respondent 48-W) accepted a position at a clinic only if she could work through her lunch hours and leave at 4 P.M. each day rather than the normal quitting time of 5 P.M. This was a condition of her acceptance of the offer and a condition met by the clinic director. Other women arranged to work from their homes in order to spend more time with their preschool-age children. If this could not have been arranged, these respondents said they would have temporarily ceased working.

These and many other examples made it quite apparent that the professionally employed wife and mother does not live in the state of unmanaged role strain. She has, by and large, created a position for herself which is psychologically comfortable.[6]

A college professor expressed the situation quite well (and in a manner with which most of the respondents would have heartily agreed):

I think it is perfectly possible to combine a profession and marriage— as long as you have these basic premises: as long as the man is not threatened by the woman's capabilities and achievements; as long as he sees it as adding to his stature and not as diminishing it; as long as a woman has worked out her own role as a mother; and as long as she is not ambivalent about her roles. If a mother feels secure about leaving her children with a housekeeper and feels she is a better mother because of it, there is nothing intrinsically difficult about it. [36-W]

Role Conflict and Limitation of Career Aspirations

Most of the women interviewed expressed an awareness of the fact that their professional involvement had less priority than their husbands' and was more subject to fluctuations in family demands. This was viewed as being essential to making a dual-profession family "work." Here again no signs of any serious unresolved role conflict were found. A woman physician who had ranked number one in her medical school class, who had had only minor professional commitments when her three children were younger, and who was stepping up her involvement as they left the nest explained it in the following way:

I think I would have been very unhappy if I hadn't been allowed to kind of "have my fling" and a career too. But as I look at it, the women that did have a career and gave it up, or the ones who had a career and never got married, are not to be envied at all. I think they are very lonely in later life. I think that the sort of satisfaction that comes from having a happy marriage and having children is pretty hard to replace with even a very successful career. I think that in that case you'd almost sublimate all of your other drives and instincts into your career, which I suppose could be deeply satisfying, but I have no question in my mind that I would prefer the other. [15-W]

This wife and mother speaks for many others in the sample who felt that they had experienced the best of both worlds by having a limited career involvement and a full family life.

There is evidence that this compromise of career goals for a normal family life is one that some women may struggle with. This struggle, it must be emphasized, is one that was (at least in the author's sample) generally resolved. One respondent (51-W) felt that it was a "big hurdle" at first for her to say and really believe that she could not be "the *best* doctor and the *best* wife" all at the same time. As she put it, "You are going to have to make certain compromises."

Some women observed that, given our present society, it is impossible to combine a career in the real sense of the term ("uninterrupted, full-time work with a high degree of commitment") with the demands of a family. All except four of the female subjects made a conscious decision to place the home demands first on their list of priorities, and these women were satisfied with the situation the way it was. Being aware that complete feminine emancipation brings *duties* as well as *rights*, they asked for neither.

A middle-aged female attorney described the situation in the following manner:

It is the fortune of women to be able to choose whether or not they *want* to work. I know that I do not have to be trapped in any job that I don't like. If I had a hateful job, I could quit and wait for something better to come along. . . . I really hate to see feminists go overboard—not everyone wants a career. I am sorry that so many graduate programs are demanding full-time involvement or nothing; this excludes many women. [28-W]

The women were aware of the fact that they were operating in an open system as far as the work world was concerned. Unlike their husbands, on whose shoulders the breadwinning role rested, they were free to stop working temporarily or permanently if conditions were aggravating or too demanding. Eventually another more favorable opportunity, it was felt, would present itself. These women seem to appreciate the freedom in their situations rather than regret the constraints forcing curtailed professional involvement. As we shall see, women who were denied this freedom to choose whether or not to work may be subject to greater and less readily managed role strain.

Situations of Unresolved Role Strain

In only eight of the fifty-three cases were there indications of persistent unresolved role strain presently causing difficulties for the wife. In three cases

(#03, #07, and #25) the wife was forced to work because of the husband's inability to make an adequate living. The wife was working primarily for the income and would have preferred either to minimize her professional involvement or to discontinue it completely. In each of these cases the theme of the wife's dissatisfaction could be traced throughout the transcribed interview.

Three other cases (those of respondents 02-W, 30-W and 32-W) provide illustrations of the importance of considering the time of the interview in analyzing the findings. Each of these respondents was interviewed during what appeared to be the height of a conflict-producing situation. An embittered academic woman (respondent 02-W) asserted that she felt "trapped" by her career, which she had started before marriage. But it is not without significance that she had been informed only shortly before the interview that her application for a much-desired promotion had been rejected. When this is coupled with the fact that this wife (unlike most wives interviewed) had placed her career on the same level of importance as her husband's and had earlier refused to move to another location when her husband received an offer for an exceptional academic position, her bitterness and frustration may be better understood. Prior to this "fiasco" (as the respondent herself expressed the difficulties she and her husband were having in their present academic positions), she had, as we have said, felt that both her and her husband's careers were of equal importance. Now the wife realized that if she wished to remain married, her career would have to take a second place to her husband's.

A physician (respondent 30-W) who was also the mother of a three-year-old child and who was an intern at the time of the interview provided an illustration of those difficulties of the training period which had been recalled by many other respondents. This year of tension and strain was relieved somewhat by the woman's plans for a half-time residency for the following year. Prior to this year the strain was reportedly not as great, and the respondent believed the situation would be greatly improved by half-time involvement following the internship.

Respondent 32-W was an attorney who had recently received a promotion, but whose husband greatly resented her newly-found success. Up until this time, the husband had been most supportive of his wife's professional activities; if it had not been for this support, she said, she would not have had the self-confidence even to attempt combining a law career with her family life. Once he began to withdraw his support, the wife experienced some role strain. At the time of the interview, the wife appeared to have the strain somewhat under control, and was possibly prepared in the near future to opt for her career rather than for her present marriage.

In addition to the interview's occurrence at a time of transition, case #32 also represents an illustration of the importance of the husband's attitude in easing role strain. Only in one other case (#14) did the author find a husband who was strongly opposed to his wife's career. The physician and mother in case #14 had serious doubts about her feminity—doubts, judging from her spouse's interview, that were planted and nurtured by her disapproving husband, who is also a physician.

Failure to establish a salient role may also cause role strain to be less readily resolved. In case #37 we found a highly successful physician and her equally successful spouse. Having married after achieving a high degree of success, she still retains a career in the most demanding sense of the term. While two other couples followed this same success-marriage-more-success pattern, these couples did not have children. It appears that in case #37 there is some relation between the emotional problems of the respondent's daughter and the respondent's own unresolved role strain. The marriage itself seemed ideal, with a high degree of personal and professional sharing between spouses, but the child was an unmanageable source of strain for the mother. While she herself was not able to explain this strain, it appeared that she, unlike most of the respondents, had never consciously set her list of priorities (between home and career) and thus continued to feel torn between two sets of demands.

Analysis and Conclusion

Although from a structural point of view a considerable degree of role strain is inevitable between the woman's "professional" and "home" roles, most of the respondents had not internalized such strains. Seen from an interactionalist or processual perspective, strain between home and professional roles is far from unavoidable. Rather, it is capable of being managed through the use of a number of techniques through which women are able subjectively to control any structurally induced role strains. Four kinds of tension-management techniques may be found in this data:

1. Favorable definition of the situation ("I spend more actual time with my children than my nonworking neighbors who are very active in volunteer work," or "I am a better mother *because* I work and can expend my energies on something other than the overmothering of my children").

2.. Establishment of a salient role in the particular role constellation. For example, if a conflict situation occurs between family demands and career responsibilities (e.g., the baby-sitter does not show up, a child is sick, there is a parent-teacher meeting, etc.), the family demands are first on the list of the woman's priorities.

3. Compartmentalization. As much as possible the wife tries to keep her home role distinct and separate from her professional role. This may occur even to the extent where a female lawyer (respondent 31-W) refrained from talking about her legal practice at home so that the children would not think that her work was more important than their father's. Very few female respondents brought work home with them, although their husbands frequently did.

4. Compromise. The wife is careful to control the extent of her career involvement to fit in with a number of factors, including the attitude of her husband toward her profession, demands placed on the wife by her husband's profession, the ages of the children, the wife's personal philosophy on the role of the mother, and the amount of sheer physical and psychic energy she can muster in order to withstand the demands of her two roles. *When one or more of these factors is out of kilter, the wife makes the necessary adjustment to manage role strain.* She generally expects little and asks nothing of the family to better enable her to adjust to family and career demands.

If all married professional women are viewed as "marginals" (in the structural sense of "marginal status"), it is apparent from these data that they need not (and usually do not) develop marginal personalities. This conflict between the achieved and ascribed statuses may be reconciled as has been done by most of the respondents through creating a role for themselves with the family demands as salient in the role hierarchy and career demands assuming less importance. Once this hierarchy is established, the wife and mother can utilize it to solve individual conflict situations that inevitably do arise between home and career. Due to the nature of the focus and corresponding sample in this study, single women involved in a profession were not included. Some of the respondents had opted for a career over a previous marriage, demonstrating the possibility that other divorcées and single career women may avoid role strain in this fashion. In any case, the marginal situation (role conflict in a structural sense) does not usually result in a permanent state of marginal personality (role conflict internalized).

This is not to say that role conflict is always resolved or that it is instantly managed, as the data have shown. It seems more difficult to resolve (1) when there is a clash between the wife's achieved career status and her husband's ascribed status as breadwinner;[7] (2) when the wife has failed to decide upon a role constellation complete with a salient or cardinal role; and/or (3) when the husband withdraws or withholds his support. In addition, certain stages of the profession and family cycles may produce strain that is resolved only once the tension-filled stage is completed or abandoned. It seems that role conflict among professionally employed married women is neither widespread nor very severe. When a conflict-ridden situation does occur, the woman's list of priorities with its salient role comes to the rescue to alleviate the problem.

It is quite significant that the data clearly suggest that the married professional woman is basically satisfied with life the way she lives it. Among the women interviewed most found being a wife and a mother very satisfying and taking precedence over their professional lives. Despite cries from radical feminists for the complete "emancipation" of women, most of our respondents showed no real desire for such emancipation. Their assertion is strong that, in light of our contemporary social structure, the family must come first for a woman. Call them Aunt Tabbys if you will, but they seem quite satisfied with their lot.

Notes

1. For some theoretical articles pertinent to role conflict and the highly educated women, see Davis and Olesen (1963), Simpson and Simpson (1961), Toby (1952), and Stouffer and Toby (1951). Angrist (1967) has reviewed other articles, including empirical studies, pointing out many discrepancies in both assertions and findings.
2. For examples of such studies see Komarovsky (1946), Wallin (1950), Seward (1945), Rose (1951), and Heilbrun (1963).
3. The numbers in parentheses after the quotations throughout this paper refer to the interview number, with the letter "W" indicating that the quotation came from the wife's interview.
4. This notion of compartmentalizing was one frequently expressed in the interviews. (It also appears in the last sentence of the quotation cited earlier from respondent 05-W.) But when a conflict situation occurs between demands in the areas of home and profession, in almost all cases the home is clearly seen as the salient area.
5. Judgments as to the nature and extent of role strain were made jointly by the

author and T. Neal Garland (who also conducted all interviews) and are subjective, based solely upon the reports of the interviewees. See the following article by T. Neal Garland, "The Better Half, The Male in the Dual Profession Family."

6. A number of female respondents in the sample commented about "creating" their own roles as wife-mother-career persons. Those more familiar with the language of social science indicated that they did not have a role model after which to pattern their particular role constellation. For a further discussion of how persons may construct their own roles, see McCall and Simmons (1966).

7. It is significant that no woman in the sample *wanted* to earn more than her husband. For most women there was no possibility of her salary equaling that of her husband. In a few cases the wife actually cut back on her career involvement rather than exceed her husband's income. Those cases where the wife's income was greater were also cases where the wife was forced to work due to her husband's inadequate salary.

References

ANGRIST, SHIRLEY S. "Role Conception as a Predictor of Adult Female Roles." *Sociology and Social Research* 50 (July 1966): 448–459.

――――. "Role Constellation as a Variable in Women's Leisure Activities." *Social Forces* 45 (March 1967): 423–431.

――――. "The Study of Sex Roles." *Journal of Social Issues* 25 (1969): 215–231.

DAVIS, FRED, and OLESEN, VIRGINIA A. "Initiation into a Woman's Profession: Identity Problems in the Status Transition of Coed to Student Nurse." *Sociometry* 26 (March 1963): 89–101.

DICKIE-CLARK, H. F. *The Marginal Situation.* New York: Humanities Press, 1966.

FELDING, HAROLD. "The Family and the Idea of a Cardinal Role: A Sociological Study." *Human Relations* 14 (November 1961): 329–350.

GOODE, WILLIAM J. "A Theory of Role Strain." *American Sociological Review* 25 (August 1960): 483–496.

GROSS, NEAL; MCEACHERN, ALEXANDER W.; and MASON, WARD S. "Role Conflict and Its Resolution." In *Role Theory: Concepts and Research.* New York: John Wiley & Sons, 1966.

HEILBRUN, ALFRED F. "Sex-Role Identity and Achievement Motivation." *Psychological Reports* 12 (1963): 483–490.

KOMAROVSKY, MIRRA. "Cultural Contradictions and Sex Roles." *American Journal of Sociology* 52 (1946): 184–190.

LINTON, RALPH. "Status and Role." In *Sociological Theory: A Book of Readings* edited by Coser and Rosenberg. New York: The Macmillan Company, 1957.

MCCALL, GEORGE J., and SIMMONS, L. *Identities and Interaction.* New York: Free Press, 1966.

MERTON, ROBERT K. *Social Theory and Social Structure*, pp. 368–384. Glencoe, Ill.: The Free Press, 1957.

PARSONS, TALCOTT. *The Social System*, pp. 230–283. New York: Free Press, 1951.

PODELL, LAWRENCE. "Sex and Role Conflict." *Journal of Marriage and the Family* 28 (May 1966): 163–165.

ROSE, ARNOLD. "The Adequacy of Women's Expectations for Adult Roles." *Social Forces* 30 (1951): 69–77.

SEWARD, H. GEORGENE. "Cultural Conflict and the Feminine Role." *Journal of Social Psychology* 22 (November 1945): 177–194.

SIMPSON, RICHARD L. and SIMPSON, IDA HARPER. "Occupational Choice among Career-Oriented College Women." *Marriage and Family Living* 23 (1961) 377–390.

STOUFFER, SAMUEL A. and TOBY, JACKSON. "Role Conflict and Personality." *American Journal of Sociology* 56 (1951): 395–406.

TOBY, JACKSON. "Some Variables in Role Conflict Analysis." *Social Forces* 30 (March 1952): 323–327.

WALLIN, PAUL. "Cultural Contradictions and Sex Roles: A Repeat Study." *American Sociological Review* 15 (1950): 288–293.

The Better Half? The Male in the Dual Profession Family*

As the level of feminist activity in the United States begins once again to increase, a familiar image can be expected to put in a parallel appearance. This image would seem to stem from the assumption that whenever one sex gains, the other automatically loses. The stereotype of the henpecked husband is no stranger to our society. It is, in fact, a common theme in many so-called "family comedies" aired daily on afternoon and evening television and serves as the central subject matter for many comic strip and cartoon artists. Author Myron Brenton (1966, p. 129) has aptly labeled this image of the American male as the "Dagwood Bumstead Syndrome"—a syndrome in which father is pictured as a likable enough but bothersomely incompetent inconvenience to the other family members. Mom, who is inevitably pictured as pretty, witty, and wise, really runs the show and manages to keep the family going in spite of Dear Old Dad, who is always left in somewhat of a fog by the end of the story, wondering What Happened Anyhow? . . . but feeling that he has adequately handled the situation.

That the fear of becoming a "Dagwood Bumstead" has long haunted men in the Western world can be seen by glancing through almost any historical account dealing with relations between the sexes—and a good many other sources as well. The writers of the Old Testament saw fit to include many bits of advice urging (and ordering) women to be submissive and obedient to their husbands, thereby indicating that a goodly number of women probably were not adequately discharging their divinely appointed womanly duties, for where no deviations occur no admonitions are needed. William Shakespeare took great pains to offer advice on how a man could deal with a headstrong wife when he wrote *The Taming of the Shrew*—and all ends well when Katherine learns the virtues of obedience to her husband.

Many writers have noted the changes brought about in the American family system by the coming of the Industrial Revolution. As women moved out of the home and into the labor market, they supposedly gained greater power within the family. Hoffman explains this situation by theorizing that "the person who receives wages in exchange for services has more control over his money than other family members; and this control can be used, implicitly or explicitly, to wield power in the family" (1960, pp. 32–33).

* An earlier version of this paper was delivered at the annual meetings of the American Sociological Association, Washington, D.C., August 31—September 3, 1970. The study was carried out with the assistance of the Lena Lake Forrest Fellowship, granted by the Business and Professional Women's Foundation, Washington, D.C.

Curiously enough men are underresearched, while considerable effort has been expended upon the problems which the Industrial Revolution and modern education have created for women (for example, Myrdal and Klein 1956; Smuts 1959; Nye and Hoffman 1963; Epstein 1970). A noticeable gap in sex-role literature has been pointed out by writers who have attempted to search out the corresponding problems of the masculine half of married pairs (LeMasters 1970; Hacker 1957; Benson 1968; Brenton, *op. cit.*; Kendall 1965). Useem has correctly noted that

> The changing concepts of women's roles are inextricably tied up with the changing concepts of the place of men and children in our society and all of these are interwoven in the overall changes which are taking place in the American life itself.
>
> (Useem 1960, p. 20)

Despite such warnings, however, the majority of writers concerned with sex roles seem to have concentrated almost exclusively on the problems connected with the much-publicized "feminine mystique" (Friedan 1963), often leaving the reader with the feeling that men (especially husbands) are somehow irrelevant to the whole female world except insofar as they, in the role of gatekeepers, discriminate against talented and beleaguered women. Hacker (*op. cit.*) attempted to bring to light the fact that changes in the roles of women involve correspondingly problematic changes in the roles of men, but researchers have been slow to follow the path which she suggested. As a result, little empirical evidence is available to help either support or refute the popular notion that a man will feel "threatened" by his wife's participation in the world of work. Safilios-Rothschild (1969, pp. 2–3) has commented perceptively upon the fact that there exists a great body of sociological literature dealing with the "egalitarian family" in the United States—a type of family which apparently exists mainly and almost exclusively in the minds of family sociologists, for almost all empirical research indicates that the vast majority of American families are a long, long way from being "egalitarian" in structure. Another notion prevalent in popular, and to some extent in professional, literature is the idea that an employed wife—especially a wife employed in a high-status, highly paid professional position—will by definition be a threat to her husband's position as main breadwinner and head of the household, and to his image of himself as a man. Do the empirical facts support or refute this notion? It is to this question that the study reported herein was addressed.

Who Were the Husbands

While the wives in the study were selected on the basis of their professions as lawyers, physicians, or college professors,[1] no attempt was made to control for the husband's occupations, for the research focus was the patterns of adjustment utilized by families in which the wife is a practicing professional. One possible mode of adjustment may be that the professional woman tends to marry a particular type of man. To control for husband's occupations would, therefore, have been equivalent to controlling on a dependent variable.

The names of married professional women associated with a midwestern university which has large medical and law schools were chosen as beginning contacts for the study. Each couple interviewed was asked to suggest other couples who fit the criteria of the study and who might be interested in participating in the project. Careful referral charts were kept to assure that we did not simply tap pockets of close friends. The final sample contained couples in all stages of the career cycle, from those on the brink of completing graduate or professional training to those who had been practicing their profession for thirty or more years. The occupational pairings of the respondents are shown in Table 1.

Table 1   *Occupational Pairings*

Wife's Profession	HUSBAND'S PROFESSION OR OCCUPATION				
	Medicine	Law	Academia*	Other	
Medicine	14	0	0	4	
Law	1	6	0	7	
Academia*	4	2	9	6	
Total	19	8	9	17	N = 53

* Academia is defined for the purpose of this paper as consisting of teaching at the college or university level combined with scholarly research and/or administrative duties. No distinction was made between the various academic disciplines.

It will be noted that even though no attempt was made to control for husbands' occupations, the majority of the husbands in the sample were professionals themselves. This pattern was also found by Ginzberg (1966, p. 25), Epstein (1968), and Simon (1967). In general, it would seem that professional women tend to marry professional men.

Included in the "other" category were 7 administrative-level businessmen, 2 city government officials, 2 biomedical engineers, 1 chemist, 1 clinical psychologist, 1 civil rights administrator, 1 mechanical engineer, 1 civil engineer, and 1 lower-ranking civil servant.

Structure of the Dual-Profession Family

A number of sociologists have attempted to develop typologies describing various aspects of family structure. Rodman (1965, pp. 249–257) has summarized a number of these typologies and has noted the differences and similarities which they exhibit. Other writers, such as Gans (1962) in his study of the "Urban Villagers" and Frazier (1939) in his study of the Negro family, have attempted to characterize families according to the various patterns which they observed in the life styles of the people they studied. The responses given seem to indicate the existence of four rather distinct family types, to which the following labels might be attached.

1. *Traditional.* In this family type, the male acts as the primary bread-winner, while the female regards the home and children as her first concern. The wife's occupational commitments are seen by *both* husband and wife as clearly secondary both to her husband's occupational plans and to her domestic duties. This type seems to bear strong resemblance to the "institutional" family described by Burgess, Locke, and Thomes (1963, p. 3), with the relationship between spouses resembling what Bott (1957, p. 3) and Rainwater (1965, pp. 28–60) have labeled the "segregated conjugal role relationship." Twenty of the couples were placed in this category.

2. *Neotraditional.* In the neotraditional family, the husband and wife are in equal or nearly equal occupational statuses. Twenty-seven of the couples were placed in this category. While in all of these cases the husband earned more than his wife, the potential existed that the wife could, at a future date, equal or exceed his income through her own professional activities. Two main characteristics differentiate the neotraditional from the traditional family type: (1) the wife's income may be needed or utilized to maintain the family's standard of living, and (2) the wife's professional involvement is viewed by *both* members of the pair as being a significant factor to take into account whenever decisions are to be made which would affect the career of either spouse. This family type resembles somewhat the "colleague" family identified by Miller and Swanson (1958, pp. 199–200) and as exhibiting more of the "intermediate conjugal role-relationships" described by Bott (*op. cit.*) and by Rainwater (*op. cit.*).

3. *Matriarchal.* Here the woman has willingly or unwillingly achieved the primary position within the family through outdistancing her husband in either educational achievement, career success and prestige, or income. Frazier (*op. cit.*) has described the matriarchal family form as he found it in the lower classes. While the interviewed couples tended to be from the upper middle class, many of the same characteristics Frazier described can be seen in operation here. Five couples seemed to fit in this category.

4. *Egalitarian.* In this family type the significance of the spouse's biological sex is reduced to an absolute minimum. Both members are equally involved in their professions, and domestic duties are not divided along any rigid lines, with both husband and wife sharing equally in the care of the home and the raising of the children. This family type approaches the "companionship" family of Burgess, Locke, and Thomes (*op. cit.*) and closely approximates the "androgynous" conception of sex roles suggested by Rossi (1964). Role relationships in this family type took the form of the "joint conjugal role-relationships" of Bott (*op. cit.*) and Rainwater (*op. cit.*). One couple appeared to fit the egalitarian pattern. This contrasts with the high percentage of egalitarian relationships found by Rainwater and is due, no doubt, to the very strict definition of "egalitarian" used in this study (i.e., *no* sex-related division of labor).

Respondents were placed in one of these four categories on the basis of the overall evaluation of the interview responses given by husbands and wives. The relationship between husband's occupation or profession and family type is shown in Table 2.

Table 2 Distribution of Professional or Occupational Types
Among Family Types

| Family Type | Husband's Profession or Occupation | | | | |
	Medicine	Law	Academia	Other	Total
Traditional	9	3	3	5	20
Neotraditional	10	3	4	10	27
Matriarchal	9	2	1	2	5
Egalitarian	0	0	1	0	1
Total	19	8	19	17	53

Discussion of the Wife's Career Before Marriage

If one makes two assumptions, namely, that (1) man is a rational being and (2) males will indeed be threatened if their wives are practicing professionals, it seems logical to assume also that men will discuss their wives' career intentions before marriage. Male respondents were, therefore, asked about the extent to which they had discussed their wives' career plans before actually walking down the aisle. Table 3 indicates the distribution of responses.

Table 3 Did the Couple Discuss the Wife's Career Before Marriage?

Family Type	Not at All	Some	Extensively	Can't Remember
Traditional	7	5	6	2
Neotraditional	8	9	6	4
Matriarchal	3	0	1	1
Egalitarian	0	1	0	0
Total	18	15	13	7 N = 53

Traditional Responses

While the frequency with which males in the traditional and neotraditional categories discussed their future wives' career plans does not seem to have differed greatly, the content of the discussions does seem to have been different. Traditional males seem to have been much more likely to have set certain conditions under which they would allow their future wives to practice their professions—and they wanted these women to know what the conditions were going to be. An administrator in the public school whose wife is an attorney gave a typical reply:

> We discussed her working before we married. Being sort of old-fashioned—maybe traditional—I told her there were a few things I did not want. I didn't want to holler when we talked to one another—I didn't want to argue. The other thing was that if the job interfered with her being a good wife and a good mother, . . . it would be eliminated to the point that it wouldn't be. [31-H][2]

In other cases, the traditional man found it unnecessary to discuss his future wife's career plans, for she had already made abundantly clear just where her main allegiances lay. When asked whether or not he had discussed his wife's career before getting married, a professor (respondent 35-H) whose wife is also a professor replied, "No, on the contrary. It was quite clear that she was much more interested in a family than in being a career woman. This was quite clear. She enjoyed working, but it wasn't the most important thing in her life."

Many of the men whose responses fell in either the "Not at All" or the "Some" categories gave the impression that they had not felt it necessary to discuss their wives' career intentions either because the wives had already let them know in other ways that a serious career was not their main interest or because the couple had taken a let's-wait-and-see-what-happens approach toward the future. A male attorney (respondent 49-H) married to an attorney noted, "Well, we just assumed that she would [complete law school and practice her profession]. She said she wanted to, and it was all right with me, so she just took classes in law school as she could fit them into her schedule." This man's responses to other questions in the interview, however, made it quite clear that he also "just assumed" that his wife's career would definitely be secondary in importance to his own and that she would abandon her profession if it interfered to any great extent with the demands of her domestic duties.

Because a man is placed in the traditional category does not mean that he feels a woman's place is in the home *only*. It does mean that he sees the husband as the main provider and the wife as mainly in charge of what Parsons would call the "expressive" functions, but at the same time he may exhibit great pride in the fact that his wife is not "just a housewife." When asked about discussing his wife's career before marriage, an academic man married to a woman who is also a professor replied that they had discussed it and that he was well aware before they married of the fact that she did not enjoy housework. When asked how he felt about her desire for a career as well as marriage, he replied:

> It was all right with me. My mother worked, so I was never brought up with the idea that the woman belonged only in the home. She has a career she wants to follow, fine—let her follow it. And as I said, we have never had any conflict over it. I am very happy with her decision. I am very proud when we go out to a faculty party or anywhere else and my wife doesn't have to feel out of it. [46-H]

Neotraditional Responses

Neotraditional males seem much more likely than the traditional males to take their wives' careers seriously and perhaps for this reason seemed to express somewhat more concern over how the two careers would interrelate once they were married. While traditional husbands often regarded their wives' careers almost as avocations or hobbies (some of the wives in the traditional category actually used this term to describe their professional activities), neotraditional husbands realized the status and earning potential that professional involvement offered to women who seriously pursued such endeavors. A civil rights organization director (respondent 03-H) whose wife is an attorney stated, "My only concern was that she not go into medicine or dentistry where the monetary compensation would have been greater. I had no apprehension about her in law because she was dedicated to the idealistic conception of law and not to the law career."

But this husband also expressed very positive feelings about his wife's professional activities, thus indicating that even though he did not want her to make more than he did, he did view her working as a benefit to the marriage. His response to "How do you feel about your wife's employment?" was, "It's fine. If she is happy in her job, she is happier in the house—and then I am happier. She is a more interesting person for having been employed."

A professor whose wife is a professor also noted:

> My generation tends to be more willing to have a wife work and pursue a career than a generation five or ten years earlier was. My wife prefers to sit around and talk about literature with my colleagues rather than sitting and talking about knitting with their [nonworking] wives—and she has my support in this. We are quite convinced that my wife is happier, the children are happier, I am happier [when she works], and that, in general, this is the way of the future. This is the way things should be organized—it is our culture that is behind in not recognizing the kinds of things that women can do. [04-H]

While this neotraditional husband strongly supported his wife's professional involvement, it must be pointed out that he left no doubt regarding whose career was the primary one in this family. He had recently accepted a job offer at a large eastern university even though his wife had not received a parallel offer. He expected that she could "find a suitable position in a year or two."

Matriarchal Responses

Since only five cases fell in this category, it is difficult to say much about them except on a very tenuous basis. In all of the matriarchal cases the wife's performance or achievement was greater than her husband's on one or more variables. She either had a higher education, made more money, was more successful in her profession than he was in his, or represented a combination of these factors. Respondent 07-H, an attorney married to an attorney, noted that "we talked about her going to law school. I had decided that I was going, and before our marriage she decided she was going to go to law school too." One gains the impression from the interview that this was a unilateral decision on the part of the wife and that she would have gone to law school with or without her husband's approval.

A middle-aged assistant professor (respondent 25-H) whose wife is an associate professor realized at the time of marriage that his wife was quite involved in her career, but hoped things would change as time went on: "Yes, I knew that she would continue working and I hoped, then, that eventually she would quit. But things have developed into such proportions so that I don't know if this will be the outcome or not. The cost of living and other things. . . ." As this man's voice trailed off into unspoken hopes of things he realized would never be, he presented an image which could have fit the other four matriarchal cases equally as well as his own.

In fourteen of the families the wife could be said to have exceeded her husband's performance in one or more of the dimensions mentioned above.[3] However, it was only when her *income* was greater than his that the characteristics of the matriarchal family appeared. This is perhaps best illustrated by the case of a male high school graduate married to a very successful attorney (case #23). Even though the wife's busy practice brought her an annual income which was high in the five-figure range, the husband in this case was literally a self-made millionaire and was greatly admired by his better-educated wife for his rugged and ambitious "drive." Although the wife emphasized that she could "take care of herself" financially, the husband was regarded by both spouses as the head of the household. Such a case lends strong support to Parson's statement regarding the key role played by bread-winning in the male role constellation.

The Egalitarian Family

This couple (case #42), though unique in their life styles insofar as almost no sexual division of labor could be seen, does not seem to have exerted a great deal of effort to make things turn out as they have. They met and dated while both members of the pair were in graduate school, with marriage coming toward the end of their student careers. Throughout the husband's interview, he consistently answered questions in terms of "we," instead of the "I" and "she" division which most of our respondents made. He indicated that throughout their marriage one spouse would not take a job unless the other also received an offer—a decision which definitely places limits upon the academic careers of both persons. Both spouses reported that they would accept a solo job offer only under special circumstances, such as if one member of the team preferred to take a year or two off to write or do research.

It should be pointed out that the life style exhibited by this couple was one which the present researchers expected to be much more prevalent among dual-career couples, especially in the academic world. His teaching schedule was set up for Mondays, Wednesdays, and Fridays, while hers was set for Tuesdays, Thursdays, and Saturdays. Thus they seldom had need for a baby-sitter, and their child always had one or the other parent home to look after him. The life pattern of this couple may well become the family pattern of the future as more and more highly educated women marry and raise families—but it definitely is the deviant pattern in our sample.

Feelings About Marrying a Professional Woman

A fear which has long haunted young women in college is the thought that "nobody wants to marry a brainy girl" (Komarovsky 1946). Male respondents were asked how they felt about the prospect of marrying a woman who either already had or would have a profession of her own. Responses are shown in Table 4.

Table 4   Husband's Feelings About Marrying A Professionally Employed Woman

Family Type	Not Applicable	Definitely Wanted a Woman of This Type	Wanted Active Intellectual Companion, but Not Concerned about Her Practicing a Profession	Never Thought about It	Some Doubts	Serious Doubts
Traditional	4	6	5	2	1	2
Neotraditional	2	7	8	7	2	1
Matriarchal	1	0	1	3	0	0
Egalitarian	0	0	0	1	0	0
Total	7	13	14	13	3	3

For both the traditional and the neotraditional categories, men were more likely to report that they wanted to marry a woman who would either have a career of her own or be intellectually active and stimulating to them than they were to say that they harbored any doubts about having such a wife. An academic man whose wife is a physician reported:

> My sister is married to an obstetrician, so there have always been a lot of M.D.'s hanging around the house and there was no "magic" about medical doctors for me. I always wanted to marry someone who was interested in some particular discipline. I don't think I ever would have married someone who wanted to be just a housewife. This I knew way, way early, and this is probably one of the reasons I never went with anybody in high school. I never had a date then. My sister and my mother were always worried about me because I never dated, and when I went to college I worked and didn't have time, so I never dated then either. I dated some in the army, but I never got very interested because I knew I wanted someone who had a career, and this career thing was apparently something I recognized way early, back in high school. When I met my wife, she was in the psychology department and I was in the psychology department, and it just seemed a worthwhile thing to follow up on. When she went to medical school, it didn't make much difference to me. She could have gone to medical school or stayed in the psychology department—she still had a career orientation. [52-H]

An attorney married to an attorney stated:

> I was thrilled by the prospect of marrying someone who would also
> have a career. I believe in education, so I was very glad. I don't take
> that narrow view that a woman belongs in the home. I think it is
> healthy for our society if women are competitive—maybe someday
> we will have a woman President. I wouldn't want to be married to
> some conniving woman who is trying to get ahead no matter what—
> but I don't like these kinds of men either. [24-H]

A physician married to a physician noted:

> I really wasn't afraid of marrying a woman physician at all. Really
> not. First of all, I found my wife to be a very intelligent, smart, at-
> tractive person. I never thought otherwise. I am not really sure that
> I would want to live with someone who would be inferior to me. I
> found the commonality of interests to be an asset even to the present
> time. So the thought that there might be anything really negative
> about such a marriage didn't enter my head. I think there is another
> very important factor—we were married in 1942. I was thirty-six
> years old at that time; my wife was thirty-three. It was a marriage
> of mature individuals. I think that this makes a tremendous differ-
> ence. I think that this helped to make for a very good marriage. I
> will say that we are both very grown-up people—I can say this of
> her and I hope she can say this of me. So that when there have been
> any problems—and there have been almost none—we have been
> able to resolve them without any fighting. [45-H]

This respondent pointed out the important fact that, for the most part,
the members of this sample married at an age considerably above the national
average. Thirty-six of the fifty-three men interviewed either had completed
their graduate or professional training or were near completion at the time
of their marriage. Given the fact that satisfactory performance of the breadwinner role has a powerful influence on the male's self-image, the male who
is well on his way to entering, or who has already entered, a relatively
high-paying professional or occupational career is less likely to see his wife's
profession as posing any real threat to his own image. This interpretation is
supported by the response of a younger physician, whose wife is also a
physician:

> For a long time I was dead set against marrying a female doctor.
> But after a while I began to ask myself why I was so set against
> it. I think it was a definite underlying fear of competition. But also
> I always tried rationalizing, saying, "Well, a woman can't be a
> doctor—she can't be a doctor and a mother at the same time." But
> that was the layman's view of what medicine was like. I quickly
> learned that there were many facets to medicine and that it could
> be combined with a family. [10-H]

Once this young doctor learned more about the nature of medicine and
decided that a woman did not necessarily have to make an "either-or" choice
between practicing her profession and running the home, his objections
melted away. It should be noted, however, that he followed the pattern pointed
out among traditional males earlier: he established early in the courtship that

motherhood was to be his wife's *first* concern. Her interest in medicine was to come second in case of any conflict. No conflict seems to have arisen, mainly because the wife shares his idea of priorities completely.

Finally, an associate professor married to a female assistant professor seems to have summed up the feelings expressed by many of the traditional and neotraditional males when he responded in these words to the question regarding his feelings about marrying a career woman:

> I don't think I ever thought about it very seriously, but I think I *probably* preferred it. I find the nonworking wives of many of my colleagues . . . dull . . . [chuckle] . . . frankly. It seems to me that for a girl like my wife, with her kinds of interests, from my point of view it is preferable that she work. I didn't think very seriously about this at the time that we were married, but now I'm quite certain I'm right about it. [06-H]

Men who fell in the matriarchal category also do not seem to have been intimidated by the idea that their future wives would have careers. Their main regret instead seems to be that their wives have outearned them, rather than that they have not remained by the hearth. An assistant professor whose wife is an associate professor stated:

> I had no reservations at all about marrying a professional woman. I've always had a great deal of respect for her working. And I knew her family and knew her very well after having worked with her on our previous jobs—I knew she was a very good person. It seemed all right with me, because most of the fellows I've known have had wives who have been teachers, or public service workers, or something like that, so I had no qualms about it. [25-H]

This response suggests that the fact that most of the men interviewed were quite willing to accept their wives' professional activities, at least up to a certain point, can be explained also on the ground that they tend to associate mainly with other working-wife couples. Rapoport and Rapoport (1969) found this to be the case in their study of dual-profession couples in London, but the data of this study do not support such a conclusion. When asked to describe their closest friends, the respondents indicated no such clear-cut patterns.

The husband of the one egalitarian couple in the sample seemed just to accept his wife's career as matter-of-factly as he accepted her hair color. When asked whether he was concerned about marrying a professional woman, he replied:

> No, I suppose I just assumed she would have a career. And I think we've been together more than most of the couples I know. We see each other at the office as well as at home, and of course in this profession [academia] you don't have that much time that you are committed to be somewhere specific. In this way I see her far more than if she were a lawyer, for example, and I were a teacher. [42-H]

Thus on at least two counts, discussion of the wife's career before marriage and the husband's own subjective feelings regarding the prospects of marrying a woman who already was or who would be professionally employed, the majority of the men expressed few of the doubts and fears which American males supposedly possess regarding the "professional woman."

Husband's Present Feelings About Wife's Career

It will be noted that both questions about discussion of the wife's career before marriage and the husband's own feelings before marriage require the respondent to reach back into time for the answers, to remember how he felt prior to his marriage—a reach which in some instances exceeded thirty years for the men interviewed. A physician (respondent 36-H) aptly summed up the dangers of such questions when he noted, "As time goes on and you get older these things take on the coloration that you want them to have. They begin to look the way you wish they had been, rather than the way they actually were."

The men were, therefore, questioned regarding their present feelings toward their wives' professions. Deutscher (1966) has pointed out that what people say and what they actually do may not be one and the same; an attempt was made to avoid this danger, which faces all social research based on interview data, by looking at various parts of the respondent's interview transcription before placing him in a given category. Thus, if a respondent reported that he was all in favor of his wife's professional activities and that he supported her all the way in every way he could, we noted the degree to which he helped with the housework and the extent to which he shared in the caring for the children was noted before he was placed in the "Unconditional and Active Support" category.

Husbands' present feelings about their wives' professional involvements are indicated in Table 5.

Table 5   Husband's Present Feelings About His Wife Practicing Her Profession

Family Type	Unconditional and Active Support	Unconditional but Inactive Support	Conditional Support	Resigned	Actively Discouraged Her
Traditional	4	3	13	0	0
Neotraditional	11	5	7	3	1
Matriarchal	1	0	1	3	0
Egalitarian	1	0	0	0	0
Totals	17	8	21	6	1

Traditional Responses

Traditional husbands were most likely to fall in the "Conditional Support" category—that is, they supported their wives' professional activities upon the condition that the wives place home and family first on their lists of priorities.

A very successful physician whose wife is an attorney employed by a law firm responded as follows when asked how he would feel if his wife were to expand her professional duties:

> Oh, I would be most unhappy. I would think that this was a confusion about the way a family is put together. I think we live in a society in which there is a sort of patriarchy as to who goes out and makes the bread. Conversely, I do believe that the American family is run on a sort of matriarchal principle in which Mama makes a great bulk of the decisions. I think it is very obvious—if the [wife's] career began to overshadow the home and began to infringe on my interests, I think I would be very resentful. [22-H]

While this man was quite proud of his wife's professional accomplishments, he left no doubt that he would withdraw his support if he felt her career was harming the children or if it were in some way hampering his own career. His statement is quite typical of the thirteen traditional men whose responses placed them in the "Conditional Support" category.

It is interesting to note that, of the four traditional men who fell in the "Unconditional and Active Support" category, three were older men—two with families in the empty nest stage and one who had never had children. The fourth was a younger academic man whose academic wife had made arrangements with neighbors and relatives to care for their preschool child for a large part of the time she was required to be out of the home. This man's great affection for their child seemed to prevent him from viewing the times he was required to care for her as any sort of burden—he seemed instead to welcome the escape from his work.

Neotraditional Responses

Neotraditional men were more likely to offer "Unconditional and Active Support" to their professional wives. An engineer (respondent 05-H) whose main work has been on space-launch vehicles noted that he shared to a very large extent in the raising of their three children to enable his wife to pursue her professional interest (his wife's interview substantiated this claim); he stated that he felt no competition from his wife because her field (psychology) is so different from his, but he nevertheless regarded the home and children as primarily *her* responsibility. When asked about organizations pertaining to the children to which the couple belonged, he replied, "We probably belong to the PTA, or did. We attended PTA meetings at ——— school, or I think we did. My wife takes care of that sort of thing."

While the neotraditional men saw their wives' careers as second in importance to their wives' domestic roles, they nevertheless gave strong evidence of positive attitudes toward their wives' work. A clinical psychologist whose wife is a medical doctor stated:

> I think that frankly if you are going to marry a bright woman, you had better realize that it is advantageous for her to have a job. If you want some degree of contentment in your home, you have to be aware that she will not be content washing walls and cleaning refrigerators. [48-H]

A civic administrator married to a woman physician explained:

> I want her to work. I don't think that a woman should be saddled with the chores of home and family exclusively. I think this is the point at which my mother really lost out. She stopped teaching as soon as she married my father; now she's in a position where she doesn't feel competent enough to do anything. She doesn't want to go back to teach, and yet she has no kids around the house and she feels somewhat irrelevant. I don't ever want my wife to get into that boat. I don't worry about the fact that she ever will. [50-H]

These husbands seem able to offer full support to their wives' professional activities because (1) they feel the wives' professions make them more interesting, enjoyable marriage partners; (2) they have defined the dual-profession situation as one characterized by a sharing of intellectually stimulating interests, rather than as one characterized by competition; (3) they feel the wives have adequately integrated their professional duties into their domestic ones without causing any disruption in the household or harm to the children; and (4) they feel that the wives' lists of priorities place home, children, and husbands' careers above their own careers. As a professor (respondent 41-H) married to a professor noted when asked if his wife had ever had to make a choice between home and career responsibilities, "Oh, yes. And in such cases she chooses the home. For example, if the baby is sick and she has to teach a class, she will cancel the class."

Matriarchal Responses

Matriarchal husbands—those whose wives had a substantially higher income—were more likely to be resigned to their wives' careers and to feel a sense of competition. An attorney whose unsuccessful practice has forced his attorney-wife to maintain her profession (against her will) noted:

> I could always take another lawyer "second-guessing" me better than my wife. That sort of thing may happen in a marital relationship when both partners are in the same vocation when they have occasion to discuss professional matters. You find that the two relationships [marital and professional] sometimes overlap. You start discussing something with your wife as a lawyer and naturally the discussion may become somewhat animated, and before you know it you are talking to her more as a wife than as a lawyer, and by the same token she may start talking to you more as a husband than as a lawyer, so sometimes you are not able to maintain the kind of relationship necessary to discuss legal matters. We practiced together for a while. We had our own law office, so we had opportunity to discuss legal matters. I would approach her the same way I would approach another lawyer. It wound up as husband-wife, rather than as lawyer-lawyer. [07-H]

While this man had trouble keeping the marital and the professional roles separate, men in the traditional and neotraditional categories reported few such difficulties. The relationship with the greatest conflict-producing potential in the sample was probably that between the doctor and his neuropathologistwife, who was in charge of performing autopsies on patients who had died in spite of her husband's best efforts to save them. This husband reported no feelings of competition or conflict and instead regarded the autopsy sessions as a valuable learning experience. The difference between this case and case #07 (the attorney married to an attorney, referred to in the preceding paragraph) may be partially due to the fact that the physician-husband is extremely successful in his own right, with over 120 published articles in his field.

Egalitarian Responses

The husband in the one egalitarian couple did not give primacy to the career of either spouse. Their careers were for them as much a natural part of their lives as eating or breathing. When asked if he regarded their child as primarily his wife's responsibility, he replied:

> No, we've never distinguished in any way. The kid was even bottle fed. I've probably done more child care than she has, from newborn on. The first night he was home he cried and she woke up. The next day she gave me a long lecture on maternal instinct, and she never woke up when he cried again. So much for that! [42-H]

Conclusion

The idea that the American male will automatically resent having a wife who is practicing a high-status profession and that he will, by definition, be emasculated and dominated by her does not seem to be supported by the empirical evidence collected in this study. Twenty of the fifty-three men sampled saw themselves as undisputed heads of their households, as did their wives. These traditional men valued their wives' professional interests and supported their professional activities to varying degrees. Another twenty-seven of the men (the neotraditionals) saw their wives' professions as being of significant importance whenever decisions were to be made (whether to take a position in another city, accept a promotion which would involve greater time demands, etc.). The one factor which seems to have a negative effect on the quality of marital life is money, when the wife makes more money than the husband. The wife's status as a professional does not, by itself, seem to affect the structure of the family significantly. Even in those cases where the wife is a physician and the husband is not, few problems were observed— probably because in all such cases the husband was extremely successful financially and both spouses regarded his career as the primary one in the family. It should also be noted that in *no* instance did any of the wives desire to be more successful than their husbands. Thus it seems even though the structure of our society may be slowly changing, in that career opportunities are opening up for married women in many areas that had heretofore been closed to them, the cultural norms of the society are changing ever so much more slowly. The sample included men and women in their twenties as well as those beyond the age of sixty—yet little difference which could be attributed to age was found in the responses.

Far from being threatened by their wives' professions, the great majority of the husbands sampled defined their wives' careers in positive terms. Among the benefits of the dual-career family, the most frequently cited was that the wife's professional involvement made her a happier and more interesting marriage partner. Also brought out by many of the extremely busy men (a number of whom averaged a seventy- to eighty-hour work week) was the fact that the wife's profession kept her busy and "out of his hair," thus freeing the husband to devote more of his energy to his own demanding career. A third benefit suggested by a number of the men is that, in many ways, the wife's career functions as an extension of the husband's own interests. Thus, if we are to accept Blood and Wolfe's idea that "a resource may be defined as anything that one partner may make available to the other, helping the latter satisfy his needs or attain his goals" (1960, pp 12–13), we may say that the husband possibly welcomes this added diversification of interests as just such a "resource" and does not necessarily see it as any form of threat to his masculinity.

Among the main negative features of the dual-career family pointed out by these men were (1) both members of the pair are often too physically tired at the end of a busy week to partake of many of the leisure-time activities they enjoy; and (2) there is never enough time to do as many things as they would like to do. Neither of these complaints seems connected in any way with feelings of inadequacy on the part of the husband.

While the sample cannot claim to be representative of all men married to professional women, and is certainly not representative of American men generally, the study nonetheless implies, to some extent, a refutation of certain notions concerning employed women (particularly those with high-status jobs) and their husbands. It would seem that much more empirical research is needed before American husbands of working wives are summarily relegated to the back wards reserved for the neurotically insecure.

Notes

1. For description of the research design, see the previous article by Margaret M. Poloma, "Role Conflict and the Married Professional Woman."
2. Numbers given in parentheses following direct quotations indicate the case number from which the quotation is taken. "H" indicates husband's response.
3. Cases of female excellence have been treated by Poloma (1970, pp. 15–20).

References

BENSON, LEONARD. *Fatherhood: A Sociological Perspective*. New York: Random House, 1968.

BLOOD, ROBERT O., and WOLFE, DONALD M. *Husbands and Wives*. Glencoe, Ill.: The Free Press, 1960.

BOTT, ELIZABETH. *Family and Social Network*. London: Tavistock Publications, 1957.

BRENTON, MYRON. *The American Male*. Greenwich, Conn.: Fawcett Publications, 1966.

BURGESS, ERNEST W.; LOCKE, HARVEY J.; and THOMES, MARY MARGARET. *The Family: From Institution to Companionship*. 3rd ed. New York: American Book Co., 1963.

DEUTSCHER, IRWIN. "Words and Deeds: Social Science and Social Policy." *Social Problems* 13 (Winter 1966):235–254.

DURKHEIM, EMILE. *The Division of Labor in Society*. Translated by George Simpson. New York: Free Press, 1933.

EPSTEIN, CYNTHIA F. "Women and Professional Careers: The Case of the Woman Lawyer." Ph.D. dissertation, Columbia University, 1968.

―――. "Encountering the Male Establishment: Sex-Status Limits on Women's Careers in the Professions." *American Journal of Sociology* 75 (May 1970):965–982.

FRAZIER, E. FRANKLIN. *The Negro Family in the United States*. Chicago: University of Chicago Press, 1939.

FRIEDAN, BETTY. *The Feminine Mystique*. New York: Dell Publishing Co., 1963.

GANS, HERBERT. *The Urban Villagers*. New York: Free Press, 1962.

GINZBERG, ELI. *Life Styles of Educated Women*. New York: Columbia University Press, 1966.

HACKER, HELEN MAYER. "The New Burdens of Masculinity." *Marriage and Family Living* 19 (1957):227–233.

HOFFMAN, LOIS W. "Effect of the Employment of Mothers on Parental Power Relations and the Division of Household Tasks." *Marriage and Family Living* 22 (February 1960), pp. 27–35.

KENDALL, ELAINE. *The Upper Hand*. Boston: Little, Brown & Co., 1965.

KOMAROVSKY, MIRRA. "Cultural Contradictions and Sex Roles." *American Journal of Sociology* 52 (1946):184–190.

LeMASTERS, E. E. *Parents in Modern America*. Homewood, Ill.: The Dorsey Press, 1970.

MILLER, DANIEL R., and SWANSON, GUY E. *The Changing American Parent*. New York: John Wiley & Sons, 1958.

MYRDAL, ALVA, and KLEIN, VIOLA. *Women's Two Roles: Home and Work*. London: Routledge and Kegan Paul, 1956.

NYE, F. IVAN, and HOFFMAN, LOIS W. *The Employed Mother in America*. New York: Rand McNally & Co., 1963.

POLOMA, MARGARET M. "The Married Professional Woman: An Empirical Examination of Three Myths." Ph.D. dissertation, Case Western Reserve University, 1970.

RAINWATER, LEE. *Family Design: Marital Sexuality, Family Size, and Contraception*. Chicago: Aldine, 1965.

RAPOPORT, RHONA, and RAPOPORT, ROBERT N. "The Dual-Career Family: A Variant Pattern and Social Change." *Human Relations* 22 (February 1969):3–30.

RODMAN, HYMAN. *Marriage, Family and Society: A Reader*. New York: Random House, 1965.

ROSSI, ALICE S. "Equality Between the Sexes: An Immodest Proposal." In *The Woman in America*, edited by Robert J. Lifton. Boston: Beacon Press, 1964.

SAFILIOS-ROTHSCHILD, CONSTANTINA. "Marital Expectations and Marital Experience: Why Such a Discrepancy?" Paper read at the ICOFA meetings, April 3–7, 1969, in Rennes, France.

SIMON, RITA JAMES. "The Woman Ph.D.: A Recent Profile." *Social Problems* 15 (1967):221–236.

SMUTS, R. W. *Women and Work in America*. New York: Columbia University Press, 1959.

USEEM, RUTH HILL. "Changing Cultural Concepts in Women's Lives." *Journal of the National Association of Women Deans and Counselors* 24 (1960).

RHONA RAPOPORT and ROBERT N. RAPOPORT

The Dual-Career Family:
A Variant Pattern and Social Change*

Families in which both husband and wife pursue careers (i.e., jobs which are highly salient personally, have a developmental sequence, and require a high degree of commitment) and at the same time establish a family life with at least one child concern us in this investigation. This is part of a larger interest in the relationship between work and family life (Rapoport and Rapoport 1966) and a specific interest in factors affecting highly qualified women's participation in the world of work (Fogarty, Rapoport, and Rapoport 1967).

Massive changes are under way as contemporary society enters the post-industrial era. These changes affect the patterning both of work and of family life. The dual-career family is instructive to study in relation to these changes because while this is a variant pattern now, it may become more prevalent given current trends. Assuming that postindustrial society emerges structurally as a presence based on advanced technology, it is likely to be followed by a variety of consequent structural and value shifts. At work, the new values are likely to emphasize self-expression, personal development, and rewarding inter-personal relationships in place of individual achievement and the capacity to endure distress while continuing to perform competitively as an individual. In the face of rapid social change, individuals may be expected increasingly to pursue serial careers and to be required to readapt to new situations continuously throughout the life cycle. The preindustrial emphasis on kinship as a fundamental social institution in the area of family life gave way in industrial society to an increased emphasis on the nuclear family and sharp sex-role differentiation between men and women. In postindustrial society, however, the emphasis is increasingly on partnership in family life: equality between husband and wife, joint activities and collaboration in decision-making so as to maximize the possibilities of each member of the family sharing the benefits of participation external to the family—leisure, political, educational, as well as occupational. Thus external relationships of the postindustrial family are

* The research on which this paper is based has been sponsored by the Leverhulme Trust in a grant to Political and Economic Planning (P.E.P.). We have collaborated in this research. For a preliminary statement on the research, see Fogarty, Rapoport, and Rapoport (1967). We are grateful to the following people who have participated with us in the part of the research with which we have been concerned: Janet Philps, William and Elizabeth Collins, David Armstrong, Stephanie White, Andrew Bebbington, and Gerhardt Christiansen.

The couples in the study must remain anonymous so cannot be thanked except generally. In addition to the insights derived from the research, we have benefited from discussion with many of our professional colleagues—particularly Nora and Anthony Lewison, and Peter and Phyllis Willmott.

likely to be more diverse. Aspects of these points have also been argued by Bell (1967), Goode (1963), Trist (1968), and Willmott (1968).

The dual-career family, though a tiny minority in contemporary society, expresses both in structure and in value one variant that may be expected to emerge in the postindustrial society which is in the making. The value systems of contemporary society are incompletely evolved to support social structural changes of the kind under examination. Indeed, as Trist (*op. cit.*) points out, there is not only cultural lag but strong resistance to value changes even though the old values are maladaptive to the new structural requirements. The dual-career families illustrate this in the pattern of strain they encounter at the present point in the change process. These strains are not intrinsic to the phenomenon of the dual-career family, but [apparent] in the relationship between this phenomenon and its present social context. Given this, an analysis of strains may be useful for indicating short-term social change processes. Planning implications are touched upon briefly.

The Increase in Married Women at Work

Following the Industrial Revolution in Western countries there was a radical separation of work and family spheres (Weber 1947). This was accomplished partly in the interests of fiscal accounting [as] important for the enterprises of the emergent capitalist society and partly to minimize particularistic bases for employment so that competiveness could be maximized. The net effect of this pulling apart of work and family has been to consolidate the world of work under the control of men and the world of home and child-care under women. The attitude of many people toward married women working in Victorian England is expressed by Tennyson in "the Princess":

> Man for the field and woman for the hearth:
> Man for the sword and for the needle she:
> Man with the head and woman with the heart:
> Man to command and woman to obey;
> All else confusion.

Both in Western and Eastern European countries sex roles are becoming somewhat more egalitarian. In both groups of countries, for somewhat different reasons, there has been an increase, following World War II, of married women in the labor force (ILO 1958, Hunt 1968, Wrochno 1966). This has been accompanied by the trend toward a higher proportion of women marrying, younger marriage, and compression of fertility into a narrower band in the life cycle. Consequently there has been a tendency for married women to reenter the labor force while still relatively young and vigorous.

While the proportions of married women working have risen, women's ascent into higher-status positions and occupations has lagged behind the general trend (Jefferys and Elliott 1966, Sommerkorn 1966, Fogarty, Rapoport and Rapoport, *op. cit*). Women still tend to favor occupations which are traditionally sex-typed as "feminine" (the arts, nursing, teaching), entry into or advancement in the business, industrial, and science worlds requiring a considerable "pioneering" orientation (Robbins 1962, Rossi 1964, Baude and Holmberg 1967).

Many reasons have been put forward in explanation for women not rising to the top occupationally in great numbers. Polemical single-factor arguments (e.g., economic exploitation by men or men's vested psycho-biological interests in domination) have given way to a more complex analytic framework. Myrdal and Klein (1956) and Wrochno (*op. cit.*) stress role conflicts and incompatibilities between expectations placed on women in the two spheres of work and family. Alice Rossi (1964, 1968a) depicts the interplay between psychological and socio-cultural factors at different stages of the life cycle to produce the observed behavior.

At the point of graduation from university in Britain the differences between the level of men's and women's aspirations are clear. In our survey of 1967 graduates, we found that while about a quarter of the men indicated that their ambition was to "get to the top" in their line of work, only 5 percent of the women indicated this level of aspiration. Another 45 percent of the men aspired to hold high positions, as compared with only 30 percent of their fellow graduates of the opposite sex. These differences become much more marked over time, as our survey of "eight-year out" graduates shows. Women tend to shift their levels of aspiration downward as they encounter difficulties in trying to pursue careers and family life at the same time, while these experiences act in the reverse for men.[1]

Furthermore our data indicate that men's ambitions tend to be channeled into specific fields of work and toward success in a material and public recognition sense, while women's are more diffuse and oriented to service or personally meaningful and aesthetic goals. Some data for the U.S.A. show similar patterns (Turner 1964, Rossi 1968).

Changes in Family Structures

While more married women have been entering the labor force, there have been concomitant changes in the organization of the family. Looking at the structure of families in relation to their environments, some social scientists have emphasized the isolation of the nuclear family as an adaptive response to the necessity for increased mobility in industrial society and the increased differentiation of interests and involvements of members of the ascriptive kin group (Parsons 1943). Parallel to the same broad cultural trends manifested in the educational experiences of boys and girls there has been a trend toward the more democratic or "companionship" type of family life. This has been evident both in the husband-wife relationship and in the child-rearing patterns of the modern family, where there has been a trend away from authoritarian bases for organizing all of the family role relationships.

The process of change in the direction outlined has been uneven. Many writers have marked out residual extended functions, i.e., as reference groups (Litwak 1960), mutual support groups in financial and other crises (C. Bell, *op. cit.*), and local community functions reminiscent of more folklike situations (Young and Wilmott 1957, Mogey 1963, Fried 1963, Gans 1965).

Obviously the structural and cultural dimensions of the change process in marital role relationships are interlaced. Recent British studies show an increase in "joint" participation in the family division of labor as families move from relatively well integrated, urban, working-class neighborhoods to new, individualistic housing developments in suburbia or other urban districts. Bott (1957), for example, stresses the structural interpretation, indicating how, when individuals are freed from the constraints of the more tightly knit community with its traditionally defined sex-typed patterns of expectation and behavior, new patterns of sharing between husband and wife may emerge. Young and Willmott (*op. cit.*) and Mogey (*op. cit.*) tend to place more emphasis on the importance of historical and class-cultural factors which differentiate life in the new communities from that in the old. Willmott points out that the change, toward a partnership type of family structure, does not follow the simple paradigm of dissemination of changes downward through the class system from the upper to the lower classes. Some "successful" middle-class families show less partnership than do some working-class families (Willmott, *op. cit.*).

To summarize, recent social changes have brought about a change of traditional kin-centered, locality-based social networks; various substitutions have replaced or developed alongside the traditional pattern. In some situations, there has been a superficial continuation of the old pattern, in some it has been done away with; and, in still others, there have been substitutions of different patterns of the traditional close-knit extended family and friendship networks (Bott, *op. cit.*; Laumann 1968). The trend has been one of diversification. Similar diversification has occurred in the internal relationship of families. The old pattern of male authority and female subservience and a segregated division of labor has become increasingly untenable as equality of access to education and to the world of work has increased. However, this has not always led to partnership in the sense used here. The ideal of an egalitarian partnership is one that is increasingly held, but as Leach (1968) has pointed out, the gap between sentiment and reality remains great and is not easily bridged. Leach has indicated some of the sources of strain in juxtaposing an outdated traditional set of family norms to the complexities of contemporary life.[2] It is the purpose of this paper to fill out the picture somewhat and to indicate (on the basis of an intensive study of several dual-career families) some of the stresses and strains that are being experienced as well as some of the satisfactions enjoyed in experimenting with postindustrial social structures in the contemporary environment, which is for the most part still geared to the values of industrial society.

Stress and Social Change:
A Microsociological Approach

Some kinds of social change occur through interventions at a macroscopic level, some through changes of a diffuse kind at the microscopic levels of social organization. Some occur through self-conscious, deliberate, and purposeful goal-directed action, others through adaptive responses to dissatisfactions or strains intrinsic in the situation. The analysis reported here is a microsociological one though we are concerned with larger societal implications.

The essence of the *dual-career* family as a variety of the partnership family is that there is a division of labor in relation to family functions that is distributed between the partners on an equal-status basis. Thus (aside from pregnancy and childbirth) the division of functions in relation to household cleaning, shopping, child-care and discipline, supervision of domestic help, food preparation, and so on may be arranged according to the skills and inclinations present in the specific partnership. We do not accept the traditional view that this set of activities is and always has been "expressive" in nature and therefore feminine in role allocation. The argument that women have always performed the household activities and men the work activities is considered irrelevant. In technological innovation after all, new forms are continually emerging. The couples we studied did, in fact, tend to see themselves as partners in social innovation.[3]

In analyzing the ways in which our families have divided their activities and social network involvements, we concentrate on stresses or structural sources of strain. However, we are aware of the total situations within which the stresses occur. This includes positive as well as negative aspects. After all, these are families who have remained intact despite the stresses. A study of families which have succumbed to the strains might show additional or more severe stresses, or they might lack the supports present in the families studied. In every case, the overall patterns were evolved from choices which were made, often to avoid what may have been perceived by the couple as still more severe stresses. It is important to note that we do not assume that these stresses are peculiar to the dual-career family. Many of them may exist, perhaps in less poignant form, in single-career families. Such stresses may represent issues of our culture, and the dual-career family represents a particular context within which the specific dilemmas are played out. The controls we have been able to use (e.g., the "drop-out" families) are inadequate to provide definitive conclusions. Our impression, however, is that dual-career families show the patterns of stresses in particularly acute form; the ways in which they coped with them may represent future solutions for a larger proportion of the population. We see each of the families studied as engaging, in a sense, in a microscopic experiment with social change. They are working out patterns of living—together and in relation to their network of relationships—that are without clear precedent.

The study is based on thirteen functioning dual-career families and three in which the dual-career aspect was given up by the wife's breaking off her career, at least temporarily. People may drop out for various reasons and for differing amounts of time and effort at different points in their careers— men as well as women. In some situations special provisions are made for career interruptions by women which may obviate the need to "drop-out" in the sense of resigning from a position in an organization. In other situations "dropping out" may simply mean a slackening of the pace of activity or output, e.g., in the career of an artist or sculptress. We use the term *drop-out* to refer to an indefinite cessation of activity—whether from an organizational post or less formal position.

The sixteen families studied were interviewed by a pair of interviewers (one male, one female); the interviews were tape recorded and transcribed verbatim. The course of interviews, which served as the basis for a preliminary write-up, ordinarily consisted of one or two joint interviews (husband and wife together interviewed by the pair of interviewers) and one or two separate interviews with the husband and wife separately by individual interviewers. The validity of the case write-ups was checked to some extent by presenting a preliminary form of write-up to the couples for discussion. In this further interview—the "feedback interview"—corrections were made for gross omissions and distortions. Where there were differences of perceptions, either between the couple or between the couple and the interviewers, these were discussed so that a statement might be made that would encompass the different possibilities. Each interview was approximately three hours long. The couples were chosen to represent a range of occupations for the women; they had to be intact families with at least one child still living at home.[4]

The current discussion is preliminary and tentative. We remain close to the phenomenological level in reporting the stresses and the patterns of resolution to them. Our own propositions drawn from this limited data can then be treated with appropriate skepticism and the data used for other propositions, should this seem merited on further investigation.

Five foci of stress in the couples studied are indicated. They are neither exhaustive nor more than a preliminary grouping of complexes of stress as appreciated by ourselves in interaction with the couples studied. Subsequent analyses and further research will doubtless refine the list. We believe, however, that it encompasses major dimensions of stress and that it is useful at this point to state them descriptively. They are: overload dilemmas, personal norm dilemmas, dilemmas of identity, social network dilemmas, and role cycling dilemmas. In each area we shall discuss the sources of stress and the ways in which the couples have adapted to the ensuing strains.

Overload Dilemmas

The old folk-expression "behind every successful man there is a woman" stands not only for a social psychological situation where the wife gives emotional support, advice, etc., but also for a whole culture complex of activities and relationships within which the wife is a helpmate—attending to the shopping, child-rearing, housekeeping, and general social tasks necessary to provide a smoothly operating base to which the male can retreat after the rigors of a day's work and from which he can sally refreshed and emotionally supported. One of the couples studied began the interview by reversing the expression, stating that "behind every successful woman there is a man." What they meant by this, however, was that the man encouraged his wife to face and cope with problems arising in her work, provided consultation on financial matters, and cooperated in various ways. They did *not* mean to indicate that the husband gave the same sort of backing—through shopping, mending, cooking, child-minding, and so on—that would be the obverse of the traditional picture.

In fact, when only the man is following a career, it is possible for his wife to provide the domestic "back-up," but when there is a dual-career family it is not usually possible for the man to provide this kind of total reversal of the traditional roles (though role reversals are by no means nonexistent). The most usual situation among our couples where both husband and wife pursue a career is a rearrangement of the domestic side of their lives. Some of the household tasks are delegated to others, part is reapportioned between husband and wife and children. In effect, each member pursues a career and performs some household and child-rearing activities. Among the couples we studied, the overload experienced seems to have been a function of at least four factors.

1. *The degree to which having children and a family life (as distinct from simply being married) is salient.* With the exception of one of the couples studied, family life in general and children in particular were highly salient. The couples were very concerned with the possible effects on their children of their both pursuing careers. This implied a limitation in the degree to which the couples were willing to delegate child-care, even assuming the availability of satisfactory resources. Aside from the sheer number of things to be done by the conjugal pair who are both working and at the same time value interaction with their families, there is an element of psychic strain involved in allowing two major areas of life, so different in their demands and characteristics, to be highly important. The overload, then, is not a simple arithmetical one of increased number of tasks to be accomplished, but one far more difficult to assess, which is related to the duality of emotional commitment and concern.[5]

2. *The degree to which the couple aspire to a high standard of domestic living.* Most of the couples aspired to a high-standard, pleasant home and garden, high standards of decor, cleanliness, cooking, and so on. This made the problem of management of the domestic side of their lives more complex, albeit by choice, than if they had kept to a lower standard. The notion of a lower standard materially, though, is almost a contradiction in terms to the notion of career success, for a certain standard of life is implied in occupational achievement; the process tends to become circular, in that once having acquired a taste for the high standards, the impetus to continue working and career development is increased.

3. *The degree to which satisfactory arrangements for the reapportionment of tasks is possible.* Here we found various combinations of conjugal role reorganization and delegations of parts of the domestic work to children and helpers of various kinds.

4. *The degree to which the sheer physical overload of tasks and their apportionment is adumbrated by a social-psychological overload.* These [stresses] arise from struggling with the following conflicts: normative conflict, sex role identity maintenance, network management, and role-cycling. Couples vary enormously in the degree to which these other sources of tension feed into the family system and [in] the degree to which they can manage them once present.

For all the couples the overload issue was salient; they all emphasized the importance of physical health and energy as a prerequisite for making the dual-career family a possibility. They regarded it as important for their children to be healthy too. Generally speaking, there was little room for illness in the systems that were evolved.

To deal with the overload issues, all of the dual-career families studied spent much thought and effort on arranging a system of domestic help. This problem can be seen as having two sides to it—the availability of different kinds of domestic helpers on the one hand, and the preferences of the couples as to which elements of the domestic role they wish to delegate.

Our survey data indicate that at a point [sometime] after graduation, domestic role tasks become differentiated into different types. Graduate women become aware that they would like to delegate the activities which are impersonal—the washing, cleaning, ironing, etc., tasks which can absorb a great deal of time, particularly in households with a high standard of living.[6] They tend to wish to retain the more people-oriented activities, particularly in relation to child-care and feeding. Among the couples studied intensively, the delegation of the less desirable aspects of domestic labor was both the expected and the observed tendency. Given the low value placed on domestic work as an occupation in our society, the dual-career couples have all had to devote considerable energy to improvising viable arrangements. A wide range of domestic help arrangements is found: short term and long term; full-time and part-time; live-in and live-out; nannies, *au pairs*, dailies, students, secretaries-doubling-as-baby-sitters, domestic help couples with husband and wife dividing up the domestic part of the employing couple's household affairs, unmarried mothers and their babies taking over part of the premises, and so on. Most of the couples used at least a duplex system; often they would shift from one type of a system to another following a major transition like having a child, having the last child enter school, etc. Sometimes the shift was associated with a difficult experience with the prior system; sometimes it was based on the couples' conception of a better arrangement for the particular stage, e.g., the dropping of a nannie and the taking on of an *au pair* instead as the infant reaches school age. Simple as the tasks of household maintenance may be, the difficulties in obtaining reliable personnel to whom to delegate them is so great in contemporary British and American society as to call for all sorts of perquisites. In the couples studied, domestic helpers were not only offered the usual salary and private room arrangements (often with TV) but in addition were sometimes given the use of one of the family cars and in one case a specially built flat. Few of the couples studied used their parents in a major way, though many used them occasionally to look after children while they were away, say for a conference or a long weekend.

As indicated above, the area of child-care presents special problems. While most of our couples valued interaction with their children and felt that their children's welfare and development were of primary importance, they had to delegate at least part of the child-care to pursue their careers. Precisely because the children were so important to them, the issue of how to arrange child-care contributed heavily to the overload picture for these couples. As many of them put it, if the house got dirty it was unfortunate but could be ultimately remedied and anyway was not crucial. However, serious lapses in relation to the children's care simply could not be allowed to occur. Most of the families were aware of and concerned with modern conceptions of child development and the importance of parental involvement in it. As one couple put it: "We are all victims of our culture in the Spockian age" (i.e., this child-centered age). While compromises could and often were made in the domestic care areas, none of the couples were willing self-consciously to adopt a policy which would have meant possible harm to their children's physical or psychological development. It was not possible within the scope of the study to assess the effects of the dual-career couples' child-rearing practices on their children. However, in detailed interviews it was striking how low the level of reported disturbance appeared to be.[7] Although the couples were quite aware of potential negative effects, they also pointed to some of the positive effects of their pattern of life. Thus, their pattern was seen as possibly fostering independence and responsibility, e.g., in getting children to help with household chores; redistributing domestic roles resulted in fathers spending more time with their children; providing a student companion for the children was seen as useful in giving them someone to "talk nonsense" with—something enjoyable to the children when their parents were away or preoccupied with work tasks; and so on. Most of the families interviewed had read or heard about the relevant research work and were concerned with the issue of whether or not a mother's working would constitute for the child a potentially harmful "maternal deprivation" situation.

The majority of the couples studied took precautions against placing complete reliance on any one helping figure, and they tended to monitor very carefully the interaction between children and domestic helpers. One mother described the degree to which she had to rely on help and how distaseful it was to a strong and independent-minded person to have to be made to feel dependent in this way: "I had no one, so I had to go from hand to mouth. I never knew, in fact, when I could make appointments ahead. It was such a strain that I got not ill but terribly upset, unable to cope, you know, and I put a high value on being able to cope. . . ."

The vulnerability of the woman, in particular, to malfunctioning in the domestic help area is expressed by Mrs. Y., who indicated that even when she is working or traveling, there is a "little corner of my mind somewhere that is thinking and worrying about the management of the children." Mr. Y., in contrast, reserves the comparable "little corners" in the back of his mind for forward planning of their work and the family's finances. The general tendency among the couples studied was to place high value on having children and developing a close relationship with them. Even in the rare instances where children were sent to boarding school, the reason for doing so (with one possible exception) was not to unload the care of the children onto an institution but rather because of tradition (father and grandfather had gone to that school) or the child's own wishes.

In general, most of the couples interviewed thought that the main consequence of their both working was that there was "very little slack left in the system." Several indicated that they were both "whacked" by the time they got home and that they had very little energy left over for extra activities, particularly on week-nights. The following quotes indicate the kinds of expression frequently used:

A husband: ". . . after a hard day in the office she is sometimes very spiky in the evening. . . ."

A wife, speaking of their situation, where her husband's job keeps him out days as a producer and her job keeps her out evenings as a performer:

> [talking of shared leisure] it's something that strongly has to struggle for existence, really. It's a matter of a night off every now and then and a weekend that we try and organize every few weeks to try and keep something apart from our work. . . . We'd like to have more time off when we can see one another, but what happens is that when I'm off he might be on and it creates a sort of tension. . . .

While leisure activities tend to be sacrificed first under the impact of overload, the repercussions may spill over into the work lives of one or both of the partners, and couples vary in the degree to which they protect this as a higher priority than other areas, like activities with the children, or the reverse. Mr. S. illustrates part of this pattern of spillover into work (in discussing how he concerns himself with his wife's business problems):

> one takes up time during the day thinking over these problems instead of perhaps dining with someone one ought to dine with for one's own business career . . . or, one comes home to commiserate, to work out a problem, or even to have a quiet evening, and one can't because the wife is really worn out and exhausted and can't cope with it. . . .

Thus, the overload issue seems to arise acutely as a stress when both members pursue careers. The strains are felt, first, in relation to leisure and recreational activities, which are often sacrificed very early; second, in relation to the children and the degree and quality of relationships with them *or* in relation to one's work. Characteristic patterns of coping with these strains are:

1. Deliberately to "work" at leisure—to discipline oneself to take holidays, weekends in the country to "unwind," frequent trips away, etc. To conserve health and energy deliberately as a human resource.

2. To delegate as many as possible of the less desired domestic chores and to provide adequate care for child-rearing—"suitable mothering" influences and other relevant companionship as seen to be needed by the growing child. Strategies to provide the child with the best possible environments—home, school, etc.—consume major proportions of the time of the couples studied. Some of this is described in greater detail [in the following section].

3. To modify one's work involvement in such a way as to be compatible with the other partner's and to diminish the strain of "overspill," e.g., from an excessively complicated, demanding, or otherwise difficult work situation. If one travels or gets too deeply involved with complex relationships at work, it is likely to impinge more on the other's capacity to function at work. Thus, most of the couples made choices that attempted to avoid unnecessary involvements of this kind so as to optimize participation of both partners in work and family spheres. Some of this is described in detail [in the discussion of] conflicts in role cycling.

Dilemmas Arising from the Discrepancy Between Personal Norms and Social Norms

The women in the intensive case study reported here have found ways to continue their careers even after childbirth, stopping work only for a minimal period which did not interfere with their career development. In doing so they have had to deal with dilemmas arising from the clash between their personal norms (i.e., what they felt was right and proper behavior for themselves) and social norms (i.e., the norms they felt people around them held) (Bott, *op. cit.*).

These dilemmas arise, as indicated above, because of the fact that most women, even highly qualified ones, tend to drop their careers to fulfill traditional domestic roles even if this is accompanied by personal frustration (Gavron 1966). It is accepted as the right and proper thing to do by the majority of people in our society and supported from childbirth by a pervasive set of cultural symbols and manifestations: the importance attributed to "mothering" (assumed to be always by the biological mother except in abnormal cases), the sanctity of the home, and the housewife role, etc. The men and women in our study have deliberately adopted a variant pattern, extending the universalistic elements of their educational experience (i.e., where boys and girls were assumed to have similarly valuable potentials and were assumed equally to be able to realize them in work). For various reasons and under various circumstances they arrive at this pattern and the dilemma for them becomes resolved and dormant.

Under some circumstances, however, the dilemmas become reactivated. Three examples are given of instances which reactivate the normative dilemmas causing the variant norms to collide with the more traditional norms and requiring a resolution again. These examples are:

1. at critical transition points in the family life cycle (particularly birth of the first child)

2. at critical transition points in the career (or occupation) life cycle of *either* partner (role enlargement or contraction)

3. at critical events in the life space of the children (e.g., illness, school problems, etc.).

A critical point in the family life cycle that reactivates these dilemmas is the birth of the first child.[8] For example, when Mrs. O's baby was born, she had to overcome the feeling of distress when "well-meaning" neighbors who had got to know her better while she was at home during the final phase of pregnancy and expected her to remain at home following the birth of the baby made such remarks as: "Oh well, I suppose you won't mind when your baby doesn't recognize you as its mother." It took her some time to overcome the heightening of the conflict aroused by such remarks before she resumed her preferred pattern of pursuing both career and family interests.

These remarks are manifestations of a larger set of cultural norms related to child-rearing practices. Most of the couples studied experienced pressure from these norms. Mrs. O., a civil servant with a good social science degree, sums up how she resolved her dilemma as follows:[9]

> When I first went back to work [after having the baby] there were the women who quoted [a noted child-psychiatrist] to me, you know. I got so fed up with this man. I got all his books out before I went back permanently. Really it made me feel a criminal . . . but I came to the conclusion that he was taking for his children those who had been in institutions on the one hand and comparing them with the

kind of children who were in an ordinary mother's care . . . and it seemed to me to be such a long way off from what I was going to do. . . . I think a lot of mothers have gripped onto him to justify staying at home. I went to see a number of friends of mine who have combined both and whose children are, in the main, older and who have turned out into well-adjusted, independent, happy, thoroughly sort of normal children who seem to have a perfectly normal relationship with their parents, as far as one could judge. I was a bit unconvinced.

An example of how a critical transition in the occupational situation can reactivate this dilemma is seen with the S.'s. Mrs. S., a clothing designer, discussed how she had been thrown into conflict (which immediately became a family conflict) when an offer was received from a large fashion group of companies to take over her firm and promote her products in a really "big" way. Mrs. S. says that this conflict was exacerbated by its timing, coming at a period of her life (age about forty) when she was in any case reviewing her personal norms and values (Jaques 1965). She felt that before she would realize it, the children would have grown up and left home. In attempting to resolve this Mr. and Mrs. S. each played devil's advocate with the other. When Mr. S. was arguing in favor of maximizing familial values, he would say it was bad enough that the father could not spend more time at home with the children but to have mother away so much in addition was "terrible." Mrs. S. would counter this with how a more senior position would enable her to be more flexible with her work hours, have more assistance and how they would have more and better holidays and be able to remove financial worries about the children's future. Then, when she took the position that she should stay at home, spend more time with the children, pursue cultural interests, and so on, Mr. S. would argue that it would be doing something to her which they would both regret later as she had so much invested in her career and derived so much satisfaction out of it, etc. They indicated that this was a period of "brinkmanship" in which each pushed the other over the brink until they had worked their way through the feelings of both of them about a new resolution to the dilemma. The resolution finally adopted was one in which she agreed to the take-over but with a number of new perquisites allowing for more time with the family and contractual safeguards against her being drawn too deeply into the firm's business involvements.

There are several instances reported of events in the children's life space reactivating this dilemma. This may occur around a major focused crisis—e.g., the child's disturbance or poor performance at school. More usually it is aroused by small occurrences. Most of the working mothers cite the feelings aroused when they see other mothers wheeling their prams in the park, e.g., while they are at the office, but they tend to put down these feelings relatively easily, saying that probably many of these mothers would rather be going to work, or that they would soon be bored with doing only this every day. Occasionally, however, the dilemma is made more acute—e.g., when the child "uses" the fact that the mother works for "playing up" the mother's guilt (e.g., by saying that she prefers her granny's house, or the house of a nonworking mum of a school friend). In continuing their work, most of these dual-career family mothers emphasized the positive elements of the situation with which the children are reported by and large to have agreed (e.g., having a happier and more interesting mum; having a mum who designs things—in one case the child's school uniform; having a mum who is on TV; etc.).

Dilemmas of Identity

We are concerned here with dilemmas arising within the person about the very fundamental characteristics of the self—whether one is a "good" person, a "good" man or woman, and so on. This is at a deeper level and more internally generated than the conflicts arising over specific behavioral patterns, as in the discussion above on normative dilemmas. This set of dilemmas stems from the socio-cultural definitions of work and family as intrinsically masculine and feminine. The quintessence of masculinity is still, in our culture, centered on work and competing successfully in the "breadwinning" roles. The quintessence of femininity is still centered on the domestic scene. While these are some occupations which have come to be defined as acceptable for women—even preferably feminine—such as nursing, primary school teaching, and social work, these tend to be as temporary, part-time or for unmarried women. Conversely, where men enter these occupations it is probable that they encounter internal dilemmas of identity stemming from the same source of social stereotyping. In analyzing the dilemmas observed in this area, it is important to note that we consider these dilemmas to be a product of our contemporary socio-cultural situation. They would be different under different circumstances or at different points in the social process.[10]

Taking the specifically sexual component of the identity dilemmas—i.e., whether the individual feels himself to be a "good" or a "real" man or woman— there seem to be at least three levels at which the issues are discussed in the literature—the physical, the psychological, and the socio-cultural. Some observers seem to assume that confusion arising at one level will necessarily be reflected in confusion at other levels. Thus we were told by one psychiatric colleague at the outset of the research that men and women who cross sex lines socio-culturally (as have all of the women in our study to some extent) would be characterized by a psychological confusion of sexual identity as well. The assumption, furthermore, was that women who wanted to enter the male world of competition would be highly motivated by competitiveness with men and, as a consequence, would emasculate their husbands and there would tend to ensue a sex life characterized by impotence and frigidity. This would be enhanced by their tendency to choose mates who fit into their needs in this regard.

While we did not focus in the study on the sex lives of the couples in detail, the data that we have seem to indicate that while these stereotyped conceptions may be present in some cases (doubtless the types of cases most seen in clinical practices), this is not the universal picture by any means. Our impression of a "normal" range of types of sexual experience makes sense when one goes into greater detail about the actual patterns of motivation that seem to be present among these people and also their ways of coping with dilemmas and issues that arise in their relationships. We find that while competitiveness with men may be a prominent motive among some of the women, it is only one of many that seem important among the women studied. Most of these women are involved (to the extent that they are fighting battles in relation to this) in issues relating to financial security; the need to be creative (in ways that are difficult for them if [their lives are] focused on the household); and the desire to be effective as an individual person. However, while autonomy is a prominent part—financial, psychological, and otherwise—it is coupled with, rather than exclusive from, the wish to be interdependent with their husbands. The occupational world is used by all of our women as the area in which they develop their separate personal identities. This makes it possible for both husband and wife to relate as two individuals, *each* having a separate identity as a person. To the extent that each has a clear personal sexual identity associated with his physical make-up, the issues of physical relationships may even be enhanced in such a situation. But it would take a more focused and detailed study to investigate this.

What actually seems to happen in the couples studied is that they are able to go a certain way toward their ideal establishment of individual identities which are independent of socio-cultural definitions, but in each case indications of discomfort arise at a certain point. They seem to say, in effect: "This is as far as I go in experimenting with a new definition of sex roles without having it "spill over" into my own psychological sense of self-esteem and possibly my physical capacity to carry on in this relationship." This point represents a limit to which an individual's psychological defenses are felt to be effective, and in each of the couples studied one or more points seem to have evolved beyond which each knew it was dangerous to push the other. We have called these points identity "tension lines."

Manifestations of "tension lines" are as follows:

In the O. family, the matter of income is a crucial point. Mr. O. encourages his wife to pursue her career and to be successful and effective in her work, but the amount of her income relative to his is a point of some tension between them.

With the X.'s the central issue is authority. Mr. X. wanted his wife to follow her profession and to achieve the security that she wished in it; even welcomed her earning more than himself and stabilizing the family income so that he could get on with what he valued more highly, namely, creative designing work. However, he did not wish actually to have her in authority over jobs on which he himself was working.

Manifestations of the sex-identity "tension line" are sometimes seen in subtle, often unrecognized undercutting behavior by the husband toward the wife. This seems to be an indication of strain and a defensive manifestation, rather than the preferred mode as it occurs in couples where the husbands make such statements as:

> My wife has at least as good an education as I have; she earns as much as I do, I don't see any reason why we shouldn't regard ourselves as equal partners, and that is what we do. . . .
>
> We see our family as a collection of individuals, each with different skills and interests and as having evolved the capacity to live together.
>
> Our marriage is a form of partnership, and has to be understood in terms of the characteristics of partnerships. . . .

Clearly these are statements of fundamental ideals on which the dual-career family is based. In actually observed or reported interactions, when the tension point was approached, the men tended to undercut their wives. Examples of this were seen in the way some husbands cut across their wives in the interview situation, not allowing them to answer fully, as though to say, "I'm really better at this than you dear." One husband actually prefaced his interruptions with statements of that type. Another example was when a husband described his wife's business practices; he tended to make a bit of a joke of them, not expecting her to deal with her management role as "for real," as he did himself. He expressed surprise when a larger firm thought his wife's business worth a take-over bid but was reassured when they offered a ridiculously low sum. In another instance the husband indicated that he thought that his wife was basically unemployable except for his help. It must be emphasized, however, that these manifestations were subordinated to the more dominant aspect of their relationship, which was that the husband did in fact support, sponsor, encourage, and otherwise facilitate his wife's career. It is to be expected that there would be some "backwash" of other feelings about it stemming from the sacrifices and threats that the pattern involved. These processes of "undercutting" and supporting are also present on the women's side of the symbiotic relationship. Where the dual-career situation persists, as it has in the couples studied, a balance is achieved which constitutes a resolution of the dilemma. In the families which are also a professional partnership (as with the Y.'s, an architectural husband-wife partnership) these processes are accentuated.

Where the working partnership is conducted at home, there must be developed a way to soften the cut-and-thrust of critical competitive work modes of relationship lest it erode the husband-wife relationship. The Y.'s recognize that criticism is important for the maintenance of work standards and to stimulate creativity. Mr. Y. indicating how they resolve this, says: "It is important if one is to preserve this kind of relationship to learn to criticize with love; and to accept criticism in work matters as different from attacks on the person. . . ."

The Y.'s themselves recognize that it is easier said than done and have learned to accept a good deal more overt conflict in their relationship than, for example, their parents were accustomed to.

Some of the wives developed distinctive ways of handling their dilemmas in relation to the sex role identity issue. Where their occupational roles called for aggressive behavior or other patterns of behavior sharply inconsistent with their conceptions of the wifely role, they more or less consciously segregated the two sets of roles. An example of the segregation mechanism is: "When I'm at work I'm very authoritarian. I wear a white coat at work and I try to hang up my working personality with it when I leave the office."

To this was added her husband's view: "I once visited my wife's company on business and by chance I saw her there. She was so different, I hardly recognized her. She seemed like someone else—some sort of tycoon—certainly not my wife."

In another case, the switch-over was not so deliberate but nevertheless decisive:

My friends who know me in both capacities say that I am two different people at home and at work. . . . I am much more domineering and aggressive in the office than I am at home in that I will fight a point in the office in a way that I would never fight in a domestic situation, or want to.

Another way that at least two of the wives dealt with identity dilemmas that would tend to arise if they gave too much emphasis to their career ambitions was to play them down almost deliberately. They presented their careers as a series of improvisations which allowed them to do something interesting rather than as a series of steps taken toward a career ambition or goal. A given couple may have more than one tension line operating, and the tension lines may shift through time. When either individual is pushed into a pattern which is too discrepant with his or her sense of personal (and sexual) identity, defensive behavior begins to develop. The form this takes—attack, withdrawal of support, etc.—varies according to the couple. . . .

Social Network Dilemmas

Each of the couples relates to its social environment through a network of relationships. This social network of each family is variously composed of kin, friends, neighbors, work associates, service relationships, and so on. The networks vary in their size, multidimensionality, interconnectedness, and so on. Network composition is affected by many sorts of things, e.g., personal preferences, convenience, obligations and pressures of various kinds. Family phase and occupational affiliation are of central importance in determining the composition and the quality of relationships. At different stages in the life cycle one may add or drop people from "active" network, some people being carried along from stage to stage in a relatively more "latent" capacity. For example, when a woman works, some of her work relationships may be important for the family in a way similar to the work relationships of her husband. (In both cases, these will vary according to the general importance of work relationships in the specific occupations and in the national cultures concerned.) When a family has children, [the parents] may enter into relationships with service personnel relating to children's care and activities and they may form relationships with families of their children's friends with whom they might otherwise not have related. As well as sheer quantity of relationships, there is the matter of quality of relationships, some being kept rather superficial and others "deeper," some relating only to a sector of one's interests and others being more general.

The population with which we are concerned has several characteristics. They are very busy people, committed to occupations which are very demanding. In addition they have their own families whom they value highly; as these families are at the stage where there are growing children at home, this creates yet another very demanding situation. Because of the heavy demands in these immediate spheres, the couples tend to have a relatively smaller amount of active involvement with kin and friendship relationships than may prevail among other professional middle-class families, where there is a greater "slack" for visiting and sociability outside the round of pressing work and family duties. . . . While some of the couples in our sample interacted frequently with relatives and some kin were drawn on to help with children occasionally, the more general pattern was for difficulties to appear in this area because of the divergence of the dual-career family from expected norms of kin behavior. This is one of the areas in which network dilemmas tended to arise. The second area in which distinctive dilemmas arose was that of friendship formation. Each of these can be illustrated. They both involve difficulties in reciprocating conventional role expectations, and they both give rise to dilemmas, as in each case there is both a wish to sustain a relationship and also a wish to protect oneself from it because of the criticism that is usually entailed in the reactions a career wife and mother gets in these relationships.

The kin dilemma is illustrated in Mrs. O.'s experience. Because her husband was very close to his widowed mother, who lived with his spinster sister, she wished to be as nice to them as possible. On the other hand, Mrs. O.'s in-laws found it difficult to accept that she was not only a working wife but one with a very heavy, demanding schedule.. Mrs. O. described a characteristic incident as follows:

> She [mother in-law] will call up and ask if she can just drop around for a visit. I've got her pretty well trained now to realize that I cannot just have a chat with her or prepare things for her. . . . Early on, even my husband didn't realize what a problem this was. When she telephoned once, I heard him say, "Yes, she'll be home on Thursday, drop in anytime in the afternoon." He didn't realize how precious that afternoon was for me . . . how many things I'd saved and planned to get done on that day. I couldn't spend it chatting with his mother. I've got her trained now to accept every third weekend.

Mrs. S. describes similar difficulties with her husband's mother. Mr. S. as with most of the men in our study, felt that he had a special relationship with his mother. In his case, although Mr. S. had four brothers, it was he who had always been close to her and in later years it was he who always carried the burden of his mother's difficulties. This was a recurrent source of conflict of loyalties in relation to his own wife and family, and a high level of tension developed when his mother became seriously ill with a long terminal illness. Mrs. S. says:

> This was the first time I felt that my marriage might break up. He would return late at night from staying up with her and then be so disturbed about it that we couldn't get any rest. This was at the same time as there were very heavy demands being made on me to keep my business going. Even when none of the others in the family would lift a finger and he acted on doctors' advice to have her put into a home, he felt so guilty about it that it disturbed our own relationship.

In one of the couples where the husband's mother lived in a self-contained flatlet in a wing of their large house, the wife and mother have worked out a routinized daily contact for a few minutes between the wife's arrival home from work and the beginning of the television program that the mother watches each evening in her own quarters. Aside from this contact, communication is largely by notes left by the wife in the morning about how to deal with the matters that might arise, e.g., with tradesmen expected.

The dilemma over friendship is less a matter of obligations being modified in the light of the wife's career demands than a matter of deviating from the usual choice patterns for friends. There seems to have been established, particularly among professionals and executives in the business world, a pattern of friendship based on the male's occupational associates (Lazarsfeld and Merton 1954, Babchuk and Bates 1963). Typically, however, the male's occupational associates are married to women who do not themselves pursue careers, though there is some variation in this. It is far less likely that a businessman's associates would be married to women pursuing careers than might hold for the professionals. In both cases, however, there was a tendency for the women in our sample to report a discomfort with social situations in which the wives of the relevant couples were not themselves working or, if not working, at least positively orientated toward it and perhaps intending to work themselves later. In other situations there tended to be at best a lack of shared interests and at worst an awkward situation arising out of expressions of criticism.

The circumstances of the dual-career family tended to produce, among the couples studied, a situation in which friendships are formed in different ways from what might be expected in mono-career families. Aside from the general tendency for overload to crowd out many contacts with friends and to make relationships very selective (as with leisure activities generally), there are other tendencies too. Neighborhood is perhaps less important than in the mono-career family because, as Mrs. O. indicates above, casual visiting patterns are impossible. In only one family was the neighborhood a source of friends, and in this case the neighborhood was a suburb and one with people of the same type as themselves, i.e. [a neighborhood with] a high density of dual-career families or families in which the women had high qualifications and wanted to work at some point. A striking feature of the dual-career families in the study is the tendency to form their friendships on a *couple* basis. While traditional families, particularly in the middle class, assume a minimal degree of acceptance by both partners of any friendships that they form, the tendency has been for the wife to accommodate to the husband's choice and for the women and men to relate separately according to traditional lines of division in activities and interests. In the dual-career families, because of the sharp difference in outlook and situation between the career wife and the noncareer wives, most of our families have tended to associate primarily with other couples like themselves in so far as the wife's involvement in an occupation went. This produces a situation in which it is the wife who has a determining role in selection of friendships though the end product is a couple-based relationship. This is because there is a greater range of acceptable couples purely from the man's point of view than from the woman's point of view, leaving the selection process to center on her sense of comfort and acceptance. This is further accentuated by the fact, as mentioned above, of overload falling most heavily on the wife, making it up to her to indicate whether she can handle friendships which are both gratifying and demanding.

Role Cycling Dilemmas

There is a good deal of literature on the life cycle and on cycles within specific spheres of life, e.g., the family life cycle. The family, for example, goes through phases which are named in the culture—engagement, honeymoon, marriage, parenthood, and so on. Each culture distinguishes different subphases, and not all possible phases are named and identified as separate. For example, in ordinary usage in our own culture we do not have a designation to distinguish the phase of the family life cycle before having children and, later, the phase in which children leave home. In our culture, we call them all "parenthood," referring not to the whole family situation but only to roles of the marital partners. In other spheres, e.g., the occupational, there is a plethora of terms, depending on the specific occupation—training, apprenticeship (internship, residency), establishment, etc., to retirement. In complex organizations there are specific hierarchies that contain named stages, e.g., in the administrative class of the British civil service there are the stages of assistant principal, principal, assistant secretary, under secretary, secretary. Other classes of the civil service have other grades. Other organizations have other hierarchies and stages of the career associated with them. In both spheres sociologists have evolved a more precise terminology (Duvall 1957, Hill and Hansen 1960, Rodgers 1964). Alice Rossi (1968) indicates the utility of thinking in terms of role cycles. A young man marrying enters the role of husband and he has a cycle of experiences in the husband role. When he takes the additional role of father, he has another set of experiences which has its own cycle. In some of our earlier work (Rapoport 1963, Rapoport and Rapoport 1964, 1966) we outlined the critical importance of events at the transition points from one role to another, discussing the processes of unorganization, disorganization, and restructuring that occur to accommodate the shifts in role. The life cycle of the larger units—families, careers, organizations of different kinds—is seen as punctuated by these points of reorganization, which tend to be accompanied by a certain degree of turbulence and conflict. Put into a more general framework, the role cycle may be seen as having an *anticipatory* or preparatory phase; the establishment phase (called the "honeymoon" stage by Rossi) in which efforts are directed at stabilizing ways of managing the role and [in which these efforts are] usually accompanied by heightened interest and involvement; and a *plateau* (or steady-state) stage during which "the role is fully exercised" (Rossi 1968a, p. 30). Then there eventually comes a stage of *disengagement* from the role, which is given up voluntarily or under the force of circumstances.

The couples studied and reported here were mostly in the stage of familial roles that would be termed the *plateau*, in that they were married, had children, and were functioning as parents in a family that was established and growing, with children still at home. In three instances, there were new first babies, so the plateau stage was barely entered at the time of the study. In all the others it was well established. Our data indicate two basic types of role cycling conflicts: between the occupational roles of husband and wife and their family roles; and between the occupational role of the husband and the occupational role of the wife. Two potential conflicts will be discussed: the career-family cycling dilemmas and the dual-career cycling dilemmas.

In relation to the career-family role cycling dilemmas, the parental role is one into which women are to some extent pushed by cultural expectations. The woman is, in addition, particularly vulnerable, as she may be catapulted into becoming a parent accidentally, even with modern methods of birth control (Rossi 1968a). The parental role is largely irrevocable and one for which parents tend to be relatively poorly prepared. While none of our couples report having been catapulted into parenthood, it is clear that the pressures to become parents were more keenly felt by the women than by the men, and several of the couples described the decision to have their first child as one that was pressed by the woman and with which the man tended to acquiesce. The timing of this step in relation to the career role cycle was something that received considerable attention from our couples, and two points of view were expressed.

Some couples stressed the importance, in their continuing to work, of their having been occupationally established before having children. This meant that they had a high income, a secure position with flexibility and perquisites of one kind or another, and could therefore afford a great deal of domestic help and were able to take time off to see that things worked out well. Their commitment to work was, by this time, so well established that dropping out seemed unthinkable.

One of the "drop-out" couples argued, in contrast, that as they had both reached the plateau stage of their careers, there was no need for the wife to work any longer, as her husband's earnings would be high and they had accumulated savings through having had a surplus income for so long. The couple felt that for those in the establishment phase, struggling to make the grade, the pressure on women to continue working after becoming mothers was greater. As Mrs. K. had previously established herself, they felt she could reenter occupationally whenever she wished; had she become a parent earlier, she might not have had sufficient status and contacts to make this possible.

The differences between these viewpoints seem to depend to some extent on the specific occupational situation and to some extent on the values and style of life of the specific couple. An example of the latter is the style of life of the K.'s (above), who lived at a level set by what one income would allow; other couples lived at levels that required both incomes. An example of the way the specific occupational situation affects whether or not women stay in after becoming mothers is seen in architecture. Martin and Smith (1968), in a survey of women architects, show that if they are married to architects, they have a higher chance of continuing their careers than if they marry men of other occupations. The early marriers, restricted as their social lives tend to be to fellow students, are more likely to marry architects than are late marriers.

None of the couples expressed strong feelings about the degree to which women had to curtail involvements in favor of family demands as compared with men. This might have been more pronounced had we studied a series of "captive housewives." For the most part the women felt fortunate that they had been able to work out a situation where they had as full a career as they had managed to achieve. They tended to accept as "inevitable" for the present that the women would have to bear the main brunt of child-care and domestic organization, so that there would "naturally" tend to be more strain on the wife's career-family [role cycling] than on the husband's.[11] The general tendency was to be "thankful for small mercies," such as having a husband who did not invite guests home to dinner at the last minute or who did not mind running a vacuum cleaner over the carpets. There were only a few who were very outspoken about their views that "jointness" and equality in the marital relationship should be equality in the degree to which *each* must curtail the demands of career in favor of their joint familial commitments.

The second type of role cycling conflict, i.e., between demands of the two careers, was expressed by most of the couples. When Mrs. O. wished to diminish the demands being made on her by her career so that she could have more time to spend with her growing children and as she wished to continue in a senior professional job of some kind, she considered taking a different post in a remote part of the U.K. Mr. O., however, could find no job in that area comparable to the one he held. So Mrs. O. had to give up that opportunity. When Mr. P. was offered a promotion with his industrial firm if he would move to the north of England, he turned it down because there was no chance there for his wife (a research scientist) to obtain a job comparable to the one she held in the London area. Mr. S. gave up a promising career in politics in order to stabilize a home base and income to underpin the development of his wife's career as a designer.

An example of a dilemma arising between the woman's career role and the parental role is seen most crucially at the point of childbirth. As indicated, this is when most women drop out, at least for an extended period. Our data from the 1960 graduates survey indicate that there is a point following childbirth when the woman's occupation aspirations soar (having been depressed in the face of difficulties following graduation from university and kept down by the counterbalance of the glow of early parenthood).

In all these instances there was stress—both within the individual making the career sacrifice and to some extent between the pair. However, in all cases, resolutions were made on the basis of a recognition of joint interest in optimizing family-career decisions so as to keep the three sets of role systems functioning with minimal tension.

Summary and Discussion

There is a trend toward increased participation of women in the work force. Women are doing this not at the expense of marrying but along with it and increasingly expect to combine marriage and career. This is producing, more and more often, the phenomenon of the dual-career family, in which husband and wife are not only companions and equal on different scales of evaluation but are both participating on the same evaluative planes. Thus, while there has been a good deal written about "women's two roles" (Myrdal and Klein, *op. cit.*), the point of reference of the present paper is not the role of women but the family in relation to its social environment. The dual-career family is one in which both "heads" of the family pursue careers. The implication is not, as with the concept of women's two roles, that men do not also have two roles. Both men and women, in the dual-career family, have both career roles and familial roles, and with the exception of pregnancy and childbirth, there is no assumption that any of the activities are inexorably sex-linked. This is not to say that there are categorically no biologically linked sex differences in the capacities of men and women to perform specific activities, e.g., "mothering." The probability is that there are "overlapping curves" of characteristics such that some men may have more of an attribute (say, nurturance) than some women and, conversely, some women may have more of an attribute (say, mechanical skills) than some men (Riesman 1965). At the same time more women may turn out to be more nurturant biologically than most men and more men may turn out to be biologically more "mechanical" than most women.

At present there are strongly held socio-cultural beliefs about sex-linked attributes which affect self-conceptions and interaction patterns. Different subsystems within society change at different rates.[12] Within the socio-cultural domains, a very complex interrelationship exists between ideology, social structure, and behavior. In contemporary society, egalitarianism is a dominant ideological theme. This is expressed, for example, in the educational subsystem. Boys and girls at school are taught and compete with one another on a single set of evaluative scales. When they leave school or university, however, the sex differential becomes more marked. It is to be noted that egalitarian education is a tendency, not an actuality. Many graduate women accommodate to the traditional sex-differentiated norms of the postuniversity role systems without apparent strain. Some similarly highly educated women conform to the traditional pattern but show great strain (the "captive wife" syndrome). Others extrapolate the egalitarian norms of their educational period into the adult stage, working out new patterns as they go because role models and precedents for equality in the work-family relationships of married couples with children are largely lacking. For the men there would seem to be less discontinuity.

The level of analysis which we have conducted is "microsociological," in that we have concentrated on the small innovating units—the dual-career partnership famil[ies]. Though our study does not attempt to encompass a cross-section of such units so as to estimate the prevalence of each of the patterns observed, we believe that it covers a sufficiently broad range of examples to provide insight into some major contemporary process of change. Because each of the units functions in a larger cultural system of norms and values and in a larger social system of relationships and interactions, the innovating patterns which are attempted may be seen as going "against the grain" of society in various ways. As society itself is changing, the strains outlined in this paper are not presented as permanent or intrinsic in the dual-career family situation but rather [offered as] a matter of contemporary concern. The contemporary concern has policy implications, but looking at the issue more theoretically, we suggest that the analysis of structural sources of stress [is] relevant for social change. In Goode's terms (1962), each couple strikes a series of "role bargains" to reduce or otherwise deal with the strains and dilemmas they experience. Taken all together, these role bargains form new structures, which are more collaborative, in the sense described for postindustrial society as a whole by Trist (*op. cit.*).

The structures evolved by dual-career families of the type studied are more than of private interest. These are couples who are unusually visible and articulate. They provide models for a wide range of less distinguished members of the society and may be seen in varying degrees as exemplars, or at least "trial balloons," for those who follow. In addition, they tend to participate in more complex and dispersed clusters of relationships (Trist, *op. cit.*).

In the immediate situation, the new behavioral models which are evolved may be evaluated in various ways. Personal satisfaction is a dimension which provides one element of evaluation but which is too diffuse and complex for our current form of analysis. It would involve matching specific personality constellations to the different structural models. For the present, a structural form of analysis is suggested. Structural sources of stress may be detected and the consequent patterns of strain described. Individual differences in capacity to absorb the strains will affect satisfaction, but, as indicated, we do not go to this level here. Within limits, the economic metaphor of a cost-benefit analysis is useful. Each family works out for itself whether the "costs" of pursuing the variant life career of a dual-career family—in any of its various forms—is worth it to them in relation to the "benefits" they derive.

These costs and benefits may be summarized for the couples studied in relation to five structural dimensions of stress:

1. *Role overloads.* Dual-career families benefit in taking on an additional set of occupational roles by the increased family income, the stimulation and personal development afforded the wife, her utilization of her training, the closer relationship between father and the children, and so on. These benefits, which are consistent with the values of postindustrial society, are realized at the cost of taxing the energies of both members through role overloads and possibly restricting of the husband's career participation. The couples generally tend to reduce the overload effect by curtailing nonessential, particularly leisure and social, activities.

2. *Normative dilemmas.* [These] arise through the discontinuities in ideology as between educational and adult roles, producing strains. One way of reducing this kind of strain is to extrapolate the earlier role ideals into the later behavior—continuing the wife's career development. This leads to benefits for the woman (and indirectly for the husband) of a sense of integrity, of feeling "true to oneself," as distinct from having to "put the lid on" or to compromise one's ideals or waste one's capacities. This may be accomplished, however, at the "cost" of diverging from the norms and expectations representing the other side of the dilemma—the more traditional female role norms, holding it right and proper for a woman to be at home looking after her family. The strains, both intraphysically and in significant social relationships, are dealt with by various devices of insulation and compartmentalization.

3. *Maintenance of personal identity.* [This] becomes a problem when one departs from the standard patterns of behavior that are institutionally supported in the traditional role structures. Where men and women continue to

pursue their personal development through the same rather than different channels of roles with their different norms and sanctions, they may find themselves confronting the issue of how to maintain their distinct identity. The "benefits" of equal participation are in terms of fairness and equity in access to society's valued resources. The "costs" may entail competitive rivalries and their concomitants, interpersonal discord, difficulties in sexual relations, and so on. The couples studied seem to deal with the identity issue by constructing (in their psychic and interpersonal world of reality) a "tension line" which demarcates areas within which they feel they can comfortably function as separate and distinct individuals.

4. *The social network dilemmas.* [These] provide structured sources of strain in reconciling obligations (e.g., in kinship relations) with desires (e.g., in friendship relations) and responsibilities (e.g., in erecting a network of effective service relationships), all in the face of overloads in the work and family role systems. The "benefits" of a fairly decisive limitation on network relationships and concentration of them on gratifying components (e.g., by eliminating unwanted relationships, delegating obligations to service personnel, etc.) may be reckoned in comfort and an enhanced capacity to function and develop in work and family roles. On the other hand, the process of network construction which this tends to represent may lead to feelings of guilt by the individual, and resentment by others, and these must be reckoned among the "costs."

5. *Role cycling.* The husband and wife in the dual-career family are involved in three role systems: the work system of each spouse (except where they are partners, in which case the two work systems are merged) and the family system which they share. Each system makes different demands according to the position of the role in the system, and each role makes different demands on the individual according to phase. The tendency for heavy demands to be made on people in work roles [occurs] when working upward toward senior positions (more than once one actually reaches an established senior role), and within roles shortly after the initial ("honeymoon") period when the new structure of person-in-role is being worked out. In the family, the heaviest strain is at the time of having young children of preschool age. There are different costs and benefits according to what the correspondence is between the peak demands on roles in these three spheres. If the couple arrange their lives so as to have the family role demands "peak" first, they may miss opportunities for career advancement. If they allow the two career role strains to "peak" first, they may pay the costs in family life of the additional strains imposed through fatigue as they are older, and a greater age gap between themselves and their children. If one spouse "peaks" while the other defers heavy involvement, the one that defers may have to pay a price in career development as well as perhaps bear a heavier brunt of family role strains. This is, obviously, an oversimplified picture and many combinations are possible, but the issue of role cycling and the "fits" in the family among the various role cycles is only beginning to be understood (Rossi 1968*b*).

Finally, we are concerned with indicating briefly what social changes may facilitate diffusion of the dual-career family structure. The policy implications of these considerations are apparent but will not be dealt with in depth here.

It is suggested that the dual-career family structure is likely to become more prevalent in our society to the extent that three arenas of change provide compatible arrays of factors to support the diffusion of the pattern:

a. the arena of work role relationships
b. the arena of domestic role relationships
c. the arena of the built environment.

Many occupational groups and organizations are working toward a reduction of the crude forms of discrimination linked to archaic sex role stereotypes. The issue of similarities or differences between men's and women's capacities is increasingly seen as part of the more general issue of individual differences, and the entire range of jobs in the world of work is becoming increasingly open to women on an equal basis with men. However, the capacity of women, particularly married women with children, to grasp the increasingly available opportunities and to exercise to their fullest capacities the available career roles will depend on the degree to which these roles can be made compatible with the demands of women's other roles. Many current ways of organizing the world of work are not intrinsically necessary and yet make participation difficult for women because of being based on "male" assumptions about times of accessibility, etc.

The arena of domestic role relationships, similarly, will provide a set of factors affecting the diffusion of the dual-career pattern. The greater diffusion will depend on the extent to which husbands as well as wives redefine the marital role relationship so as to give explicit recognition to the interconnectedness of domestic and occupational roles. If the pursuit of a career by the wife is to become a possibility for more than the "amazons" of this world, it will depend on men having an attitude more supportive than "it's all right so long as it doesn't affect me." The whole area of child-care seems to be the most important element in this constellation of roles. To the extent that husbands can participate more in child-care and that auxiliary roles and arrangements are developed, the pattern may diffuse more.

The "built environment" can be expected to play an important part in the extent to which the dual-career family becomes more viable and pervasive in the future. This seems to be most relevant in two areas: the journey to work, and the pooling of services in the areas of domestic arrangements. The tendency following the Industrial Revolution to remove the work place as well as the husband from the home is no longer as relevant, given the more agreeable general conditions of work. To the extent that new complexes of living bring work and family into more easy interplay, as in some of the new towns organized with industry as well as housing in mind, the impediment of the arduous journey to work now placed on women and men, and contributing to their role overloads, will be diminished. If housing developments are oriented in the future to the sharing of domestic care facilities—cleaning, food buying and preparation, child-care, etc.—rather than simply [to the multiplication of] individual living units as seems to be the present tendency, a greater diffusion of the pattern is possible. New mixtures of individualism and communalism may be expected in postindustrial society, with an increase in the latter for the Western countries (D. Bell, op. cit.).

The situation, in summary, is that the trend toward cultural norms which are compatible with the dual-career family seems to be well underway. In many instances the mono-career family structure will be chosen for self-expressive rather than traditional reasons. However, where there is the wish to choose the dual-career structure and there are normative conflicts, these are due, in our view, partly to cultural lag and partly to defensive reactions from people in the environment who have not been able to succeed in evolving a dual-career family on a microsociological level. The structural changes which are necessary to fully implement these changes are not yet in effect, particularly in the areas of organization of work, organization of domestic role relationships, and the conception of the built environment.

In conclusion, what is being suggested is that the availability of these facilities [and structural changes] will be important in making it possible for individual families to have a choice of potential arrangements. It is not implied that the dual-career family is advocated as a universal pattern.

Notes

1. Our survey results will be reported fully in subsequent publications. They are mentioned here only fragmentarily to provide a context in the analysis of the small series of case studies. We are deeply indebted to Alice Rossi for allowing us to use a modified form of the survey instrument which she and F. Spaeth developed for their survey of American university graduates. Some of the survey data [were] gathered for us by Research Services Ltd. Professor Kelsall was extremely helpful in locating a sample of 1960 graduates. We are also grateful for help received in different parts of the analysis [from] Survey Analysis Ltd., and from the School of Social Sciences, Brunel University, and the Atlas Computer Centre, Chilton.

2. The cultural lags in the Eastern European countries also resemble those in the West. Sokolowska reports, for example, that when working hours were shortened, this resulted in an increase in leisure for working men and in an increase in *housework* for working wives. This was presumably based on the traditional assumption that housework is a feminine area of responsibility (Sokolowska 1963).

3. The couples in our study valued the rights of women as well as of men to pursue careers. However, the general line of our analysis is in agreement with Goode's point that ". . . the kernel of the psychological problem of extending human rights to a given group. . . . [is] that each right is someone else's obligation, that to grant a right requires that someone loses what he had formerly considered his right. . ." (1966).

4. Couples who fitted our criteria for inclusion were obtained through establishment or personnel officers in the civil service, BBC, and large industrial organizations and through professional and business association representatives, for the architects and small-business women.

5. It is interesting to note that this duality of emotional commitment is put into practice by only a small number of people. It would appear, however, that many more highly qualified people value this duality than are actually able to carry it out. Preliminary analysis of a sample of 1960 graduates shows the relative salience of work, family, and leisure in relation to marital status and family stage. Degree of satisfaction was used as a rough index of salience, and respondents were asked which area of life gave them greatest satisfaction, which next greatest satisfaction, and which the most dissatisfaction. For men there is a sharp contrast between those who are single and those who are married and have children. For the single men, "career" is the most frequently chosen as

the area giving most satisfaction (55 percent), with "leisure" second (17 percent), and "family" third (12 percent). For married men with children, "family" is the most frequently chosen area (55 percent), with "career" second (30 percent), and "leisure" dropping alongside the other areas of little importance—i.e., under 5 percent choosing it as the most satisfying. Single women, like single men, choose "career" as the most important (45 percent), with "leisure" second (22 percent), and "family" third (15 percent). For married women without children, the pattern is like that of the married men with children; 57 percent indicate that "family" is the most important area of satisfaction, 19 percent indicating "career," and 10 percent "leisure." The married women with children, however, overwhelmingly look to family as their greatest satisfaction, with over 80 percent indicating that this is the main area. It is interesting that only 4 percent indicated "career" as their main area of satisfaction; this is about the same proportion of the married women with young children who work at jobs for over thirty hours a week.

6. From a communication with Alice Rossi, it appears that this pattern holds even in the U.S.A., where there are a great many labor-saving devices in the home. In countries where households are less mechanized and shopping is less rationalized (e.g., no "supermarkets" and shopping centers), the burden of overload in the situation is even greater.

7. Terence Moore's work (1964), though not on dual-career families specifically, supports the impression that the maternal separation entailed in mother's working does not *per se* produce disturbance. American research reported in Nye and Hoffman (1963) leads to a similar impression. We are aware that we are unable to make scientifically conclusive statements on the effects of the dual-career family structure on children's development. We hope, however, to study this more closely in a subsequent project.

8. Our survey data also support this, showing that while nearly 90 percent of single women graduates are working thirty hours a week or more eight years after they leave university and this pattern is sustained for 65 percent of the married women without children, only 4 percent of the married women with children continue working this amount.

9. While all of the dual-career families made similar resolutions, sometimes less scientifically based, the "drop-out" cases differed in this. Two of the three drop-outs resolved this dilemma in favor of the traditional norms at the point of the birth of the first baby. The third drop-out was occasioned by a crisis in the area of the children's life space (breakdown of care facilities accompanied by incipient signs of disturbance in the child).

10. For an interesting discussion of how cultural norms affect the role of psychotherapists, see Knoblochova and Knobloch (1965). In Czechoslovakia, the tendency in family psychotherapy (where identity problems of the type being described here are encountered) is to assume employment as a part of the feminine role concept. If there are marital difficulties associated with a dual-career situation, [psychotherapists] are as likely to see the issues as [resulting from] the husband's difficulties in allowing his wife equal opportunities as [they are to see them as resulting from] the wife's deviance in relation to a narrow domestic role conception.

11. For an account of how the ideal-real discrepancies are absorbed into everyday life in Finland and Hungary, see Heiskanen and Mannila (1967). These writers distinguish between "formal ideology" and "everyday ethic," the former representing the "ideal" pattern, the latter the "real" one.

12. It seems to be generally assumed that technological subsystems not only change more rapidly than socio-cultural subsystems but . . . are "open-ended." That is, they can change in ways that open up new possibilities never before experienced, e.g., for increased speed, power and control over nature. At the socio-cultural level there seems to be a much greater assumption that socio-cultural changes are limited by the relatively unchanging biological condition of men.

References

BABCHUK, N., and BATES, A. P. "The Primary Relations of Middle-Class Couples: A Study in Male Dominance." *American Sociological Review* 28 (June 1963), pp. 377–384.

BAUDE, A., and HOLMBERG, PER. "The Position of Men and Women in the Labour Market." In *The Changing Roles of Men and Women,* edited by E. Dahlstrom. London: Duckworth, 1967.

BELL, C. "Mobility and the Middle-Class Extended Family." *Sociology,* vol. 2, no. 2 (May 1968), pp. 173–184.

BELL, D. "Notes on the Post-industrial Society," pts. 1, 2. *The Public Interest,* nos. 6, 7 (Winter and Spring), pp. 24–35 and 102–118 respectively.

BOTT, E. *Family and Social Network.* London: Tavistock Publications, 1957.

DAHLSTROM, E. *The Changing Roles of Men and Women.* London: Duckworth, 1962.

DUVALL, E. M. *Family Development.* Philadelphia: Lippincott, 1957. (Revised 1962).

FOGARTY, M.; RAPOPORT, R. N.; and RAPOPORT, RHONA. *Women and Top Jobs.* London: Political and Economic Planning (P.E.P.), 1967.

FRIED, M. "Mourning for a Lost Home." In *The Urban Conditions,* edited by L. Dahl. New York: Basic Books, 1963.

GANS, H. *The Urban Villagers.* New York: Free Press, 1965.

GAVRON, H. *The Captive Wife.* London: Routledge and Kegan Paul, 1966.

GOODE, W. J. "Theory of Role Strain." *American Sociological Review* 25 (August 1960), pp. 483–496.

———. *World Revolutions and Family Patterns.* New York: Free Press, 1963.

———. "Family Patterns and Human Rights." *International Journal of Social Science,* vol. 18, no. 1 (1966), pp. 41–54.

HEISKANEN, V. S., and HAAVIO-MANNILA, E. "The Position of Women in Society: Formal Ideology and Everyday Ethic." *Social Service Information* 6 (December 1967), pp. 169–188.

HILL, R. L., and HANSEN, D. A. "The Identification of Conceptual Framework Utilized in Family Study." *Marriage and Family Living* 22 (1960), pp. 229–311.

HUNT, A. *Survey of Women's Employment.* Government Social Survey, 55.379 (March 1968).

INTERNATIONAL LABOUR OFFICE. *Year Book of Labour Statistics, 1958.* Geneva, 1958.

———. *Year Book of Labour Statistics, 1967.* Geneva, n.d.

JAQUES, E. "Death and the Midlife Crisis." *International Journal of Psychoanalysis* 46 (1965), pp. 502–514.

JEFFERYS, M., and ELLIOTT, P. M. *Women in Medicine.* London: Office of Health Economics, 1966.

KNOBLOCHOVA, J., and KNOBLOCH, F. "Family Psychotherapy." Public Health Paper, vol. 28 (Geneva: World Health Organization, 1965), pp. 68–89.

KOMAROVSKY, M. *The Unemployed Man and His Family.* New York: Dryden Press, 1940.

LAUMANN, E. O. "Friends of Urban Men." Mimeographed. 1968. *Sociometry* (in press).

LAZERSFELD, P. G., and MERTON, R. "Friendship as a Social Process." In *Freedom and Control in Modern Society,* edited by M. Gergerstal. New York: Octagon Books, 1954.

LEACH, E. *A Runaway World.* London: Oxford University Press, 1968.

LITWAK, E. "Occupational Mobility and Extended Family Cohesion." *American Sociological Review* 25 (1960), pp. 9–21.

MARTIN F., and SMITH, H. "Women in Architecture." Mimeo memo, no. 1068. London Political and Economic Planning (P.E.P.), 1968.

MOGEY, J. *Family and Neighbourhood.* Leiden: Bull, 1963.

MOORE, T. "Children of Full-Time and Part-Time Working Mothers." *International Journal of Social Psychiatry*, special congress issue no. 2, vol. 10 (1964).

MYRDAL, A., and KLEIN, V. *Woman's Two Roles, Home and Work*. London: Routledge and Kegan Paul, 1956.

NYE, F. I., and HOFFMAN, L. W. *The Employed Mothers in America*. Chicago: Rand McNally & Co., 1963.

PARSONS, T. "The Kinship System of the Contemporary United States." *American Anthropologist* vol. 45, no. 1 (1943), pp. 22–38.

PARSONS, T., and BALES, R. F. *Family Socialization and Interaction Process*. Glencoe, Ill.: The Free Press, 1955.

RAPOPORT, RHONA. "Normal Crisis, Family Structure and Mental Health." *Family Process* vol. 2, no. 1 (1963), pp. 68–80.

RAPOPORT, RHONA, and RAPOPORT, R. N. "New Light on the Honeymoon." *Human Relations* vol. 17, no. 1 (February 1964), pp. 33–56.

———. "Work and Family in Contemporary Society." *American Sociological Review* 30 (1966), pp. 381–394.

RIESMAN, D. "Some Dilemmas of Women's Education." *The Educational Record*. Washington, 1965.

ROBBINS, L. C. *Report on Higher Education*. 3 vols. Education and Science: Her Majesty's Stationery Office, 1961, 1962, 1963.

RODGERS, R. H. "Toward a Theory of Family Development." *Journal of Marriage and the Family*, vol. 26, no. 3 (August 1964), pp. 262–275.

ROSSI, A. "Equality Between the Sexes: An Immodest Proposal." *Daedalus*, vol. 93, no. 2 (Spring 1964), pp. 607–652.

———. "Transition to Parenthood." *Journal of Marriage and the Family* 30, no. 1 (February 1968a), pp. 26–39.

———. *Head and Heart*. Manuscript in preparation (1968b).

SOKOLOWSKY, M. "The Household; Unknown Working Environment." *Studia Socjologicze* vol. 3, no. 10 (1963), pp. 161–182. Edited by M. Sokolowska. Warsaw: Ksiazka and Wiedza.

SOMMERKORN, I. "The Position of Women in the University Teaching Profession in England." Ph.D. dissertation, University of London, 1966.

TRIST, E. "Urban North America: The Challenge of the Next Thirty Years." Keynote address to the Annual Conference of the Town Planning Institute of Canada, June 1968. Tavistock Institute, H. R. C. Document no. 153.

TURNER, R. *The Social Context of Ambition*. San Francisco: Chandler, 1964.

WEBER, M. *The Theory of Social and Economic Organisation*. London: Hodge, 1947.

WILLMOTT, P. "The Influence of Some Social Trends of Regional Planning." Mimeographed. London: Centre for Community Studies, 1968.

WROCHNO, K. "Women in Directing Positions About Themselves." *Kobieta Wspolszesna* (1966).

YOUNG, M., and WILLMOTT, P. *Family and Kinship in East London*. London: Routledge and Kegan Paul, 1957.

The Making of a Confused, Middle-aged Husband

When I was in my twenties, I would try to convince marriage-oriented women to become involved with me by predicting on the basis of experience that, within six months of such involvement, they would very likely be getting married—though not to me, because the association with me seemed to drive women to marriage. In my forties, I find that young women's work association with me seems to correlate highly with their movement into Women's Lib. Whether proximity to me induces a liberation spirit or whether it could possibly be due to larger cultural forces, my female co-workers have led me to think much more about sexism of late, and to review my own experiences over the decades in that framework.

Two interchanges with my colleagues particularly struck me. One wrote me a strong note asking why was I not publicly active in fighting sexism if I thought that I was so good on the question. I was somewhat stung by this passionate indictment, and in cool, clear, parsimonious prose replied that I did not consider myself to be very good on the sex issue, but looking around at most men of my own and perhaps younger ages, I was constantly surprised to find myself much better in my attitudes and behavior than they, but not good enough, etc., etc.

But a nagging vision persisted despite my measured rejoinder. True, my wife worked and always had worked, and I pushed her to do more professional writing to establish herself solidly in her professional life; true, I had played a major role in bringing up our children, especially when they were young and she was going to school; true, in arguments with friends I had always taken pro-Liberation positions. For decades I had argued against the then fashionable *Kinder-Küche-Kirche* motif of the suburban existence and had counseled students against it. I advised husbands whose wives were diffusely unhappy that they should drive their talented and educated, if unsure, spouses into work, for staying home all day and taking care of a household made for a malcontent, which was compounded by social disapproval of the expression of unhappiness in mothering and wifing. Yes, all that was true, but how different was the present pattern of my own family from that of a family with a more obviously backward husband than I?

Another female colleague, more disposed to be kindly to me, told me when I questioned a particular emphasis of Women's Lib that I did not realize how backward men now in their twenties and thirties were: they had been brought up in the suburban sadness where their mothers played the required "good mother-wife" role, where their sisters and their dates accepted the necessity of catering to men in order to make a "good catch." And [she told me] that these men had not been confronted on sexist issues—this conversation preceded the mass media's appointing Women's Lib to celebrity status—indeed, they were largely unaware that there might be some injustice in the present ordering of the world.

My experience, I told her, had been different. In the left-wing ambience of New York City in the forties and fifties, "male supremacy" and "male chauvinism" were frequently discussed. True, my male friends and I discussed the issues with our female friends and then often proceeded to exploit them, but a dextrous awareness we did have. (Yet I add, in order to avoid a reassuring self-debasement, that we did encourage our women friends and wives to think and to develop themselves; I even believe that I was less exploitative than most.)

And yes I am dogged by the feeling expressed in the notion that if you're so smart, how come you're not making money? Where was the equalitarian family life one would reasonably expect from my sophistication on Women's Lib issues and my personal experience with them in my younger adulthood?

I have never had an intellectual problem with sexism. One reason may well have been the women who surrounded me as a child—my father's mother, my mother and two considerably older sisters—although I know it sometimes goes quite the other way. My father slept and my mother dominated—partly out of force of character and partly, one sister informed me fairly recently, because of the occupational and other failures of my father. He had tried to make it in America—and could not. His was the immigrant's rags-to-rags story, for he started as a factory worker, became a small businessman, only to be wiped out by the 1921 depression; he worked again as a machine operator and then started a dress store where he did the alterations and my mother was chief saleswoman. Again, his enterprise was rewarded by a depression—this time, that of the 1930s. He went back to working a machine in the lowest paid part of the garment industry, where he stayed until he retired in his early seventies. From the depression days on my mother worked as a saleslady. I was a "latchkey kid" from an early age, warming up the meals that were left for me by my mother.

My mother was very smart and witty and so was my older sister. They were obviously intellectually well endowed, although not well educated. My mother had a few years of formal schooling; my sister just managed to graduate from high school. (I think I developed my repugnance to credentialism because I recognized that these were two very smart though not well-educated women.)

From this experience, I grew up regarding women as competent and capable of making family and economic decisions. (By contrast, my mother disliked cooking, and it was a shock to me when I began to eat away from home to discover what a bad cook she was.) Women worked and ran things well.

On the other hand, there was a notion that people frowned on women working, so we tried to hide the fact that my mother worked. I think I felt both shamed that my mother worked and irritated that "society" thought that it was wrong for women to work, especially when their incomes were needed.

Furthermore, sexism was, in principle, alien to the equalitarian and participatory circles in which my closest friends and I were passionately involved. We were out-of-sorts with the intellectual climate of the forties and fifties because of an egalitarian, populist, antielitist spirit. We criticized Stalinist democratic centralism and American "Celebration"-style pluralist democracy because of their inadequate attention to equality and participation for all. We could no more subscribe to intellectual rationalizations for female low status than we could condone the miseries of oppression and deprivation among other parts of the population.

A third reason I see myself as intellectually escaping sexism has more manifest emotional roots. Looking back, I don't believe that I could accept a woman who would center her life completely on me and devote herself to making me happy. (Children were not part of my purview.) At one level, the intellectual, how could one individual be worthy of such dedication by another? At the deeper and, I suspect now, more significant level, I rejected or stayed away from easily giving or male-centered women because I did not consider myself worthy of another person's total devotion or capable of evoking the sentiments which would sustain it beyond the initial impulse. Furthermore, it demanded an emotional response that I possibly could not make. In short, I did not think so well of myself that I could live with (overwhelming) devotion. As a consequence, I was usually involved with young women with strong career goals who were seeking their identity through work and not through family. They were my intellectual equals, if not superiors.

Thus, I had a good beginning, it seems to me, for having a marriage that did not embody sexist currents. But I don't see that my current life is very different from [that of] those who espoused or expounded more sexist values. Years ago a good friend told me that I had the reputation among the wives in our circle of being "an excellent husband," and he said, "You know, that's not a good thing." I now have the feeling that families that openly embrace both bourgeois and sexist values don't live very differently from us. I sense that we are engaged in a "lapsed egalitarianism," still believing in our earlier commitments and concerns about equality but having drifted from the faith in our daily life.

What happened? Probably the most important factor which accounts for the direction we took was our amazing naïveté about the impact of having children—a naïveté incidentally which I see today having a similarly devastating effect on many young parents. We just had no idea how much time and emotion children captured and how they simply changed your lives—even when we were able, as we were, to afford a housekeeper as a result of my wife's working.

The early years of child-rearing were very difficult. Our first son was superactive and did not sleep through the night. We were both exhausted. My wife insisted that I not leave everything to her; she fought with me to get me to participate in the care of our son and apartment. I took the 2 A.M. and 6 A.M. feedings and changings, for our ideology did not allow me to just occasionally help out; I had to "share" and really participate in the whole thing. I resented that degree of involvement; it seemed to interfere terribly with the work I desperately wanted to achieve.

Indeed, I have always felt put upon because of that episode of many months. To make matters worse, I did not know of other work-oriented husbands who were as involved as I with their children. True, I realized that my sons became much attached to each other and a lovely new element entered my life, but I resented the time and exhaustion, particularly since I was struggling to find my way in my work. I did not consider myself productive and was in the middle of struggling to clarify my perspective. I looked at the problem largely in terms of the pressure of my job, which required a lot of effort, and, more importantly, in terms of my personality and my inability to work effectively. While I wrote memoranda with great ease, I wasn't writing professional articles and books.

In retrospect, I think that it was the period of the McCarthy and Eisenhower years that was more significant in my lack of development. My outlook and interests were not what social science and society were responding to. That changed later, and I was able to savor in the sixties that infrequent exhilaration of one's professional work and citizen concerns merging and of gaining both a social science and popular audience and constituency. But I did not know in the 1950s that this would ensue and I felt resentment.

What I experienced was that I was working hard to make things easier for my wife, unlike my friends, and . . . I did not see rewards. Yes, she told me that she appreciated my effort, but my activities were never enough, my sharing was never full in the sense that I equally planned and involved myself with initiative in the care of child and house. She was tired too and irritated by child-care, and in turn, I was irritated by what seemed to be her absorption in taking care of children.

And there were always those male friends who did so little compared to me. I could and did tell myself that at some point along the line they would be paying heavy "dues" for their current neglect of their wives' plight, but it was small balm now. I wondered if I was not rationalizing my irritation by an intellectualizing metaphor about how you pay prices sooner or later and by a plaintively reassuring injunction never to envy anyone else, for who knew what lurked beyond the facade of family equanimity.

Things were further complicated by another factor—less typical of today's young marrieds—incomplete early socialization as a family member. For example, since I ate meals by myself as an adolescent and preadolescent, I developed the habit of reading while eating. Indeed, I am a compulsive reader, a "print nut." If there is nothing around to read, I will study the labels on ketchup bottles. The result is that marriage required a resocialization into talking to someone at mealtimes, not turning inward to my own thoughts or the *New York Times*.

Of course, the reading is only the personal iceberg tip of a larger problem of not closing myself to others and becoming inaccessible because of stress or intellectual absorption. I am now, again, in a conscious period of trying to make myself more accessible emotionally to my family, but it is a struggle. For example, when we vacation, I spend the first days devouring three to four mysteries a day, decompressing I call it, hardly talking to anyone. And, of course, when I am at a deadline or caught in my inability to work out an idea, or just unable to get to work—there are few other conditions for me than these three—I am rather inaccessible, to say the least. I work against this tendency but don't do notably well. While I do the mundane tasks of the household, psychologically I am often not much there. I think that I am winning the struggle against withdrawal, but what is a giant step to the battler may appear as a wiggle of progress to the beholder.

My wife has accommodated to my dislike of fixing things and "wasting time" on such things—not great matters in themselves, but symptomatic of the process of my disengagement from the burdens of home and family.

From a narrow perspective, I have useful incompetences, protecting me from diversions of my energy and focus. I don't like to fix things and don't do them well (or soon). In my youth, in my proletarian-near-idealization, I felt that Arthur Miller was right when Willy Loman says a man isn't a man unless he can do things with his hands. So I tried adult education shop courses and the like for a brief time. I went in a "klutz" and came out a "klutz." Now in a spirit of reactive arrogance or greater self-pride, I boldly assert the counter-position that I believe in the division of labor and prefer to pay for specialized labor. I do little around the house—and that usually long delayed. Since skilled labor is hard to get at any price, things are undone or my wife does them, but my principle of specialization (for me) remains unimpaired.

Similarly, I have been relieved of the task of paying bills. With my usual speed and disdain for trivia, I did this job very rapidly and made mistakes. Now my wife spends time doing this task. It is easier, in her view, for her to do it than to keep after me to do a competent job. Failure is its own reward: I have escaped another task.

Of course, I have been after my wife to have a part-time secretary and bookkeeper and have located several people for her. But she resists, as they do not provide enough help to make it worthwhile. The result is that my personal efforts reduce my feelings of guilt when she spends evenings writing out checks. After all, I did try to get her out of that function. But I am still irritated by her doing the checks—for that is another indication that she is failing me by not showing our true equality, by not spending more time on her professional writing and research.

I guess what dismays me and makes me see my marriage and family as unfortunately typically upper-middle class, collegial, pseudo-egalitarian American—especially in light of my own continuing commitment to an equalitarian, participatory ethos—is that I assume no responsibility for major household tasks and family activities. True, my wife has always worked in her profession (she is a physician) even when our sons were only some weeks old. (I used to say that behind the working wife with young children, there stands a tired husband.) True, I help in many ways and feel responsible that she have time to work on her professional interests. But, I do partial, limited things to free her to do her work. I don't do the basic thinking about the planning of meals and housekeeping or the situation of the children. Sure, I will wash dishes, "spend time" with the children; I will often do the shopping, cook, make beds, "share" the burden of most household tasks; but that is not the same thing as direct and primary responsibility for planning and managing a household and meeting the day-to-day needs of children.

It is not that I object in principle to householding and child-rearing. I don't find such work demeaning or unmasculine—just a drain of my time, which could be devoted to other "more rewarding" things. Just as I don't like to shop for clothes for myself even though I like clothes. My energies are poised to help me work on my professional-political concerns, and I resist "wasting time" on other pursuits even when basic to managing a day-to-day existence.

The more crucial issue, I now think, is not my specific omissions and commissions but the atmosphere that I create. My wife does not expect much of me in order to let me work and to lessen the strain which I produce when I feel blocked from working. Even our sons have always largely respected my efforts to work while feeling much freer to interrupt their mother at hers. The years have been less happy than they would have been if I were more involved and attentive and my wife had not lowered her ambitions.

Outstanding academically from an early age, a poor girl scholarship-winner at a prestige college and medical school, excelling in her beginning professional work, she expected and was expected to do great things. But with children, she immediately reduced her goals. Of course, medical schools don't pay much attention to faculty members who are part-time or female. The combination of both is powerful in getting offhand treatment.

She is now coming out to fuller professional development, but I have always [felt] guilty that she wasn't achieving more. So I nagged her to publish, while not providing the circumstances and climate which would make serious work much easier. I had the benefit of feeling relieved that I was "motivating" her by my emphasis on her doing more, while I did not suffer the calls on my time and emotions that making more useful time available to her would require. In the long run, I undoubtedly lost more by limited involvement because she was distressed by the obstacles to her professional work. But the long run is hard to consider when today's saved and protected time helps meet a deadline.

What are the lessons of this saga of a well-intentioned male? One is that equality or communality is not won once and for all, but must continually be striven for. Backsliding and easy accommodation-to-the-male-is-less-troublesome are likely to occur unless there is, at least occasionally, effort to bring about or maintain true communality rather than peaceful adjustment.

What follows is that women must struggle for equality—that it will not easily be won or re-won. A male is not likely to bestow it—in more than surface ways. Some women are arguing that it is not worth the effort to have equality with men in close personal relations and not to bother with men, but equality and communality among women will not be automatic either. The struggle does not necessarily mean nastiness but the perceptiveness and willingness to engage issues not only of prejudice and discrimination but also of subtle practices requiring female accommodation to males.

I know that this point is often misused and will open me to much criticism, but let me try to make it. A third lesson is that bringing up of children must be changed and that many women are lagging in this respect although present-day concerns suggest a possible change. For all of male reluctance, resistance, and avoidance, many women, particularly when they have young children, end up structuring life so that it is difficult to make a collegial life. Indeed, the concentration, nay absorption, with children make even a low-level decent relationship difficult, let alone an egalitarian one. Yes, I realize that the subordinate group is never the main source of difficulty, that men make women embrace the mother-housemother syndrome, but cultural and personal history are involved as well as direct or more covert husbandly pressure and unwillingness to be a full partner. Overinvolvement with children may operate to discourage many husbands from fully sharing because they do not accept the ideology of close attention to children.

I am *not* saying that the problem is with women but that this part of the problem shouldn't be ignored. Even for the young parents, it is important to have some measure of agreement on the mode, the style of child-care. That is difficult to do before the actual fact of having children. But perhaps this will not be an issue for those in their twenties who may have a different and more relaxed attitude toward children. (And, of course, many no longer feel unfulfilled if they do not have children.) For some, yes; but I doubt if that will be true of most relatively "straight" parents. What is also needed is a reconsideration of what is required in parenthood and in householding.

Let me take the household case first. The easy notion that in the right atmosphere housework is not so bad seems wrong to me. A lot of jobs can be stomached, treated as routine, but that is their best—manageable, doable. But they are not exciting, stimulating, or satisfying except to the extent that they are completed and "accomplished," i.e., gotten rid of for the moment. This is especially so when one's other interests are high, then these tasks become highly competitive with other ways of using one's time and thereby dissatisfying. Householding can be a full-time job if it is not guarded against. Some agreement on a minimum, satisfactory level of household care and some efficiency and sharing in performing it are important for a couple.

I have maintained, verbally at least, the desirability of "all for the parents" and "salutary neglect" (before Moynihan incidentally). But it has been difficult for my generation, whose adolescence and early twenties were stirred by Freud and who have wallowed in the guilt of parental omniscience and ethnic parental concern, to erase the sense of responsibility and guilt for how their children develop. What if one's son doesn't graduate from college or becomes a bomb-thrower or a homosexual—isn't it the parents' fault? When a son or daughter is eighteen or twenty, it seems easier to say one doesn't have responsibility, and since so many [young people] are also in troubled times, . . . it is difficult to talk of Freudian acting out rather than of a generational change in consciousness. But at earlier ages it is much more difficult to shake the feeling of parental responsibility for how the infant or child is developing. I don't advocate callous neglect, but some less constraining and demanding views of parenthood—and probably some additional institutional aims like day care—are needed.

The problem is not always in the mother's attitudes. Some studies show that working-class women are very interested in working, but their husbands feel that it is important to the children for their mothers to be home. The issue is not so much whether the mother or father is lagging but how to move toward new child development views and institutions.

A fourth lesson is about sex, and I am rather surprised by it. It turns out that the most easy acceptance of equality is in bed—not in the kitchen. Few middle-class men, except those regarded as crude or brutes, would assert that women do not have a right to enjoyment in bed equal to that of their partner. (I doubt, however, that female extramarital affairs are treated as casually by men as they think their extramarital adventures should be regarded.) Even if the male does not generally assume great responsibility for a female's difficulty in achieving orgasm, he is expected by himself and others to try to help her gain at least some measure of fulfillment. "Biff, bang, thank you, ma'am" is more of a joke than ever before.

This suggests that the most delicate of human relations—sex—isn't that central. Men are adjusting to new requirements and incorporate them in their definition of maleness. But the other elements of equality are not so easily absorbed into the definition of maleness. The "male-ness" of many young females' attitudes to sex—ready to go to bed without much emotional involvement with the partner; sex as kicks, not love—may be misleading them. "Good sex" doesn't necessarily mean real equality. I suspect many young women are being exploited by men just as my generation exploited women with the notion that true freedom, both political and psychological, was demonstrated by an "uninhibited" attitude toward relatively casual intercourse.

The phenomenal and depressing success of *Love Story*, as trite and sentimentalized a story of romance and sexism as has come along in a long while— truly a 1950-ish romance—indicates that many young women, even when they use four-letter words, dream of the everlasting and all-satisfying flame of love, including the purity of death as authenticating it. And, I fear that they think that equality in bed means equality in other things. They are much less liberated than they think and are probably sexually exploited by their male friends. Both young men and women seem unlikely to sustain untraditional forms of bedding and wedding, which is one of the reasons that I think my experiences still have relevance.

But all these "implications" are minor, except for the importance of struggle. What strikes me as the crucial concern at least for the occupationally striving family, is the male involvement in work, success, striving. It is the pressure around which the family often gets molded. Accommodation to it is frequently the measure of being a "good wife"—moving when the male's "future" requires it, regulating activities so that the male is free to concentrate on his work or business. It isn't sexism or prejudice against women which is at work here— although they contribute—but the compulsive concentration upon the objective of achievement and the relegating of other activities to secondary concern. Egalitarian relationships cannot survive if people are not somewhat equally involved with each other and if the major commitment is great to things outside the relationship but which inevitably intrude upon it.

As long as success or achievement burns bright for the male, it is going to be difficult to change drastically the situation of the family and the women. While I am strongly of the mind that success drives should be banked and other more humanitarian urges encouraged, I don't accept that all of the drive for success or achievement is pernicious or undesirable. This drive is exciting and can be fulfilling. It is a great danger to be avoided when it becomes all embracing or when it is a success without a content that is both personally and socially satisfying or beneficial.

It should be made easier to do interesting and useful things, to feel a sense of accomplishment. As in military strategy, a "sufficing" level of achievement rather than a "maximum level" of security or position should be sought. Being "number one" should not be the goal; rather, high competence should be enough for both men and women. I have seen many talented people blighted in their work by number-oneism when they probably would have done outstanding and useful work by adopting a high-competence performance criterion.

And if women accept "success" to the same extent and in the same way that many men do, the problems will be enormous. If women simply adopt the number-oneism which dominates the workplace, the achievement drive will probably lead them into the same narrowing and unpromising obsessions which destroy many men.

A more egalitarian society in terms of the distribution of income and social respect, of course, would make it easier to escape number-oneism. But meanwhile we shall have to struggle with the values which surround us and which corrode true equality in the home.

Finally, men have to feel some gains in the growing equality in their relationship to women. Over the long run there may well be greater satisfactions for the males in egalitarian relationships, but in the short run the tensions and demands may not lead to enjoyment and satisfaction. Some short-term gains for males will be important in speeding up the road to equality. But such gains are not easy nor automatically forthcoming. Substitute satisfaction or gains for the male are needed to push out sexism. That is why I made the first points about the inevitability of struggle. But successful struggle requires modes of living and relationships to which the male can accommodate without total loss. That is hard to do without falling back again to women accommodating to men. Hopefully, what is needed is not accommodation but the growth of new or deeper mutual satisfactions arising from an easier exchange of ideas and a more profound expression of love and affection.

I recognize that I concentrate upon the upper middle class and upon the experience of one male. I don't think either is the world—I really don't. But I do perceive that some of my experiences and interpretations are not solipsistic pieces of life. And that with things changing, others are experiencing similar shocks and stresses. I wonder whether the egalitarian changes I see in some young families will mean permanent changes or "lapsed egalitarianism" once again. My hope is that the seventies will be different.

Discussion

As we saw in Chapter 4, and especially in its Discussion, American women as well as women in many highly developed countries have in general few options in all the life sectors, and marriage and motherhood drastically restrict further the few options (other than these two) still open to them. Furthermore, not only are academic and occupational efforts and achievements of women rewarded, in social and psychological terms, unequally as compared with those of men, but these efforts and achievements are, in addition, stigmatized as deviant and "unnatural."[1]

Thus, when socialization at an early or later age has been unusual enough to create "deviant" women who take unapproved and unrewarded options such as getting a Ph.D. or pursuing a "masculine" profession, these women will stay single or must find a very "understanding," supportive, and "liberated" husband. Thus, Rossi has reported that the majority of women with long-range career goals in "masculine" fields like the natural sciences, business management, medicine, law, dentistry, engineering, architecture, and economics stay single.[2] And of the women engineers and physicians who marry, six out of ten marry men in their own or related fields.[3]

The very fact that so many professional women, especially in "masculine" fields, do stay single indicates quite clearly that these occupational options are deviant and negatively sanctioned. This is not true for societies such as those of Finland, Hungary, and Poland, where, as we have seen, in the Discussion in Chapter 4, the majority of married women work and the professions of pharmacy, dentistry, chemistry, and medicine have long since ceased to be considered "masculine." But even in the United States some recent evidence tends to indicate that, at least among women of high scholastic achievement, a career (mostly in a "deviant" occupation) increasingly may be seen as a life goal that can be combined with marriage with no interruption.[4]

Because of the great amount of strain involved in the attempt by American and English women to combine a "deviant" occupational choice with the socially approved option of marriage, the plight of these women has recently attracted considerable research interest and some evidence is, therefore, available. The two American research papers presented in this chapter by Poloma and Garland indicate that American women seldom have careers even when the training for their jobs has been long and arduous, as in the case with training for the practice of law or medicine, or for academic positions requiring a Ph.D. In practically all cases the husband's career is much more important than the wife's professional involvement, this issue becoming much more important at critical times such as when a decision about a move must be made. Taking into consideration the fact that many of the women studied either worked part time or made it clear that their job was a sort of pleasant and interesting hobby (that of course would never be allowed to interfere with married life), it is surprising not that the husband's occupational concerns largely determined most of the moves but rather that at least some moves were influenced mostly by the wife's occupational outlook. In general, while the wife's occupational achievement is usually sacrificed for that of the husband (whenever conflicts arise), the husband's career is not always or completely unaffected by his wife's work especially when her degree of work commitment is significant.[5]

Why do professional women seldom have careers in the United States? First, according to values prevalent in American society, women's "true" roles are those of wives and mothers. Thus, despite unique socialization and life experiences that may have allowed them to become lawyers, doctors, or college professors, they cannot bring themselves to admit to or actually to have a commitment to their careers that is as great as their commitment to their familial roles. Second, according again to prevailing traditional American sex-roles ideology, housekeeping and child care are the woman's responsibility, and breadwinning, the man's responsibility. This ideology, coupled with the lack of adequate societal mechanisms for the performance of the household and child-care–related tasks that would free women, renders the possibility of having a career very problematic, especially if a woman wants to continue her career uninterrupted while her children are very young. And the only reason the Cleveland women interviewed in the studies by Poloma and Garland were able to work (if they chose to) even when they had small children was the high income level they enjoyed, which made it possible to hire full-time housekeepers.[6]

Actually, it is rather remarkable that at least some American women, despite the tone and content of prevalent sex-role ideologies, the lack of social or emotional support for having a career and achieving significantly, the lack of readily available societal mechanisms for the performance of household and child-care tasks, and their own efforts to subordinate their work to their family and their husband's career, have been able to make significant contributions to their fields, to become famous, and occasionally to become financially or in terms of status more successful than their husbands. But the fact remains that many women, even those in "masculine" fields requiring a long training or those with Ph.D.'s in various fields, work part time or intermittently, and even when they work full time, their occupational ambitions are low, their degree of work commitment rather low, and their achievements insignificant.[7] Available research on husband-wife law partnerships indicates that even when the husband and wife are legally equal partners, the wife most often does the "dirty," uninteresting, and nonvisible work, acting as an assistant lawyer, a highly skilled legal secretary, or the manager of the enterprise.[8]

It must be noted that in societies in which women have the option to work after marriage, even when the children are young, in a variety of professions (in America considered "masculine"), women can more often be found to have significant careers. This is true for Finland,[9] Poland,[10] as well as Greece;[11] women do hold high-status, responsible positions, and a considerable number among them have a high work commitment that makes them, in some cases, place their work before family responsibilities when the two are in conflict. But even in England, where women are not provided with many choices (although with relatively more than in the United States), well-educated women can be found to have genuine careers.

While American women entering "masculine" fields and occupations often stay single, when married they are much more concerned about their femininity and their "feminine" talents than other women. This preoccupation makes them embrace motherhood with a great enthusiasm and makes them unwilling to choose the option of childlessness. This is not true for women in other countries. In Greece, for example, in a survey conducted in 1966–67, it was found that 52.2 percent of women with master's degrees or Ph.D.'s and 37.1 percent of all women college graduates were childless.[12] Childlessness in this case does represent an option chosen by Greek women, since in Greece, as demographic research indicates, the maternal role (even during the children's first years) is quite compatible with the working role, while in the United States the two roles are not compatible.[13]

Furthermore, full-time working women in the United States, despite the great strain imposed on them by a triple role (working woman, mother, and housekeeper), make a great effort to be good housewives and pride themselves on being able to do so. There is considerable evidence that these wives' preoccupation with being able to maintain the traditional housewife role prevents them from achieving truly egalitarian marriages.[14] They are often reluctant to have their husbands share family responsibilities or to relegate most responsibilities to housekeepers. Of course, it cannot always be claimed that the American husbands in these marriages are anxious to share familial responsibilities, although in some cases they do voice their willingness to do so to a greater extent than they are actually permitted by their wives. Miller's autobiographical article in the chapter presents clearly and vividly the dilemmas of an intellectual husband who would like to be an egalitarian partner but cannot escape from the sex-role behaviors for which he was socialized. It is rather striking that English career women seem to be able to find husbands whose primary source of satisfaction is their family rather than their career and that these women seem more able to delegate responsibility to different types of paid help than American "career" women. It seems that when women who try to integrate a family with a career orientation are matched with men who place relatively greater importance on their family than on their work, the result is a very good mix that leads to high marital satisfaction for both spouses, despite the necessary time and role strains involved.[15]

But let us see what kinds of unique experiences enable American women to take deviant options. The most frequent positive socialization experience has come from the father who, most often because his daughter was an only child or one of an all-girl family, encouraged her (as he would encourage a son) to enter a "masculine" field and have a "career." A second, somewhat less important life experience has been an encouraging husband, who in a few cases is the one responsible for the wife's enrollment in a professional or graduate school and her entrance into the occupational world.[16] Similar findings have been reported by the Rapoports in their research on English dual-career families.[17]

Indeed, recent studies have shown the decisive importance of the nature of women's early socialization and have indicated quite clearly how unambitious, nonachieving, nonworking women are created through a sex-role differentiated socialization process and how, as children, women are sensitive to even qualified changes toward a more unified sex-role treatment of children.[18]

Notes

1. Alice S. Rossi (Address to Massachusetts Institute of Technology symposium), reprinted in John Lear, "Will Science Change Marriage?" *Saturday Review,* December 5, 1964, pp. 75–77.
2. *Ibid.;* James S. White's article, however, "Women in the Law," included in Chapter 6 of the volume, indicates that in his sample 69.0 percent of the women and 83.2 percent of the men lawyers were or had been married.
3. Rossi, *op. cit.*
4. While they were still in college or after they had graduated, 46.4 percent of the women who had won National Merit Scholarships gave this type of response (see Donivan J. Watley and Rosalyn Kaplan, "Career or Marriage? Aspirations and Achievements of Able Young Women," *Journal of Vocational Behavior,* vol. 1 (1971), pp. 29–43).
5. Actually, another study including intensive interviews with twenty husbands and their wives, both with professional careers, concluded that in most of the couples that had moved (each couple making multiple moves), the decision to move or not, and where to, had been significantly influenced at least once by the wife's career (see Lynda Lytle Holnstrom, "Career Patterns of Married Couples" (Paper delivered at the Round Table in Honor of Everett C. Hughes, Seventh World Congress of the International Sociological Association, Varna, Bulgaria, September 14–19, 1970).
6. In regard to the research carried out in Cleveland by Margaret M. Poloma and T. Neal Garland, two papers in addition to those presented in this section provide a wealth of information: Margaret M. Poloma and T. Neal Garland, "Jobs or Careers? The Case of the Professionally Employed Married Woman," pt. 2, *International Journal of Comparative Sociology* (in press); and Margaret M. Poloma, "The Myth of the Egalitarian Family: Familial Roles and the Professional Employed Wife" (Paper delivered at the national meeting of the American Sociological Association, Washington, D.C., 1970).
7. Poloma and Garland, *op. cit.*
8. Cynthia Fuchs Epstein, "Law Partners and Marital Partners: Strains and Solutions in the Dual-Career Family Enterprise" (Paper delivered at the Eleventh International Family Research Seminar, London, September 1970).
9. Veronica Stolte-Heiskanen and Elina Haavio-Mannila, "The Position of Women in Society: Formal Ideology versus Everyday Ethic," *Social Science Information,* vol. 6, no. 6 (December 1967), pp. 169–188.
10. Jerzy Piotrowski, *Family Needs Resulting from an Increased Employment of Married Women: Adequacy of Existing Resources to Meet These Needs* (Warsaw: Chair of Sociology of Work, Institute of Social Economy, 1969).
11. Constantina Safilios-Rothschild, "The Influence of the Wife's Degree of Work Commitment upon Some Aspects of Family Organization and Dynamics," *Journal of Marriage and the Family,* vol. 32, no. 4 (November 1970), pp. 681–691.
12. Constantina Safilios-Rothschild, "Quelques aspects de la modernisation sociale aux État-Unis et en Grèce," *Sociologie et sociétés,* vol. 1, no. 1 (May 1969), p. 30.
13. J. Mayone Stycos and Robert H. Weller, "Female Working Roles and Fertility," *Demography,* vol. 4 (Fall 1967), pp. 210–217; Robert H. Weller, "The Employment of Wives, Role Incompatibility and Fertility," *The Milbank Memorial*

Fund Quarterly, vol. 46 (October 1968), pp. 508–526; Constantina Safilios-Rothschild, "Socio-psychological Factors Affecting Fertility in Urban Greece: A Preliminary Analysis," *Journal of Marriage and the Family*, vol. 31 (August 1969), pp. 595–606.

14. See also Constantina Safilios-Rothschild, "Companionate Marriage and Sexual Inequality: Are They Compatible?" in Chapter 2 of this volume.
15. Lotte Bailyn, "Career and Family Orientations of Husbands and Wives in Relation to Marital Happiness," *Human Relations*, vol. 23, no. 2 (April 1970), pp. 97–113.
16. Poloma and Garland, *op. cit.*
17. Rhona Rapoport and Robert N. Rapoport, "Early and Later Experiences as Determinants of Adult Behavior: Women's Family and Career Patterns," *British Journal of Sociology*, vol. 22, no. 1 (March 1971), pp. 16–30.
18. For more details on this issue, see Chapters 1 and 6.

Women in "Deviant" Occupations

PATRICIA ALBJERG GRAHAM

Women in Academe

American colleges and universities, struggling to accustom themselves to the state of siege mentality in which, it seems, their present and future work must be carried out, are in for another round of crisis—this one dealing with the "woman question." In colleges and universities throughout the country, high pressure has been applied by women intent on securing rights equal to those of men in academic position and preferment. In this atmosphere, many academic administrators must look wistfully back to the first two centuries of higher education in the United States, when women were simply excluded from collegiate precincts. From the founding of Harvard in 1636 to the opening of Oberlin in 1837, it was not possible for a young woman to attend college in this country. By the mid-nineteenth century, some American colleges had begun to admit women to their classes, in response to pressures similar in some respects to those affecting higher education in the United States today. One source of the pressure was ideological—the conviction that women were entitled to the same educational opportunities as men. From this stimulus, which, significantly, was contemporaneous with the abolition movement, came the establishment of certain colleges designed specifically for women, and of others which admitted both men and women. But the major impetus for women's higher education came in the second half of the nineteenth century, a time of dire economic need for many colleges, caused chiefly by shrinking masculine enrollments. The sag in college attendance was attributed to the Civil War, to economic depressions, and to dissatisfaction with the college curriculum. College trustees and presidents saw women as potential sources of tuition revenues that would permit the colleges to remain open. The principal reason, then, for the nineteenth-century breakthrough in admitting women to colleges with men was economic rather than ideological, and these circumstances were not highly conducive to developing plans than would take particular account of the educational needs of women. Even such state institutions as the University of Wisconsin first admitted women during the Civil War when many men students had joined the army.

After the Civil War very few colleges were established solely for men, the major exception being Roman Catholic institutions. The most important women's colleges were still in the East, where traditional institutions of the Ivy League—as it would later be called—dominated the educational scene; these, on the whole, saw no need to include women. In the West, where endowments were small or nonexistent and the financial pressures were greater, resistance to the admission of women was much less. There the critical institutions were state universities, and by the turn of the century most were coeducational. There, too, the denominational colleges, limited as they were in endowments and dependent upon tuition, and now in competition with the less expensive public institutions, frequently became coeducational. The argument is sometimes made that the important role the women on the frontier played is substantially responsible for the greater degree of coeducation in the West. Although this may have been a factor, it seems not to have been as determining a one as the economic considerations or as the nascent women's rights movement, which was heavily centered in the East. Well into the twentieth century the single-sex colleges in the East remained the prestigious places for young women to be educated.

By 1920 women constituted 47 percent of the undergraduates in the country and were receiving roughly 15 percent of the Ph.D.'s. In 1930 the proportion remained about the same. Today women constitute only 40 percent of the undergraduate student body and receive about 10 percent of the doctorates. The total number of students, of course, has increased enormously during these years. Although the percentage of women receiving doctorates is rising gradually from a low in the late 1950s and early 1960s, it still has not reached the high attained in the late 1920s. Various studies have also shown that between 75 and 90 percent of the "well-qualified" students who do not go on to college are women.

In the present movement toward coeducation at some of the well-known single-sex colleges, particularly Princeton, Yale, Vassar, and Sarah Lawrence, economic considerations are again an important basis for the decision to admit members of the opposite sex. The current financial dilemmas of many colleges and universities are well known, but the cure is no longer simply a matter of enlarging the student body. Although these institutions are not short of applicants, some of them at least believe that the most outstanding high school graduates are choosing other, coeducational colleges because of a desire not to be isolated from young persons of the opposite sex. This is an economic argument of a rather more sophisticated type, based on considerations of human capital. In some cases the admission of women follows by several decades the abolition of quotas for Jews and, more recently, the initiation of efforts to admit blacks. Again, the parallel with the mid-nineteenth century is striking: the women's rights advocates rode the coattails of the abolitionists much as the current feminists are trailing the black power movement.

The Current Situation

What, then, is the current situation for women in academe? Women constitute about 18 percent of the staffs of institutions of higher education, being distributed principally at small colleges and universities and in the lower ranks of other institutions. They tend to be concentrated in such fields as education, social service, home economics, and nursing. For example, 6 of the 11 women who were full professors at the University of Chicago in 1968–69 (there are 464 men full professors) were in social work. At present 2 percent of the full professors at the University of Chicago are women, in contrast to 8 percent at the turn of the century, when Chicago was (as it still is) one of the top half dozen universities in the nation. Alice Rossi[1] reports that 30 percent of the Ph.D.'s awarded in sociology go to women but that only 1 percent of the full professors in sociology in top graduate schools are women, 5 percent are associate professors, and 39 percent are subprofessional appointees, such as "research associates."

The 2 percent figure for the proportion of full professors who are women also applies at Stanford University where 15 percent of the graduate students are women. At Columbia University, which has probably granted more doctorates to women than any other institution and has for years enrolled a high proportion of women in its graduate departments (about 20 percent), just over 2 percent of the full professors are women. Barnard College, the women's undergraduate division of Columbia, which has its own faculty, for many years in the first third of the twentieth century hired women primarily, as did most of the other women's colleges. Since World War II the proportion of men professors has risen steadily. Barnard still has a higher proportion of women on its faculty than any other of the "Seven Sister" colleges (only six of which have separate faculties), probably because there are more highly educated women in New York City than in South Hadley or Poughkeepsie. The representation of women at Barnard in 1968–69 in the professorial ranks is still weighted heavily at the bottom, with women constituting 82 percent of the nonprofessorial teaching staff, 64 percent of the assistant professors, 54 percent of the associate professors, and a mere 22 percent of the full professors. Nonetheless, Barnard still has a woman president, whereas only one of the other five faculties (Wellesley) is presided over by a woman. Mary I. Bunting heads Radcliffe, but it does not have a separate faculty. In the last five years men have replaced women presidents at Vassar, Bryn Mawr, and Sarah Lawrence. Both Smith and Mount Holyoke have men presidents. Kirkland, the newest bidder for prestige as a women's coordinate college, has a man president.

Recent studies, such as Helen S. Astin's,[2] indicate that, contrary to the dire pronouncements of some graduate school officers, women who receive Ph.D.'s are likely to use them in a professional capacity. Ninety-one percent of the women who received doctorates in 1957–58 were employed in 1964, and 79 percent of them had not interrupted their careers during that time.[3] Even more startling to those of both sexes who assume that the reason women are not in better positions is that they do not publish enough is the research of Rita Simon, Shirley Merritt Clark, and Kathleen Galway,[4] which showed that married women Ph.D.'s who were employed full time published slightly more than either men Ph.D.'s or unmarried women Ph.D.'s.

Other studies, such as one made by Lindsey R. Harmon and another by the National Academy of Sciences (NAS), report, on the basis of various measures, that women doctorate holders have somewhat greater academic ability than their male counterparts.[5] Further, women who were married at the time of receiving the Ph.D. were more capable academically than their unmarried female contemporaries. Nonetheless, the fate of married women Ph.D.'s is somewhat discouraging. The NAS report states:

> In general, the rate at which women achieve the status of full professor is slower than for men, the average lag varying from two to five years in the bio-sciences and up to as much as a decade in the social sciences. There is a marital status difference also. Considering data on women for all fields combined, the single women lead the

married ones by five to ten years. At any given time, 10 to 20 per cent more of the single than married women have achieved full professor status.

Not surprisingly, the NAS also found that the salaries received by married women in general were 70 to 75 percent of those received by men at the same interval after receipt of the doctorate. Salaries of single women were more variable, but on the average they were somewhat higher than those of the married women, though still markedly lower than men's salaries.

Possible Explanations

Discrimination

One can think of various explanations for the considerable discrepancy between the ability and the professional position of women Ph.D.'s. One possibility is overt discrimination, but obvious disregard of women scholars is not as common today as it was in earlier years. The confident announcement of a senior professor in a leading history department less than ten years ago that, as long as he was a member of the department, there would never be a woman professor in it was at the time accepted without a murmur. His view held sway until his retirement. Now, in that department of nearly fifty full-time members, one full professor and one assistant professor, both in esoteric specialties, are women. Explanations given by the department for the absence of women from the populous fields of European and American history are vague. For many years about 15 percent of the graduate students in that department have been women. The discrimination is now much more subtle and less easily countered.

Internal Ambivalences

Preeminent among the reasons for the poor representation of women in the higher echelons of the professional world is a psychological-cultural one. Ellen and Kenneth Keniston of Yale University have written perceptively about the "internal ambivalences" that most American women feel about combining career and family.[6] These ambivalences are especially acute in the years between eighteen and twenty-five, years which, in this society, men generally devote to intense preparation for a career. For women these years are likely to be a time in which they seek affirmation of their femininity, an activity likely to be at variance with serious vocational commitment. These activities are certainly not the only ones young people engage in, but they are likely to be the ones invested with the greatest psychic energy.

Some young women are able to do graduate work and to do it well in these years, but few pass through this period without severe qualms about the desirability of planning for a demanding professional life. Men, too, are beset by a variety of doubts during these years, but for the majority of them, at least, academic success does not bring substantial psychic problems as it does for women. Matina Horner has recently given unfinished stories, identical except for the name of the protagonist, to groups of young men and women for comment.[7] In one set "Bill" is at the top of his medical school class; in the other set "Anne" is at the top. Both the young men and the young women believed that Bill was headed for a bright and happy future whereas many believed that Anne would face many problems as a result of her academic achievement. Matina Horner concludes:

> For women, then, the desire to achieve is often contaminated by what I call the *motive to avoid success.* I define it as the fear that success in competitive achievement situations will lead to negative consequences, such as unpopularity and loss of femininity.

To expect young women to buck the cultural standards for females is to demand of them much more than is expected of any man attempting to succeed in his field, since men are supposed to be successful. The problem for young women is not eased by the fact that they see few women occupying positions of importance in the academic, professional, and business worlds. Some of those who are there are unmarried, and few young women deliberately choose the single life. Others are the rare individuals who manage to marry a brilliant and successful husband, have five children, write intelligently on a variety of topics, assume a major administrative position, and, at the age of forty be featured on the beauty pages of a woman's magazine. Most young women rightly recognize such an achievement as truly exceptional, and girls in this society do not think of themselves as conquerors of the world. "Models" of this sort sometimes lack effectiveness because undergraduates simply refuse to aspire to such heights.

Aspiration and Expectation

The problem of aspiration is closely tied to the internal ambivalences. If one is uncertain about whether one should have a career, one cannot aspire, either publicly or privately, to be an art historian, a plasma physicist, or a professor of philosophy. Women's low expectations for themselves so infect the society that both men and women refuse to think of women as generally likely to occupy important posts. A riddle currently popular in the cocktail party circuit concerns a father and son driving down a highway. There is a terrible accident in which the father is killed, and the son, critically injured, is rushed to a hospital. There the surgeon approaches the patient and suddenly cries, "My God, that's my son!" The group is then asked how this story can be true. All sorts of replies requiring immense ingenuity are forthcoming: complicated stepfather relationships are suggested, sometimes even artificial insemination. Almost invariably the storyteller must supply the answer: "The surgeon is his mother."

The problem, then, of aspiration and of expectation is acute. The Kenistons have pointed to the absence of an aristocratic tradition in America as one factor depressing the level of women's aims. They point out that in Europe "women of the upper classes have had enough leisure and freedom from family needs to permit them, if they choose, to 'work' outside their homes." Except in the South and possibly in the Boston area—both places which have nurtured a number of unusual and talented women—the United States has lacked, not to say discouraged the growth of, such a leisured class. The

South, which in this respect as in so many others does not fit the usual generalizations, has produced some of the best-known contemporary writers in America, such as Flannery O'Connor, Katherine Anne Porter, Eudora Welty, and Carson McCullers.

But Boston and the South cannot change the nation, much as both have sometimes wished to try. There are few hard data on the question, but the number of women Ph.D.'s in the United States today who have close ties to another cultural heritage is probably substantial. For example, both the first woman full professor at Princeton (who was appointed to the professorship in 1968) and the recently named special assistant to the president for co-education, at Yale, the former a Ph.D. in sociology and the latter a Ph.D. in chemistry, came to the United States as young girls, one from Austria and the other from Germany. The author of the most recent major work on women Ph.D.'s herself grew up in Greece. A leader of the Columbia Women's Liberation Movement is English. All these women have direct experience with another culture and presumably recognize a greater variety of options for women than the stereotype of middle America currently exemplified by Mrs. Nixon and Mrs. Agnew.

Another substantial category of women Ph.D.'s is comprised of the daughters of professional women. Learned pediatricians and psychiatrists to the contrary, the daughters of working mothers seem more inclined to pursue definite career patterns than other women are. My own mother received her Ph.D. in 1925 and taught in Alabama State College for Women until her marriage and then only sporadically (she was a victim of the nepotism rule). When Princeton hired its first female assistant dean this year, the university selected a woman whose mother is director of the New Jersey State Council on Aging. Mary Bunting's mother was a leader in public education in New York City.

No doubt Princeton and other universities are completely unaware of the way in which their women fit into these three major categories [coming from Boston or the South, coming from another cultural heritage, being the daughter of a professional woman], but the fit is striking. Incidentally, Princeton's second woman full professor, who will join the faculty in the fall of 1970, is a Virginian by birth.

The "internal ambivalences" remain for the girl of more or less ordinary ability. If she wants to marry, bear children, and also have a serious and responsible position, whom can she find to exemplify such a pattern? Unless she has gone to one of the women's colleges, which still have larger proportions of women faculty than coeducational institutions have, she is not likely to find many models, although probably more now than she would have found five or ten years ago. If she is impolitic enough to suggest that something is wrong with a society in which it appears so difficult for a woman to achieve these kinds of goals, she is likely to be subjected to the harshest kind of argument—not anger but ridicule, as evidenced by the recent article in *Harper's* by a young Harvard graduate who had returned to the United States after several years in Europe and found to his consternation that a feminist movement was under way. In her formative state she may well opt out of a Ph.D. program or accept a "research associate" position instead of holding out for the degree or the assistant or associate professorship she deserves.

Publication

Another major reason usually given for the low proportion of women in top positions in universities is that they do not publish. This may well be true, despite the Simon-Clark-Galway study which indicated that married women Ph.D.'s publish slightly more than men Ph.D.'s do. Simple numbers of items on bibliographies are not a guide to quality. Probably one of the most important reasons why most women Ph.D.'s do not publish as widely as men Ph.D.'s do, if this is indeed true, is that they are not put into positions in which they must. Research and writing for publication are not easy, and a great many people would not publish unless it was necessary. For example, if a young man is appointed an assistant professor at a major university shortly after receiving his Ph.D., the chances are better than nine out of ten that he is married. Presumably he is supporting his wife and his growing family. He knows that if he expects to remain at the university beyond his six or so allotted years as an assistant professor, he must publish. Furthermore, as his family grows he needs more money, and his wife, whose status in a community is largely a reflection of her husband's position, is usually eager for him to be promoted and may even be willing to help him with his research. Most important, a man expects to be a success, at least in a modest way, and most men are willing to exert some effort to achieve this.

A woman's situation is very different. One of the cardinal social rules is that she should not be more successful than her husband, especially in his line of work. Nearly half of the recent women Ph.D.'s who are married have husbands who also have professional degrees. For example, all but one of the husbands of the married women Ph.D.'s holding professional appointments at Princeton in 1970 have doctorates. The remaining one expects to receive his Ph.D. at Harvard soon. But people in some circles question whether a woman with an advanced degree should succeed at all. The chances are that, if she is married, her place of residence has been selected because it offers the best position for her husband, not for her. Often, if she is teaching, it is in an institution less prestigious than her husband's, and there she is under less pressure to publish. Sometimes she rationalizes her nonresearch on the basis that research would not be helpful to her professionally anyway, so why should she bother. Her chances of having secretarial help and graduate-student assistance are probably less than those of men professors. In short, incentives for her to do research are generally missing.

Single women, who theoretically have much greater geographic mobility than married women, can seek a position in an institution in which extensive publication is not expected. In fact, until very recently that was about the only place in which they were likely to be hired, since the faculties of the most prestigious institutions were almost entirely male. Unless she published, she would probably not be hired away from the small institution at a higher academic rank. Often she need not publish because departments frequently assign onerous committee duties to women, who accept them too willingly and then use them as excuses for not doing research.

The Problem of Time

Another serious obstacle to women's (particularly married women's) professional advancement is the simple one of time. There are just not enough hours in the day to do all she must. A recent UNESCO study[8] revealed that the average working mother had 2.8 hours of free time on a typical weekday, as compared with 4.1 for a working man.

Another way of viewing this question is to note that women Ph.D.'s in the United States spend about twenty-eight hours per week, on the average, on household tasks.[9] Although we are fond of talking of the great advances made by technology in freeing women from domestic tasks, the working mother's concern for her children is not eased by possession of an automatic washer-dryer or dishwasher. What she needs, and what she finds increasingly difficult to find, is household help—persons who are competent and reliable and will assist her in caring for her children and running her house. Day-care centers are certainly needed, but even they do not solve the problem of having to vacuum the living room and change the beds.

The Suburban Syndrome

Related to the problem of time and of inadequate household help is the suburban syndrome, in which both of these problems are accentuated. More and more Americans live in outlying urban areas, and it becomes harder and harder for wives to find jobs that do not take them away from their homes for long periods of the day. If one must spend three hours each day commuting and then come home to perform the customary domestic chores, the amount of energy left at the end of the day is small indeed. In suburban communities domestic help is notoriously difficult to find. Complicating the picture even further is the usual social custom of such towns, in which people generally entertain at dinner parties in their own homes. In a city it is still possible to entertain one's friends by taking them to restaurants or concerts, but in many suburban communities there are no public facilities where one can spend a pleasant evening. The home and the overtired woman are expected to provide the serene environment in which friends can enjoy themselves. An obvious solution is simply to reduce one's social life to the barest minimum, but this exceedingly common way of dealing with the problem works hardships on the professional woman's family and on the woman herself.

The Nepotism Rule

A final obstacle that a woman Ph.D. (or sometimes her husband) faces is the nepotism rule, written or unwritten, that still prevails on many campuses. Although more and more institutions are now willing to have two members of the same family teaching in one institution, few regard with enthusiasm the prospect of having a husband and wife in the same department, particularly if both are at the professorial level. Since many professional women met their husbands in graduate school (the proportion of women Ph.D.'s married to Ph.D.'s in the same field is very high in all fields except that of education, where women are less likely to be married), the question of husbands and wives being employed in the same department is very likely to occur. Rarely is the wife given the superior appointment. Typically she takes a job in another institution or works part time as a "research associate" at her husband's institution.

Corrective Measures

If these are the problems that affect professional women on academic faculties, what are some of the steps institutions might take to alleviate them? Until very recently universities were, on the whole, not conscious of discrimination against women. Administrators were—and many still are—fond of making pious statements to the effect that all persons were treated equally, that none was discriminated against. To say this is to raise the question of what "equality" really is. Is it simply applying the same rule in all situations, or is it rather recognizing that the rules themselves may favor one group over another? For many years we gave standardized IQ and achievement tests to youngsters and assumed that we were treating them equally because we were giving all students identical tests. In recent years we have come to see the fallacy of this policy, and we recognize that tests have a "cultural bias." Although they met the standard of abstract equality, they failed to meet the comparably important one of actual equality. So it is with many of the policies in the university, which apply primarily to men. Women who wish to teach must meet these similarly "culturally biased" standards, and what is called equality in academe is only abstract equality and not actual equality.

Appointment to Senior Faculty and Administrative Posts

In order to achieve genuine or actual equality for women, colleges and universities need to make some adaptations. Preeminent among these is the need to recognize women's situations in their own academic communities and then to support them adequately. Probably the most important single factor in creating an environment that is as hospitable to the aspirations of women as to men is to appoint women in significant numbers to senior faculty and administrative posts in the university. Just as "tokenism" has been rejected for the blacks, so it must be rejected for the less militant feminine majority. The appointment of women to faculty posts will provide evidence for both male and female students, and for faculty colleagues, that teaching and scholarship of the highest standards can be attained by women as well as by men. The presence of women in senior administrative positions will also encourage the able young undergraduate and graduate women at the university to believe that a secretarial career, even a glorified one, need not be their vocational ambition, and it will remind the young men who will later be employers of women that women too can be expert executives. Male professors should see successful women of their own age among their colleagues, in order that the entire faculty can justifiably encourage women students to pursue additional studies or accept demanding positions that are in line with their talents.

No doubt it is also necessary on most campuses to increase the number of young women in the junior faculty and administrative positions at the university, but this is generally neither as crucial nor as difficult as the senior appointments. Many mature male professors find it much easier to appoint young women to junior and subordinate positions (where they have little power) than to appoint women of their own age to positions truly equivalent to their own. Sometimes it is possible to appoint women of mature years to junior administrative positions which might otherwise be filled by bright young men, but this kind of appointment may be more damaging than no female appointment at all. Few intelligent, alert coeds look forward to being rewarded in their middle years by promotion from departmental secretary to administrative associate when other administrative associates are twenty-five-year-old men. At one leading university three assistant deans were men in their twenties or thirties; the fourth was a woman in her fifties. Many traditionally coeducational colleges are now replacing the separate dean of women and dean of men by a dean of students. Generally this reorganization, which is thought to be "progressive," means that a man is appointed. At one midwestern state university where this was done the dean of women was nationally known and widely respected. The dean of students, who became her immediate superior, had no standing outside the community and not much locally, but he was of the same sex as the all-male administration of the university, which had been coeducational since its founding in 1869.

Ideally the women at the university should represent a variety of styles, just as the male faculty members do. Some should be dedicated, and probably single, scholar-teachers, and others should be women who manage successfully to cope with the demands of academic life and of home and family. Some may be concerned with the particular educational needs of women students, but others may not. In appointing women professors the institution will look first for scholarliness and teaching ability, not militant feminism. As the number of women on the faculty grows, the responsibility of individual women for exemplifying female academic accomplishment will decline, and this is as it should be. When there are but a few women on a faculty, excessive demands are made upon them; not only must each fulfill the usual academic requirement but she must serve as the token woman on all kinds of committees.

Part-Time Professorial Appointments

If the academic institutions do move vigorously to appoint more women to their faculties, they might well consider expanding the number of part-time professorial appointments with full perquisites. "Part-time" has a poor reputation among academic administrators, largely because it is assumed that the part-time person is one who is in effect "moonlighting" from a full-time job. With women scholars this is not quite the case. They have no prior institutional loyalty or obligation. Women scholars, particularly those who are married, might welcome the opportunity to teach on a part-time basis with full professional recognition. The demands on their time and energies at home are often considerable, as noted above, but at present, if they wish to be taken seriously in their fields, they must accept full-time positions. To do so frequently requires an unusual endowment of energy. If they do not wish to teach full time, they are generally consigned to the ranks of lecturers and instructors, where they are not eligible for sabbatical leaves and other academic perquisites. Such circumstances tend to depress the status of women in the university and do not foster conditions in which they are likely to do research, which is the major means of getting out of the lower-ranking positions.

If universities permitted and even encouraged departments to appoint persons to assistant, associate, and full professorships on a part-time basis, they would be able to staff their institutions with persons of diverse interests and specialties whom they could perhaps not afford to employ on a full-time basis. In large departments these persons could supplement the traditional offerings, and in small departments which are not scheduled for substantial growth they could provide some of the necessary breadth. At senior levels, the university could select outstanding persons of proven accomplishment at salaries roughly comparable to, or less than, those now paid to lecturers and instructors. More imaginative research appointments for women might also be made along these lines.

Full provision needs to be made for opportunities for part-time faculty to shift to full-time status when the individual and the department agree that such a change would be desirable. Similarly, tenure should be available to part-time professors, just as it is to full-time professors, and the same standard should be used in determining qualifications for promotion. Anything less would create a category of second-class citizens. Committee obligations, student advising, and the other duties associated with professional appointments would be apportioned to part-time faculty members roughly on the basis of the full-time equivalent position; thus, for example, a half-time associate professor would have half the number of student advisees that a full-time associate professor had.

Obviously men as well as women might be interested in these part-time appointments and should be eligible for them. Departments should be cautious, however, about permitting large numbers of their members to be on part-time appointments, and they should look with some skepticism upon persons who want continuing part-time appointments in order to devote more time to remunerative activities for other institutions or businesses. These difficulties should be construed not as insurmountable but merely as requiring some additional consideration before a part-time professional appointment is made.

Maternity Leave

The appointment of women in significant numbers to faculties must involve a policy concerning pregnancy and maternity leave. Most universities currently have no such policy, and many administrators, when queried, reply that none is necessary. The principal reason why none seems necessary is that women have never been on these faculties in substantial numbers. Typically, a woman faculty member either manages to have her baby in midsummer or simply loses her appointment when she takes time off to have the baby. Not all women have been as fortunate as Millicent McIntosh, who was debating whether to accept the position of headmistress of the Brearley School in New York City. Her aunt M. Carey Thomas, the illustrious president of Bryn Mawr, is supposed to have advised her, "Take it, you can have your babies in the summer." Mrs. McIntosh accepted the advice and went on to have five children and to become president of Barnard College. In short, academic women who become pregnant must handle this part of their life as they do all other parts—they must pretend to be as much like men as possible and not permit this event to interfere with the regular performance of their duties.

No university should be exploited by women professors who keep having children and expecting the university to pay them while they are on maternity leave. A more rational policy than the present one ought to be developed, so that pregnancy, of itself, does not discriminate against a woman scholar. It would seem that guaranteeing a woman a maximum of two sixteen-week maternity leaves, with pay, during her academic career would not bankrupt most colleges or universities. This would in effect be a one-semester leave with pay, twice in a woman's life. Additional pregnancies would be the woman's own financial responsibility.

Tenure

In many institutions the hurdles that must be run in order to achieve tenure are considerable. It is now standard in many fields to receive a Ph.D. when one is in one's late twenties. If the new Ph.D. accepts a teaching appointment at the assistant professor level, then ordinarily within six or seven years the tenure decision is made. In many universities this means that the dissertation must have been converted to a publishable manuscript, and that some other scholarly research, ideally another book, has been completed. This six- or seven-year period coincides with a woman's childbearing years, and, if one assumes that the couple wants two children, both are ordinarily born before a woman is thirty-five. Therefore, the greatest pressures both for scholarly publication and for domestic performance coalesce in these years between the ages of twenty-eight and thirty-five.

One way of handling this difficulty is to grant women assistant professors an automatic one-year extension, before the tenure decision is made, for each pregnancy they have, up to a maximum of two, during their nontenure years. This addition of one or two years before they are subjected to the scrutiny of their colleagues for the tenure decision would give them some additional time to complete the scholarly work necessary to justify promotion. Should they prefer that the tenure decision be made earlier, this could be done.

Husbands and Wives on the Same Faculty

Another policy that colleges and universities would do well to adopt is one that permits husband and wife to serve on the same faculty. Twenty percent of the wives of junior faculty members at one prestigious university have

Ph.D.'s, yet none is a member of the faculty. At a large Midwestern university throughout the 1930s, 1940s, and 1950s, one faculty wife published over two dozen articles and one book and coauthored two other books with her husband, yet was never permitted to become a member of the department, despite a research record superior to that of all but two members of the department. Obviously, having both husband and wife on the faculty can lead to some awkward circumstances, particularly if both are junior members of the same department and only one promotion can be made. The other frequently cited difficult case is that in which one spouse is a tenured member of the department and the other is up for promotion. The supporters of nepotism rules cite such cases with great alacrity, and they are absolutely right in pointing to the possibilities for hard feeling that can develop within a department. Nonetheless, the case is rarely made for the advantages of having two members of a family employed at the same institution. In this era of considerable faculty mobility and declining institutional loyalty, one way of insuring faculty support is to employ both husband and wife in positions commensurate with their ability and training. A husband and wife who both enjoy their work will be much less inclined than a single individual to heed the siren call of another university. In those fields in which collaboration is essential to research, husbands and wives are often much more effective as a team than either would be alone; hence the university is brought distinction by having both members on its faculty.

Although the problems should not be minimized and any department thinking of hiring such a husband-and-wife team should examine the situation carefully, any university rule which explicitly forbids such a practice should be abolished. Departments and senior faculty members should be strong enough to say starkly that only one spouse will be hired because only one is really wanted or needed, rather than dragging out a university regulation that officially prohibits the practice. The proportion of women Ph.D.'s who are married is increasing, and the nepotism question will become more acute.

Day-Care Centers

A greater boon to women faculty members with children would be the establishment of university day-care centers. In these days of constricted university budgets this recommendation is perhaps the most expensive of all to implement, but it does deserve careful consideration. On those many campuses which now have nursery schools in connection with their school of education programs for training nursery and primary school teachers, it would probably not be very difficult to convert these laboratory schools, which now function for the convenience of the school of education, to all-day centers. For mothers to have a place where they can leave their children, confident that they will be well cared for, would be a tremendous help. Ideally these centers should be open to all employees and students of the university, with preference in admission given to children of women attached to the university. Thus the women graduate students who have children would have a real chance to finish the work for their degrees despite their maternal responsibilities. Similarly, women employed by the university in food services and custodial capacities would have a much better place to leave their children than is frequently now the case.

A less ambitious aid than a day-care center would be a placement service for domestic workers maintained by the university for the use of women faculty, administrators, students, and employees. Most universities have an extensive employment office in which they screen applicants for various jobs in the university. If this office would also supply names and references for persons willing to do cleaning, housekeeping, or babysitting, this would be a tremendous help to women working at the university. Astin found in her study of women receiving Ph.D.'s[10] that the difficulty of finding adequate domestic help was their single greatest problem.

Curriculum Changes

A recommendation less directly tied to insuring the full participation of scholarly women in the university life, but nonetheless related to it, concerns the curriculum. Departments within the university should be encouraged to review their departmental offerings to be sure that women's experience is given adequate treatment. English courses in biography, for example, might well cover women subjects as well as men. Anthropology courses might give considerable attention to male and female sex roles in various cultures. Courses in American social history could probably do better by the experience of American women in the nineteenth century than the usual hasty reference to the Seneca Falls convention and the suffragette movement. Much greater sophistication is needed to deal appropriately with women's historical experience; the particular psychological and cultural factors affecting women at a given time are poorly understood. In this connection the professional associations, such as the American Historical Association or the American Psychological Association, can be of genuine service by sponsoring sessions at their conventions on questions of this kind, so that historians and psychologists can become aware not only of the issues but also of what some of their colleagues are doing about them.

Continuous Review

Finally, most colleges and universities would benefit from appointing a senior administrator, or establishing a committee, to keep under continuous review the status of women on their own campus. This would in effect be an individual or a group lobbying effort for the cause of women at that institution. The administrator or committee would be concerned with matters such as faculty salaries, making sure that women and men received equal compensation for equivalent services. On most campuses some change needs to be made if women are to have truly equal access to the opportunities of the institution, and change usually does not come, in a university or any other institution, simply on the basis of goodwill. Some steps need to be taken to assure that the needed alterations will take place, and these are not likely to be taken unless some person or group recognizes that the responsibility for change is theirs.

Generally a university does not create a lobby within itself in order to create change. In fact, too often administrations are forced to modify policies as a result of lobbies within the university that the administration did not foster. Unlike many other constituencies within the university community, women undergraduates (and to a lesser degree women graduate students) have not yet pushed for the cause of women on their own campus. Many women scholars on the faculty have not done so either, although such activity is now being initiated on some campuses chiefly among the younger women faculty members and among women teaching assistants and graduate student.

The frequently drawn analogy between the status of blacks and of women in this society is perhaps least appropriate here. There is indeed much historic similarity between the two groups, particularly in regard to the way in which their respective heritages have been ignored, the patronizing manner in which both are treated, the economic discrimination both suffer, the inability of both to "pass" as members of the dominant race or sex, and, finally, the reluctance of some of the successful members of both groups to assist younger and more militant members to attain more satisfactory situations. In two critical areas, however, the analogy does not hold, and both of these are germane to the academic situation. One is the reluctance of young women, unlike young blacks, to band together to push for their own causes, and the other is the vastly more complicated relationship that women have with their so-called oppressors, males, than blacks have with whites. Unlike blacks, who can indeed develop a separatist mode of life, women as a group cannot. In the core of their lives they are deeply involved with men (whereas blacks are not inevitably tied to whites), and the nature of that bond is such that, for many women, an overt attack upon the male establishment is not possible. A major goal of the rapidly developing militant feminist groups is to increase women's sensitivity to their plight in this society. To do this many rely heavily upon informal conversations of women in small groups in which an effort is made to build a group solidarity. The hope is that these closer ties with other women will help "emancipate" women from their dependence—economic, social, and psychic—upon men.

A Rare Opportunity

So far the radical feminists have been most successful among women in their twenties and thirties, not yet among undergraduates. This laggardness in feminine militancy on the campuses gives university administrations an opportunity to act to improve the status of women on their campuses before being confronted with demands—an opportunity of a kind that is rare these days. Difficult as it is for an academic institution to gird for change when danger is not imminent, the present moment is a time when universities can assume the leadership they have so rarely exhibited in these years of confrontation politics.

Notes

1. Alice Rossi reported these figures and other related data to the general business meeting of the American Sociological Association on September 3, 1969.

They were summarized in a mimeographed document, "Status of Women in Graduate Departments of Sociology: 1968–69," circulated by the Women's Caucus of the American Sociological Association; for excerpts, see *Science*, vol. 166 (1969), p. 356.

2. H. S. Astin, *The Woman Doctorate in America: Origins, Career, and Family* (New York: Russell Sage Foundation, 1969).

3. *Ibid.*, p. 57.

4. R. J. Simon, S. M. Clark, and K. Galway, "The Woman Ph.D.: A Recent Profile," *Social Problems*, vol. 15, no. 2 (Fall 1967), pp. 221–236.

5. L. R. Harmon, *High School Ability Patterns, A Backward Look from the Doctorate?* Scientific Manpower Report no. 6 (Washington, D.C.: National Research Council, Office of Scientific Personnel, 1965); *Careers of Ph.D.'s, Academic v. Nonacademic, A Second Report on Follow-ups of Doctorate Cohorts, 1935–60* (Washington, D.C.: National Academy of Sciences, 1968).

6. E. Keniston and K. Keniston, "The American Anachronism: The Image of Women and Work," *American Scholar*, vol. 33, no. 3 (Summer 1964), pp. 355–375.

7. M. Horner, "Fail: Bright Women," *Psychology Today*, vol. 3, no. 6 (November 1969), pp. 36, 38, 62.

8. Reported in *New York Times*, March 5, 1967.

9. Astin, *op. cit.*, p. 95.

10. *Ibid.*, p. 101.

JAMES J. WHITE

Women in the Law

Introduction

In 1869 Belle A. Mansfield, reputedly the first female lawyer admitted to practice in the United States, was admitted to the state bar of Iowa.[1] Others soon followed her and this dribble of women entering the legal profession has grown to a persistent and continuous trickle in the twentieth century, but it shows no signs of becoming a flood.[2] At last count approximately 7000 out of America's 300,000 listed lawyers were women.

Since the practice of law—even in the most masculine and aggressive Perry Mason style—does not require a strong back, large muscles, or any of the other perculiarly male characteristics, one might ask why women account for less than 3 percent of all lawyers. That question is only part of a larger and equally puzzling inquiry about the status of women in medicine, engineering, business, and government, but this study cannot hope to answer the larger question and does not endeavor to do so;[3] rather, its purpose is to investigate a ten-year segment of the small female contingent in the American bar.

In the legal world, both in law school and in practice, one hears a multitude of inconsistent rumors about the composition and status of this female segment of the bar. One source will say that almost all women lawyers are tough, masculine, and querulous; another, with quite the opposite implication, will state that women come to law school only to achieve the feminine goal of capturing a husband by placing themselves in a most advantageous marriage market. One woman will report that she has been turned away by one potential employer after another because she is a woman. Another will report that she is working for an outstanding large city law firm and that she has received treatment from both her employer and other firms which was in no way discriminatory. One counselor will tell a woman to seek a job with a large firm where they can "afford to hire a woman"; another will tell her to find a job with a small firm where her individual abilities and capabilities will be appreciated and where she will be treated fairly.

One purpose of this article is to report data from a large sample of the women who are recent graduates of the country's law schools in order to give some basis for drawing conclusions about what women do and what opportunities are open to them. A second purpose is to compare the status of these women with that of a matched group of male graduates and to examine the possible causes for some of the differences in their status. Finally, we shall make a tentative examination of the forces at hand which might permit a narrowing of the gap which exists between female and male status where such a narrowing seems desirable.

The Status of Women in the Legal Profession

The Sample

In October of 1965 we wrote to each of the 134 accredited law schools in the United States and asked each of them for the name and address of each of its female graduates in the classes of 1956 through 1965 inclusive, and the name and address of one male from the same class for each such female; 108 schools ultimately replied to this request and supplied 2219 female names and 2151 male names. We mailed questionnaires to each of these women and men: 1298 female and 1329 male respondents ultimately returned usable questionnaires; 303 questionnaires were returned as undeliverable; and 26 members of the sample refused to participate in the study. The women who returned usable questionnaires constituted 64.8 percent of those women whom we believe to have received a questionnaire. The corresponding percentage with respect to men was 66.4.

The careful reader will bear in mind several important qualifications in considering the following discussion and in extrapolating from its results. First, he should not assume that either the female or the male sample is an exact replica of the entire male or female lawyer population. The sample comes entirely from the last ten years' law graduates and omits the 30 to 40 percent of the males and females in the sample who did not respond. Conceivably these silent figures would have slipped into the calculations without the change of a decimal point in the tabulations; on the other hand, it is possible that they would have changed the results extensively. In the male sample, this problem is aggravated by the fact that not all of the law schools selected their male names on a truly random basis.[4] So *reader beware*: "Males" means those men in the sample who responded; "females" means the same with respect to the opposite sex.

Finally, this report assumes that the respondents' memories were accurate and their reporting truthful. Undoubtedly the statistics have been rendered somewhat inaccurate by the failure of some to recall and record correctly all of the data. In a few cases the figures themselves hint at forgetfulness, disingenuousness, or distortion in the sample. For example, approximately 50 percent of all the respondents stated that they were in the top quarter of their graduating classes and only 5 to 6 percent acknowledged residence in the bottom quarter. Perhaps these figures can be explained by the fact that many graduates do not know their quartile rank and gave themselves the benefit of the doubt. Whatever the explanation, to the extent that this report focuses on the differential between male and females, discrepancies of this kind may not be significant if we can assume that the males and females each gave themselves a uniform benefit of the doubt when their recollections were faint or inaccurate.[5]

Money

The questionnaire asked the respondent to state his adjusted gross income (1) for his "first nontemporary job" after law school and (2) for the calendar year 1964. The respondent did not state his actual income but only marked an annual range (for example, $5001–$8000). The conclusion is clear: the males make a lot more money than do the females. The differential in present income is approximately $1500 for those in their first year after graduation, and, with the passage of each year, the males increase their lead over the females until they reach a point at which the differential is represented by a $17,300 to $9000 lead, and with no substantial appearance of abatement in their rate of gain. In 1964, 9 percent of the males earned more than $20,000, but only 1 percent of the females had reached that level; 21 percent of the males exceeded $14,000, as compared with only 4.1 percent of the females. The converse is true at the levels below $8000, where one finds 56.3 percent of the females but only 33.6 percent of the males. These figures are not distorted by the inclusion of housewives or others who are not employed full time at a paying job because only those employed full time at a paying job were included.

Doubtless the reader can imagine a variety of rival hypotheses in addition to discrimination which might explain the enormous income difference between males and females. Some of these, such as class standing, school, type of employer, and type of work, will be considered [in later sections] of this article.

Job Profiles

Approximately 25 percent of the respondents, both male and female, found their first jobs with firms of 4 or under (including solo practice).[6] There were only statistically insignificant differences in the percentage of males and females taking their first jobs with firms of over 29 and with the federal government. However, men far exceeded women in obtaining jobs with firms in the 5- to 30-man category, and women had a substantial edge over men in state and local government.

A comparison of male and female migrations from starting to present jobs shows several significant differences. The percentage of women in government work increases by more than 5 percent, while the corresponding male percentage decreases by approximately the same amount. Women increase their representation in firms of 15 and under by only 2.4 percent, but nearly 10 percent more men find their present jobs with firms of 15 and under than started there. Other migrations are less significant.

These statistics are consistent with two commonly held notions: (1) men often use the government as a stepping-stone to private practice; and (2) a large part of all women lawyers (about one third) find long-term employment in government.

The comparative distribution of men and women in small, medium, and large firms is puzzling. Women have roughly comparable representation with men in small and large firms, but have substantially less representation in medium-sized firms. The questionnaire offered only tantalizing fragments of information to explain these phenomena. The comparative lack of female representation in the medium-sized firm may be explained by the function which the female law graduate performs. If her function in the large firms is to do research, mind the library, and perform other specialized tasks which fall somewhat short of practice on the same scale as her male colleagues, her comparatively small representation in the medium-sized firm can be explained by the fact that such firms are not large enough to justify hiring her. However, since the small firm is no better able to hire women exclusively for research or library work than is the medium-sized firm, this analysis cannot explain the extensive representation of women in the 4 or under category. The answer here may lie in the peculiar status of lawyers in these firms, which include solo practice and practice in which the starting lawyer is something more than an ordinary employee. For example, it includes cases in which a woman forms a partnership with her husband, her father, or with another person of approximately her own age. The questionnaire did not yield data on the number in solo practice, nor did it give the number in practice with husbands, fathers, or other relatives. Nonetheless, my discussions with lawyers and my own observations of female practice suggest that this form of practice is common for many women. Thus the comparatively large representation of women in the 4 or under category may be attributable to the fact that [the woman lawyer] does not face the usual employer's discrimination either because she is not an employee at all or because she has a familial relationship with a member of the firm which overcomes any such discrimination.

First Jobs: Ten-Year Change

It is quite possible that the jobs available to the class of 1950 one year, five years, and ten years after graduation differ considerably from the jobs available at the corresponding periods after graduation to the members of the class of 1930. Since the data cover only a ten-year time span, however, there is very little information about changes in job profiles from one class to another. This is particularly true as to the respondents' present jobs, and it would be misleading to compare the present jobs of a class only two or three years out of law school with those of a class which had been out eight years. In such a comparison, the change in profiles between two classes would be obscured by the fact that one class had been in practice longer than the other. For that reason, we have presented a comparison of only the starting jobs of the two oldest and three youngest classes. Certain changes were common to both males and females: (1) more now find their first jobs with firms of 30 or more, in clerkships, and in state and local government than they did eight to ten years ago; and (2) fewer find their first jobs in firms of 4 or under. Since our data did not effectively distinguish between firms of 4 or under and solo practice, it is not possible to tell what percentage of this decrease is attributable to the fact that fewer lawyers are starting out in solo practice. Once again, the 5- to 30-man firm plays the villain. A substantially larger percentage of the men started with such firms in the 1963 to 1965 period than ten years ago [1957], but the corresponding percentage of women starting with such firms has diminished. Except to the extent that the data show discrimination generally, they give no explanation for the opposite movement of men and women in this case.

Work Performed

The survey disclosed interesting differences between the areas of work of men and women. Most of the respondents indicated that they performed more than one kind of work; many acknowledged the performance of all of the types indicated in Exhibit 1. The proportion of females engaged in trusts and

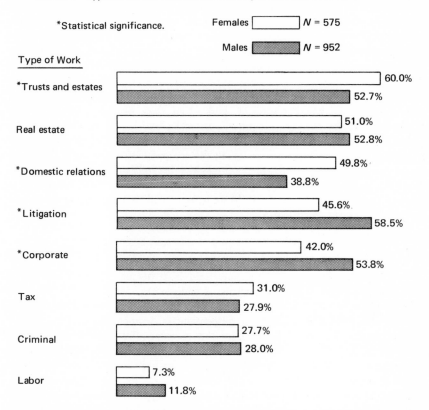

Exhibit 1   Types of Work Performed (Excluding Those Employed by Government)

*Statistical significance.   Females [   ] *N* = 575

Males [▨▨▨] *N* = 952

Type of Work

*Trusts and estates
60.0%
52.7%

Real estate
51.0%
52.8%

*Domestic relations
49.8%
38.8%

*Litigation
45.6%
58.5%

*Corporate
42.0%
53.8%

Tax
31.0%
27.9%

Criminal
27.7%
28.0%

Labor
7.3%
11.8%

estates (60 percent), domestic relations (50 percent), and tax (31 percent) was higher than the proportion of men engaged in those activities. These data accord with the commonly held beliefs about women's practice. The fact that 45.6 percent engage in litigation and 27.7 percent in criminal work is more surprising. Since the question did not limit "litigation" to actively contested adversary court proceedings, some may have acknowledged participation in litigation even though their court appearances amounted to nothing more than procuring a signature on a probate order or obtaining an occasional uncontested divorce. However, even if the number is reduced somewhat to account for those who marked litigation but do not engage in adversary proceedings, the size of the female response to this question and to the question about the number of court appearances per year indicates that a substantial part of the practicing women carry on an active trial practice and are not hidden away in the "women's specialties."

Another question asked the respondent to state his "type of work performed" (singular) in one or two words and suggested "general practice" as a sample answer. Although the question did not define "specialty," any answer other than general practice probably indicates that the respondent devoted a substantial amount of time to the type of work listed.

Only 30 percent of the women stated that they were engaged in "general practice," but nearly 50 percent of the males so characterized their practice. The study produced no data which explain this apparent female propensity to specialize. One can speculate that the woman makes a conscious choice to avoid general practice because she believes that a special skill will reduce or overcome sex discrimination. Or, the relative absence of women in general practice may mean only that some employers hire women for specialized positions in probate, tax, and other fields. Whatever the explanation, the data show that women who listed a type of work other than general practice usually made more money than their sisters in general practice.[7] Although the woman is likely to increase her earnings by moving out of general practice, the data also show that her chances of reducing the margin between herself and males in the same kind of practice are only slightly better than even, for in several cases the incomes of the male specialists exceeded those of their general practitioner brethren by as much as the female specialists' income exceeded that of female general practitioners.

Family

Twenty-eight percent of the women and 25.6 percent of the men had at least one lawyer among their parents, grandparents, uncles, and aunts. This difference between men and women in the aggregate is not statistically significant. On the other hand, the percentage of women who had a female relative in the law was greater than the corresponding percentage for men by a statistically significant margin.[8] However, this was not a factor of great importance in explaining professional choice, for only 47 out of 1300 women had a female-lawyer relative.

A more fertile ground for inquiry is the respondent's own marital and maternal status: 890 (69.0 percent) of the women and 1098 (83.2 percent) of the men were or had been married at the time of the study.[9] . . . Exhibit 2 summarizes family-work relations:

Previous studies have indicated that marriage alone does not usually cause a women who is working to cease working, and our data are consistent with those findings.[10] More than half of the full-time employed women were married, and only nineteen (6.1 percent) of the women who were not practicing at the time they answered the questionnaire acknowledged that they had left practice "to get married." Of all of those who had ceased practice, only 5.4 percent left in the same year as their marriage without having a child. Eighty-five (27.3 percent) of the females who were not practicing acknowledged that they ceased practice to have a child, and another seventy-three (23.5 percent) acknowledged having ceased practice to "devote time" to their families. The

Exhibit 2   Family-Work Relations

	Males	Females	Single Females	Married Females without Children	Married Females with Children
Full time	85.5%	65.3%	83.5%	74.5%	44.5%
Part time	3.8%	12.1%	5.5%	4.0%	22.2%
Not working	—	12.9%	—	4.0%	25.7%
Not responding to this question	10.6%	9.7%	11.0%	10.3%	7.6%
	N = 1329	N = 1298	N = 475	N = 276	N = 534

data indicate that 54.0 percent of those who left practice did so in the same year or in the year following the birth of their first child. Although the birth of a child will necessarily cause some interruption in a woman's practice, the data suggest that it is also an event which may cause a more lengthy, if not necessarily permanent, departure from practice. However, it is by no means true that the birth of a child always means departure from practice. 27.8 percent of all full-time employed women were married and had children. Moreover, most of these children were less than seven years old.[11]

The following exhibit reflects the relation between type of employer and marital and maternal status for the full-time employed women who responded to the relevant questions:

Exhibit 3   Type of Employer by Marital-Maternal Status of Female

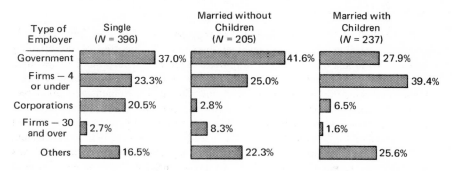

The women who continue full-time practice after the birth of a child are heavily concentrated in the 4 or under category and their ranks in larger firms and government are reduced, but the data do not reveal the reasons for these results. Higher earnings alone are not a satisfactory explanation, for the women with children both in large firms and in government earned more money than did their sisters in the firms of 4 or under. It is possible that solo practice and small firms have a flexibility which suits the mother of a small child. Many large firms and government agencies may not offer the necessary flexibility because of their size and attendant bureaucratic rigidity, or they may offer it only when it is accompanied by a second-class status which the woman will not accept.

Although married women without children are more heavily represented in government and in firms of 30 and over than are either single women or women with children, these data do not necessarily mean that childless married women are more likely to find places with government agencies and large firms than are unmarried women, for many of the childless married women were unmarried at the time they took the jobs reflected in the exhibit.[12]

One might expect married women to earn less money than their unmarried female colleagues for two reasons: married women presumably need less money because they are married to men who are expected to support them; and a married woman's devotion to the job and resulting productivity may be less than that of a man or an unmarried woman, since both of the latter presumably seek their primary satisfaction from job success. However, the data contradict these expectations. The full-time employed married women in the classes of 1956 through 1960 earned significantly more money in 1961 than did the unmarried women in the corresponding classes. One can make a variety of interesting speculations about this finding.[13] It might be explained by the fact that some married women practice with their husbands and are able to make more advantageous monetary agreements than if they were dealing with other males. On the other hand, it may simply reflect a relationship between the emotional qualities which lead a woman to take a mate and those which make her acceptable to clients and colleagues. Unfortunately, the data do not give any satisfactory explanation for the higher earnings of married women.

Attitudes and Opinions

Nearly half of the women stated that they believed that they had "certainly or almost certainly" been the object of discrimination because of sex by their present, a former, or a potential employer. Another 17 percent of the women thought that they had "probably" been the object of such discrimination.[14] Upon observing this widespread conviction among the women, and upon seeing that many women either have ceased practice or are earning much less than their male counterparts, one might expect that many women would regret their decision to become lawyers. The study contradicts such a conclusion. In response to a question [asking] whether they would again become lawyers if they "had to do if over," 1150 (94.1 percent) of the women answered affirmatively; only 72 (5.9 percent) said they would not. These responses do not differ significantly from those of the males.

Another indication of female optimism is given by the women's answers to a question which asked what advice they would give a present-day female law student seeking employment. 10 percent of the women would instruct her to work hard and prove herself; another 6 percent would counsel patience and perseverance; and nearly 13 percent would tell her to do well in school. On the other hand, only 3 percent of the men think it is important that she work hard to prove herself; only 2.2 percent counsel patience and perseverance;

and only 6.3 percent think it important that she do well in school.[15] No women would have told the prospective female graduate to "forget it," but nearly 8 percent of the men would have so advised her. It appears, therefore, that the women have a continuing, and perhaps irrational, belief that hard work, good grades, and perseverance will overcome the obstacles which they face, whereas the men are less sanguine about the effect of these factors upon the success of the potential woman lawyer.

Motives for Studying Law

It is sometimes suggested that differences between male and female status in the bar are attributed to the different motives which men and women have for entering the profession. The argument is as follows: Women are really social workers who wish to become lawyers for the unselfish reason of helping the poor and oppressed; although these motives are laudable, they render the woman a less able representative of the profit-motivated business client than is a standard male lawyer who, like the businessman, is strongly influenced by monetary motives. In an attempt to test this theory, one question sought the respondent's motivation for going to law school. He was asked to state whether each of six different motives was "very important," "important," "so-so," or "not important" to him in his decision to enter law school. The answers to that question are inconsistent with the "social worker" characterization of women lawyers. The percentage of women who marked "desire to help society" as "important" or "very important" exceeded that of the males by a margin which was not statistically significant (59 [as compared with] 53 percent), while the percentage of females who marked "good remuneration" as "important" or "very important" exceeded [that of] the males by a margin which was statistically significant (70 [as compared with] 60 percent). Indeed, twice the percentage of women as men stated that good renumeration was a "very important" reason.

For two reasons, these data probably do not justify the conclusion that the prospect of monetary gain more strongly influenced women than it did men to take up the practice of law: (1) women more than men tended to mark "very important" or "important" as to all of the motives and the women's responses may simply reflect this female inclination to depict each of the motives as "important" or "very important"; and (2) a large number of the women placed no mark at all in the "good remuneration" boxes. We cannot state whether these women would have rated the monetary motive as relatively important or unimportant, but if [we infer] from the absence of any mark that the motive was only "so-so" or "unimportant" to them, then [we] may conclude that the women as a whole were less strongly influenced by monetary considerations than were the males. Nevertheless, it is clear that a substantial part of the women were strongly motivated by a desire to make "good money" and that the "social worker" characterization does not fit them to any greater degree than it fits the men. One wonders whether other assumptions about the woman lawyer's motives and beliefs are equally as inaccurate as the one that they are uniformly motivated to become lawyers by a desire to help society.

Analysis of Discrimination

[The second part] of this study is an examination of some of the possible explanations for the male-female income differential reported in [the previous section]. The principal reason for selecting income as the focal point of the discrimination analysis is my belief that it is the most universally recognized single measure of success in American society. It is an even more universal measure when one limits his inquiry to a single profession, for this limitation renders irrelevant any special recognition which may inhere in membership in a particular group, such as the medical or legal professions. Another reason for using income as the focus is that adjusted gross income, unlike nonmonetary rewards, is a specific thing which is capable of certain measurement. Except for exceedingly modest deviations, its meaning is the same for all American taxpayers; thus one comparing the adjusted gross income of two persons faces none of the definitional problems which he would have in comparing recognition or status within the profession. Finally, it is my impression that the income associated with a particular mode of practice (that is, large firm, house counsel, small firm) is closely related to the status of that mode within the profession. Thus, when one finds that women earn less than men, he is likely also to find that they are concentrated in jobs of less status than those of men.

In his study of income differential, the hurried traveler on the devious way of statistical analysis is tempted to end his journey by a shortcut from the observation of a wide income difference between the males and the females to the conclusion that it was caused by unjustified discrimination against the females. However, the more careful traveler will take the slower route of examining the other plausible causes for such a differential and may find that his data cannot carry him all the way to his conclusion. The following discussion will deal with ten of the factors other than discrimination which might have caused or contributed to the observed income differential.

Obviously many things other than one's sex have an effect upon how much one earns. If any factor inherent in the psychology or intellect of "woman" is excluded for the moment, there are still many factors which, solely or in combination, could have caused the observed difference between the incomes of the males and females or which could have caused the incomes of the males and females in our sample to fail to be representative of the incomes of male and female lawyers of their age groups in the bar generally. In attempting to examine the other plausible hypotheses, we have arbitrarily classified them in the following way: (1) failure of the women to work full time; (2) greater experience on the part of the men; (3) class rank and law review participation; (4) school attended; (5) type of employer; (6) type of work performed; (7) type of work sought by men and women; (8) composition of the 35 percent of the sample who did not respond; (9) failure of the male sample to be representative of males in the bar generally; (10) forgetfulness and disingenuousness of the respondents.[16]

We can dispose of the first two of these objections at once. While it is true that many women in the sample did not work or worked only part time, the comparative income figures were not distorted by that fact because only women who were working full time were included in computing those figures. Second, although experience in law practice is not exclusively a function of the passage of time since graduation from law school, time since graduation in a sample greater than 1000 probably is a satisfactory measure of experience for the purposes of a gross comparison of aggregate income. Since the income comparisons were made by year of graduation from law school and since an income differential existed between the male and the female members of each class, the differences cannot be adequately explained by arguing that the men had had more experience than had the women in the sample.

Class Rank and Law Review

Several studies support the proposition that one's starting and [one's] ultimate incomes as a lawyer are related to his class standing and law review participation.[17] Our findings are consistent with that proposition and show that, as a general rule, the law review participant will earn more than the non-law review participant and, with some exceptions, the higher one is in his class, the more money he is likely to earn. Our data, however, show that this factor does not account for the difference between the incomes of the female and the male samples, for neither the entire female sample nor the full-time employed females differed significantly from the male sample in class rank or law review participation.

School Attended

For a variety of reasons, one might hypothesize that the graduates of the most widely known and highly respected law schools would have higher aggregate incomes than the graduates of other schools. If so, and if a larger part of the men than the women in the sample came from such schools, this could be a contributing factor to the income differential. To test for this kind of bias in the sample, we divided both the men and the women into those who were graduates of nine schools which we considered to be relatively high in prestige and those who were graduates of all the remaining law schools.[18] There was no statistically significant difference between the percentage of men and women in each of the two groups. Thus, whatever the effect of the type of school attended upon a lawyer's income, that factor cannot explain the male-female income differential revealed by this study.

Our statistics did cast some doubt upon the accuracy of the hypothesis that attendance at a prestige school results in higher income. The starting salaries of the men from "nonprestige" schools in six out of the nine classes which we tested, and the present salaries in five out of the nine classes, exceeded the respective average salaries of the male graduates of the prestige schools. These figures are not conclusive, however, for the present income of prestige male graduates in the classes of 1956, 1957, and 1958 exceeded the salaries of their "nonprestige" counterparts, and the margin appeared to be growing. Perhaps the graduates of prestige schools concentrate in jobs which have greater ultimate income potential but which pay less for the first five or six years. The prestige-school hypothesis appeared to be more uniformly accurate for the women; the prestige females' average starting income exceeded that of the other women for seven out of the nine graduating classes examined, and the present salary of the prestige women exceeded that of the other women in six out of the nine classes.

Type of Employer

In 1964, approximately one third of the full-time employed women worked for federal, state, or local governments, while only 15.7 percent of the men found their jobs in government. One might argue that women, for whatever reason, hold those jobs which are uniformly low-paying irrespective of the sex of the holder and that the income differential between the males and females is caused by these differences in the type of employment. Our data show that the income differential between the men and the women indeed varied from job to job. Yet they also show that the average present income of the men exceeded that of the women by substantial margins in almost all of the possible combinations of year of graduation and job type.

Contrary to what one might expect, the heavy concentration of women in government does not increase the income differential. If the women in the government jobs are removed from the sample, the aggregate female income decreases and the differential between [the females] and the males grows larger. On the other hand, if the same percentage of women as men were employed by each kind of employer, at the present average salary of women currently working for each such employer, the aggregate income differential between males and females would decrease; but the reduction would be only a few percent. Thus, the concentration of females in the service of certain employers can explain no more than a small part of the income differential.

Type of Work Performed

The questionnaire did not define or explicitly solicit information about the various specialities. As indicated above, however, it is probably safe to assume that anyone stating his "type of work" (singular) to be something other than "general practice" devoted a substantial amount, perhaps the bulk, of his time to the type of work which he listed. Our data show that the type of work performed is relevant in determining income, but they also show that the income of the males exceeded that of their female counterparts in almost every category.

Because of the wide income differences which exist between men and women within nearly every category of work performed, the data suggest that the differences in the type of work performed do not explain the male-female income differential. This conclusion must be more tentative than some of those reached above, for two reasons. First, the question was not explicit and it is possible, for example, that some who should be considered tax specialists listed general practice as their type of work, while others whom one would consider general practitioners may have listed tax because 10 or 15 percent of their work lay in that area. A second and more important deficiency in the data is that they do not tell us anything about the level of responsibility which the respondent has or about the sophistication and degree of difficulty of the work which he performs. It is possible, for example, that the women who listed litigation as a specialty engaged mostly in "nickel and dime" cases and that the men dealt principally in litigation involving more money and greater responsibility. Of course, the converse may as well be true; we simply cannot say.[19]

Type of Job Sought

The data presented above show that a substantial income differential exists between the men and the women even when one limits the examination to a single kind of employer. However, the data also show that both men and women earned more money from certain employers than from others. If, therefore, a larger percentage of the women found employment with the higher-paying employers than is presently the case, and if there were no corresponding shift by males, the aggregate income differential between the males and the females would be reduced. Consequently, it may be argued that at least a part of the income differential is attributable to the fact that women seek employment in those jobs which pay less money.

The law student's typical method of seeking employment is to write a prospective employer, interview the employer, or both. The questionnaire asked each respondent to state the number of such interviews he had and the number of such letters he wrote with respect to various kinds of employers. At least insofar as the type of job sought is reflected by the numbers of letters sent and interviews held, the data show a significant difference in the kinds of jobs sought by men and women. A significantly larger portion of the women sought jobs in federal, state, and local governments, as judicial clerks, and in banks and trust companies. A significantly smaller share sought jobs with firms of 5 to 15. The female decision to seek more jobs with the federal government and to seek fewer jobs with the firms of 5 to 15 may have actually caused them to earn more, not less, money and [it may have] reduced, rather than increased, the income differential between the males and the females. On the other hand, it appears that the jobs with banks and trust companies and in state and local government probably paid less money than the women might have earned elsewhere, thereby contributing to the income differential. Had each kind of employer hired a percentage of women equal to the percentage of interview and letter contacts, and had they been hired at the average income of the women in fact employed by that type of employer, the female income would have increased rather than decreased.[20] To put it another way, the women appeared to be seeking higher-paying jobs than those they ultimately acquired. However, because of the wide male-female income difference with respect to almost every kind of employer, it appears that no amount of female job seeking would have significantly closed the income gap.

Evidence of Discrimination

As it is used in this article, "discrimination" includes every differentiation, whether or not it is rational or functional. It includes both the racist's selection of one of his own race in preference to a more able member of another race and an ill person's selection of the best neurosurgeon in preference to the next best one. Initial support for the conclusion that the male-female income differential is caused principally by discrimination against women comes from the fact that our statistics rule out or render unlikely the other most plausible explanations. On the basis of the figures and analysis set out above, one can conclude with near certainty that the income differential between the men and the women was not caused by any of the following factors: (1) the fact that women were employed only part time; (2) a lack of experience on the part of the women lawyers; (3) lower class rank and less law review participation by the women; (4) a difference in schools attended; or (5) different types of employers. In addition, the statistics and analysis indicate, although with less certainty, that the income difference was not caused by (1) response bias among the members of the sample; (2) differences between the general type of work performed by the men and the women; or (3) differences in the type of jobs sought. If one rejects forgetfulness and lying as plausible explanations for the large income differential which was observed, he is left with only one plausible hypothesis[21] to explain the income differential, namely, discrimination on the basis of sex against women lawyers by employers and clients.

A second and more direct piece of evidence of this discrimination is the response of the 63 placement directors and deans who answered our placement questionnaire: 6 stated that any discrimination against female law graduates is "insignificant"; 43 believed that such discrimination is "significant"; and 14 stated that it is "extensive." These observers speak with authority and from long and extensive experience with the interviewing and hiring processes at a number of our busiest law school placement offices.[22]

Further evidence of discrimination is provided by the response of women to the question: "Do you believe that you have been the object of discrimination because of your sex by your present, former, or by any potential employer from whom you sought a job?" The following exhibit shows that more than half believe they probably [or certainly] have been the object of such discrimination and that more than a third are "certain" that they have been discriminated against.

Exhibit 4   Beliefs of Females Concerning Discrimination

Degree	Percent of Females ($N = 1148$)
Certainly discriminated against	38.2
Almost certainly	9.6
Probably	17.6
Probably not	15.8
Certainly not	18.8

Doubtless many disappointed female lawyers blame their lack of success upon discrimination, and, for that reason, the figures [showing positive discrimination] on the above table should probably be [reduced] by a certain percentage. The question gave the respondent an opportunity to say that she was only "almost" certain or that it was only "probable" that she had been discriminated against, yet 38 percent of the women chose to state that they were "certain" that they had been the victims of discrimination. In view of lawyers' notorious propensity to qualify and equivocate, the absolute quality of these answers, made exclusively by lawyers who had the opportunity to select several degrees of equivocation, suggests that one should not discount the answers too greatly.[23]

Finally, discrimination against women lawyers is suggested by the female response to the question, "How many of each of the following types of employers stated a policy to you against the hiring of women as lawyers?" On 1963 separate occasions, potential employers are reported to have actually stated to a female respondent a policy against the hiring of women lawyers. Even if we discount this number by a considerable margin, it still constitutes persuasive evidence of employer discrimination on the basis of sex.

Exhibit 5   Employers Who Stated a Policy Against the Hiring of Women Lawyers

Type of Employer	Number of Statements of Discrimination Policies	Number of Women to Whom at Least One Statement Was Made
Law firm—30 and over	474	218
16 to 30	322	141
5 to 15	325	149
4 or under	271	125
Federal government	88	79
State and local government	95	63
Judges	78	52
Corporations	125	66
Banks and trust companies	111	56
Unions	22	5
Nonlaw jobs	52	28
Totals:	1963	982

It does not necessarily follow that one who states he has a policy against the hiring of women in fact has and carries out such a policy. However, one can imagine few circumstances under which it would be beneficial for the employer to state a policy of discrimination which he did not practice. In some southern societies, the pressure to discriminate against Negroes might be so great that even one who did not oppose Negroes would feel compelled to express opposition, but surly the pressure to discriminate against women has not reached such a pitch.

The combination of this evidence—the apparent failure of other hypotheses to explain the income differential, the statements of the placement officers and deans, the opinions of the female respondents, and finally the reported statements of the employers themselves—convinces me that discrimination against women lawyers by their potential employers is at least a substantial cause, and probably the principal cause, for the income differential which we have observed between men and women.

Is the Discrimination Functional?

For present purposes, discrimination by any private employer may be considered functional to the extent that it is likely to produce a greater economic gain for him than he would have received had he not so discriminated. For example, the failure of the Green Bay Packers to select women as defensive linemen is discrimination, yet it is entirely functional and appropriate; women do not exhibit the massive size, strong backs, and powerful limbs which are the requisites of the position. Similarly, women may have psychological or intellectual limitations which make them less effective lawyers than are men. If this is true, some or all of the discrimination against women lawyers is functional and, perhaps, defensible.

Because the qualifications of a defensive lineman are relatively simple and obvious, it is easy to tell which discriminations in selections for that position are dictated by its function and which are not. However, there is no such agreement about the necessary, or even the desirable, attributes of an "effective lawyer." Indeed, such attributes are kaleidoscopic, elusive, and difficult to generalize. At one end of the legal spectrum is the lawyer who does nothing but appear before juries; at the other end is the man employed by a governmental agency or a very large firm who is an expert on some obscure and complex statute or body of law. The latter in his relish for and mastery of the statutory intricacies resembles the scholar; the former in his enjoyment of the pomp and show of the courtroom resembles the actor. The same personal characteristics which are vital to the success of one of these men would spell the doom of the other. And between these two extremes lie 300,000 American lawyers who exhibit infinitely varied mixtures of a number of roles, including actor, scholar, and counselor.

Nonetheless, it probably is possible to identify a few characteristics which are desirable for the performance of every lawyer [by] function (for example, intelligence), and others which would be helpful to sizable slices of the legal profession (for example, ability to inspire confidence in clients). The data produced by this study are not extensive, but they do provide a basis for comparing men and women as to certain of these functional attributes—intelligence, emotional suitability, probable length of service, and ability to inspire confidence in clients.

Intelligence

Both class standing and law review participation probably bear a direct relation to intelligence.[24] These are two common indicators of intellectual ability used by employers, who often specify that only persons on law review or with certain grades or class standing may apply for jobs with them. The data provide no basis for discrimination against women on either of these grounds. There was no statistically significant difference between the men and the women in either class standing or law review participation.

Emotional Suitability

I know of no data which give a suitable inventory of the emotional makeup of women lawyers, nor do I know of any which compare female lawyers either with other women or with male lawyers.[25] [In the absence of] systematic psychological inventory, one should take care to avoid two inviting errors in analyzing the emotional composition of women lawyers. The first is to attribute the common characteristics of all women to that tiny percentage of women who happen to be lawyers. One random selection of 15,663 female college graduates netted only 44 who were going to become lawyers.[26] Whatever the process which culled out these 44, it is a hasty judgment which says that they exhibit all of the attributes of the remaining 15,619. On the contrary, it is entirely possible that "women" exhibit certain attributes and that "women lawyers" exhibit substantially different ones. The second error is to color all 7000 female lawyers with the attributes of one or two of them. Since women make up no more than 3 percent of the bar, it is possible to engage actively in practice and yet not have extensive contact with women lawyers. Nevertheless, I have quizzed few lawyers or law teachers who did not have definite, and often outspoken, views about the emotional composition of that group, although often these generalizations are based on only a handful of experiences with one or two women lawyers. Since this study is limited to women who are lawyers and includes approximately 1300 of them, it suffers from neither of these errors.

Two areas of our study—one dealing with trial practice and the other with motives for attending law school—yielded information which is relevant to the question of emotional suitability. First, the idea that women shrink from the combat of litigation is not supported by the data, which show that the women appeared in court with nearly the same frequency as did the men.[27] Seven percent of the full-time employed women listed "litigation" as the type of work (singular) they performed; 7.2 percent of the men listed litigation. Moreover, 45.6 percent of all the females in full-time private practice stated that they engaged in litigation and 27.7 percent stated that they did criminal work. The study did not compare male and female success in litigation, but it showed at a minimum that a sizable [number] of the women were actively engaged in trial practice.

It is sometimes suggested that women are less able at certain kinds of practice because, unlike men, they are not motivated by a wholesome ambition to earn money and get ahead. However, the thought that women are exclusively or even principally motivated to enter law by "bleeding heart" motives or that they are untouched by crasser motives is contradicted by the data discussed, above.[28]

We know far too little about the psychological composition of the female lawyer to state with certainty how she differs from other females or from male lawyers. Clearly some current ideas about the female lawyer's psychological composition cannot be empirically supported. Such incidental data as the study produced on motives for attending law school and frequency of court appearance should inspire a vigorous skepticism about other notions concerning a woman's emotional suitability for various kinds of practice.

Probable Length of Service

It is often stated that a woman is a less desirable employee-lawyer than is a male because she will quit working to get married, to have a child, or to devote more time to her family just when she is gaining sufficient experience to be a valuable employee. The data show that many women had changed jobs several times [by] the time they answered the questionnaire and that a larger share of the women than men had ceased practice entirely.[29] However, they do not support the common expectation that there is a vast difference between male and female performance on this point. Rather, the striking thing about the data is that both men and women changed jobs quite frequently. At the end of three years, only 30 percent of the males in the class of 1962 and 29 percent of the females in that class were still at their first jobs. At the end of seven years, the corresponding percentages fall to 14.5 and 11.1, respectively. Except for the class of 1959, the percentage of women in each class who were still at their first jobs at the time they answered the questionnaire did not differ from the corresponding percentage of the males by a statistically significant margin. However, if the men from all classes are compared with all of the women, the difference is statistically significant.

A significantly larger percentage of women than men had left their *second* jobs, in four of eight classes. The fact that the male turnover with respect to the second job is lower by a significant margin in the three oldest classes might suggest that this job turnover differential grows wider with the passage of time, as more women leave practice because of growing family commitments. Yet the first-job data show no such trend, and the number of women permanently reentering practice after a spell of child-rearing and housekeeping may actually cause a reduction in turnover among female lawyers who have been out of law school for more than ten years. The data give us no reliable answers to these questions.

In summary, our gross data show a slightly greater female job turnover in the first job after law school;[30] they also suggest that job turnover of women is higher than that for men thereafter. Moreover, if a large share of the female nonrespondents are housewives,[31] and if no corresponding percentage of the male nonrespondents are not working, the actual job turnover of all female lawyers may be even higher than that reflected in our data.

But, even if the total female job turnover is higher than our data suggest, that fact alone does not prove that a woman is a less desirable employee than is a man, for high turnover can result from many causes. It can be caused by employee fickleness, but it can also be caused by poor pay or other inadequacies of the job. If women are as effective lawyers as are men but are nevertheless paid less money than are comparably employed men, one might expect women to seek new jobs more frequently. On the other hand some of the standard female motivations for job change—the urge to motherhood, the need to devote time to one's family or to move with one's husband to a new location—are all peculiar to women and may be less subject to control by employer offers of more money and greater status than are the typical male motivations for job change. Without information indicating which changes are caused by employer discrimination and which are caused by the demands of a husband or a family, high job turnover neither proves nor disproves that discrimination against women is functional. The naked statistic of frequent job change is equally consistent with either hypothesis.

The data do explode the myth that few married women and no mothers practice law. Few women ceased work because of marriage alone, and more than 25 percent of the full-time employed women were mothers of small children. One can only guess how many more might work full time if more employers tailored positions so that the hours and responsibilities were compatible with a mother's other responsibilities.

Client Confidence

Every law firm, except one with a shrinking practice, has the problem of transferring a client's sometimes fragile allegiance from senior men to competent younger men without losing the client's patronage. If the young lawyer is a Jew, a Negro, or a woman, this problem may be aggravated by the clients' own prejudices.[32] One of the most frequently stated fears about women lawyers is that clients will not place their confidence in them. Our data did indicate that women see fewer clients than do men by a statistically significant margin. This difference was particularly great among those who were employed by large firms and who had been out of law school for four or more years.

Despite this statistically significant difference in the frequency of client contact, the data do not really support the conclusion that clients will not place their confidence in women lawyers. First, it is not possible to tell from our data whether the lower frequency of female client contact was due to clients' resistance or to mistaken beliefs of women lawyers and their employers about client resistance. Second, the data show a very substantial amount of client contact on the part of women employed by corporations and by firms of 15 or under. If the hypothesis about client resistance were correct, one would expect women to be concentrated in jobs which required little or no client contact. Yet in the smaller firms and corporations, women saw approximately seven clients for every ten seen by men.

Of course these data do not prove that all clients will place their confidence in a woman lawyer as readily as in a male lawyer. The figures tell nothing about the kind of clients which the women saw. Perhaps they were spread across the spectrum of legal practice, but they may have been concentrated in the probate and domestic relations field.[33] Furthermore, the figures do not indicate whether the clients were satisfied with the service, nor do they indicate whether the employers had to undertake a more extensive and careful introduction than would have been required with a male. They do show, however, that any vision of the woman as exclusively a back-room and library worker is badly distorted.

The Weight of the Evidence

The survey did not solicit conclusive or comprehensive data on the question [of] whether discrimination against women lawyers is functional. It tells us nothing about the relative ability of men and women to acquire clients or about the importance of the function to employers. Moreover, the information on court appearances and frequency of client contact falls far short of the systematic psychological inventory which we need in order to begin evaluating the contention that discrimination against women lawyers is functional. Nonetheless, the information which the survey did gather makes some of the stoutest citadels in the rational discrimination fortress look vulnerable. "Women can't stand the rigors of trial practice"—but the full-time employed women appeared in court nearly as often as did the men. "Clients won't put up with a woman"—but, except in one kind of practice, the women saw seven clients for every ten that men saw. "Women quit work to marry and have children"—but 27 percent of the full-time employed women were married *and* had children. "Women lawyers are just bleeding hearts who do not understand the usual business motives"—but equally as many men admitted the importance of the "bleeding heart" motive and a large share of the women rated monetary motives [as] very important in their choice of law as a career. These data have convinced me that much of the enormous income differential between the males and the females is attributable to nonfunctional discrimination.

Notes

1. Dorothy Thomas, *Women Lawyers in the United States* (New York: Scarecrow Press, 1957), p. vii.
2. F. A. Hankin and D. W. Krohnke, *The American Lawyer: 1964 Statistical Report* (Chicago: The American Bar Foundation, 1965), p. 29, gives the following female listings:

Year	Total Lawyers Listed	Female Listings	Percent of Lawyers Listed in U.S.
1948	171,110	2997	1.8
1951	204,111	5059	2.5
1954	221,600	5036	2.3
1957	235,783	6350	2.7
1960	252,385	6488	2.6
1963	268,782	7143	2.7

3. The following bear upon the larger question of the female's status in twentieth-century American society: Jessie Bernard, *Academic Women* (University Park,

Pa.: Pennsylvania State University Press, 1964); T. Mattfeld and K. Van Aken, *Women and the Scientific Professions: Proceedings*, M.I.T. Symposium on American Women in Science and Engineering (Cambridge, Mass.: M.I.T. Press, 1965); *Report of the Committee on Federal Employment to the President's Commission on the Status of Women* (Washington, D.C.: U.S. Government Printing Office, 1963); *Report of the President's Commission on the Status of Women* (Washington, D.C.: U.S. Government Printing Office, 1963); "The Woman in America," *Daedalus*, vol. 93 (1964), p. 579.

4. Three hundred seventy-nine males were chosen by the selection of the male name on an alphabetical class list which next followed the matching female. We believe that this is a random selection method. Three hundred thirty-two males were selected by a process unknown to us but characterized as "random" by the responding schools; 323 were selected for having the academic average which most nearly matched that of the female in the class which they were chosen to match. The remaining 295 were selected by methods unknown to us.

5. The percentages of males and females in each quartile of class standing were surprisingly similar. The widest deviation was only 1.9 percent.

6. The category "firms of 4 or under" includes an undetermined but probably significant number of respondents who were in solo practice or were partners and not employees. This fact contaminates that category and renders it unreliable as a basis for generalization about the small firm as an employer.

7. Many of the respondents believed that specialization would improve the woman's opportunities. In response to a question about the advice they would give a neophyte female lawyer, 6 percent of the female respondents and 9 percent of the male respondents recommended that she specialize.

8. The mothers of only 4 of the males and 20 of the females were lawyers; 15 males and 25 females had an aunt who was a lawyer. The following table summarizes the data on relatives of the respondents:

Relation of Lawyer-Ancestor	Females	Males
Father	185	176
Mother	20	4
Uncle	155	199
Aunt	25	15
Grandfather	77	72
Grandmother	2	4
	464	470

9. The questionnaire did not ask the respondent to state whether or not he had been divorced. Some volunteered that information in response to a question about their marital status, but the absence of a specific question renders the data on divorce unreliable. All references to "married" females and males mean those who were or had been married at the time they answered the questionnaire.

10. See A. S. Rossi, *A Plan for the Analysis of Women College Graduates* (Chicago, Ill.: National Opinion Research Center, 1965), p. 5.

11. The following table summarizes the maternal status of the women who were employed full-time in 1964:

Age of Children for Full-Time Employed Females

Age of Youngest Child	Number of Females (N = 237)	Percent
Child under 5	162	68.5
Child 5 to 7	30	12.6
Child 7 to 10	15	6.3
No response to age of child	30	12.6

12. The data may mean only that women who go with large firms marry colleagues there.
13. The higher earnings of married women are not attributable to the fact that married women demand a job with relatively high pay or accept none at all, for an analysis of the figures shows that married women were spread over a wider spectrum on the income scale than were unmarried women. They had a higher average income not because of an absence of their numbers in the lower ranges but because of an abundance of their numbers in the higher ranges.
14. For a summary of the responses to the question concerning beliefs about discrimination, see Exhibit 4.
15. Our data show that the advice with respect to grades is sound in that a female's income tends to increase in relation to her grades. The questionnaire solicited no information which accurately tells whether hard work and perseverance are effective, but the aggregate income figures suggest that the male pessimism may be nearer to the truth than is the female optimism.
16. A final factor which may play some part in this income differential is that a disproportionately large part of the females may be Jewish or members of other minority groups. If so, part of the observed income differential may be attributed to discrimination against these groups. The questionnaire solicited no data on the respondents' racial, ethnic, or religious backgrounds; therefore we can neither prove nor disprove this possibility.
17. Harvard Law School, *Class of 1955—10th Year Class Report* (1965); Wellman, Memorandum to the Law Faculty and Law Class of 1951 (University of Michigan Law School, 1966).
18. I have selected the nine schools on the basis of the mean LSAT scores of their student bodies and on the basis of my own subjective observation of the esteem in which they are held by others on law faculties and in law practice.
19. In at least one case, the data do hint that women of comparable experience with men are performing different functions for certain employers. These data (reported more fully in the text accompanying note 32 *inf.*) are that females see significantly fewer clients in firms of 16 or more than do males in those firms; perhaps they also have less authority and responsibility.
20. The increase in income would be as follows: The graduating classes of 1956–58, 8.4 percent increase; 1959–61, 1.9 percent increase; and 1962–65, 4.5 percent increase.
21. If a disproportionate share of the females are Jewish, some of the income differential may be explained by discrimination against them because they are Jewish. Since the questionnaire did not collect any information on race, religion, or ethnic background, I could not calculate the effect, if any, of such discrimination, and, absent data showing a disproportionate percentage of Jews among the females and lacking evidence about the extent and effect of anti-Semitic discrimination against lawyers, I have chosen to classify this hypothesis as "not plausible."
22. Among those indicating a belief that discrimination against women in hiring is significant or extensive are representatives of the placement offices at six out of the nine schools which we classified as prestige institutions.

23. The women who were most certain they had been discriminated against also earned the least money. Perhaps this fact proves the accuracy of their opinion. On the other hand, it may only indicate that their belief is a rationalization for low income. The average present income of the full-time employed women in relation to their responses to the discrimination question is as follows:

1964 Income

Discrimination	Classes of 1956–58	Classes of 1959–61	Classes of 1962–65
"Certain"	$8700	$7000	$6400
Balance of responses	$9100	$8100	$6600

24. Since law review participation is usually determined in part by class standing, the former may be only an additional indication of the latter's effect.
25. Alice S. Rossi, who is with the National Opinion Research Center at the University of Chicago, is conducting a study of a large sample of female college graduates. This study should ultimately produce information about the characteristics of women who undertake practice in the traditional male professions, but it probably will not give specific information about female lawyers.
26. This sample is random in the sense that it was chosen from colleges which were randomly selected.
27. [However,] the difference between the average number of court appearances made by the males and the females is statistically significant.

Average Number of Court Appearances Per Year

Year Graduated	Females	Males
1964	2.4	4.1
1963	4.0	7.7
1962	5.8	7.9
1961	9.2	10.0
1960	7.4	9.2
1959	9.6	10.2
1958	7.3	9.1
1957	7.8	10.5
1956	8.2	10.3

28. See page 285.
29. Only 65.5 percent of the female respondents reported that they were in full-time practice, and 85.5 percent of the males reported that they were in full-time practice.
30. Because the sample was not large enough, we could not make a meaningful comparison of female turnover by type of job. Such data might reveal quite different patterns among jobs and between male and female employees depending upon the type of job.
31. We have no reason to believe that they either are or are not.
32. Despite the fact that employer discrimination based on clients' prejudices is functional, it has been prohibited by the Civil Rights Act of 1964.
33. Some members of the bar assume that probate and domestic relations clients find female counsel more acceptable than other clients do. One can question why these clients should react differently to female lawyers than do others.

Psychological and Social Barriers to Women in Science

Talented and educated women with family responsibilities often face special problems of identity and self-esteem when they attempt to continue their professional activity. Although many do so successfully and encounter few problems, others find it more difficult. I first became aware of some special aspects of these problems when I interviewed women scholars at the Radcliffe Institute—women with outstanding intellectual and creative ability who had been awarded fellowships so that they might continue their professional interests on a part-time basis.[1]

The Institute members were particularly questioned about their feelings of identity as a professional. Did they feel any more professional as a result of their fellowship at the Institute? What made a person feel professional? Had their commitment to their work changed as a result of their Institute experience? At the time, I hypothesized that one outcome of the fellowship, of the opportunity to work deeply and seriously on a project, would be a greater sense of competence. The greater the sense of inner competence, my reasoning went, the greater would be the sense of commitment to future productive work. This proved to be only partially true.

Many indicated that the fellowship program had resulted in a genuine change in their conceptions of themselves as professionals, but their responses suggested that this change was rarely due solely to the opportunity to work on their projects. Although this was important, equally significant was the access to stimulating colleagues, both within and outside the Institute, which the special status conferred by the fellowship made possible. Appraisals of their work by others, coupled with acceptance and recognition by people whose professional opinions were relevant and appropriate, made a significant difference in determining whether a woman felt like a professional, and whether she in turn had a strong sense of commitment to future work.

Challenging interaction with other professionals is frequently as necessary to creative work as is the opportunity for solitude and thought.[2] Yet comments from many women indicate that it is particularly difficult for them to attain, especially for the woman who seeks reentry. As one woman astutely noted: "Those of us who have interrupted our careers because of children or moving with our husbands across the country have special difficulties. Our departments maintain no ties with us. Often no one knows us, and the articles and books on which we are working may not be published for another three to five years. Meanwhile, if we are to be productive, we need to be professionally involved again."

Although women offer unique qualities to intellectual and creative endeavors, one of the main barriers to women's achievement of excellence and commitment is the expectation that women's career patterns and motivation will be the same as men's. When they are not, there are many phrases ("lost to marriage," "didn't pan out," "dropped out") which indicate the disappointing nature of their acts, the hopelessness of their making choices which are uniquely theirs as women. Many, possessing energy and talent, will choose the same career paths and find great personal satisfaction in meeting the same demands as many men. But others who live life differently, and who may choose differently from the traditional career pattern, also have much to offer, and our gain is greater if we can include their talents among those which society and science utilize. Attracted to scholarship and scientific research, they continue on to graduate school or professional school after college because of their deep interest in a field. Many have clear and well-defined plans for a career, while others wish to combine "worthwhile work" with homemaking. Because of their serious intellectual interest and involvement, such women usually do well academically and are excellent students. Yet they find that their interest in learning and in excellence does not receive the same recognition after college or graduate school as it did before unless they determinedly indicate that they plan a full-time uninterrupted career. But clearly the dominant (and in many cases preferred) life pattern for many a highly trained woman still includes multiple roles, dual commitments, and occasional interruptions. If she wishes to continue her professional activity on a flexible or modified schedule, or faces temporal or geographic discontinuities, she is frequently excluded from important aspects of what the sociologists call "socialization into a profession."

Professional Socialization

In the normal course of men's and women's professional careers, only a part of their professional training takes place in college, in graduate or professional schools, or in a training program. Many professions and occupations have periods analogous to that of the medical intern or resident (though these stages are frequently informal and rarely explicitly recognized) during which the individual learns to behave in ways which other people in the field regard as "professional." Such "socialization" usually occurs during graduate school as well as during the first decade of employment after one is launched on a career, and consists of learning the roles, the informal values and attitudes, and the expectations which are an important part of real professional life. During this stage of a career, the person not only learns occupational roles and skills, but gains a firmer image of himself as competent and adequate. Appraisals of his work by others permit self-criticism to grow and standards of judgment to develop. Such a sense of competence may come quickly and early for some, but develop slowly and gradually for others. Once a person has this sense of competence and regards himself as a professional, it is probable that he has less need to learn from colleagues and indeed may have greater freedom to diverge from the accepted way of doing things, seeking his own pathway instead. It is this firm sense of professional identity and capability which women, regardless of their ability, may find difficult to achieve, or achieve only at a high personal price.

Many people are unaware of this period of role learning in scholarly, scientific, or academic professions and fail to realize how important such a stage is and how lengthy it has become because of the increased complexity of professional life. Everett Hughes, the sociologist, has noted that many still think of professions as they were in the nineteenth century, although they have vastly changed since then.[3] Many professions are practiced in complicated organizations, with consequent nuances of status and levels of organization to contend with. There are elaborate social systems in all parts of academic and business life, and purely technical training is rarely enough. The aspiring young scientist must be knowledgeable about many aspects of institutions, journals, professional meetings, methods of obtaining source materials, and funding grant applications. Knowing how to command these technical and institutional facilities requires numerous skills, many unanticipated by the young student. But once gained, such skills often seem very simple in retrospect and even thoughtful professionals forget that they were once not second nature. This is the kind of learning we speak of as "caught," not "taught," and it is a valued by-product of acceptance and challenging association with other professionals.

Sponsorship

Studies of professions and professional identity have also stressed the importance of sponsorship as a device for influencing commitment and affecting the self-image. Referred to by some writers[4] as the "protégé system," sponsorship is common to the upper echelons of almost all professions, including the scientific fields. One must be "in" both to learn crucial trade secrets and to advance within the field. Unfortunately a man may be hesitant about encouraging a woman as a protégé. He may be delighted to have her as an assistant, but he may not see her as his successor, or as one who will carry on his ideas, or as a colleague. He may believe that she is less likely to be a good gamble, a risk for him to exert himself for, or that she is financially less dependent upon a job. Because of subtle pressures from his wife, he may temper his publicly expressed enthusiasm or interest. He may fail to introduce her to colleagues or sponsor her for jobs. And as one of Anne Roe's studies of eminent scientists indicated,[5] the advancement and success of protégés are important to [the sponsor's] own feelings of satisfaction in his professional efforts; nonachieving protégés reflect on the sponsor's public and private image.

In addition, sponsorship affects the recognition an individual receives. One might assume (or hope) that excellence and productivity in scientific work is all that is needed for recognition, but in reality ideas are more likely to be accepted if they are promoted or mentioned by eminent sponsors, or if they are the products of joint authorship with a well-known professional or derive from a well-known laboratory or university. Whether a woman is "sponsored" in these ways will partially determine who reads her work, listens to her reports, or even offers friendly comments on the draft of a paper. Such informal signs of recognition increase motivation and affect one's subjective feelings of commitment to a field, as well as feelings of professional identity.

Are Women in the Club?

A recent study of women Ph.D.'s[6] showed that the full-time employed woman Ph.D. published as much as her male colleagues and was more likely than the average male scientist to be in research. She was involved in the activities of her professional organization, was sought out as a consultant, and was more likely to be awarded fellowships and be accepted in honorary societies. Despite all this evidence of productivity and commitment, the authors of the study noted that the women often felt left out, and suggested that

> the problem which bothers the woman Ph.D., who is a full-time contributor to her profession, is that she is denied many of the informal signs of belonging and recognition. These women report that even on such daily activities as finding someone to have lunch or take a coffee break with, or finding someone with whom she can chew over an idea, or on larger issues such as finding a partner with whom she can share a research interest, the woman Ph.D. has a special and lower status.

This exclusion from the informal channels of communication is of particular importance in fast-moving science, where, as Sir Alfred Egerton has noted, "of the total information extant, only part is in the literature. Much of it is stored in the many brains of scientists and technologists. We are as dependent on biological storage as on mechanical or library storage." Jessie Bernard astutely comments: "It is this access—[to] the brains of fellow scientists—that may be more limited for women than for men."[7]

The need for stimulating colleagues was also attested to in a study by Perrucci of women engineers and scientists.[8] She found that women were more apt than men to endorse as important the opportunity "to work with colleagues who are interested in the latest developments in their field" and "to associate with other engineers and scientists of recognized ability." Interestingly enough, no differences appeared between men and women of comparable education as to whether they desired challenging work or work involving "people versus things."

The evidence also seems to indicate, however, that in many cases women are reluctant to put themselves forward or to protest their being left out. It is a vicious circle: men indifferent or unaware of excluding women; women insecure and hesitant of intruding. The remedy is not necessarily more individual boldness, but must include new institutional arrangements and programs which do not depend on individual initiative.[9] However, as the Radcliffe data indicated, such arrangements and programs are not too difficult to achieve.

There have been lone individuals who have flourished on society's neglect and produced great ideas or masterpieces, but this is not characteristic of those in the professions or the majority of people. For most people, acceptance by others and interaction with challenging groups or organizations are a source of deep personal significance and of creative energy as well. Yet it is this acceptance and this interaction which [are] often denied, both purposefully and inadvertently, to women, whether they participate full time or on a flexible schedule, whether they remain continuously in the field or seek reentry.

A New Career Concept

Because of their life patterns, many women with scientific training have nonprofessional roles and identifications to which they are deeply committed. They seek an occupational or professional identity which recognizes and takes into account this dual commitment. For women with these values, a new concept of professional "career" may be necessary.

Numerous women, either because of their own inclination or their personal situations, enjoy and competently manage full-time work and a full-time career. Others, however, seem to be seeking to invent for themselves a new and more varied conception of career, one which has not existed before and for which there are few models or patterns available. They have a full-time commitment, but do not always plan to work on a full-time basis; their lives and where they work are governed to a greater degree by nonoccupational factors. As a result of the smaller size of the families, and the shorter span of child-rearing, few of these women see their maternal role as bringing their professional life to an end. They think of themselves as a permanent part of the working force, and regard flexible schedules and part-time work as a necessary part of the solution. Some seem to be seeking an alternative career model which is neither upward moving nor "success oriented," but which recognizes their commitment to family responsibilities as an important part of their choice. To accommodate this lateral career, or "career of limited ambition,"[10] they seek to improvise a new professional role which is more differentiated and diversified than the accepted pattern. (I should note parenthetically that this interest in new career patterns is by no means limited to women.) Such an alternative mode might be represented schematically by an ascending spiral movement, indicating career choices which are upward in direction but slowly paced, with long horizontal stopovers. Deeper knowledge or more varied experience would be the goals of such a career: not greater status, but greater esteem; not primarily extrinsic rewards, but intrinsic satisfactions.[11]

Such new models are long overdue. Almost a century of experimentation has been spent in attempting to fit women's career patterns into those followed by most men, and the result has not been phenomenally successful. If such alternative career patterns can gain general recognition, the result may be more productive, creative work. As Epstein[12] has so succinctly noted, the barriers to women's advancement and achievement are not merely a function of prejudice or incapacity. The structures of professions, narrow and inflexible as they often are, may create limits which are largely unintended. But groups and colleagues are powerful forces in shaping attitudes and behavior; the institutional settings and social mechanisms which inhibit commitment and identity can also be used to promote change and to encourage different consequences.

Suggestions

What can women do to cope with these barriers and discriminatory practices which intensify the effects of discontinuity in their lives? How can they fully utilize their talents, yet make choices that are suitable to their goals and life styles? What constructive action can be taken to remedy the inadequate socialization which the current structure of the professions makes inevitable for many women?

In overcoming the barriers, the importance of sponsorship and the maintenance of communication with stimulating colleagues should not be underestimated. When a woman has to interrupt her training, graduate study, or employment, she should talk over future alternatives or avenues of return with an adviser and ask for letters of recommendation which may be used when a return is contemplated. She can seek ways to keep in touch with her department or work group. As one successful woman observed, "She should leave no gap unfilled."

Women with similar fields of interest can often profit by forming or joining other women in associations which provide professional stimulation and motivation, as well as information and access to new opportunities. Such groups can be particularly effective in assisting women who have temporarily retired to return to or keep up with their field. Several studies[13] suggest the possibility that women who are more ambitious in the traditional male-career sense may be more stimulated to achieve by the presence of men who are achieving, while women who regard intellectual achievement as part of the feminine role may react more favorably to the presence of capable women colleagues. This at least suggests that many talented younger women might be more encouraged by knowing and observing in the professional role other women who value the feminine family role. Such models are still too often a rarity.

Part-time work has only begun to be utilized effectively. Many men have long known that they are most productive when they engage in a variety of functions, carrying out activities which complement, but may have very little immediate relation to, each other. Although the initial stages of learning how to accomplish this are not easy, many women are discovering that such juggling can work even in complex and demanding scientific and engineering fields. Pilot projects using women scientists in the federal government have found both a shorter week and [a] shorter day successful.[14] Enthusiastic women report that they get almost as much done, while employers note that they get more than their money's worth, since there is little wasted time and important thinking time often comes free. In fields with hard-to-find skills such as data processing, part-time job opportunities may make it easier to recruit employees. An innovation which has been used with great success in education, social work, library work, and medical residencies is to have two women share one job. Thoughtfully and carefully planned, the partnership job has proved not only eminently suitable to the needs of women, but of benefit to employers as well.[15] Partnership teaching has proved so useful in education that one wonders why it was not thought of before.

Sometimes women create their own part-time opportunities. In the San Francisco area, a group of women biologists found they lacked opportunities for part-time work and for keeping up with their fields while their children were small. They organized a talent pool, incorporating as an educational group, Natural Science Education Resources. They have since offered a unique series of classes on plants and animals to mothers and their preschool children, served as consultants to teachers and schools, developed new ecology programs, presented adult education courses, and obtained a pilot National Science Foundation grant. Several women have now moved on to other jobs, leaving a vacant place [which is] eagerly taken by someone else seeking such a part-time opportunity.

Although all of these part-time approaches serve to prevent technical obsolescence, retraining programs and reentry techniques are also needed. Although some writers counsel noninterruption as the only answer, it seems more realistic to assume that discontinuity will continue to be a fact of life for many women. A woman's interests change between the time she is in college and the point at which she decides to involve herself more deeply again. Fortunately mid-career retraining is becoming mandatory for many scientific fields; if reentry opportunities for women can only be included by companies, universities, and professional societies along with the continuing education programs for full-time professionals, these transitions can be more easily accomplished.

Some women have planned their own transitional reentry programs. One woman chemist talked to a local college professor and offered to assist him in his laboratory courses during the year in order to bring her knowledge up to date. She proved so capable that he admitted her to advanced seminars, supervised her in tutorial reading, and is now working to retain her in a permanent capacity in the department.

Master's degree programs aimed at updating skills are particularly promising. Rutgers University has had one for mathematicians, and Wellesley College has had a two-year program for chemists.

Some may raise the question: Aren't women now insisting on the same opportunities as men? Do women want the same opportunities or do they want special opportunities? The answer is simply that they need both. Career commitment takes a variety of forms for women and may increasingly do so for men. Longevity, population pressures, and the explosion of knowledge have created new needs and life stages for us all. If we become obsessed with simply giving women the same opportunities as men (important though this may be), we not only obstruct effective recognition of the differences in women's lives, but may fail to note what is already a trend—more complex educational and occupational patterns for both men and women. Many of the programs and innovations developed to suit women's needs are needed for men as well. They too are feeling the impact of new knowledge, the expectation of intellectual retooling every decade, and the need for part-time refresher courses to update proficiency. They too have discovered that interests change after twenty years in a field, that challenge can outweigh security, and that mid-life may bring a desire to shift the focus of a career. And surely we are all learning the lesson that education is most useful when one is most ready for it. Many young students are no longer so eager to cram all their education and professional training into the beginning of their adult years.

While the patterns of women's lives may be more varied, the interruptions more pronounced and profound, and possibly the needs for guidance greater, our attempts to foster a social climate which meets the complex needs of women today may well be pointing the way toward meeting the diverse needs of both the men and [the] women of tomorrow.

Summary

Commitment and creativity in science are not merely a function of an individual's competence or excellence, but are a product of the social environment as well. Acceptance and recognition from significant other people (one's peers and other professionals) and opportunities for stimulating and challenging interaction are essential for developing a strong occupational or professional identity, and for creating the inner sense of role competence which can lead to greater commitment and productivity in professional work. Unfortunately women, especially those who have experienced interrupted or discontinuous careers, find such opportunities and acceptance difficult to obtain.

The scientific community can foster the professional development and effectiveness of women in science by permitting women more flexible opportunities for professional participation, by being more aware of practices which exclude women on the basis of gender rather than ability, and by separating standards of excellence from time schedules.

Women can help themselves by keeping up contacts with others in their fields, participating in professional groups, becoming familiar with new part-time approaches and reentry skills, creating their own retraining and employment opportunities, and instituting new programs appropriate to their needs.

"Restriction of opportunity not only blights hope; it excludes the person from the chance to acquire the knowledge and skill that would in turn enable him to surmount the barriers to effectiveness."[16]

Notes

1. M. S. White, "Conversations with the Scholars" (Report submitted to the Radcliffe Institute, 1966). The Radcliffe Institute supports part-time scholars, provides funds for domestic and child-care help, a place to work, and access to the library and intellectual resources of Radcliffe and Harvard. The scholars neither work for a degree nor take courses, but engage in creative or scholarly work within their fields. Many already have their doctorate, or its equivalent in achievement. In addition, the Institute sponsors other fellowship programs for part-time graduate study and medical residency training, and conducts a research program.
2. D. C. Pelz, "Creative Tensions in the Research and Development Climate," *Science*, vol. 157 (1967), p. 160; H. S. Becker and J. W. Carper, *American Journal of Sociology*, vol. 41 (1956), p. 289; J. J. Sherwood, "Self-Identity and Referent Others," *Sociometry*, vol. 28 (1965), p. 66.
3. E. C. Hughes, "Professions," *Daedalus*, vol. 92 (1963), p. 655.
4. C. F. Epstein, *Woman's Place* (Berkeley: University of California Press, 1970).
5. A. Roe, "Women in Science," *Personnel and Guidance Journal*, vol. 54 (1966), p. 784.
6. R. J. Simon, S. M. Clark, and K. Galway, "The Woman Ph.D.: A Recent Profile," *Social Problems*, vol. 15 (1967), p. 221.
7. J. Bernard, *Academic Women* (University Park, Pa.: State College, The Pennsylvania Press, 1964), p. 303.
8. C. C. Perrucci, "The Female Engineer and Scientist: Factors Associated with the Pursuit of a Professional Career" (Unpublished report, 1968).

9. See U.S., Civil Service Commission, *Changing Patterns: A Report on the Federal Women's Program Review Seminar* (Washington, D.C.: Government Printing Office, 1969); A. L. Dement, "The College Woman as a Science Major," *Journal of Higher Education*, vol. 33 (1962), p. 487.

10. M. K. Sanders, "The New American Female: Demi-Feminism Takes Over," *Harper's*, vol. 231 (1965), p. 37.

11. R. H. Turner, "Some Aspects of Women's Ambition," *American Journal of Sociology*, vol. 70 (1964), p. 271.

12. Epstein, *op. cit.*

13. E. G. French and G. S. Lesser, "Some Characteristics of the Achievement Motive in Women," *Journal of Abnormal Social Psychology*, vol. 68 (1964), p. 119; C. A. Leland and M. M. Lozoff, *College Influences on the Role Development of Undergraduates* (Stanford: Institute for the Study of Human Problems, Stanford University, 1969), pp. 46–90.

14. U.S., Civil Service Commission, *op. cit.*; Dement, *op. cit.*

15. I. Zwerling, "Part-Time Insured Staff," *Hospital and Community Psychiatry*, vol. 21 (1970), p. 59; W. A. Thompson, et al., "An Answer to the Computer Programmer Shortage, *Adult Leadership*, vol. 18, no. 7 (January 1970), p. 213.

16. M. B. Smith, in *Socialization and Society*, ed. J. A. Clausen (Boston: Little, Brown & Co., 1968), p. 313.

Discussion

The articles in this chapter deal with the women who have made occupational choices that are considered to be "deviant" within the context of the American society (and to varying degrees within the context of some Western European societies as well). These occupational choices, including law, medicine, dentistry, pharmacy, engineering, natural sciences, or an academic career, are considered "deviant" only because these fields are dominated by men. For example, in the United States in 1960, 1.1 percent of the architects and the engineers were women; 5.6 percent of the physicians, the surgeons, and the dentists; 8.1 percent of the chemists, the geologists, and the physicists; and 3.5 percent of the lawyers.[1]

When, however, one looks at occupational distributions in other societies, the emerging picture clearly indicates that there is nothing inherently "masculine" or "feminine" about the various occupations. Only the sex-linked stereotypes attached to different occupations vary (and widely so) from society to society. While in the United States the "feminine" need to help others is stereotypically channeled into nursing and social work, in Russia it is channeled into medicine.[2] And in Greece the most feminine occupations are considered to be pharmacy, dentistry, law, and, in the last decade, also architecture.[3] Also it must be noted that in all countries in which women have a considerable number of choices in the marital, parental, familial, educational, and occupational areas, the occupations of pharmacy and dentistry have been redefined as "feminine" fields and women largely predominate in them. This is true in Poland, Finland, Hungary, Denmark, and to a somewhat lesser extent in Sweden and Greece.[4] In the Philippines also, pharmacy (but not dentistry) had become almost an all-female occupation.[5] Chemistry and medicine follow in most societies, but their redefinition as appropriate "feminine" occupations does not lead to the virtual exclusion of men, who continue to choose them but a little less often than women. Law and architecture in the most "liberated" societies never become redefined as "feminine" (with the recent Greek redefinition of the field of architecture as the only exception[6]), and some fields, despite a greater participation of women (in the "liberated" countries), still remain stereotyped as "masculine." These fields are engineering, agriculture, physics, aeronautics, and veterinary medicine.[7]

Moreover, it is interesting to note that some occupations, which American women are discouraged from entering, are the very ones that could provide them with maximum flexibility and a satisfactory and highly remunerative source of work. Dentistry and medicine provide two outstanding such examples, since the practice of these professions can be limited for some years to only certain hours each day, those hours being chosen on the basis of a schedule best suited to the needs, for example, of a mother of young children.[8]

Despite the "masculine" image of medicine, law, engineering, executive jobs, and academic positions which is prevalent in the United States, a few women do enter these fields. This fact raises a number of interesting questions, such as: Why do these women seek masculine jobs? In what characteristics do these women differ from other women and from men in the same professions? What is the type of "career" and occupational success that they are able to achieve in these fields and how does it compare with that of men? What factors facilitate or inhibit their occupational success?[9]

While there is not an abundance of relevant studies, the few studies available provide sufficient information to answer the above questions. First, women who enter these occupations seem usually to have received from their parents, a socialization different from that received by the majority of American women. As compared with mothers of women choosing "typical" occupations, twice as many of these mothers (of women choosing "deviant" occupations) provided, by their own example, a model of a working woman who successfully combined work with family life and responsibilities, and in some cases these mothers were employed in "deviant," male-dominated occupations.[10] The fathers have symbolically treated them as boys either because they were the only child or because, thanks to large age gaps between them and other siblings, they were in effect an only child or because all the children were girls and one was selected to "play the role of a son." Or, finally, they may have been treated as boys because a brother refused to be a doctor, or a lawyer, like the father or refused to manage the family business, and they are thus used as substitutes.[11] It is, therefore, very interesting to note that the "deviant" occupations are not open to women and that women are not socialized to enter them, unless they actually or symbolically substitute for a son.[12]

The findings presented in James J. White's article on women lawyers indicate that men and women lawyers do not differ very radically. Both are equally motivated to become lawyers by the potentially high income (the "social work" element of law practice by no means being more important for women); they equally often work in litigation cases; and women appear in court with the same frequency as men.

A comparative study of male and female engineering students showed that the female engineering students were as feminine as a general sample of college coeds (as measured by a masculinity-femininity test[13]). Female engineering students, however, much more often than male students see their role as involving more tolerance of ambiguity both in the professional sphere as well as in their relationships with other people. They place a greater value on a liberal arts background, have "intellectual" expectations, and "see their social relationships in the area of engineering as having more autonomy from their technical performance."[14] Thus, female engineering students tend to introduce feminine norms and behavior into their role, which leads to lower grades (despite their high intellectual capacity), less faculty approval, and a greater tendency to drop out (and change majors) before graduation. Only the female students who score high on masculinity tend to define the role of student engineer more as the boys do; they get better grades, and a higher proportion of them graduate than is the case for more "feminine" students.[15] This finding tends to suggest that those girls who not only are intellectually capable but also think and behave more like the boys do are more successful than the more feminine ones in engineering studies and probably also later on, in the practice of engineering. This finding may be better understood in the light of the fact that, as mentioned earlier, only approximately 1 percent of engineers in the United States are women and, therefore, they represent an extreme case of occupational deviance.

Actually, research evidence on the existing relationship between degree of femininity and the choice of a "deviant" career is not conclusive, some studies showing a correlation between masculine traits and such a choice, and others showing a correlation between femininity and a "deviant" career choice.[16] But one trend that seems to be quite persistent and valid for all fields is that the most outstanding women enter "deviant" fields, probably because girls just above average (or below this level) are "counseled" out of their occupational aspirations and guided toward more feminine occupations. In architecture, for example, while women make up 2 percent of the students, scholastically they all belong to the upper 5 percent of the class.[17] Another type of evidence indicates that "women scientists do not enjoy the same things as do women who are in occupations where beauty is an essential asset" (such as fashion modeling or working as an airline stewardess or nightclub, TV, or other entertainer).[18] Women in the latter category tend to prefer the dramatic to the routine, the unstructured situation to the structured; they prefer exciting, adventuresome activities, including those with the abstract feeling of danger, and they strongly dislike working with numbers in precise, disciplined settings. The opposite, however, seems to hold true for women scientists.[19] This evidence does not, though, indicate a "basic incompatibility between women's beauty and their involvement in science," as has been implied.[20] Women scientists may be quite beautiful, but still they may like to work with numbers, and in structured, "safe," and "nonswinging" places. But, of course, the degree of attractiveness of women scientists drawn to any of the "deviant" fields may be directly related to the percentage of women in the field, which in turn reflects the degree to which such occupational choices are considered "deviant" in a particular society. It can be, thus, hypothesized that the more "deviant" a field, the less attractive the women who enter it in our present society.

A study of Finnish women physicians (in 1968, 25.2 percent of the physicians in Finland were women) showed that they were more patient-oriented than men, who conversely, gave greater importance to research, recognition, prestige, and high income. Women physicians liked "the opportunity to help and serve," the "opportunity to work with and among people," and the "opportunity to fulfill humanistic, religious or other ideals" more than men, although the differences were small.[21]

It would be important to have comparative data about women versus men physicians in the United States, where women constitute a small and very deviant group, and in Poland or the USSR, where women physicians are not only socially acceptable but also in the majority group. Only when such data are available will it be possible to assess the influence of the "deviant" status of an occupation upon the type of women attracted to it, and to separate the influence from that of the occupation's desirability because of the nature of the work involved.

Finally, a study of women psychologists, psychology being a "borderline" type of occupation between "feminine" and "masculine" ones, has shown that the women attracted to the field now (and in the past) have "more intellectual, scientific, and verbal-linguistic interests than does the average woman, and fewer interests in the traditional feminine roles."[22] In another study successful academic women (born before 1910) in the field of psychology were compared with women in the general population, college women, and successful academic (research) men (not only in psychology). The findings indicate that successful women psychologists share with eminent men researchers certain characteristics, characteristics not possessed, at least to the same extent, by other adult and college women. Both women psychologists and prominent academic men differ from the general population in that they tend to be more aloof, introspective, intelligent, assertive, flexible, adventuresome, sensitive, radical, and self-sufficient. However, successful academic women in psychology tend to be even more intelligent and radical than successful academic men, probably because these are prerequisites in order to break away from traditional female roles and succeed in "a man's world."[23]

Another analysis of women psychologists which took into account also the characteristics of two younger generations—those born between 1910 and 1925, and those born after 1925—has shown that 50 percent of those in the oldest of the three generations (those born before 1910) spent most of their time teaching, while the younger women have increasingly taken up research (a higher-prestige activity). Furthermore, it was found that women psychologists of all three generations were significantly "more socially aloof, intelligent, dominant, flexible, adventuresome, unconventional, confident, radical, and self-sufficient" than women in the general population. Comparisons among women psychologists of the different generations showed that those born after 1910 were significantly more intelligent and unconventional but also less composed, less rigid, less trusting, and less shrewd than those born before 1910. Thus, it seems that while women psychologists have always tended to be more intelligent than average women, those who entered the profession during or after the Second World War were more intelligent and unconventional than those who entered the profession in the "pioneering" days in the United States. The reason for this, as the authors of this research study have correctly pointed out, is the fact that especially after the end of the Second World War societal expectations pressured a woman toward home and motherhood and it thus required a very talented, dominant, and unconventional woman to resist these pressures and do what she wanted. But because women had to go against prevailing values and societal definitions of sex roles and sex-appropriate behavior, they may have ended by feeling less confident about their identity as women.[24]

In examining, furthermore, what type of "careers" women have in male-dominated fields and the extent to which they are successful, one is struck by the fact that even when women enter these fields, they tend to (or are encouraged to?) select some specialties which are usually the least well paid and least prestigious ones. For example, American women lawyers concentrate, as we have seen in James J. White's article, in trusts and estates, real estate, and domestic relations, while women physicians are found mostly in pediatrics, psychiatry (and to a lesser extent in anesthesiology and gynecology and obstetrics), women architects in residential design, and women engineers in industrial engineering.[25] The Finnish study of women physicians shows also that they tend to concentrate in pediatrics, pulmonary diseases, psychiatry, and ophthalmology, while men specialize in surgery, internal diseases, obstetrics, and also psychiatry;[26] and the majority of West German physicians are also pediatricians.[27] Evidence from another masculine occupation, kept masculine by "sacred" tradition, that of the clergy, shows quite clearly that the women who have entered it are "marginal" from all points of view. They tend to be older and much less educated than clergymen of the same age and race, to be accepted much more often by sect-type than church-type groups, and when ordained by a church-type group, not to be permitted to perform marriages or administer communion.[28]

This concentration of women in the lowest paid and less prestigious specialties of the male-dominated occupations accounts to some extent for women's lower income and lower prestige than men in the same profession. But as White showed in his comparative study of men and women lawyers, regardless of all other reasons, women receive less pay for the work they perform because they are discriminated against on the basis of their sex. Furthermore, women very infrequently reach high prestigious and/or administrative positions partly because they do have low aspirations and partly because they are not given the opportunity to do so or are frankly precluded from doing so on the basis of prevailing prejudice against them.[29]

But as a Canadian study of women in the public service has shown, there is a very small percentage of women in high administrative jobs; women are aware that their promotion chances are poor or very poor (especially in the professions and in administrative jobs); and if they are in administration, they tend to think that they should have been two or more grades higher and do not expect that they will ever reach that level.[30] Similarly, in Russia, even in occupations in which women abound (such as medicine), as the level of authority and social significance increases, the percentage of women in high administrative posts decreases. Thus, while 4 out of 5 Russian physicians are women, 4 out of 5 physicians holding a high rank are men.[31] While this type of evidence tends to be interpreted as proof of women's low level of expectation from their career development, it may simply mean that a vicious circle is operating, whereby women with high career expectations, faced with the fact of clear-cut discrimination against them, adjust to the situation by lowering their expectations. It is very taxing for all women to become revolutionaries trying to change the entire social structure, and an encouraging wider social movement did not exist until 1967. But, of course, for the sake of objectivity, it is only fair to mention that many married women in the United States and Canada tend to shy away from high positions that entail many responsibilities because of the burden of familial responsibilities, which, almost in its entirety, they must simultaneously carry.[32] It is the combination of all these factors that is responsible for women's rather conspicuous absence from top positions, administrative and otherwise, in the professions, administration, business, government, unions, etc.

But let us see what the actual work history of women in male-dominated occupations is. There seems to be general agreement that women work relatively fewer hours than men, partly because some of them opt to work part time for some stages of their family cycle (or throughout their careers) and partly because they are not inclined to work overtime as some of their overachieving male colleagues tend to do. This has been found to be true for American engineers and college science professors[33] as well as for all women professionals[34] and for Finnish physicians.[35] Finnish women physicians were also found to see fewer patients on the average than men doctors and to spend more time on the average with each patient than men physicians, another proof that they are patient- rather than profit-oriented. But as the Finnish authors of this study correctly point out, the fact that women physicians live on the average 2.2 years longer than men (both die before age sixty-five) makes up with length of service for their relatively shorter working hours.[36]

Furthermore, women are often rejected by prestigious and high-paying employers who allegedly do not want to risk giving "important" positions to women upon whose commitment and continuity they cannot always rely.[37] For example, it has been reported that about 40 percent of industries do not offer jobs to women engineers, but there is no information as to the nature of these industries.[38] But even when men and women professionals are employed by the same employer and have the same qualifications, they are often assigned different tasks, the women assuming the "dirty" or boring work and being paid less than the men. Probably one of the most clear-cut and outstanding cases is provided by the study of law partnerships in which at least a husband and a wife lawyer are involved. In practically all instances the woman is relegated to the function of a glorified legal secretary or legal assistant and manager rather than treated as a full-fledged legal partner.[39]

It seems, therefore, that, at least in the case of American women, even when they escape the low-paying, low-prestige "feminine" occupations that mostly entail the boring detailed work that nobody really wants to do, they often end up in the same position even after having entered a more prestigious and profitable male-dominated profession.

The professional advancement of women in male-dominated occupations is inhibited by, among other things, the difficulties of establishing a man-woman protégé relationship and by the exclusion of women (by the men or through self-exclusion mechanisms) from informal discussions and cliques, as discussed in more detail by Martha S. White (in this chapter) and by Cynthia Fuchs Epstein.[40] But women in the United States tend to be more accepted by their male colleagues on different institutionalized occasions, such as cocktail parties and dinners at meetings or luncheons in everyday professional life, and they have more of a chance of coming under the "sponsorship" of an important male figure if they are physically unattractive or old. The less their potential for being sexually attractive to their male colleagues, the more women may be taken seriously and aided up the occupational ladder. And one cannot but think to what extent this masculine assessment of the situation is correct, since up until very recently the majority of highly committed professional women were ugly and single[41] or were older women whose time-consuming familial responsibilities were out of the way. Probably a considerable number of young and attractive women will have to prove their continuous and high commitment (more than their excellence) before *any* young and attractive woman is take seriously and treated equally by her male colleagues and given the same treatment as that given to men and other women.

Notes

1. U.S., Department of Commerce, Bureau of the Census, *1960 Census of Population* (Washington, D.C.: Government Printing Office, 1961), vol. 1. pt. 1.
2. Cynthia Fuchs Epstein, *Woman's Place* (Berkeley: University of California Press, 1970), pp. 158–159.
3. It is interesting to examine the nature of the cultural stereotypes that have permitted the redefinition of these occupations in Greece. It is said that women make better pharmacists than men because they are much more patient and careful in preparing prescriptions, thanks to the skills they have developed in learning cooking. And women can be better architects than men because they know how to design a comfortable house, since they are more aware of and sensitive to the needs and preferences of all family members. Thus, again the redefinition of these occupations is still based upon the traditional role of women (see Constantina Safilios-Rothschild, "Quelques aspects de la modernisation sociale aux États-Unis et en Grèce," *Sociologie et sociétés*, vol. 1, no. 1 [May 1969], p. 35).
4. Constantina Safilios-Rothschild, "A Cross-Cultural Examination of Women's Marital, Familial, Educational and Occupational Options," *Acta Sociologica*, vol. 14, nos. 1/2 (Spring 1971).
5. Chester L. Hunt, "Female Occupational Roles and Urban Sex Ratios in the United States, Japan, and the Philippines," *Social Forces*, vol. 43, no. 3 (May 1965), pp. 407–417.
6. In 1960–61, 46.9 percent of the architectural students who successfully passed the highly competitive and high-standard entrance examinations of the Athens Polytechnic Schools were women. See: Constantina Safilios-Rothschild "Quelques aspects de la modernisation sociale aux États-Unis et en Grèce," *op. cit.*, p. 35.
7. Constantina Safilios-Rothschild, "A Cross-Cultural Examination of Women's Marital, Familial, Educational and Occupational Options," *op. cit.*
8. The greater potential flexibility of medicine as an occupation (and therefore its suitability for women) has been also recognized by Joseph Katz: "Career and Autonomy in College Women," in *Class, Character and Career: Determinants of Occupational Choice in College Students*, eds. Joseph Katz et al. (Stanford, Cal.: Institute for the Study of Human Problems, Stanford University, 1969), pp. 146–147.
9. Having a career does not necessarily imply occupational success. "Career" connotes uninterrupted employment (in the same job) and a high work commitment that places work most of the time above all other things (including familial obligations). Thus, although having a career (and therefore, a high work commitment) increases one's chances for occupational success, it does not guarantee it.
10. Elizabeth M. Almquist and Shirley S. Angrist, "Career Salience and Atypicality of Occupational Choice Among College Women," *Journal of Marriage and the Family*, vol. 32, no. 2 (May 1970), pp. 246–247. See also James J. White, "Women in the Law," in this chapter.
11. Anita Lynn Micossi, "Conversion to Women's Lib," *Trans-Action*, vol. 8, nos. 1/2 (November–December 1970), p. 83; Margaret Hennig, "Career Development for Women Executives" (Ph.D. Diss., Harvard Graduate School of Business Administration, 1971), as reported in Marilyn Bender, "A Profile of the Woman Boss," *New York Times*, February 23, 1971; Carol Lopate, *Women in Medicine* (Baltimore: Johns Hopkins Press, 1965), p. 23.
12. See also the Discussion in Chapter 5.

13. See also the Discussion in Chapter 1.
14. Stanley S. Robin, "The Female in Engineering," in *The Engineers and the Social System*, eds Robert Perruci and Joel E. Gerstl (New York: John Wiley & Sons, 1969), pp. 203–218.
15. *Ibid.*
16. Becky J. White, "The Relationship of Self-Concept and Parental Identification to Women's Vocational Interests," *Journal of Counseling Psychology*, vol. 6, no. 3 (1959); Katz et al., *op. cit.*, p. 143.
17. Beatrice Dinneiman, "Women in Architecture," *Architectural Forum*, vol. 131, no. 5 (December 1969), p. 50.
18. David P. Campbell, "The Clash Between Beautiful Women and Science" (Paper delivered at the American Psychological Association meetings, San Francisco, August 31, 1968).
19. David P. Campbell, "The Vocational Interests of Beautiful Women," *Personnel and Guidance Journal*, vol. 45 (June 1967), pp. 968–972.
20. Campbell, "The Clash Between Beautiful Women and Science," *op. cit.*
21. Elina Haavio-Mannila and Risto Jaakkola, *Sex Roles and the Medical Profession*, Institute of Sociology Research Report no. 150 (Helsinki: University of Helsinki, 1970).
22. D. P. Campbell and A. M. Soliman, "The Vocational Interests of Women in Psychology: 1942–1966," *The American Psychologist*, vol. 23 (1968), p. 163.
23. Louise M. Bachtold and Emmy E. Werner, "Personality Profiles of Gifted Women: Psychologists," *The American Psychologist*, vol. 25 (1970), pp. 234–243.
24. Louise M. Bachtold and Emmy E. Werner, "Personality Profiles of Women Psychologists, Three Generations," *Developmental Psychology* (in press).
25. Epstein, *op. cit.*, pp. 154–164; Alice S. Rossi, "Barriers to the Career Choice of Engineering, Medicine or Science Among American Women," in *Women and the Scientific Professions*, Jackelyn A. Mattfeld and Carol G. Van Aken eds. (Cambridge, Mass.: M.I.T. Press, 1965), pp. 58–65; Lopate, *op. cit.*, p. 56; Beatrice Dinneiman, *op. cit.*, p. 51; James J. White, "Women in the Law," in this chapter.
26. Haavio-Mannila and Jaakkola, *op. cit.*
27. Epstein, *op. cit.*, p. 163.
28. E. Wilbur Bock, "The Female Clergy: A Case of Professional Marginality," *The American Journal of Sociology*, vol. 72, no. 5 (March 1967), pp. 531–539.
29. This is true not only for the United States and Canada but also for the Scandinavian countries and Australia. See Harriet Holter, "Women's Occupational Situation in Scandinavia," *International Labour Review*, vol. 93, no. 4 (April 1966), p. 394; Jean I. Martin and Catherine M. G. Richmond, "Working Women in Australia" (Background Paper no. 11, HRH The Duke of Edinburgh's Third Commonwealth Study Conference, Australia, 1968), pp. 11–12.
30. Stanislaw Judek, *Women in the Public Service*, Ottawa: Canada Department of Labour, Economic and Research Branch, 1968, pp. 12–38.
31. Norton T. Dodge, *Women in the Soviet Economy* (Baltimore: Johns Hopkins Press, 1966), pp. 193–205.
32. U.S., Department of Labor, Women's Bureau, *Women in Higher-Level Positions* (Washington, D.C.: Government Printing Office, 1950), p. 26.
33. Rossi, *op. cit.*, pp. 69–72.
34. Epstein, *op. cit.*, pp. 182–183.
35. Haavio-Mannila and Jaakkola, *op. cit.*
36. *Ibid.*
37. Rossi, *op. cit.*, pp. 66–68.
38. S. Scott Hill, "Women Engineers in Industry," in *Women and the Scientific Professions*, eds. Mattfeld and Van Aken, pp. 196–197.
39. Cynthia Fuchs Epstein, "Law Partners and Marital Partners: Strains and Solutions in the Dual-Career Family Enterprise" (Paper delivered at the Eleventh International Family Research Seminar, London, September 1970).

40. Epstein, *Woman's Place,* pp. 167–182; Cynthia Fuchs Epstein, "Encountering the Male Establishment: Sex-Status Limits on Women's Careers in the Professions," *American Journal of Sociology,* vol. 75, no. 6 (May 1970), pp. 965–982.
41. David Campbell of the University of Minnesota, for example, found that there was a negative correlation between women in "masculine" occupations and attractiveness, a fact that tends to reinforce the stereotype that pretty women are not serious about work, especially "masculine" work.

Projections About the Women's Liberation Movement and the Future of Men and Women

BARBARA BOVEE POLK

Women's Liberation: Movement for Equality

With the protest of the Miss America contest in Atlantic City in 1968, the Women's Liberation Movement burst upon public consciousness. Despite widespread publicity on the activities, groups, and individuals associated with the movement since that time, most people are still confused about exactly what it is that women want.

Basically, the movement seeks equality between the sexes—an end to the male chauvinist myth that men are superior to women and an end to the institutions and practices of society which perpetuate this myth. Beyond this, the apparent disunity of the movement is largely a reflection of the many different changes which must be made in order to institute equality between the sexes. Although disagreements do exist, especially over the question of reform versus revolution, groups with divergent viewpoints find themselves working together on such projects as setting up child-care centers and supporting change in laws prohibiting abortion.

Divisions of the Women's Liberation Movement

The Women's Liberation Movement is composed of three types of groups: those seeking the expansion of women's rights, those seeking women's liberation, and those seeking a socialist society which includes equality for women. An understanding of these groups is an aid to making sense of the divergent activities of the movement.

Typical of groups seeking the establishment of women's rights is the National Organization for Women (NOW), the only large national organization in the movement. It draws its membership heavily from among well-educated professional or would-be professional women. NOW accepts the basic structure of the society and of social relationships, but seeks to improve the status of women through legal, economic, and political means. The organization has a national structure, holds conventions, hires lobbyists, pursues court cases on discrimination against women, participates in orderly demonstrations, and publishes pamphlets and leaflets on the legal and economic status of women. Among its major concerns are ending discrimination against women in the obtaining of employment and in pay, reforming abortion laws, equalizing educational opportunity, and providing child-care facilities. Many other small *ad hoc* groups organized around similar issues in specific communities, professions, or places of employment also fall into the category of women's rights groups. In most cases, these groups feel themselves to be part of a general movement on behalf of women, but do not accept the Women's Liberation label for themselves.

Independent Women's Liberation groups, the second type of group in the movement, usually have no official name, referring to themselves by such labels as "the Tuesday night group." A few, with more picturesque designations such as SCUM (Society for Cutting Up Men), Redstockings, the Radical Feminists, and WITCH (Women's International Terrorist Conspiracy from Hell), have captured the imagination of the mass media and received national attention. The typical Women's Liberation group (including most of the groups listed above) is composed of no more than ten to fifteen women who come together in "consciousness-raising" or "rap" groups (to be discussed further) for the purpose of developing their own understanding of the condition of women on the basis of their own experiences. Although most such groups are entirely autonomous of each other, or have only weak ties to other groups through a coalition structure, the political analysis they develop is remarkably similar. They agree generally with the need for the reforms pursued by the women's rights groups but go well beyond them to criticize the basic institutions and power relationships of the society. All Women's Liberation groups agree that the institutions of our society are male-dominated and account for the oppression of women. They tend in particular to be critical of marriage, religion, and the law, as well as of political and economic institutions. They differ, however, over the role of men in the institutionalized oppression of women. Some groups view men as oppressors who use social institutions to hold down women, while others see men as themselves suffering oppression from these institutions. Whatever the position on the culpability of men, Women's Liberation groups agree that men derive economic, political, and psychological benefits from their superior status and will therefore be reluctant to relinquish their position. But even the most anti-male groups tend to aim most of their attack at institutional and role systems. For example, the final stanza of a long WITCH hex says:

> WITCH calls down destruction
> on Babylon.
> Oppressors:
> the curse of women is on you.
> DEATH TO MALE CHAUVINISM.[1]

The final concentration of this hex upon an ideology rather than on men is indicative of the position of even the most strongly anti-male groups.

The independent Women's Liberation groups participate in actions from the most conventional to the most unconventional. They have captured the attention of the media through various guerrilla theater actions,[2] including the beauty pageant demonstrations, and certain WITCH actions (publicly and dramatically hexing individuals or groups, as in the quotation above), but these are only the most dramatic, not the most frequent, actions of these groups.

The third type of group in the movement is the women's caucus of the left-wing political groups (for example, International Socialists, Socialist Workers Party, and various New Left splinter groups). Although women in these groups typically accept the Women's Liberation label and concur with many of the views and analyses espoused by independent Women's Liberation groups, they differ in that they subscribe to a basically Marxian analysis of society which serves as a framework for their understanding of the oppression of women. They generally do not see the "consciousness-raising" group as a vehicle for developing a political analysis, as do the independent groups, although they may hold similar kinds of meetings for the purpose of identifying and fighting male chauvinism in their political organizations. A fundamental belief is that a socialist revolution is a necessary precondition for women's liberation. In addition, they differ from independent groups by emphasizing the necessity of having structure and discipline within the movement; of organizing women, particularly working women; and of supporting other movements (for example, by having women's contingents participate in peace demonstrations). These groups tend to favor more conservative activities such as demonstrations as forms of political action and would rarely be found participating in guerrilla theater. Because these caucuses are a part of organizations which are dominated by men, these women's groups tend to be distrusted by members of the independent Women's Liberation groups, who see them as willing to give first priority to the socialist revolution rather than to their own liberation. Nevertheless, they make an important contribution to the Women's Liberation Movement through their attempts to integrate the issues of women's oppression into a broader social theory and through their efforts to help women see their experiences as similar in type to those of other minority groups.

The remainder of this paper will be devoted to a discussion of the activities of only one of the three types of groups in the movement—the independent Women's Liberation groups—primarily because of their unique form of organization.

Organizing for Equality

The independent Women's Liberation groups have three basic ways in which they are attempting to achieve the liberation of women. The first two, personal liberation through consciousness-raising groups and social liberation through political activity, have been given wide publicity in the mass media. The third, the attempt to build a social movement which reflects the kind of society in which women would like to live, has been ignored. We shall briefly consider the first two approaches and their relationship to each other, then turn our attention to the third.

Personal Liberation/Consciousness Raising

As has been pointed out previously, the focus of attack in the Women's Liberation Movement is the doctrine of male supremacy. Since we have all been reared with this doctrine, women as well as men tend to accept the belief that men are superior to women. For this reason, women interested in the movement find that they typically have to begin with themselves in their attempts to attack the male chauvinism of the society. The heart of the movement, then, is the small "consciousness-raising" or "rap" group in which women gather to attempt to understand their lives and problems in terms of the pressures which impinge on all women in the society. The purpose of these groups is not therapy; it is to develop both an analysis of the society and an appropriate politics based on the experience of being female—the personal becomes political. As members of the group share experiences and attitudes, they become aware that the problems they thought were theirs alone are less a function of their own personal hang-ups than of the social structure and culture in which they live. Through sharing experiences, women find that personal problems related to being a woman cannot be solved without an understanding of the society and, often, without attempting to implement changes within it as well.

The changes which women attempt to implement usually begin with altering attitudes and interactions in relationships with husband, boyfriend, employer, co-workers, and female friends, with the goal of seeing oneself, and being seen, as an equal in interpersonal relationships. This change is perhaps the most difficult and the most fundamental for the Women's Liberation Movement. For to change interactions, a woman must begin to change her entire concept of herself and begin to present a self-image which deviates from the accepted norms of the society.

Examples of the types of changes which women attempt to make in their lives vary considerably with their position and concerns. A single woman may begin to insist that her ideas be taken seriously in mixed groups, although she realizes that this will decrease her acceptability as a girl friend or date. A wife may insist upon her husband taking over much of the housework and supporting her continued education as she has supported his, although this is not socially acceptable behavior for men. A working wife may insist that her husband iron his own shirts, even though poorly ironed shirts reflect on her abilities rather than on his. Or a female employee may demand salary and title commensurate with her responsibilities although she risks being fired for insubordination. Meanwhile, in all interactions, women begin to object to being referred to as "girls" (how often are adult men referred to as "boys"?), to assert their right to be heard, and to demand equal participation in the decisions which affect their lives.

Most such changes are actively resisted by men, who, in addition to being accustomed to the norms of the society, also derive psychological and physical benefits from the submissiveness and domesticity of women.[3] Thus, women, in attempting to change interactions between the sexes, frequently encounter hostility from men and, in turn, begin to be hostile toward men. The consciousness-raising group becomes a place where women can express their rage and begin to find constructive outlets for it. The group serves the important functions of helping a woman assess the reality of her oppression, helping her identify ways in which *she* is not being egalitarian, and encouraging her to continue her quest for equal treatment in the face of negative sanctions. In this process, women come to respect each other's views and to take each other seriously, often for the first time. Women, then, through sharing the struggle to attain egalitarian relationships with men, begin to form egalitarian relationships with each other and come to rely less heavily on the approval of men and more on the judgments of women.

Social Liberation/Political Action

In the process of attempting to change their own lives and interactions, women are confronted with the necessity of effecting changes in the structure of society. The mother who wishes to return to school or get a job finds that adequate day care is not available and organizes action groups to seek day-care funding from political agencies, employers, or schools. Women seeking dignity in society find themselves outraged by advertising practices and protest by organizing boycotts, writing letters, invading business offices, and pasting "This Insults Women" stickers on the offending advertisements. Meanwhile their sisters work for equal pay and employment opportunities, attack school textbooks and television programs for their sexist images of women, or challenge the legality of marriage laws, using political actions ranging from circulating petitions, passing out leaflets, or holding rallies to participating in guerrilla theater actions. All of these activities are attacks on the institutionalization of the male chauvinist myth. Some are engaged in with the hope of actually changing an institution or practice, but most at this point in time are designed largely to draw attention to the position of women and to help raise the consciousness of women who have never before seen the sources of their discontent in clear focus.

Organizational Liberation/Equality

Hand in hand with the search for personal liberation through the consciousness-raising groups and for changes in social institutions and practices has come an attempt to build *within* the Women's Liberation Movement a new form of organization and new way of living which does not import the oppressiveness of traditional male-dominated forms in the society. This third method of achieving liberation is one which should command the greatest attention of those concerned with social movements and social change, for it is an attempt to build an egalitarian movement which serves as a model for an egalitarian society.

Women's Liberation is perhaps the first social movement in recent times to take the idea of equality seriously. Throughout the country, wherever groups associating themselves with the Women's Liberation idea have sprung up—often with little or no communication with other groups—women have come to similar points of view with regard to the necessary organizational forms for Women's Liberation. The significant social development in Women's Liberation is that women can see that little will have changed in their lives if they are willing to substitute the domination of organizational leaders for the domination of men. Women who are attracted to the movement are women who are seeking individual liberation and who have felt thwarted in a variety of ways, largely, but not exclusively, through their roles as women. The women in the movement are not attempting to change the lives of others as much as they are attempting to change their own lives. In doing this, it is impossible to accept the authority of any person other than oneself.

Out of this understanding has emerged a movement without national organization or leaders. Although there have been informal conventions of women in the movement, they are for the purpose of meeting sisters in other cities and sharing ideas rather than for the purpose of passing resolutions and agreeing upon a public posture. Again, the usually unspoken belief of the women involved is that an organization tends to usurp power to assert direction, a power which more properly must be vested in each individual.

As an example of attempts at nonauthoritarian organization at the regional level, let us examine the Michigan Women's Liberation Coalition. The goal of this group is to provide flexible coordination of groups and activities in the state while preserving the autonomy of its members. In order to achieve this, it has developed a leaderless structure which diffuses responsibility for collective activities.

The primary function of this coalition is to provide a communication center for women interested in Women's Liberation rather than to make policy. It publishes a monthly newsletter (for which member consciousness-raising or action groups alternate responsibility), buys, produces, and sells literature, and is a central contact point for women seeking information about Women's Liberation, groups wanting speakers, and women trying to organize new groups. Although it holds monthly meetings to discuss actions planned or carried out by component groups, it avoids taking stands on issues, leaving the decision to join or oppose a particular action to individual members.

In place of the hierarchical structure of most action organizations, the coalition has a treasurer as its only elected officer and selects the chairwoman for each monthly meeting by lot. All other work of the organization is done on a volunteer basis. In addition, the coalition avoids the development of informal local spokesmen by always sending at least two speakers to represent the group before outside organizations and by pairing experienced and inexperienced speakers in order constantly to expand the number of women able to speak. This policy is also used to emphasize the belief that there are many viewpoints and types of women within the movement and that each women really speaks only for herself.

In addition to its attempts to avoid leadership and hierarchy, the Michigan Coalition differs from conventional political organizations in its attitude toward recruiting new members. Although it helps women organize groups when they request such aid and puts women who are interested in a group into contact with each other, it does not attempt to locate and organize groups who might be "ripe" for Women's Liberation or groups which it would be politically desirable to have as part of the movement (such as black women). The organization stands ready to support the attempts of any woman or group of women to achieve their liberation but does not feel that women should be enticed to join the movement. Thus, in recent months, groups from the coalition have picketed with women clerical workers attempting to unionize, set up picketing of the local Civil Rights Commission office which was stalling on a job discrimination case involving a woman, and supported welfare mothers in their fight for higher clothing allowances and other rights. Although the women who joined in these causes talked with the women involved about Women's Liberation, no attempt has been made to organize new groups from these contacts. This approach, unique among partisan groups, is consistent with the value placed by Women's Liberation on each woman's ability to make decisions regarding her own life, free of all pressures.

Another group which illustrates the effort to employ the concept of equality in organizing the Woman's Liberation Movement is The Feminists, a New York–based Women's Liberation group. This group takes as its basic assumption the belief that all women are capable of developing any talent equally, provided they have the opportunity to do so. The Feminists were the first group to identify several subtle forms of inequality which occur in many Women's Liberation groups and which prevent equal opportunity for development. One form of inequality is the tendency of articulate women to do a disproportionate share of the talking at meetings and to dominate the group through verbal aggressiveness. As The Feminists have pointed out, verbal ability tends to follow class lines, so that middle- or upper-middle-class women tend to dominate in any group. Starting with a fundamental belief in the validity of each woman's experience, regardless of her ability to express herself, The Feminists were the first to point to this domination of groups by members of certain social classes and to view it as a serious deterrent to recognition of a sisterhood which transcends class lines, as well as to see it as tending to perpetuate within the movement the pernicious effects of social-class divisions which exist in the society. They contend that in a movement for equality, it is as improper for women to dominate because of social status or verbal ability as it is for the movement to establish formal authority structures which allow the domination of some women by others.

To offset these problems, the group instituted a plan called the "disc system" which has since been adopted by many other groups. At meetings, each member is given an equal number of discs as she arrives. When a member speaks during a meeting, she surrenders one of her discs. After she has used up her tokens, she may no longer speak. This system encourages articulate women to consider seriously, before speaking, whether what they are about to say is really an important addition to the discussion, and it opens up space for more reluctant members to speak. Apparently it is an effective system, for women who have never participated in a group discussion before becoming involved with The Feminists rapidly become poised public speakers.

A second system developed by The Feminists for equalizing the opportunity to learn speaking and writing skills is the "lot system." Here, each woman puts her name on a slip of paper for creative tasks and on a separate lot for routine tasks. When an opportunity to speak or write arises, an individual is assigned to the job by the drawing of a name from the "creative" lots. When typing or other routine matters must be done, a name is taken from the "routine" lots. No woman does two creative or two routine jobs until each other member of the group has had an opportunity to do one of each. In this way, the group expresses faith that each member is capable of performing any job, no matter how demanding, and through the opportunity to do so, women indeed develop the ability to perform well in varied situations.

Problems in the Movement

Although the attempt to implement egalitarianism within the structure of Women's Liberation groups is clearly commendable, it is not without its difficulties. The entire Women's Liberation Movement is often seen by males, especially by the mass media, and to some extent by females within and outside the movement as being ineffective because of its lack of organization, leaders, and clearly agreed-upon goals and tactics. Men who have been active within left-oriented groups are quick to offer their organizational talents, revealing their male chauvinist belief that women lack organizational abilities and know-how. Some observers have suggested that the no-leadership policy of the movement is a necessary protection against the ambitions of many women who have had little prior opportunity for leadership and who could destroy the unity of the movement through competition if they were allowed free rein.

These criticisms all fail to take note of the fact that the structure of the movement flows directly from its egalitarian ideology and is itself a strategy in the implementation of that ideology. Nevertheless, the criticisms must be taken seriously if there is a danger that Women's Liberation will bury its important demands on the society in its idealism. In this final section, we will consider two major problems of the attempt at egalitarian organization—the degree to which the movement has, in fact, avoided the formation of leaders and elites, and the degree to which the lack of structure limits the activities of the movement.

Elitism

The attempt to avoid the development of generally recognized leaders is baffling to the mass media, which count on personalities to add human interest to their stories. Partly to avoid letting the media create leaders within the movement, and partly because of misrepresentations of the movement's actions and ideas, many groups throughout the country have imposed a ban on communications with the mass media. Nevertheless, leaders have arisen through the media. Although Women's Liberation groups use these "media personalities" to draw attention to their rallies and teach-ins, there is no automatic acceptance of their ideas within the movement. For example, in Detroit recently, members of Women's Liberation groups attended speeches and informal discussions with nationally known figures such as Marlene Dixon, Betty Friedan, Florynce Kennedy, Gloria Steinem, and Robin Morgan and discussed their ideas seriously and thoroughly. But an equally large number of women sought out two completely unknown women representing The Feminists and at least as eagerly considered their ideas. At this point, it appears that women in the movement seek the stimulation of ideas and information but do not rely on the personality or authority of "name" people.

There are, however, other problems created by the attempt to avoid leadership. One lies in the natural process of elite formation in groups which exist over time, partly in response to differing abilities and talent within any group and partly in response to the tendency of people who have been in the movement longer to have a more clearly developed viewpoint. We have already indicated the ways in which Women's Liberation groups are attempting to deal with initial differences in talents and abilities by providing growth and participation opportunities for the weaker members. Although The Feminists are the clearest example of this attempt, most groups are conscious of this problem and attempt to encourage participation by weaker members, a process which is facilitated by the small size of most groups. In addition, the belief that while each woman has her own unique experience, that experience has elements in common with the experiences of other women enables women to listen more openly to each other.

Another problem, which is the outgrowth of the attempts to avoid elites, is that women who have been in the movement for some time may feel that their ability to develop their capacities is retarded by the egalitarian ethic of the movement. One solution for this problem lies in the coalition-type organization made up of many small groups. Longer-term members can form their own small groups, where they will have more leeway in speaking and developing their ideas. Through such a coalition, they will be able to share their ideas with newer members but within a format which prevents them from dominating decision making. Ideological insights and suggestions for action presented in coalition meetings will be debated again by the small groups, enabling newer members to proceed at their own pace without undue influence from older members, but with the benefits of their insights and experience. The experience of the Michigan Women's Liberation Coalition, which is organized in this way, is that the greater autonomy of newcomers in this structure enables them more freely to bring forward insights which are both valuable and challenging to older members.

As each member grows in the understanding that she is her own authority, it becomes less and less important to set up artificial restraints on informal leadership. It is becoming increasingly true that the woman who feels she has something to say is encouraged to speak and write, for other women are confident that they will follow only when, and for as long as, she speaks to their experience and their needs. Thus, the ideas are important, but the leaders are not.

Effectiveness

It is probably premature to attempt to assess the impact of the lack of discipline and organizational structure upon the effectiveness of Women's Liberation. The movement at the present time is in the process of developing an understanding of the condition of women and increasing the awareness of the problems of women both in its adherents and in the society as a whole. When a group or number of groups have decided to take action (as in establishing child-care centers or working for the repeal of abortion laws), more structured organizations have emerged to coordinate activities. However, these structures last only as long as the activity and then dissolve, leaving no permanent leaders or organizational apparatus. It is likely that the movement will solve the problem of achieving coordination while avoiding the ill effects of hierarchical organization by continuing to see action groups as *ad hoc* organizations, while the movement itself remains centered in the small groups. In this way, the movement may be able to combine small-group autonomy, flexibility of organization, and effective action. It is an attempt well worth watching, for if it proves to be stable, it may in fact become a model for a new society based on tolerance, diversity, and equality.

Notes

1. Robin Morgan, ed., *Sisterhood Is Powerful* (New York: Vintage Books, 1970), p. 553.
2. Guerrilla theater is the use of brief, sudden dramatic events in public places for the purpose of calling attention to a new definition of the situation. A simple example would be a group of young women on a street corner whistling at men.
3. Yet men also have something to gain in changing their interactions with women, for men carry the burden of having continually to prove their superiority (see Polk and Stein, Chapter 1). A few men are beginning to recognize this fact and are forming groups parallel to and sympathetic with the Women's Liberation groups. Among these are Men's Liberation groups in Michigan and New York, Men Against Cool in Illinois, and several men's auxiliaries to women's groups in various parts of the country.

HARRIET HOLTER*

Sex Roles and Social Change

Introduction: Theories and Strategies

The following is a tentative outline of perspectives on changing sex roles in present-day society. First a brief summary of some theories on sex roles and social change is given. It is of course impossible here to give justice to the great variety and depth of sex-role theories, but attention is drawn to a few systematic descriptions of how and why sex roles are established and maintained. Secondly, an elaboration of important points of theoretical descriptions, as seen by this author, contains the substance of this article. The focus is here on fairly recent changes in sex roles and their links with society at large. Finally, questions of strategy, that is, questions as to where in the social structure—in the light of theory—actions toward change should be directed in order to result in desired consequences, are discussed.

Some Theories of Sex-Role Change

Most theories about change in sex roles have a global character. They are often formulated with a view to understanding the very existence of gender differentiation and at the same time purport to explain changes in the position of women especially.

A considerable number of authors simply point to changing "traditions" or "attitudes" as the main basis for changes in sex roles. Since traditions and attitudes are among the phenomena to be explained, only theories that attempt to do so are mentioned here. Also sex-role theories that give constitutional features of men's and women's psychology a main explanatory status must necessarily be excluded here, since they do not lend themselves to an understanding of changes in the system.

The sociological, anthropological, or social psychological theories all seem to point—ultimately—to changes in the requirements of the economic system as the prime moving forces of shifts in sex roles or changes in the status of women.

The American sociologist Goode, for example, points to industrialization as a main explanation for a trend toward egalitarian relations within and outside the family. The industrialized economy [with] its need for a mobile, flexible labor force, is best served with a small, independent family. Goode postulates a "fit" between the conjugal family and the modern industrial system, stressing the individual's right to move about and the universalistic evalu-

---

* I am indebted to stud. mag. art. Annemor Kalleberg and stud. mag. art. Lars Hem for discussions and criticism of my views on sex roles and social change.

ation of skills. The increasing demand for skill and mobility tends to eliminate barriers of race and sex, and, in addition, forces within the conjugal family a press for equality between husband and wife (Goode 1963).

Bott (1957) especially has shown how the social network of a family—that is, its total web of friends and social contacts—may influence the division of tasks in the family. The families with looser social ties cannot count on stand-ins in traditional roles, and husband and wife are forced to give up a traditional arrangement and to share more than the families with more close-knit networks. Mobility combined with urbanization, which is likely to produce socially isolated families, may thus develop more egalitarian relations between spouses.

"The crisis theory of women's equality" furnishes another illustration of a view of changing sex roles. Rapid modernization as well as war and crisis often seems to bring women into "male" positions at least for some time (Boulding 1966), a fact which may be interpreted as a national mobilization of all resources, even secondary ones. In times of crisis the economic or military demands may, at least temporarily, lead to a breakdown of cultural norms and ideals pertaining to men's and women's tasks. The fact that gender differentiation is reestablished, although often in novel forms, when crisis conditions disappear does not render the "crisis theory" useless. It serves to illustrate the importance, not only of material resources, but also of the time necessary for changing ascribed roles. The possibilities and limitations for sex-role change inherent in a society are likewise demonstrated during crisis.

Also relevant is the notion that sex differentiation is caused by gender differences in physical strength, which suggests that when technological development renders physical strength unimportant, as in highly mechanized production, this will eventually diminish sex differentiation.

In Marxist thinking strategy can hardly be separated from theoretical descriptions without doing injustice to both. Nevertheless, for the sake of analysis and since Marxist theory is the theory of social change par excellence, a few points concerning Marxist ideas on changes in sex roles are presented here, rather than in the last section. Traditional Marxist theory is mainly developed by Engels (1942) and later by Bebel (1946) and Lenin (1952); Marx never formulated a comprehensive view on the subject [of sex differences], although his works contain several references to it. In general, Marxist analyses of sex differentiation and sex discrimination are of course formulated in terms of historical development, starting with changes in material conditions. With the development of surplus capital in prehistoric times, the man—who through a natural and nondiscriminating division of labor with women had access to the surplus—took possession and instituted private property. Private property again necessitates individual as opposed to collective households and rules of inheritance. This is the foundation of the patriarchal family in which the father rules, and in which women and children are subjugated to the father.

Engels as well as Lenin saw women's participation in modern, collective forms of production and the disappearance of individual household work as a condition for equality and liberation of women. Lenin (1919) advocated strongly the establishment of child-care institutions and partly collective household functions in the Soviet Union, and seemed to believe that the USSR was on the road to liberation of women.

It is recognized, however, even among Marxists, that important elements of traditional gender discrimination have survived in Eastern Europe and that additional theoretical considerations must be brought to bear on Marxist ideas about the subject. Simone de Beauvoir (1953), Evelyn Sullerot (1969), Juliet Mitchell (1966), and others have started this work, bringing forth rather different conceptions of sex roles and the forces which influence them. Most important is de Beauvoir's attempt to link historical materialism to a conception of man as a being of transcendence, seeking always to dominate the Other, to exercise his sovereignty in an objective fashion. Men would not have used their early material advantage to dominate women had this not been embedded in their existential condition. According to de Beauvoir, then, a change in sex roles requires not only changes in the economic and social order, but first of all women's attainment of authenticity.

Recent Marxist theories on women's position are all very vague with respect to the crucial distinction between equality in a capitalist versus a socialist society. This is perhaps most evident in Mitchell's analysis, which focuses on women's situation with respect to production, reproduction, socialization, and sexuality. Only changes in all these four structures can bring about equality between men and women, but they are at present in different stages of development. [Mitchell does not deal with] the problem of structures in which women are not integrated, for example the political power structure [and] the relation between class struggle and sex equality is left undiscussed in [her] article (Mitchell, op. cit.). One is further led to forget that some of the repression and manipulations to which women are subject are shared by men.

One of the difficulties of a strict Marxist analysis of gender differentiation is that such differentiation is common to all productive relationships but less important than the more specific relationship expressed by social classes. Gender differentiation as such cannot be linked to capitalism. The task of Marxists is to place gender differentiation as an element in the productive relationship and in the superstructure, not as a property of the productive forces. The Marxist specific historical elaboration of the differentiation must, however, be seen in light of the class structure, a [topic] to which [we will] return in the discussion of strategy.

The—mainly sociological—analyses of sex roles cited above offer a natural mixture of pessimism and optimism with respect to the possibility of changes in sex differentiation in current society. The same is true of writers who have developed theories in which sex roles are seen as consquences of specific biological and sexual differences between men and women. Montagu (1953, 1963), for example, postulates women's biological superiority over men, and men's unconscious striving to dominate and take revenge [on] women. The Norwegian psychologist Nissen (1971) maintains that a different sexual cycle applies to each gender and shows some of the implications of such a possibility, in terms of male-dominated societies.

Such deeper psychosocial elements of sex differentiation are not discussed in this article. The present modes and the present maintenance of sex roles rather than their ultimate origin, causes, and historical development are the themes in what follows. Furthermore, the discussion builds on the assumption, among others, that sex roles are of secondary importance as a force of social change in general. Also, the importance of basically economic forces, combined with technological developments and ideological shifts—as summarized in this section—is recognized. The analysis stresses, however, a trend toward *latent sex differentiation* and *latent discrimination* in industrial societies, as opposed to manifest differentiation in traditional society. It differs from some theories of changing sex roles in viewing sex differentiation not as something which either exists or is eliminated, but as a social arrangement which may take on different forms and functions.

Theoretical Elaborations

Sex Differentiation and Potentials for Change

Anthropologists have labeled gender differentiation "the primary division of labor," and with good reason. Gender differentiation is more ancient, more stable, and more widespread than any other type of social differentiation. It appears under all known economic systems and political orders. The very existence of sex roles cannot be attributed to special forms of production or subsistence conditions.

But the *extent* to which sex—or, rather, gender—constitutes a differentiating element in society varies considerably culturally and historically. This is true of the modes and substance of gender differentiation as well. It may be maintained, for example, that the degree of task differentiation between men and women has been kept stable over the last hundred years, since a number of "new" job openings for women actually are extensions into modern work life of their traditional tasks. At the same time this shift in women's production from a primary to a secondary social frame for their work constitutes a change in the mode of sex differentiation. Such shifts also point to changes in those social forces which maintain sex differentiation.

Gender differentiation is here used primarily to include a division of tasks between men and women which is accompanied by a consistently different personality formation of the two genders. Such differentiation usually also contains a discrimination of women, and it is the contention of the present author that discrimination against women necessarily follows from most known gender differentiations (Holter 1970).

The consequences of social changes for the extent and modes of sex differentiation practiced in a society—including degree of discrimination—are a main theme in the following discussion. It is an assumption, then, that extent and modes of sex differentiation are more results than determinants of changes in other social and economic relations. This does not imply that changes in gender differentiation are without consequences for social structure and cultural conditions. The opposite is the case, since gender differentiation contributes to the maintenance of a number of other social arrangements (Holter, *op. cit.*). But sex differentiation contains less of a dynamic potential for conflict and change than, for example [do] social classes or technological [advances]. The very stability of sex differentiation should therefore also be exposed, at least in part, by the analysis presented here.

Sex Differentiation and Social Structure

The modes and degree of sex differentiation are partly a reflection of requirements of the economic system at large and of more specific demands for a suitable labor—and consumption—force. Sex differentiation is also directly influenced by technological changes, such as the invention of contraceptives. The changes in cultural values which have developed, partly in harmony with and partly in opposition to the postindustrial economic demands, have sometimes direct bearing on the current ideas about differentiation, ideas which to a large extent are contradicted by sex differentiating practices.

The shift from a production-oriented to a consumption-oriented economy has changed women's position more than men's, and in at least two ways. First, women's services have increasingly been extended directly to production outside the home, and employers take a novel interest in the female labor force. Second, the "consumption-and-fun-ethos" has brought women into focus as consumers—and as fun. The last pattern is supported by the invention of a number of contraceptives, which has also implied new freedom to women as well as men.

Modern economy requires a mobile, partly well trained labor force, and men are more mobile than women. Young women, however, have proved willing to move in great numbers to the urban centers, a development that has created population imbalances in the cities as well as in the rural areas. The changes in the structure and function of the family facilitate mobility for men as well as women, and the institutional changes in the family have probably provided increased sex-role equality between husband and wife. Physical strength has become less important for unskilled and semiskilled jobs [and] this should tend to eliminate sex differences in the lower echelons in industry. The expansion in white-collar jobs and the stagnation in blue-collar work favor women to a certain extent. The same may be true of a shift from labor conflict and industrial struggles to an atmosphere of negotiation, human relations skills, and attempts at psychological manupulation of employers.

Most of these changes in the desired properties of the labor force should favor women in the lower positions in firms and corporations, and may in time produce a certain pattern of equality in these sectors. Developments, however, have not at all been conducive to equality in the middle and higher levels of industrial work units. The demands for leadership, devotion, education, efficiency, and stress-taking [where] higher-level work is concerned, effectively shut out women from the business elite and other types of elites.

Women's confinement to routine and service work is balanced, as it were, by their important function as consumers who are flexible and sensitive to advertising and status consumption. Women are even increasingly consumers of education, which partly serves to solve a main problem of modern economy: the absorbtion of surplus (Hem 1971). This is [all] the more evident, since women to some extent make no use of their education. But there is still a large group of women who work all day, nowadays because they have two jobs, and another group who are full-time consumers. Women's work in the home constitutes part of the infrastructure of modern economy. Women's poorly paid, isolated work with children and family is clearly one of the conditions for the efficient, collective organization of "official" production.

In all spheres men still have the leadership positions, and women do the serving.

Since a large number of women are fairly isolated housewives, their conceptions of themselves and each other are mediated to them through "a third party"—especially the mass media. Such stereotyped self-images of women are less conducive to feelings of solidarity among women than direct contact and cooperation.

At the same time new values constantly question this lack of changes in the basic differentiation according to gender. Ever since women came to be regarded as human beings, a comparison between the situations of men and of women has been legitimate. Secularization and universalism have furnished a new standard for such comparison: equality. Scientific rationalism and [the belief that] "criticism is a duty" have strengthened these ideas.

The main effects of the economic and social changes outlined above points to some forms of increased equality, but also to strong elements of inequality and covert sex differentiation. An elaboration of the changes that have taken place in sex differentiation may furnish some explanations for this situation.

From Traditional Sex Roles to Quasi-Egalitarianism

The first type of change to be discussed is one from an openly recognized and accepted differentiation which is expressed in legal rules or other codes to a more covert differentiation, a quasi-egalitarianism (Holter, *op. cit.*). The present sex differentiation is neither officially accepted nor manifested in legal codes and constitutes a contrast to the official ideology. This discrepancy between ideology and reality is a "modern" phenomenon, the maintenance of which is closely related to the complexity of industrialized society.

The term *quasi-egalitarianism* refers to elements of latency in present-day sex differentiation as well as to certain mechanisms of covert or latent sex differentiation.

Latent structures are [those] for which there exists a psychological and social preparedness, and which come into operation under certain circumstances. For example, some kinds of sex differentiation in the labor market or in education appear only under the condition of scarcity. When jobs are abundant, that is, when the business cycle is rising, women are in demand and may get jobs which would be denied them under economic downturns. When parents can afford to give all children an education and they don't have to choose between sons' and daughters' education, the fact that parents usually would give priority to the education of a son is not expressed in action. There exists, nevertheless, a constant psychological propensity for sex differentiation—should the situation change.

The mechanisms for covering up sex differentiation are numerous. An emphasis on legal definitions or official ideology may distract attention from actual practice, and the same is true of ritualized selection of women for a small number of official positions.*

---

* A practice otherwise known as tokenism. [Ed.]

It may also be suggested that one of the covering-up processes is a tendency to increase women's influence in institutions which are, in some respects, becoming obsolete in present-day society. For example, as the family has lost its importance as an economic and political institution, egalitarianism between spouses has become increasingly common. Women are today probably the main decision-makers in a large number of families in which the father is a rather absent and diffuse figure. The father's absence is dictated by the demands of his work, which again necessitates the mother's role as decision-maker. Nevertheless, this coincides with the decline of the family as an important social and political unit.

Educational institutions may furnish another example of female influence in obsolete institutions. The first years of elementary schools have—at least in Scandinavia [and to some extent in] the United States (Henry 1963)—changed over the last decades from being oriented toward children's acquiring of knowledge to [being oriented toward] more diffuse purposes of primary socialization and personality formation. At the same time the male schoolmaster or teacher moved away from these beginner classes of the elementary school system and female teachers are now in an overwhelming majority as [primary grade] teachers. Later, when the "real" acquiring of knowledge is in focus, the male teacher takes over. From a strictly educational point of view the first steps have become, if not obsolete, at least more an extension of the family's primary socialization. The fact that there are a great number of female teachers does not imply that the educational tasks are distributed in an equal manner, but rather [means] that female teachers continue the mothers' family tasks.

One may, finally, consider certain aspects of women's political activity in the light of a hypothesis about female influence in institutions which are in the process of losing importance. In Scandinavian political discussions it is recurrently asserted that the parliament as an institution is becoming less powerful, that important decisions are increasingly taken outside this body, and that the parliament is losing influence vis-à-vis a strong governmental apparatus as well as powerful economic forces. This seems to be a typical postwar development. It is interesting to note that at the same time the percentages of women representatives are increasing in all the Scandinavian countries—although slowly. The number of women on the boards of banks, insurance companies, or industrial concerns, however, remains at zero.

From Unreflectedness to Self-Awareness

With respect to sex roles, the development from traditional to industrialized society is also one from unawareness to self-reflection. This is true in the sense that sex roles in older societies were seen as unproblematic, God-given, and unchangeable, whereas the roles today—for example, in Scandinavia—represent a constant subject of discussion, of reflection, and also of social research. The above description also suggests that some of the reasons for this change are to be found in the movement from legitimate to illegitimate differentiation. A social differentiation which is declared illegitimate but which nevertheless occurs will be reflected upon by some, although, almost by definition, it will be covered up by others. Today there can be no doubt that the *status quo* is questioned, discussed, and criticized.

Such awareness of social injustices in certain groups is, however, also a more general characteristic of modern society than of traditional society. The idea that the present is not good enough permeates conservative as well as radical thought in Western society—although the premises for desires for change as well as the changes advocated may be quite different. It would be strange indeed if sex differentiation should be exempted from examination. It may be suggested, nevertheless, that the discrepancies between the ideal which the criticisms are aiming at and the reality illustrate the status of opinions in current society: they result in a noticeable lack of consequences. . . .

The discrepancies between ideology and reality also indicate a powerlessness on the part of official authorities in a society. In Scandinavia, most political parties state explicitly their desire to obtain equality between men and women, but their power to influence the development seems more limited than [is] indicated by their programs. Furthermore, as can be seen in connection with a number of social problems, a "right" has become something which politicians, administrators, and "the law" would *like* people to have, not something people [do] have. If this is true, rights may be increasingly generously issued to the losers in current Western society.

From Ideological to Psychological Maintenance of Sex Differentiation

The development from a commonly accepted sex differentiation to an almost illegitimate one has had a number of consequences. One of them is, of course, that legal or open sanctions cannot be brought to bear upon those who deviate from the sex-role pattern. An employer is not free to fire women because they marry, no school or university may bar women's entrance, nobody could formally hinder a female politician from running. Formal sanctions have been replaced by informal ones, and this has come to constitute a special pressure on psychological sex differentiation. In traditional society, *ideology, division of tasks,* and *personality formation* were to some extent harmonized, for men and for women, to form two distinct patterns of life, one male and one female. In industrialized society, ideology does not justify sanctioning of deviance from the essence of sex differentiation, which is differentiation of tasks. The maintenance of task differentiation has thus become heavily dependent on the different personality formation of boys and girls. This does not necessarily mean that the socialization of boys and girls is more segregated now than it was before, but [means] that those differences which are the outcome of socialization have another social significance. Conformity must, for example, be important as a general characteristic.

From Supernatural to Rational Premises

The ideological changes which have accompanied changing sex differentiation practices have already been mentioned. The idea of a discrepancy between an official egalitarian ideology and an actual differentiation between men and women is seen as an important aspect of sex roles in current society. The presence of official egalitarian values does not imply, however, that the actual practices have no ideological premises. The beliefs [in an actual differentiation between men and women] which are in conflict with the ideas of equality and which are more less explicitly formulated, may sometimes be found as remnants of previous religious values. But even the ideas that constitute arguments *for* sex differentiation have undergone changes in that more rationality, more systematic proofs, and [more] sophistication are required of them. When research indicated that the old belief in superior male intelligence had no scientific basis, this was a blow to the arguments for a social differentiation of men and women. Other psychological data have, however, furnished arguments in favor of differentiation, such as research regarding the infant's need for motherly care. In addition, more or less well-founded ideas about psychological sex differences have gained in importance as support for differentiation, whereas religious beliefs have lost much of their force in this respect.

From Role Homogeneity to Role Heterogeneity

The development from manifest to latent sex differentiation includes a number of aspects, only a few of which will be mentioned here. A shift from cultural homogeneity to heterogeneity with respect to sex roles should, however, not be overlooked. Although in traditional society the substance of sex roles may have varied somewhat within a population, at least it varied in fairly predictable ways. To be a woman in the feudal lower class was probably a fairly well established role, even if it was somewhat different from the role of an aristocratic lady. Today the variations in sex roles [in various] subgroups are probably considerable, and this is true within and sometimes across class boundaries.

Sex differentiation has always assumed a different character in different social classes and it still does. Liberation is one thing for an educated middle-class woman and another for a working-class wife with the prospect of unskilled labor only, if she wants to work outside the home. The trend is, however, to increase women's influx into white-collar jobs and thus to decrease the class differences between women. On the other hand, new psychological dividing lines are separating women [on the basis of whether they are, for example, married or unmarried or on the basis of] more subtle choices between various versions of the feminine role.

Shifts in the Domain of Male and Female Value Orientations

There can be no doubt about the fact that the somewhat limited entrance of women into secondary institutions in present-day society has taken place on male premises. Women have accepted the dominant norms and values of secondary affairs [which may stress] "efficiency" or "competition" or "universalism," and these very values have often, in debates, provided the justifications for women's participation in work, education, and politics. No wonder, then, that the male values persist in the face of female participation.

In primary relations, however, there seems to be a decline in the influence of traditional male values. As maintained by Dahlström (1962), a feminization or humanization of the relations in the family, in the classroom, and in the work group may be observed.*

The development may thus be interpreted as an increased polarization of male and female values, feminization of primary values being compensated, as it were, by an increased dominance of male values in secondary affairs. If this interpretation is reasonable, it indicates that the structure of primary groups is such that even with an influx of male participation, traditional female orientations not only prevail but are strengthened. In the same vein, the structures of secondary institutions are kept more or less unchanged in the face of increased female participation.

Strategies of Sex-Role Change

In questions of sex roles and especially changes in sex roles, problems of strategy often take precedence over problems of theory, and sometimes, but not always, to the advantage of [both].

The first question to be asked concerns, of course, the aims of the movements toward equality between men and women. Whereas there is general agreement about the insufficiency of formal equality expressed in laws and administrative rules or in "empty rights" of women, the content of equality is still vague.

One may roughly distinguish at least between equality within the framework of the present Western societies on the one hand, and equality in a radically changed society on the other. The first may be termed equality on masculine premises, or briefly "masculine equality"; the other is equality in a qualitatively different society, that is, a society which is not dominated by masculine values as we know them.

Masculine equality would be a situation accomplished in the present type of economy and political order, expressed as a 50-50 percent distribution of men and women in almost all positions, be it care of home and children or the business elite. Such a goal, combined with an assumption that present society and institutions remain by and large intact, obviously requires women to become more similar to men [along the lines of] current masculine ideas of efficiency, profit, competition, and power, according to which Western societies operate. Half of the power, so to speak, would have to be handed over to women, with the burdens which are implied in male power today and in the female tasks that would be taken over by men.

The main strategies for attainment of this situation would be awakening of women's political consciousness, an increase in women's educational level, but above all an introduction of a number of specific, detailed laws and regulations which [would] secure women's [opportunity] and ability to compete, fight, and exercise power.

The thesis that obtaining equality is first and foremost a question of women

---

* At least in Scandinavia. [Ed.]

seizing half of the power which men have now has a ring of reasonableness, but is nevertheless the expression of a static view.

It is still a question [as to] whether equality in a reasonable sense can be at all attained within a society that builds on a capitalist economy or in a society which is not both socialist and above a certain level of technology. The interests of children as a group would be contradictory to and heavily set aside under a combination of market economy and gender equality. The practicality of full equality under the present economy must be questioned. A long-range perspective on equality [entails] the establishment of an economy subordinated to the goal of equality. In addition, a number of political and educational measures would be necessary.

[In the context of] today's economy, however, and with an eye to the description of sex differentiation offered in the [preceding] paragraphs, two examples of problems to be attacked may be mentioned. One is the problem of latent or covert sex differentiation; the other consists of breaking the psychological maintenance of sex roles. Both are closely related to the question of women's self-respect and ability to advance their own interest. The covert discrimination leads to a feeling of defeat, since the official rights are all there, and gives the illusion that it is a matter of the single woman's ability and energy to use the rights. The psychological maintenance of sex differentiation also consists of encouraging women's devaluation of themselves in various ways, a devaluation which is clearly reflected in the wages paid for women's work.

The salary and the prestige associated with one's work are in current society the main road to self-respect for men. Women have been advised to seek their rewards in love and in child rearing, which may be inherently as valuable—if it were paid [for] and respected. To get out of this vicious circle for women, all work with children, especially in child-care institutions, should be more highly paid than, say, the production and maintenance of cars. This would increase the self-respect of large groups of women and in addition change radically the desirability of child-care work. Such a manifestation of changes in a society's values and priorities would lower the prestige of competitiveness and technological advancement.

Increased higher education for women is another road to changes in women's working conditions and in their self-respect. Norwegian data indicate that women with a higher level of education are more politically active and report less submissiveness, less conflict avoidance, and more gender-egalitarian norms than do women with lower education (Holter, *op. cit.*). Higher education may, however, not be especially conducive to the development of solidarity among women. And higher education alone is not enough [if] women [are] to gain power.

The analyses in the preceding paragraphs show that the time has come to see the premises on which women work outside home as more important than such work itself. Work outside home as a policy must be judged in terms of pressure toward equal wages and working conditions and the avoidance of a female reserve labor force. The question of consequences in terms of solidarity formation on part of women—and men—is also relevant.

The last point has become very clear in statements from young Western

European Marxists: if the struggle for equality between men and women is a struggle *between* men and women, then this would lead to a weakening of the solidarity of the working class and must at present be given low priority. Marxist groups offer other reasons as well for taking a conservative stand on the question of married women's work, such as the extra exploitation of women and the pressure on men's wages in general (Ohrlander 1969).

If sex differentiation and sex discrimination are mainly the result of social forces and not [of a] deeply rooted antagonism between men and women, the solidarity between men and women is probably less served by women being isolated housewives than [it is by their being] industrial employees. Under certain circumstances, however, men and women will compete for jobs under more equal working conditions, in ways which may decrease their loyalty toward each other. The problem is, then, more to counteract competition among employees who have long-range interests in common, especially since splits in the labor movement are a much more serious and widespread problem than a hypothesized conflict between male and female workers. More of a danger to a solidary labor movement lies in the tendency of women to go into low-paid white-collar work which offers little stimulus for consciousness about equality and political work. This too, however, represents a more general problem than women's participation itself.

If the "premises of work" are one strategic point for changing current sex roles, the "premises of consumption" are another. There are a wide variety of problems related to sex differentiation, but ultimately it is a question of the direction of production. For example, from the point of view of equality it is more important to build houses in a new way and on a sufficient scale than to produce an abundance of the commodities which today dominate the consumers and which are necessary for production to be maintained. The housing industry should be nationalized and devoted to the construction of reasonable, more or less collective types of housing, building for flexible families and for the needs of children.

As has been shown by the above summary and elaboration of theoretical descriptions, the breakdown of sex differentiation is not only an economic question. The privatization and the latency of sex roles require a "consciousness raising" in small groups as well as in the existing women's organizations. Similarly, group training of young couples seeking to share work in a new way should be attempted. It is [upon] this level of attitude changes that the question of cooperation between women and between men and women [has] direct bearing. This point is of special importance, since it is sometimes maintained [that such attitude changes are] related to the all-important question of women's solidarity among themselves.

Solidarity [among one's own sex] and identification with one's own [or] the opposite gender are feelings that obviously are sensitive to social circumstances. The social devaluation and isolation of women has proved dangerous to their solidarity, and their overidentification with man, the stronger gender, is an obstacle to any attempt at liberation of women as well as men. Some of these psychological states may be broken down in the indvidual woman's work with herself and others, but the same fight will continue against the entire society.

Individual men may be antagonistic to equality between the genders, but even this is a result of social circumstances. The view that the more or less hopeless and bitter fight between man and woman within the four walls of a home can bring about a revolution in sex roles is denied by all reasonable analyses of the forces of revolution as well as of [those of the origins of] sex differentiation.

The individual consciousness of the problems of sex differentiation is, however, one of the initiators of change, and this consciousness must be brought to bear on social as well as psychological maintenance of the system. The ambiguity of the situation constitutes a temptation to passivity, [and] the individual man or woman who attempts to change current sex roles moves in a field of ambiguity not only socially but also psychologically. For the tension between practicing equality, which may be the individual's intention ("the project," to use Sartre's word), on the one hand, and his "embeddedness" in past experiences, emotions, learned norms and values, on the other (Hem, *op. cit.*), is expressed in the institutional setting as well.

References

BEBEL, A. *Die Frau und der Sozialismus.* Berlin: Dietz Verlag, 1946.

BOTT, E. *Family and Social Network.* London: Tavistock Publications, 1957.

BOULDING, E. "The Road to Parliament for Women." Mimeographed. Rome: International Seminar on the Participation of Women in Public Life, 1966.

DAHLSTRÖM, E. "*Analys av konsrollsdebatten.*" In *Kvinners liv og arbeid.* Stockholm: Studiesallskapet Naringsliv och Samhalle, 1962.

DE BEAUVOIR, S. *The Second Sex.* London: Bantam Books, 1953.

ENGELS, F. *The Origin of the Family, Private Property and the State.* New York: International Publishing Company, 1942.

GOODE, W. J. *World Revolution and Family Patterns.* New York: Free Press, 1963.

HEM, L. *Demokrati og forandring. Erfaring fra Forsoksgymanset i Oslo* [Democracy and change. Experiences from an experimental gymnasium in Oslo]. Oslo: Oslo University Press, 1971.

HENRY, J. *Culture Against Man.* London: Tavistock Publications, 1966.

HOLTER, H. *Sex Roles and Social Structure.* Oslo: Oslo University Press, 1970.

LENIN, V. *Marx-Engels-Marxisme.* Oslo: A/S Norsk Forlag Ny Dag, 1952.

MITCHELL, J. "Women: The Longest Revolution." *New Left Review,* no. 40 (1966).

MONTAGU, A. *The Natural Superiority of Women.* New York: The Macmillan Company, 1968.

NISSEN, I. "The Role of the Sexual Constellation." *Acta Sociologica,* no. 1/2 (1971).

OHRLANDER, K. *Kvinner som slaver* [Women as slaves]. Stockholm: Bonniers, 1969.

SULLEROT, E. *Kvinden og fremtiden. Demain les femmes.* Kobenhavn: Gyldendal, 1969.

Sex Equality: The Beginnings of Ideology

It should not prejudice my voice that I'm not born a man
If I say something advantageous to the present situation.
For I'm taxed too, and as a toll provide men for the nation
  While, miserable graybeards, you,
    It is true
Contribute nothing of any importance whatever to our needs;
  But the treasure raised against the Medes,
You've squandered, and do nothing in return, save that you
  make
Our lives and persons hazardous by some imbecile mistake.
What can you answer? Now be careful, don't arouse my spite,
Or with my slipper I'll take you napping
    faces slapping
    Left and right.   ARISTOPHANES, *Lysistrata*, 413 B.C.

It is 2400 years since Lysistrata organized a sex strike among Athenian women in a play that masked a serious anti-war opposition beneath a thin veneer of bawdy hilarity. The play is unique in drama [with its] theme of woman power and sex solidarity, and takes on a fresh relevance when read in the tumultuous 1960s. Women in our day are active as students, as blacks, as workers, as war protesters, but far less often as women qua women pressing for equality with men, or actively engaging in a dialogue of what such equality should mean. Until the last few years, woman power has meant only woman-power, a "resource to be tapped," as the manpower specialists put it.

It has been exactly one hundred years since John Stuart Mill published his classic essay on *The Subjection of Women* in England, and [and somewhat more than one hundred years since] the Seneca Falls Conference in New York State gave public recognition to the presence of women critical of the political and economic restrictions that barred their participation in the major institutions of American society. Nineteen sixty-nine is thus a propitious year in which to examine what we mean by a goal of equality between the sexes, rather than to persist in the American penchant for tinkering with short-run "improvements in the status of women."

The major objective of this article is to examine three possible goals of equality between the sexes, while a secondary objective is to pinpoint the ways in which inequality on sex grounds differs from racial, ethnic, or religious inequality.

Meaning of Inequality

A group may be said to suffer from inequality if its members are restricted in access to legitimate valued positions or rewards in a society for which their ascribed status is not a relevant consideration. In our day, this is perhaps least ambiguous where the status of citizen is concerned: We do not consider race, sex, religion, or national background relevant criteria for the right to vote or to run for public office. Here we are dealing with a particular *form* of inequality—codified law—and a particular *type* of inequality—civil and political rights of an individual as a citizen. There are several other forms of inequality in addition to legal statute: corporate or organizational policies and regulations, and, most importantly, those covert social pressures which restrict the aspirations or depress the motivation of individuals on the ascribed grounds of their membership in certain categories. Thus, a teacher who scoffs at a black boy or white girl who aspires to become an engineer, or a society which uniformly applies pressure on girls to avoid occupational choices in medicine and law are examples of covert pressures which bolster racial and sexual inequality. *Forms* of inequality therefore range from explicit legal statute to informal social pressure.

Type of inequality adds a second dimension: the area of life in which the inequality is evidenced. There are inequalities in the *public* sector, as citizens, employees, consumers, or students; and there are inequalities in the *private* sector as [regards] family, organization, or club members. Throughout American history, the gains made for greater racial and sexual equality have been based on constitutional protection of individual rights in the public area of inequality, [for] citizens, students, and workers. But precisely because of constitutional protection of privacy of home, family, and person, it is more difficult to remove inequalities rooted in the private sphere of life. Attempts to compensate for emotional and nutritional deprivation of preschool, inner-city children are through three-hour Headstart exposure to verbal stimulation and nutritious food from caring adults. We have yet to devise a means to compensate for the influences of parents who depress a daughter's aspiration to become a physician, while urging a son to aspire beyond his capacity or preference. In both instances, the tactics used tend to be compensatory devices in the public sphere (counseling and teaching in the schools, for example) to make up for or undo the effects of inequalities that persist in the family.

There is, thus, a continuum of increasing difficulty in effecting social and political change along both dimensions of inequality: by *form,* from legal statute to corporate regulation to covert and deeply imbedded social mores; by *type,* from citizenship to schooling and employment, to the private sector of family. Hence, the easiest target in removing inequality involves legal statute change or judicial interpretation of rights in the public sector, and the most difficult area involves changes in the covert social mores in family and social life. It is far easier to change laws which presently penalize women as workers, students, or citizens than it will be to effect social changes in family life and higher education which [presently] depress the aspirations and motivation of women.

An example of this last point can be seen in higher education. Few graduate schools discriminate against women applicants, but there are widespread subtle pressures once women are registered as students in graduate departments—from both faculty and male peers. In one graduate department of sociology, women represent a full third of the students, and, hence, the faculty cannot be charged with discriminatory practices toward the admission of women students. On the other hand, it was not uncommon in that department to hear faculty members characterize a woman graduate student who showed strong commitment and independence as an "unfeminine bitch" and others who were quiet and unassertive as "lacking ambition"—women who will "never amount to much." Since it is difficult to be simultaneously independent and ambitious, but conventionally feminine and dependent, it would appear that the informal rules prevent many women from winning the game, although they are accepted as players.

Discrimination against women in hiring or promotion may be barred by statute and corporate policy, but this does not magically stimulate any great movement of women up the occupational status ladder. Progress on the legal front must be accompanied by compensatory tactics to free girls and women from the covert depression of their motivations and aspirations through ridicule and double-bind pressures to be contradictory things.

Unique Characteristics of Sex Inequality

Many women find an easy empathy with the plight of the poor, the black, and minority religious groups—not from any innate feminine intuition, but simply because a subordinate group is sensitive to both unintended and intentional debasement or discrimination where another subordinate group is concerned. Women know from personal experience what it is like to be "put down" by men, and can therefore understand what it is to be "put down" as a black by whites. But there are also fundamental differences between sex as a category of social inequality and the categories of race, religion, or ethnicity. I shall discuss three of the most important differences.

Category Size and Residence

In the case of race, religion, and ethnicity, we are literally dealing with minority groups in the American population, whether Mexican, Indian, Jewish, Catholic, or black. This is not the case for sex, since women are actually a numerical majority in the population.

While the potential is present for numerical strength to press for the removal of inequalities, this is counterbalanced by other ways in which women are prevented from effectively utilizing their numerical strength. The Irish, the Italians, and the Jews in an earlier period, and blacks in more recent history, have been able to exert political pressure for representation and legislative change because residential concentration gave them voter strength in large urban centers. By contrast, women are for the most part *evenly distributed throughout the population.* Women can exert political pressure in segmental roles as consumers, workers, New Yorkers, or the aged; but not as a cohesive political group based on sex solidarity. It is inconceivable that a political organization of blacks would avoid the "race" issue, yet the League of Women Voters does precisely this when it takes pride in avoiding "women's" issues.

Early Sex-Role Socialization

Age and sex are the earliest social categories an individual learns. The differentiation between mother and father, or parent and child, is learned at a tender, formative stage of life; and consequently, we carry into adulthood a set of age and sex role expectations that are extremely resistant to change. Not only do girls learn to accept authority from the older generation and from men, but they learn this lesson in intense, intimate relationships. By the time they reach adulthood, women are well socialized to seek and to find gratification in an intimate dependence on men, and in responsible authority over children. They may be dominant and affirmative mothers with their own children, or as teachers in a classroom, but pliant and submissive as wives.

Sex role expectations tend to remain a stubborn part of our impulse lives. This is often not visible among young men and women until they become parents. Many young people are egalitarian peers in school, courtship, and early marriage. With the birth of a child, deeper layers of their personalities come into play. Since there is little or no formal education for parenthood in our society, only a thin veneer of Spock reading hides the acting out of old parental models that have [been] observed and internalized in childhood, triggering a regression to traditional sex roles that gradually spreads from the parental role to the marriage and [the] self-definition of both sexes.

As a result of early sex-role socialization, there is bound to be a lag between political and economic emancipation of women and the inner adjustment to equality of both men and women. Even in radical political movements, women have often had to caucus and fight for their acceptance as equal peers to men. Without such efforts on their own behalf, women are as likely to be girl Friday assistants in a radical movement espousing class and racial equality as they are in a business corporation, a labor union, or a conservative political party.

Pressures against Sex Solidarity

Racial, ethnic, and religious conflict can reach an acute stage of political strife in the movement for equality, without affecting the solidarity of the families of blacks, whites, Jews, or gentiles. Such strife may, in fact, increase the solidarity of these family units. A "we versus them" dichotomy does not cut into family units in the case of race, religion, or ethnicity as it does in the case of sex. Since women typically live in greater intimacy with men than they do with other women, there is potential conflict within family units when women press hard for sex equality. Their demands are on predominantly male legislators and employers in the public domain—husbands and fathers in the private sector. A married black woman can affiliate with an activist civil rights group with no implicit threat to her marriage. For a married woman to affiliate with an activist women's rights group may very well trigger tension in her marriage. While there is probably no limit to the proportion of blacks who might actively fight racial discrimination, a large proportion of married women have not combated sex discrimination. Many of them fear conflict with men, or benefit in terms of a comfortable high status in exchange for economic dependence upon their husbands. There are many more women in the middle class who benefit from sex inequality than there are blacks in the middle class who benefit from racial inequality.

The size of a women's rights movement has, therefore, been responsive to the proportion of "unattached" women in a population. An excess of females over males, a late age at marriage, postponement of childbearing, a high divorce rate, a low remarriage rate, and greater longevity for women, all increase the number of unattached women in a society, and therefore increase the potential for sex equality activism. The hard core of activists in past suffrage and feminist movements were women without marital and family ties: Ex-wives, nonwives, or childless wives, whose need to support themselves triggered their concern for equal rights to vote, to work, and to advance in their work. The lull in the women's rights movement in the 1950s was related to the fact that this same decade saw the lowest age at marriage and the highest proportion of the population married in all of our history.

Since 1960, the age at marriage has moved up; the birth rate is down to what it was in the late 1930s; the divorce rate is up among couples married a long time, and more married women are in the labor force than ever before. These are all relevant contributors to the renascence of women's activism in the mid-1960s. The presence of older and married women in women's rights organizations (like the National Organization for Women) is also responsible for a broadening of the range of issues that concern women activists—from the civil, political, and economic concerns they share with feminists of an earlier day, to [concern with] a host of changes affecting family roles: repeal of abortion laws, revision of divorce laws, community provision of child-care facilities, equal treatment under Social Security in old age, and a debunking of the clinging-vine or tempting-Eve image of married women that pervades the American mass media.

The point remains, however, that movement toward sex equality is restricted by the fact that our most intimate human relation is the heterosexual one of marriage. This places a major brake on the development of sex solidarity among women, a brake that is not present in other social inequalities, since marriage tends to be endogamous with respect to class, race, and religion.

Models of Equality

Courses in social stratification, minority groups, prejudice, and discrimination have been traditional fare in sociological curricula for a long time. Many sociologists studied immigrants and their children and puzzled about the eventual shape of a society that underwent so massive an injection of diverse cultures. From these writings, we can extract three potential models that will be useful in sketching the alternate goals not only for the relations between ethnic groups, but for those of race and sex as well.

Three such models may be briefly defined, and then each in turn explored in somewhat greater detail:

1. *Pluralist model:* This model anticipates a society in which marked racial, religious, and ethnic differences are retained and valued for their diversity, yielding a heterogeneous society in which it is hoped cultural strength is increased by the diverse strands making up the whole society.

2. *Assimilation model:* This model anticipates a society in which the minority groups are gradually absorbed into the mainstream by losing their distinguishing characteristics and acquiring the language, occupational skills, and life style of the majority host culture.

3. *Hybrid model:* This model anticipates a society in which there is change in both the ascendant group and the minority groups—a "melting pot" hybrid requiring changes not only in blacks and Jews and women, but white male Protestants as well.

Pluralist Model of Equality

It is dubious whether any society has ever been truly pluralist in the sense that all groups which comprise it are on an equal footing of status, power, or rewards. Pluralism often disguises a social system in which one group dominates—the upper classes (white Anglo-Saxon Protestants)—and minority ethnic, religious, or racial groups are confined to the lower classes. The upper classes may ceremonially invoke the country's cultural heterogeneity, and delight in ethnic food, art, and music, but exclude the ethnic members themselves from their professions, country clubs, and neighborhoods. Bagels and lox for breakfast, soul food for lunch, and lasagna for dinner; but no Jews, blacks, or Italians on the professional and neighborhood turf! Pluralism has been a congenial model for the race segregationist as well, rationalizing the confinement of blacks to unskilled labor, segregated schools, and neighborhoods.

In the case of sex, the pluralist model posits the necessity of traditional sex role differentiation between the sexes on the grounds of fundamental physiological and hence social differences between the sexes. This is the perspective subscribed to by most behavioral scientists, clinical psychologists, and psychoanalysts, despite the fact that the women they have studied and analyzed are the products of a society that systematically *produces* such sex differences through childrearing and schooling practices. There is no way of allocating observed sex differences to innate physiology or to sociocultural conditioning.

Freudian theory has contributed to the assumption of innate sex differences, on which recent scholars in psychology and sociology have built their cases for the necessity of social role and status differentiation between the sexes. Freud codified the belief that men get more pleasure than women from sex, in his theory of the sexual development of the female: the transition from an early stage in which girls experience the clitoris as the leading erogenous zone of their bodies to a mature stage in which vaginal orgasm provides the woman with her major sexual pleasure. Women who did not make this transition were then viewed as sexually "anaesthetic" and "psychosexually immature." Psychological theory often seems sterner and more resistant to change than the people to which it is applied. It is incredible that the Freudian theory of female sexuality was retained for decades despite thousands of hours of intimate therapeutic data from women, only recently showing signs of weakening under the impact of research conducted by Masters and Johnson and reported in their *Human Sexual Response*, that there is no anatomical difference between clitoral and vaginal orgasm.

Implicit in both psychological theory of sex difference and the Freudian, vaginal-orgasm theory was a basic assumption that women should be exclusively dependent on men for their sexual pleasure, hiding from view the realization that masturbation may be different from, but not necessarily less gratifying sexually than sexual intercourse. Much the same function has been served by the strong pressures to disassociate sex from maternity. Physicians have long known that nursing is associated with uterine contractions and have noted that male babies often have erections while nursing, but no one has suggested that the starry-eyed contentment of a nursing mother is a blend of genital as well as maternal pleasure. The cultural insistence upon separating sex from maternity, as the insistence that vaginal orgasm is the only "normal satisfaction" of a mature woman, serves the function of preventing women from seeing that they can find pleasure and fulfillment from themselves, other women, and their children and do not have to depend exclusively upon men for such gratification.

Coupled with this is the further assumption, peculiar to American society, that childrearing is the exclusive responsibility of the parents themselves, and not a community responsibility to assure every child a healthy physical and social development (as it is, for example, in East European countries, Israel, and Sweden). This belief keeps women tied closely to the home for the most vigorous years of their adulthood. The "new" look to a woman's life span, now institutionalized by over 100 centers for continuing education for women in the United States, does nothing to alter this basic assumption, but merely adapts to our lengthened life span. Women are urged to withdraw from outside obligations during the childbearing and rearing years and to return for further training and participation in the labor force when children reach an appropriate mature age. The consequences of such late return to active work away from the home are lower incomes, work at levels below the ability of the women, and withdrawal for the very years all studies show to be the peak of creativity in work, their twenties and thirties.

Why does American society persist in maintaining erroneous myths concerning female sexuality, contrary to research evidence, as it does in urging women to believe their children's development requires their daily attendance upon them, again contrary to research evidence? I believe the answer lies in the economic demand that men work at persistent levels of high efficiency and creativity. To free men to do this requires a social arrangement in which the family system serves as the shock-absorbing handmaiden of the occupational system. The stimulation of women's desires for an affluent style of life and a bountiful maternity—to be eager and persistent consumers of goods and producers of babies—serves the function of adding continual pressure on men to be high earners. The combination of pronatalist values and aspirations for a high standard of living has the effect of both releasing and requiring men to give heavy psychic and time investment to their jobs, and requiring women to devote their primary efforts and commitments to homemaking. As a result, the broad sweep of many an American woman's life span is caught by the transitions from Bill's daughter to John's wife to Johnny's mother and Billy's grandmother.

Behind the veneer of modern emancipation is a woman isolated in an apartment or suburban home, exclusively responsible for the care of young children, dependent on her husband for income, misled to believe that sex gratification is only possible via a vaginal orgasm simultaneous with male ejaculation, and urged to buy more and more clothes and household possessions, which she then takes more time but little pleasure in maintaining. Complementing the life of the woman in the pluralist model of sex roles, the American male is prodded to seek success and achievement in a competitive job world at the emotional cost of limited time or psychic energy for his marriage or his children, tempted by the same consumption-stimulating media and promises of easy credit, expected to uproot his family if a move is "good for his career," and ridiculed if he seeks to participate more extensively in home and child care as "unmanly."

The odds are heavily stacked against the pluralist model of society as a goal in terms of which racial, ethnic, or sex equality can be achieved.

Assimilation Model of Equality

This model anticipates that with time, the minority groups will be gradually absorbed into the mainstream of society by losing their distinguishing characteristics, acquiring the language, educational attainment, and occupational skills of the majority host culture. Concern for inequality along ethnic or racial lines is concentrated on the political, educational, and economic institutions of society. Little sociological interest or political concern is shown once men in the minority group are distributed throughout the occupational system in roughly the same proportion as mainstream males.

Feminist ideology is but one variant of the assimilation model, calling upon women to seek their place with men in the political and occupational world in sufficient numbers to eventually show a 50-50 distribution by sex in the prestigious occupations and political organizations of the society. The federal government has served as a pacesetter for the economy in urging the appointment and promotion of competent women to the highest civil service posts and encouraging private employers to follow the federal example by facilitating the movement of women into executive posts.

The feminist-assimilation model has an implicit fallacy, however. No amount of entreaty will yield an equitable distribution of women and men in the top strata of business and professional occupations, for the simple reason that the life men have led in these strata has been possible only because their own wives were leading traditional lives as homemakers, doing double parent and household duty, and carrying the major burden of civic responsibilities. If it were not for their wives in the background, successful men in American society would have to be single or childless. This is why many professional women complain privately that what they most need in life is a "wife."

The assimilation model also makes an assumption that the institutional structure of American society, developed over decades by predominantly white Protestant males, constitutes the best of all possible worlds. Whether the call is to blacks or to women to join white men in the mainstream of American society, both racial integration and a feminist ideology accept the structure of American society as it now exists. The assimilation model rejects the psychological theses of innate racial or sex differences implicit in most versions of the pluralist model, but it accepts the social institutions formed by the ascendant group. This is precisely the assumption numerous blacks, women, and members of the younger generation have recently been questioning and rejecting.

Hybrid Model of Equality

The hybrid model of equality rejects both traditional psychological assumptions and the institutional structure we have inherited. It anticipates a society in which the lives of men and of whites will be different, not only [those of] women and [of] blacks. In fact, it might be that this hybrid model would involve greater change in the role of men than of women, because institutional changes it would require involve a restructuring to bring the world of jobs and politics to the fulfillment of individual human needs for both creativity and fellowship. From this point of view the values many young men and women subscribe to today are congenial to the hybrid model of equality: the desire for a more meaningful sense of community and a greater depth to personal relations across class, sex, and racial lines; a stress on human fellowship and individual scope for creativity rather than merely rationality and efficiency in our bureaucracies; heightened interest in the humanities and the social sciences from an articulated value base; and a social responsibility commitment to medicine and law rather than a thirst for status and high income. These are all demands for social change by the younger generation in our time that are closer to the values and interests women have held than they are to the values and interests of men. They represent an ardent "no" to the image of society projected by the new crop of male technitronic futurists—a machine and consumption oriented society that rewards technological prowess in a "plasticWasp9–5america."

Because women have tended to play the passive, adaptive role in the past, they have not been prominent as social and political critics of American institutions. In fact, the traditional roles of women confined them to the most conservative institutions of the society—the family, the public schools, and the church. Women deviant enough to seek greater equality with men in professional, business, and academic life have tended to share the values of their masculine colleagues, while professional women who did not share these values have been quiet, either because they distrusted their own critical bent as a vestige of unwanted "womenliness," or because they feared exclusion from the masculine turf they have precariously established themselves on.

But there is a new groundswell in American society, which is a hopeful sign of a movement toward the hybrid model briefly sketched here. One finds it in Women's Liberation groups across the country, particularly on the university campus. I would predict, for example, that these young women, unlike their professional older sisters, will not bemoan the fact that academic women have been less "productive" than men, but will be critical of the criteria used to assess academic productivity. Up to now these criteria have been such things as "number of publications," "number of professional organization memberships," and "number of offices held in professional organizations." The new breed of women will ask, as many young students are now demanding, that the quality of teaching, the degree of colleagueship with students, the extent of service to both an academic institution and its surrounding community, become part of the criteria on [the basis of] which the productivity of an academic man or woman is evaluated. No one has conducted research on academic productivity with this enlarged net of criteria, and it is a moot point whether men would show greater productivity than women if such criteria were applied. Though it will be a difficult road, with all the money and prestige pulling in the opposite direction, this thrust on the part of the young, together with like-minded older humanist scholars and critics, creative artists, natural and behavioral scientists, has the potential of developing oases of health and sanity in many educational, welfare, and cultural institutions in American society.

Conclusion

A *pluralist* model of social equality is implicitly a conservative goal, a descriptive model that accepts what exists at a given point in time as desirable and good. The *assimilation* model is implicitly a liberal goal, a Horatio Alger model that accepts the present structure of society as stable and desirable, and urges minority groups to accept the values and goals of the dominant group within that system as their own. The *hybrid* model is a radical goal which rejects the present structure of society and seeks instead a new breed of men and women and a new vision of the future. Applied to the role of women, these models may be illustrated in a summary fashion as follows: the pluralist model says the woman's nurturance finds its best expression in maternity; the assimilation model says women must be motivated to seek professional careers in medicine similar to those pursued now by men; the hybrid model says, rather, that the structure of medicine can be changed so that more women will be attracted to medical careers, and male physicians will be able to live more balanced, less difficult and status-dominated lives.

An analysis of sex equality goals may start with the reality of contemporary life, but soon requires an imaginative leap to a new conception of what a future good society should be. With the hybrid model of equality one envisages a future in which family, community, and play are valued on a par with politics and work for both sexes, for all the races, and for all social classes and nations which comprise the human family. We are on the brink not of the "end" of ideology, but its "beginning."

KYRIAKOS M. KONTOPOULOS

Women's Liberation as a Social Movement

*Until women assume the place in society which good sense and
feeling alike assign to them, human improvement must advance
but feebly.*   FRANCES WRIGHT, 1830

*If . . . society will not admit of woman's free development,
then society must be remodeled.*   ELIZABETH BLACKWELL, 1848

Such voices from the past claiming nobly the inalienable humanness of
womanhood sound lately quite prophetic, full of meaning in anticipation of
a historical inevitability. Yet it is paradoxical—and by the same token, tragic
—that even today, in the last decades of our millennium, we refuse to be
fully aware of the fact that "whenever we establish our own pretensions upon
the sacrificed rights of others, we do in fact impeach our own liberties and
lower ourselves in the scale of being."[1] Tragically but truly the ecumenic
groanings remind us that the redemption of humanity is still ventured. The
Hegelian, Marxist, and Camusian paradigms of the relationship between
Master and Slave remain classical and didactic.

The case of women is by far the most iniquitous case of exploitation and
alienation in history. Women's alienation, a direct by-product of the enchain-
ment of feminine human nature and the blocking of their potentialities through
the negative reinforcements of socialization, has been experienced for a long
time. The consciousness of women's total situation has been slowly but consistently developing through the centuries; it has been the ground from which
the feminist movement has sprung up as a force of extreme societal significance. Today we are witnessing a regeneration of the feminine forces under
the new name "Women's Liberation Movement." It is wise for us to be aware
of the ongoing processes that could possibly reshape our culture, redefine the
social values and the social norms, and give birth to a new identity for both
men and women.. This essay will attempt to approach the movement from a
sociological point of view; it will describe its step functions in terms of certain
theoretical constructs[2] and explore some points that are thought to be crucial
for the future of the movement.

It is true that the area of social movements "has not been charted effectively."[3] However, one can take into consideration at least three dimensions
to create a basic frame of reference for analysis: First, the level at which the
collective action seeks to bring a change; therefore the question is whether
the change will be cultural, structural, and/or characterological. Second, the
attitude of the participants toward the existing order in terms of the change
sought, i.e., if this change has to be total (radical approach) or partial and

specific (reformist approach). Finally, the explicitness of the movement, especially regarding the articulation of its ideology and the development of its structure. This frame of reference, I hope, will enable us to describe the new feminism of the sixties and seventies and understand the power and the appeal of its preachings.

In charting its development I would like to argue here that a social movement emerges from given sociohistorical conditions of dissatisfaction and strain, which intensify the already existing, chronic feelings of alienation (grounds). It starts out as a vague, general, episodic expression of a fundamental search for new directions (general amorphous movement). It then becomes fairly rationalized and conscious, rather accepted as fact or fad, and fairly well established (general instituted movement). It probably creates an articulated ideal image of the future, a morale, an ideology (specific idealized movement); and, finally, it formalizes and structures its existence and plans its specific course of action (specific crystallized movement). This model is justifiable insofar as it is the outcome of a logical questioning of the concrete sociohistorical situation from which the movement has arisen. Indeed, given such an alienation-producing situation, a consciousness can develop in consideration of the following questions: What are the experiences and feelings of (my and/or the collectivity's) alienation at present? What are the (causal) conditions of these experiences and feelings? What and/or who can be blamed for these conditions of alienation? What would a better, or ideal, situation *be*? And, what can actually be done? The logical consequences of a conscious consideration of these questions will be a progression from alienation to consciousness formation, then to the formation of a collectivity for action, then to the articulation of a systematic morale, and finally to a structuralization of the movement for reasons of viability and praxis. This progression is one of value addition and reformulation.[4] It implies also clarification of beliefs, specification of objectives, intensification of commitment, and planning of tactics.

Concerning the levels of action and the actional attitudes, which are firmly related, this much should be said: An elementaristic attitude will be limited to some reforms of (especially legal) norms at a basically structural level; a totalistic attitude will expand to the cultural and characterological levels, with its emphasis on total change, new sociocultural values, and new images of the human being—and, of course, this will indicate a radical collectivity.[5]

With these various dimensions in mind as formal guidelines for analysis, let us turn now to the concrete example of the Women's Liberation Movement.

The origins and the current status of Women's Liberation have been treated extensively elsewhere,[6] so we may as well take these aspects for granted and present here certain second thoughts, especially relating the early development of the movement to the stages outlined earlier in our discussion.

First, one should stress the fact that conditions of exploitation and alienation of women have been in existence for a long time, causing chronic sociocultural oppression. Consequently, feelings of alienation have also been in existence for a long time, creating inertia, fear, timidity, and reactions labeled in modern times as "neuroses." The general feminist movement should be explained as a historic reaction against these alienating conditions. This wavelike insurrection of womanhood, however, was enthusiastic but episodic,[7] successful on certain issues but vague and general overall, unorganized although morally justified.

A new impetus in the direction of struggle for the emancipation and self-actualization of women was manifested in the radical sixties. This impetus was expressed:

> *as a radical search for identity* through the channels of other action groups
> —civil rights groups, SDS, socialist movements, etc.—in vain, alas; the
> dialectics of that process of participation, frustration, and negation can be
> understood in depth only with a masterful Sartrian analysis.

> *as a literary articulation by many writers,* such as M. Mead (1949), S. de
> Beauvoir (1953), and then E. Flexner (1959), B. Friedan (1963), H. R.
> Hayes (1964), L. J. Ludovici and A. Sinclair (1965), and many others,
> who made an enormous effort to articulate women's dissatisfaction, create
> awareness, and stimulate other reformist or radical thoughts and actions.

> *as the creation of neo-feminist groups,* such as the reformist National Orga-
> nization of Women (NOW), which appeared during 1966; various radical
> Women's Liberation groups emerged as radical schisms from NOW
> during and after 1968 (NY Radical Women, WITCH, The Feminists,
> Redstockings, New York Feminists, and so on).

Those events, during the sixties mark the transition from the general amorphous to the general instituted stage of the movement. This transformation carries with it the implication that new forms of consciousness and new collectivities have emerged, shaping the present sociocultural milieu. This is really the beginning, the process of the awakening of a giant majority group— not a class, a minority, or a caste.[8] To be more analytical, we may say that the new female consciousness is at the same time situational, critical, and apostolic: *situational,* for the inner feelings of alienation have been understood to be externally caused; *critical,* inasmuch as the alienating conditions are pointed out, the "oppression" is stigmatized, and, by many groups, the "oppressors" are unmasked; and, finally, *apostolic,* for in "consciousness-raising" meetings or in public protest and propaganda the young radicals preach liberation, incite their audiences, reveal the "truth," struggle against inertia and conformity, incite, and express with missionary zeal their commitment to the female cause.

Yet the emerging consciousness transcends the characterological level, where it strives to create new persons with a new philosophy of life and the ability of self-actualization and growth. It is dynamically expressed at the cultural and structural levels as powerful pressure groups are formed through totalization and mobilization.[9] Totalization breeds *coalescence*—togetherness, recruitment of comrades, rapport, collectivizing activities. Then *esprit de corps* is created, the ingroup loyalty and solidarity and the outgroup hostility, the informal fellowship and formal rituals, etc., in the way that Blumer so aptly described.[10] And, indeed, in our concrete case, coalescence and *esprit de corps* have been successfully developed; nevertheless, the ultrapluralization of the radical groups produces a certain disunity and instability and minimizes the aforesaid success.

At the present time, the movement is still general and hesitating: the enigma regarding the goal orientation (reform or revolution, elementaristic or totalistic attitude) is unsolved, always at stake. There is, however, some evidence that the radical groups are gaining in importance. On the other hand, one should not believe that there is unity among the many radical groups of Women's Liberation, and this in spite of the fact that there is an apparent coalition and fairly well expressed coactivation vis-à-vis specific issues, like abortion.

The ideological grounds of this differentiation should be sought for the clarification of this point: The movement, in terms of radicalization, begins with the reformists (NOW) and steps, first, toward the groups that advocate a total restructuring of the society and its values for the sake of both women's and men's liberation. Those groups do not claim that men are oppressors (at least not consciously, or at least not all men) but believe that men, as much as women, are victims of the sociohistorical progression of the "unconscious infrastructure" and concrete socialization practices. Another step forward is to be found in the radical feminist groups that stigmatize the oppression and name men as oppressors.[11] Their "generalized belief" is sincere but pathetic, unrealistic although consciousness-raising. The final step brings us to the position taken by some very powerful groups that preach separation from men, and possibly, rejection of marriage and the family, and, in a few cases, total sexual separation. Those are, of course, the *enfants terribles* of the movement.[12] This ideological diversification allows more intergroup flexibility and intragroup identification. On the other hand, it maintains the compartmentalization of forces and makes difficult the expansion of the movement to other segments of the feminine majority. And, of course, this is one deficiency among others.

When one refers to the "deficiencies" of a social movement, he means those functional inadequacies that hinder its effective realization. In our concrete case, Women's Liberation as a general instituted movement (at present) manifests certain characteristics that could possibly be thought of as being developmental inadequacies. We have already mentioned the ultrapluralization of the radical groups. We could also cite the lack of a specifically articulated ideology; the leaderless, memberless, protean form of the groups; the neglect of "timed" strategies; and many other "inadequacies." Such peculiarities are claimed to be beneficial, egalitarian, and ideal, yet to a skeptical sociologist they might well appear to be decisive factors against the attainment of the movement's up till now unclarified goals. To be more specific, I would argue that the movement has to advance to the specific idealized and specific crystallized stages, clearly defining its goals, morale, and ideology and properly organizing its forces.

As regards the development of a unified ideology to serve as the telelogical (aspirational/idealistic) *élan vital*, the movement has to decide about its totalistic inclination—it should specify its cultural goals and envisioned solutions (e.g., vis-à-vis the family, marriage, sexual mores, emancipation, mass media and advertising, fashions, education, cultural self-actualization, etc.); articulate its political, legal, and economic claims; and describe the ideal personality of the new free, nonalienated person. In doing so, the movement is called upon to exemplify its "utopia" and prove realistic its millennial faith in the ultimate attainment of liberation.

This quasi-religious consciousness could then unite the various groups in the name of the same idealistic hope[13]—for example, bringing the ideology somewhere close to seeking a human (male and female) liberation. Such an ideology should be humanitarian, critical, idealistic, and practical (providing for intellectual, existential, and collective praxis). And by the same token it should be the basis for a strategic rationale, which deductively will prove the inevitability of victory.[14]

As regards the structuralization of the movement, Women's Liberation has to find ways to cope effectively with problems of organization on the national (and international) level. Such a large-scale organization should provide a certain mobility and also make possible distinctions among leaders and elites, members, sympathizers and followers, and the masses. The importance of leadership, from both theoretical and practical viewpoints, is known only too well. For the time being, the radical groups, absorbed as they are in their utopian dream of a leaderless society, refuse to recognize the crucial nature of this problem. One should seriously doubt, however, whether the movement can survive and succeed without a sort of "leadership" in the broad sense of that term—a responsible (yet moral and sensitive), representative agency for decision making and ideo-crystallization. I can dare the prediction that the problem will inevitably be confronted, and in the near future.

Furthermore, the movement has to expand to other social categories of women besides intellectuals, professionals, and students. It has to approach and gain the lower classes, the housewives of suburban communities, the black women, and other multiply oppressed feminine groups. And this is another crucial criterion for the ultimate success or decline of the movement.

Moreover, the movement will soon face problems of division of labor beyond the regional level. This will lead to problems of control of rules and judgments within the groups, and of normative-structural expectancies and traditions, and it possibly, but not necessarily, will cause a secondary disunity[15] due to conflicts about value orientation (ideology), norm orientation (normative guidance and control), and action orientation (praxis and *pratiques*).

The recent behavior of the radical groups justifies an overall skepticism: To what extent is the refusal of authority structures of any sort (differentiation, ranking, stratification) a viable means in the struggle for liberation? Are the rejection of leadership and the neglect of identifiable membership powerful and positive principles that will succeed for the first time in history, or are they signs of an impractical belief that will hinder the success of the movement? Any opinion on this extremely significant point is bound to be interpreted as "ideological"—a romantic desire of the radical feminists or a wish fulfillment of male chauvinists. The difficulties are not present for the time being because of the emphasis placed on regional and local activities. But there is no indication that these inherent difficulties of every movement will not emerge when the development of Women's Liberation necessitates a national "organ" to be the bureau for decision making and action planning.

To summarize this brief account, we can say that the movement has to make some really significant decisions in order to specify and crystallize itself. Such decisions will refer to homogeneity; unified collective consciousness; mobilization and expansion in regard to other, more alienated segments; structure and organization at the national level; etc.

Turning now from the analysis to a few selected points that will help us make some final predictions, I believe we have to insist on the fact that the ingroup philosophy (morale) does not coincide necessarily with the outgroup rationale for strategy. To make myself more explicit: It is true that it will be better for its cause if the movement has a unified morale adopted by every single group and member, only one exemplified ideology, only one utopia to be realized, only one set of basic objectives. This will bring homogeneity and collective consciousness, consolidate the ideological schisms, and make possible the projection and persistence of the significant value and normative changes that are sought. On the other hand, for tactical purposes, one can advocate or at least find justifiable a "two collectivities front" (one reformist and conciliatory, the other radical and polemical).[16] All in all, the choice is between a monistic or a dualistic front, which implies, of course, that the movement will consume its pluralism of today by consolidating its forces into one or two nationwide collectivities.

Therefore the next significant point is to find the appropriate ideological position and to embody it. We alluded to that problem earlier, but let us say here for the sake of prediction that the only position that seems to be adequate for a long-range development is the one that claims the need for a basic restructuralization of both the value and the normative systems in favor of human liberation from alienation. Separatism does not seem viable: For one thing, the great majority of women will not subscribe to it in spite of any kind of sexual revolution. On the contrary, many will feel repelled. Moreover, I would argue, total separation, functionally and substantially speaking, cannot sustain any society. Philosophically and practically, it is unattainable and dysfunctional. Separation excluded, there are still other ideologies which must vie for the monopoly of radicalism: the relatively moderate ideology of human liberation in general (the belief that males too are oppressed by the existing system of sex roles) and the more radical view of female liberation from male supremacy. One can predict a dialectical synthesis in the following direction: "Yes, some (possibly many) males are oppressors and exploiters; yet the majority (or many) of them are as much the victims of the sociocultural pressures as the female group. Consequently, unmask and fight the exploiters; yet give consciousness to and liberate the others." This synthesis, I believe, could be a fundamentally realistic morale/rationale for the successful ennoblement of life. From a theoretical point of view, one can thus relate Women's Liberation to the upward-tending spirit of intellectual history—as exemplified for example, in the dialectical visions of Hegel, early Marx, and Camus.[17]

For, implicitly or explicitly, there is a utopian humanitarianism behind the facade of those episodic moments of protest of the new feminism: the dream of an egalitarian, tolerant, nonalienating, loving community of human beings. This dream, this underlying powerful utopian dream—it is believed—could possibly bring *the* miracle, *a* miracle, any kind of miracle that will create a more humanitarian society. There is, therefore, a transcendental basis[18] that idealizes and crystallizes the feminine praxis: *The Humanitas of the Future*. Thus, the dramatic character of certain radical claims is understood in this light as a sincere and sensitive existential expression, a groaning for human redemption rather than a "bourgeois" demand of selfish motivation. One has to stress emphatically those sociomoral bases of the movement in view of the dangerous, vulgar, and oversimplified association of it with sexual problematics.

Briefly, idealistic catharsis (that is, clarification of ideology, unity of morale and quest for a drastic reconstructing of society) and structural crystallization are what is needed for the successful realization of the Women's Liberation Movement. And, of course, the times are ripe for such an attempt.

Notes

1. Frances Wright, "Of Free Enquiry Considered as a Means for Obtaining Just Knowledge," in *Voices from Women's Liberation*, ed. L. B. Tanner (New York: New American Library, 1970).
2. The approach we follow emphasizes the cognitive and volitional character of collective action in the case of developed social movements. The basic assumptions held here are in agreement with the ideas advanced by Alain Touraine— although certain constructs have been adopted from the work of Blumer and Smelser.
3. These are the words that H. Blumer uses for the entire field of collective behavior (H. Blumer, "Collective Behavior," in *Review of Sociology: Analysis of a Decade*, ed. J. Gittler [New York: John Wiley & Sons, 1957], p. 127).
4. See N. Smelser, *Theory of Collective Behavior* (New York: Free Press, 1962), pp. 13 ff. This view recalls the similar work of Jean Piaget on the restructuralization of cognitive schemata.
5. It is clear that an elementaristic attitude is to be found in reform (Blumer), norm-oriented (Smelser) movements, while a totalistic attitude is to be found in revolutionary (Blumer), value-oriented (Smelser) movements.
6. See Barbara Bovee Polk, "Women's Liberation: Movement for Equality," in Chapter 7 of this volume; Gerda Lerner, "The Feminists: A Second Look," *Columbia Forum*, vol. 13 (Fall 1970), pp. 24–30.
7. H. Blumer, "Collective Behavior," in *New Outline of the Principles of Sociology*," ed. A. M. Lee (New York: Barnes & Noble, 1951), pp. 200–201.
8. Lerner, *op. cit.*, pp. 27–28.
9. *Totalization* here indicates the consciousness of being confronted with an oppressive situation; *mobilization* implies individual and collective response to the totalizing situation. Both terms as used here are quite close to the schemes of Sartre and Touraine.
10. Blumer, *op. cit.*, pp. 205–208.
11. Cf. the now famous Redstockings Manifesto: "II. Women are an oppressed class. . . . III. We identify the agents of our oppression as men. . . . *All* men have oppressed women. . . ." (July 7, 1969).
12. Outside of NOW and the various Women's Liberation groups, there is naturally the great majority of women, who for the time being stay silent, or apathetic, or conform to the given sex roles. There are also certain antiliberation voices; some antiabortion groups, for example, supported by certain churches; and, paradoxically, two or three explicitly antifeminist groups (i.e., Moms, Pussycats). The latter seem to oppose especially the totalistic attitude of Women's Liberation vis-à-vis pageants, fashion, and advertising and their perpetuations of the feminine mystique.
13. And this is the crucial moment, indeed; the moment when a humanitarian idealism has to define in terms of praxis its conception of true human nature and *telos*.
14. Such a rationale will progress as follows: Definition of True Human Nature and

Telos ⇒ Exemplification (Utopia) ⇒ Justification of the Movement ⇒ Legitimation of Praxis ⇒ Action and Tactics ⇒ Sacrifices ⇒ Inevitability of Victory.

15. Smelser, *op. cit.*, pp. 361–362.

16. Cf. Gunnar Myrdal's two types of leadership in the black community—leadership of accommodation and leadership of protest. Gunnar Myrdal, *An American Dilemma* (New York: Harper & Row, 1962), p. 720.

17. Cf. A. Camus, *The Rebel* (New York: Random House, 1956), pp. 140 ff, 197 ff.

18. From a Sociology of Knowledge perspective one can recognize three such transcendental bases: (A) God and/or The Cosmos, (B) The Future (History), and (C) *Humanitas* (i.e., Humanness and Human Solidarity).

Dialogue-Focuser: Women*

Areas of Essential Agreement

The role which women have played, their own self-image, and the image that men have had of them have varied from culture to culture and from one historical period to another. There has, however, been one factor common to all cultures and time periods—that babies were born to women as a result of sexual activity. This common factor has limited the range of variation in cultural patterns although it must be recognized that the limits have still been extraordinarily wide. Values which are considered essentially masculine in one culture are considered feminine in others: roles which are played only by men in certain areas of the world are played only by women in others.

The necessary linking of sexual activity to procreation is already essentially broken and with it the physiological basis for the double standard of sex which demanded purity in women but accepted premarital sexual activity for men. The range of contraceptive devices is now so wide that it is possible to ensure, with almost complete certainty, that unwanted conceptions do not occur. Projected developments, such as a birth-control capsule which will release its ingredients over an extended period of time, will effectively eliminate the remaining risk.

In addition, there is evidence that the taboos about abortion, as well as birth control, are dropping. There is growing agreement that the healthy emotional development of a child [into a sane, healthy individual] depends on those around him being willing to provide the love he requires. . . . The combination of these developments means that it is possible for sexual activity to be almost completely divorced from procreation.

Two other factors in this general area are also generally agreed [upon]. First, it is clear that the degree of population pressure throughout the world, and particularly in the poor countries, is now such that the average size of family must be reduced if overcrowding and famine are to be avoided. Second, it is not only possible to avoid conception when it is not desired, it is also increasingly possible to ensure conception for all those who desire it. The number of women who want to bear children but are denied this possibility has already declined abruptly and will continue to decline.

It is perhaps less clearly recognized that the linkage between procreation and sexual activity is being shattered in the opposite sense also: procreation is

---

* This is a new style of document called a dialogue-focuser. Its purpose is to summarize the state of the debate on a particular subject. Dialogue-focusers are not copyrighted for they attempt to reflect what all of society has discovered about a particular topic: they therefore belong to the total society.

362

increasingly possible without sexual activity. The first limited steps were taken in this direction with the acceptance of artificial insemination for those unable to have babies through sexual relations with their husbands. Some people are now calling for the extension of this possibility to mothers who would prefer that their children partook of the hereditary characteristics of some man whom they admired: it has been suggested that a sperm bank should be created for this purpose. Others have argued for clonal reproduction: the creation of an exact replica of a human person presently alive. Still others are working to create life in a test tube. There are few, if any, who are prepared to state confidently that none of these techniques can be achieved.

Finally, it is far from certain that sexual pleasure must necessarily be related to human sexual relationships: it might well be possible to create more "efficient" sex pleasure through the use of electrical or mechanical machines rather than through human sexual activity.

The new debate about women and the relationships between men and women therefore centers around which of these potentially possible physiological developments are desirable and what social attitudes will facilitate, hinder, or prevent them. It is clear, of course, that full acceptance of some of these techniques would make it possible, and necessary, to create female-male relationships totally anew.

Areas of Disagreement

One side of the debate claims that present definitions of masculinity—and femininity, which has been largely defined in reference to it—force man's and woman's nature into a cultural straightjacket and [that] the values presently accepted are dangerous to the survival of the world. They argue that the dominant masculine values—strength, vigor, competitiveness, power—do not fit the new conditions apparently emerging.

It is argued that the main purpose of the new society must be to permit the development of each individual to his maximum potential and to provide him with a social environment in which this can be achieved. Two key views about the nature of the good society are advanced: First [there is] the necessity of diversity, of a wide range of personalities and attitudes through providing each individual with the circumstances in which he can discover who he is. Second, life cannot consist in the setting of specific goals which must be achieved, but rather must be oriented toward process.

Effective opposition to this view hardly exists. This is not because the view is accepted but rather because it appears so irrelevant to the present leaders of governmental, administrative, and voluntary organizations, who generally see the appropriate goals in terms of a higher gross national product, more goods and services, and greater control over the environment. Man's needs are seen as unlimited and the basic goal of the society must be to satisfy these needs. It is therefore argued in much of literature that the failure of women to emerge as equal partners with men is due to the fact that they have not adopted the characteristics which can be clearly seen as crucial for success in the present socioeconomic system, and that women should therefore concentrate in developing these values and "strengths."

Disagreement with this latter view does not challenge the statement that women have been relatively unsuccessful within the present culture. Nor does it deny that women could change and be more successful. Rather it is argued that the areas *presently* valued will not be important in the future and that it is therefore absurd to abandon female values at this point. It is suggested that the major areas of work in coming periods will be education, the human care of human beings, and the creation of the good community and that these will demand empathy, intuition, and cooperation, which appear to be predominantly female characteristics.

This theme has been developed further by certain women's groups, such as Women's Strike for Peace, who have argued that feminine values are crucial to the controlling and development of the world even today. They claim that women have the capacity to do certain presently crucial tasks better than men. Believing that force is counterproductive on the national and international scene, they state women must now take the initiative because men have been taught to try to achieve "power" in all situations.

This view is countered on two levels. First, it is argued that the only way to bring about change is to force through a new idea or a new technique—that cooperation cannot be effective in changing the behavior of people. Second, it is argued that it is impossible to change people, that the world will always be ordered by force, and that it is, therefore, naïve to look for alternative techniques which would eliminate force. At the next level of analysis, these two arguments appear effectively identical: it is claimed that competition is necessary and will prevail over cooperation.

Perhaps the most rapidly growing debate is around the desirable nature of the family—and by extension the community with [which] the family or the individual has close relationships. Examination of this issue stems from a belief that we are now in the process of moving from the industrial age into a cybernated era and that this involves changing the basis of our society from a production-transportation net to an information net.

> The effective functioning of an information net, however, would require fundamental shifts in the attitudes of the society; for information can only be moved effectively in an honest, cooperative society. This statement is based on the now clearly proven fact that power and distortion of information are linked: the individual in a subordinate position passes information up the line which he believes his superiors would like to hear. The acceptance of an information net as the basis of society would therefore inherently require greater acceptance of what might be defined as female characteristics.

If the culture will, in fact, be based on an information net rather than a a production-transportation net, it will be possible to reduce substantially the degree of mobility. People could then determine for themselves, without outside constraints, how often they would like to move, how much children would like to see of their parents at what points in their lives, how much parents would like to see of their children at what points in their lives, and how the possible conflicts could be resolved.

> While a debate on this topic is just beginning, it is important to note that there are many attempts to work out these issues through living

them. The present life styles and thinking range all the way from the preservation of the nuclear family to the creation of new forms of community groups, from intense personalism to institutionalization.

This debate also appears irrelevant to many. It is argued in rebuttal that we are living in the high period of the industrial culture, that man has learned to produce what is needed for a decent standard of living, and that we have developed both the tools and the institutions to ensure that this standard will be shared by all. According to this view the basic lines of human advance for the future are still those which have been laid down in the past: there are now new factors in the environment which make it necessary for the culture to adapt fundamentally.

If this view is correct, the debate about the appropriate family structure is indeed essentially irrelevant, for the structures of the industrial age essentially foreclose debate on this topic. Overwhelming pressures force an ever-growing proportion of workers to move; this has meant that families have generally been reduced to the nuclear level, thus containing mother, father, and minor children.

Arguments about the structuring of families and communities are crosscut by a 'debate about freedom, permanency, and commitment. Some believe that the whole idea of the family as a permanent bond is a cultural hangover which should be eliminated. It is argued that it is essential that each individual be free to grow away from another as well as to grow toward him, that no substantial number of human relationships would be permanent if they were not supported, and indeed demanded, by social pressures. Individuals should, therefore, have the right to relate to one another for as long as seems good to them and there should be no expectation of permanency.

This approach is countered by the argument that permanency can only be created through commitment, that it is permanency which permits finding oneself in another and thus finding one's own self. Willingness to try to help another is essential to one's growth in this view; getting to know a person well enough take a lifetime.

All the previous issues are crosscut by yet another: the argument as to whether we will be able to improve the genetic inheritance, the emotional behavior, the intelligence of the human being through the use of human engineering. It is argued that the only possible way to improve the human race rapidly enough to face the present crises is to use all of our scientific knowledge to achieve this end. Manipulation of the genetic structure first, followed by the actual creation of life [is] essential, it is claimed.

It appears that this stance must necessarily be based on the belief that fundamental shifts in bodily functions can occur without any major unfavorable effects on the organism in either the short or the long run—that we have the power to engineer our own bodies. In this view, the physiological differences between men and women can also be expected to yield to the culture; there is an effective possibility of producing any cultural pattern which seems desirable. Such a position means that there are no effective constraints in remaking the human race: man can choose to structure his body and his culture in any way which seems good to him.

Disagreement with this approach occurs at two levels. First, it is claimed that it may be reasonably expected that there are rather severe limits to the ability of any organism—including our own bodies—to adapt and that it is extraordinarily difficult to predict the effects of any change. This argument is based on a statement in theoretical cybernetics (the science of communication and control) that change in any system will bring about further changes both expected and unexpected. It is also based on practical observations of the consequences of relatively minor bodily changes, such as the slight—but continuing—increase in body height. Most of those who adopt this view also appear to argue that there are substantial physiological differences between the sexes and that cultural standardization cannot submerge these differences without the potential for highly unfavorable consequences.

The second level of challenge is philosophical and metaphysical. It results from a belief that the important quality of a human being or social system—that of completeness or [wholeness]—does not lend itself to improvement through objective analysis alone. It is, in a very real sense, on a different dimension. [This view] involves the acceptance of mystery, of the ultimate inability to know everything. This acceptance of unknowability may derive from many sources—from religion or ethics or science—but it always leads away from an acceptance of "objective" manipulation.

In this view the problem of mankind cannot be solved by improving any one dimension of his being, such as his speed or his intelligence. Rather it is mankind's ability to define his own private self in relationship to a small number of other beings which determines the meaning of human life. Improvement in this dimension will be achieved by learning how to communicate genuinely—an ability which seems to have been largely destroyed during the industrial age. Progress in this direction does not depend primarily on "improved" physical or mental characteristics but rather on commitment to achieve communication.

In effect, this final argument is about the proper relation of ends and means. One group argues that improvement in the minds and bodies of human beings would lead to improvement in the quality of human life. The other group argues that we should aim to improve the quality of human life and that physical and mental improvement would result. It is this disagreement which leads the first group to call the second naïve and vague, and the second to call the first instrumental and manipulative, which is perhaps [the problem] most in need of resolution and yet most difficult to resolve.

Women, Marriage, and the Future

In 1927 John B. Watson, the psychologist, prophesied that by 1977 marriage would no longer exist, for by then family standards would have completely broken down and the automobile and other things would have taken the child out of control.

Some ten years later, Pitirim Sorokin, the sociologist, prophesied that divorce and separation would increase until any profound difference between socially sanctioned marriages and illicit sex relations disappeared. The home would become a mere overnight parking place, devoted mainly to sex relationships.

And ten years after that, C. B. Zimmerman, another sociologist, concluded that the family was doomed unless we turned to the domestic style of our grandparents.

Actually, marriage has never been in better shape, at least statistically speaking. The proportion of people who are married is going up, up, up, and it is now projected that with the present young generation just coming on the scene, all but 2 or 3 percent will be married during their lifetime.

But I am going to discuss a prophetic minority—the radical women who lead the Women's Liberation Movement. They are indeed a small minority, perhaps less than 15 percent of their generation, but in my opinion they represent an avant-garde that is going to modify enormously all of our projections.

Do not smile when you read that some of them have picketed the Miss America pageant, or burned their bras, or demonstrated at abortion trials. Do not laugh even at the guerrilla theater antics of one branch that calls itself the Women's International Terrorist Conspiracy from Hell (WITCH). If you ask [a member] about the name, she will give you a very learned description of witches, who were sort of learned women in the ancient past. It isn't as funny as it sounds.

These women are not cute little kittens engaged in a kind of reverse coquetry. True, they engage in attention-getting devices that are a bit on the outrageous side. If the women themselves were not so sophisticated and so well aware of the reaction they are evoking, you might dismiss them as mere nuisances. But do not approach them with preconceived ideas. These women are forearmed. They know everything you are going to say and they have an answer.

The goals and aims of radical women as they see them are revolutionary. They want to restructure society and the whole matrix of relationships between the sexes. More power to them! But I would like to emphasize here a different angle on their activities. I see them as performing the fundamental function of preparing us for the future that the technological geniuses have in store for us.

Motherhood and Housekeeping Roles Are Declining

The technologists have made it possible to salvage so many births and to extend the longevity of so many older men and women that we are about to be smothered in people. We are too squeamish to indulge in infanticide or killing off of the old, but we cannot afford to continue to have so many babies. Roughly two babies per couple would keep us well supplied. But this will leave women technologically unemployed—unemployed, that is, by motherhood.

In the twentieth century there has been a fairly steady trend downward in the proportion of married life spent in childbearing and rearing, and we are now beginning to see the magnitude of the dislocation that this creates. For [a] long [time] we have thought of population control in terms of finding suitable techniques of contraception and disseminating them widely in the population. In doing so we have forgotten that we have not given adequate attention to the repercussions in the lives of women. We take it for granted that contraception is welcome, and so indeed it is. But in the nineteenth century there were a great many domestic alternatives to motherhood for the time and energy of women; it took a great deal of effort just to run an ordinary household, and saving women the extra burden of child care did not render them technologically unemployed. But today the technological geniuses have not only made contraception feasible on a mass basis, but have also reduced housekeeping chores to almost a minimum. Give us an automatic dust filter that keeps all dust out and there will be very little left, except, of course, the perennial battle against gravity—picking up.

So two of the age-old functions of women—childbearing and housekeeping—are being vastly reduced. What does a woman do with her life when these two major functions are taken from her, especially when her own life is being spectacularly lengthened? What kind of marriage will be suitable?

All our thinking about women in the past has posited a being most of whose adult life would be dedicated to childbearing, child rearing, and household management. Everything else had to adjust itself to these rockbound fundamentals. Yes, she could enter the labor force but not at the expense of these major functions. Yes, she could even have a career. But again, not at the expense of the major functions. They always had to take priority. Home and family had to come first; it was a law of nature. Everything was arranged to fit that conception of women, marriage, birth, and career.

Marriage Is Poor Status for Women

Women were socialized to accept the situation, but marriage was not really a good status for women. Marriage was not and is not, I would repeat, a good status for women, at least not marriage as it has been institutionalized in the past. Long ago de Tocqueville commented on that sad and melancholy look of American married women. When researchers began studying marriage, they found that women made far more of the adjustments than men. In instruments for measuring the success of marriage, women evaluated their marriages lower than men did. Married women had poorer mental health than unmarried women.

In a book I wrote thirty years ago (*American Family Behavior*), I propounded, on the basis of data then available, what I called a "shock" theory of marriage. For it appeared that although the differences between married and unmarried women at marriage were minimal, the differences increased with time to the disadvantage of the married women. But since the whole social structure was organized on the assumption that childbearing, child-rearing, and household management were the major life work of women, they were in effect swept into marriage willy-nilly [with] practically no other status available to them. Marriage made sense for most women, however much an occasional dissenter might protest.

So we had a paradoxical situation: marriage, as institutionalized, was not really a good status for women; yet they were most anxious to marry. Men, for whom marriage was the best possible status, were complaining about marriage and the way women corralled them into it. Women were so thoroughly programmed for marriage that they accepted the situation. They were too brainwashed, as the radical women put it, to see the deprivations they were subjected to.

As an aside, to show how we blame women for being unhappy in this status [let me illustrate from my own experience:] I was at a meeting of the American Psychiatric Association last May and there was a caucus of radical women who protested that psychiatrists and counsellors are always blaming women for being unhappy, which is like blaming miners for black lung, or, in the 1930s, blaming people for being unemployed. You have a structural situation which produces certain results, and then you blame the victims of the situation.

Radical Women Threaten Men and Many Married Women

The radical women, like children who view things freshly and are not fooled by preconceptions, proclaim openly that the emperor has no clothes. They look at marriage and what it does to women rather than at the stereotype and at what women say it does. What the radical women say about marriage alienates both men and many married women. Men do not relish the implications of what the radical women rub their noses in, and the married women are frightened by a threat to the foundations of their lives.

Reproduction Will Be Minor Part of Woman's Life

The popular conception of modern marriage is one of equality between husbands and wives. The radical women ask, "What equality?" They are preparing us for a world in which reproduction is going to be only a very minor part of a woman's life, a world in which men and women are going to have to relate to one another in ways quite removed from reproduction, both in marriage and outside of it.

The radical women's function of preparing us for a world of changed reproductive needs is my view of their activities, not theirs. They see themselves as being revolutionaries. I see them as helping us to catch up with revolutions that have already occurred or are in process, with revolutions which the technologists have precipitated and which we must come to terms with.

But one major revolution these women are fomenting is a brand new sexual revolution. This is not the now stale revolution with which the women's magazines are still preoccupied—the work-harder-to-achieve-orgasm revolution—but one that transcends it. The new revolution is one that aims to make it possible for women not to feel that they have to be hot numbers, exuding sexuality and super orgasmic adequacy. We have become so obsessed with the idea that women are exclusively sexual beings that we have made it almost compulsory for them to demonstrate their talents to every man they meet.

Get over that, say the radical women. Here is how it looks to one of them:

> The hangup to liberation is the supposed need for sex. It is something that must be refuted, coped with, demythified, or the cause of female liberation is doomed. Already we see girls fairly liberated in their own heads, understanding their oppressions with clarity, trying deliberately and a trace hysterically to make themselves attractive to men—men for whom they have no respect, men they may even hate—because of a basic sexual emotional need. Sex is not essential to life, as eating is. Some people go through their whole lives without it at all, including fine, warm, happy people. It's a myth that this makes one bitter, shriveled up, twisted. We are programmed to crave sex. It sells consumer goods. It gives a lift and promises a spark of individual self-assertion in a dull and routinized world. It is an "in" to power—the only means they have for women.

And I could document this defense of celibacy. Unmarried women show up very well in all of the tests of mental health. Married men, of course, come out on top, but never-married women are next, then married women, and, of course, at the bottom, unmarried men.

It takes courage in this day and age to come right out and say these things. The women-need-sex image has become such a shibboleth that to contradict it hazards the worst kinds of sanctions. Men, the radical women tell us, have needed this image. Without it they are threatened. As the radical women say, men "will try to destroy you, stab you in the back, use any underhanded move to get back at you for posing this threat to them. You have done them the incalculable offense of not deferring to their sex, daring to be yourself, of stepping out of your role, of rejecting the phony sexual differentiation that makes each of them feel like a man."

Celibacy May Again Become Honorable

The next step is even more revolutionary. It is the statement that marriage is not the *summum bonum* of life, that celibacy is not a fate worse than death, but an honorable status. The radical women say we must come to realize that celibacy is a state that could be desirable in many ways, in many cases preferable. To quote a radical woman, "How repugnant it really is, after all, to make love to a man who despises you, who fears you and wants to hold you down. Doesn't screwing in an atmosphere devoid of respect get pretty grim? Why bother? You don't need it."

This is not a call for celibacy per se but for an acceptance of celibacy as an honorable alternative, one preferable to many male-female sexual relationships. "Only when we accept the idea of celibacy completely will we ever be able to liberate ourselves. Until we accept this completely—until I say I control my own body and I don't need any insolent male with an overbearing manner to come and gratify my needs—they will always have over us the devastating threat of withdrawing their sexual attentions and, worse, the threat of our ceasing to be even sexually attractive." In an era in which reproduction was, in the last analysis, the *raison d'être* for relations between the sexes, other kinds of relations, no matter how much desired, had to take second place. But radical women, who already sense that reproduction will be a minor part of life in the future, want something other than primary sexuality to become the basis of relationships.

As they put it, love and affection and recognition can easily be found in comrades—a more honest and open love—who love you for yourself and not for how docile and cute and sexy and ego-building you are.

Future Men and Women May Deal with Each Other as Individuals

The radical women are anticipating a future in which loving and affectionate companionship between the sexes will be possible, based on mutual recognition of one another as individuated human beings rather than as stereotypical male and female sex beings. The radical women are under no illusions that bringing about these new relationships is going to be easy. Men will resist and punish them. Unliberated women, brainwashed not only to accept their slavery but also to love it, will also resist.

"A man can devote himself to his work wholeheartedly," the radical woman tell us, "because he has a servant at home who takes care of the dull chores of home-making. He is not accustomed to doing the monotonous, repetitive work that does not issue in any lasting, let alone important, achievement. If it takes at least an hour a day to manage the chores of keeping for oneself, a man who foists this off onto a woman has seven hours a week, one working day more, to play with his mind."

I am all for the radical women. I think they are performing an extremely important function. I myself wouldn't have the courage to be as brave as they are. But I think they are doing what I think needs to be done. They are preparing us for a future in which we are going to have to recognize a different kind of woman and a different kind of role for women than we did in the past.

Fifty years from now we will look back and wonder what we ever thought was so avant-garde about these women. By that time, it will just seem so matter of fact.

The Effects of Population Change on the Roles and Status of Women: Perspective and Speculation*

The purpose of this brief essay is to explore some of the possible implications and consequences of population change for the roles and status of women. The discussion is divided into two parts. In the first part, attention is focused on past demographic changes that have contributed to alterations in the roles and status of women, for only by gaining some historical perspective may future changes be discerned. In the second part, some possible future changes and their implications for women are examined. Obviously, the discussion in the last part is highly speculative, since the demographic changes referred to have yet to occur.

Historical Perspective[1]

Changes in the roles and status of women as well as changes in the three demographic factors—mortality, fertility, and migration—occurred as part of the vast economic and social changes of the Industrial Revolution. The demographic changes were experienced first in Western societies, but as industrialization has spread to other parts of the world most societies have, in varying degrees, been experiencing them also.

An Overview

Women have always worked. The degree of importance, however, that societies have attached to women's work has varied greatly. At the risk of oversimplification, it may be stated that at least in Western societies there existed greater equality between the sexes prior to urbanization and industrialization.[2] Economic roles were not sharply differentiated from familial roles. Consequently, sharp status distinctions between men and women were not made. This lack of differentiation was a reflection of the concentration of economic activities within the family. Thus, women could perform their basic

---

* A number of ideas presented in this paper were developed in the course of several discussions with Joan W. Lingner, of the University of North Carolina. Her contributions are gratefully acknowledged. Also acknowledged are the research assistance of Ilene Herz and Elizabeth Kochar and the secretarial assistance of Adelaide Hirschheimer.

biological function of reproduction and the associated tasks of child care along with an economic role.

But with industrialization, economic production was gradually removed from the home. If women were to continue to fulfill their childbearing and child-rearing roles, they were restricted from engaging in economically productive work. Moreover, men found that they had to assume almost completely the economic role for the family. Since this required men to spend a great deal of time away from their homes, their participation within their families as husbands and fathers was greatly diminished. As a result, the child-rearing tasks women once shared with their husbands had to be assumed by the women more and more. In addition, it is likely that women acquired many of the housekeeping tasks that had formerly been shared with their husbands. Accordingly, a sharp division of labor within the family, based on sex, emerged.

Men, by retaining their economic role through their occupations, acquired the status that once was attached to the family as a group. Hence, the family's status increasingly was dependent on the occupational role of the husband. The woman, by having no occupation defined in the economic sense, therefore, had no claim to status in her own right.[3] The demographic developments, however, that occurred as part of the Industrial Revolution gradually permitted women to resume an economic role in society. This resumption of the economic role is evidenced by the increased rates of female labor-force participation in industrialized countries in the twentieth century.

Primarily, these demographic developments were the declines in mortality that produced marked increases in average life expectancy and hence the lessened need for prolific childbearing. For most of human history, high mortality required correspondingly high fertility. But with decreasing infant and child mortality, women were no longer required to bear a large number of children. Such factors as the rising costs of rearing children in industrializing societies further diminished the importance of reproduction.[4] Changes, also, in the mobility of families and individuals had, as we shall see, a number of consequences for the roles and status of women.

Since the effects of these various changes in the three demographic factors are so interrelated, it is difficult to disentangle them. Nevertheless, some of the more important and obvious effects that may be attributed to each of the demographic factors may be discerned.

Effects of Mortality Declines

One of the most obvious consequences of the declines in mortality was the increase in average life expectancy.[5] A newborn female in industrialized countries of today can look forward to a lifetime on the average of 70 or more years. Even in many of the more recently developing countries, average life expectancy for females has now reached approximately 60 years. In contrast, one hundred or even fifty years ago the average life expectancy in Western countries was considerably less. Estimates for the United States at the beginning of the nineteenth century place life expectancy at approximately 35 years (Taeuber and Taeuber 1958). Data for England and Wales indicate that for females born in 1840–41, average life expectancy was approximately 43 years (Glass 1965).

The following figures of life expectancy at birth for American males and females illustrate the dramatic increases in life expectancy in the twentieth century (United Nations 1968, 1970):

Year	Males	Females
1900–02	47.9	50.7
1909–11	49.9	53.2
1919–21	55.5	57.4
1929–31	57.7	61.0
1939–41	61.6	65.9
1949–51	65.5	71.0
1960	66.6	73.1
1965	66.8	73.7
1967	67.0	74.2

For females, the increase in life expectancy from the beginning of the twentieth century to 1967 has been slightly over 23 years, while for males it has been slightly more than 19 years. These improvements in life expectancy have resulted mainly from the tremendous reductions in infant and child mortality. While in 1900, 79 percent of white American females could expect to survive to age 20 and only 65 percent could expect to survive to age 45 (Bogue 1959), by 1965, 97 percent could expect to survive to age 20 and 94 percent to age 45. Moreover, American white women surviving to age 45 in 1965 had a future average expectancy of 32.9 years (U.S., Department of Health, Education, and Welfare, 1967).

Consequently, women today look forward to a large number of years at the end of their childbearing period. As Myrdal and Klein (1956) point out, these years, when women are in the forties and fifties, are ones in which most women are still healthy and energetic. In fact, for men, these are precisely the ages at which they are considered to have attained the peak of their productivity in many occupations.

These increases in life expectancy for both sexes have had many implications for marriage and family life. Most obvious have been the increases in marital duration and the reductions in the probability of early widowhood. Something of the extent of the effects on marital duration may be seen by considering the following hypothetical figures.[6] At an average life expectancy at birth of 43 years, a group of women married at age twenty may expect an average of only 28 years of married life. In contrast, with an average life expectancy at birth of 72 years, a group of women marrying at the same age may look forward to an average of 44 years of married life. This represents a gain of 16 years. At the turn of the century, average life expectancy for both American males and females was somewhat better than the 43 years assumed in the hypothetical estimates given above, being approximately 51 years for women. Glick and Parke (1965) estimate that the increase in marital duration for women in the United States during the twentieth century has been approximately 9 years. This extension of married life, of course, means that spouses may look forward to spending many more years together.

Furthermore, with an average life expectancy of 72 years, 85 percent of the women will be alive and still married at age 50, as opposed to only 48 percent when average life expectancy is 43 years. The proportions of women becoming widowed have thus changed dramatically. With an average life expectancy of 43 years, approximately 17 percent of women surviving to ages 40 to 49 would become widowed. At the higher life expectancy only 6 percent will have been widowed at those ages.

Although the chances of widowhood for women in the early adult ages have been reduced considerably as a result of the lengthening of life, the prevalence of widowhood has increased at the later ages. This is a result of the mortality differential between the sexes. At all ages, males tend to have higher mortality than females. In the United States, the mortality differential between the sexes has been increasing as life expectancy has increased. For example, between the period 1939–41 and 1967, the differential in life expectancy increased from 4.3 years to 7.2 years. Taeuber (1971) has pointed out that men in the United States are more disadvantaged in terms of mortality than men in other countries. This may reffect the differential burdens of the roles men and women are expected to perform in American society.

The Reduction in Fertility

The freedom women attained when low mortality no longer necessitated constant childbearing meant that women no longer had to face "the drain and danger of pregnancy to no purpose. . . ." Thus, this released "energy" of women "could be spent on other aspects of life" (Davis 1945). Not only did fewer years have to be spent on the bearing and rearing of children, but, because of the increasing life expectancy, the period devoted to these activities came to represent an even smaller portion of women's lives. More recently, particularly in the United States during the 1940s and 1950s, the earlier age at marriage and the shortening of intervals between births have also resulted in more time becoming available to women (Day 1958, Ryder, op. cit.).

The decline in family size can be illustrated by contrasting the average number of children had by every married white women born in the period 1835–39 with the number had by ever married white women born in 1910–14. The average was 5.3 children for women born in the earlier period, while for women born in the later period the average was 2.3 children. Moreover, 35 percent of every married white women born in 1835–39 had 7 or more children, while only 4 percent of the every married white women born in 1910–14 had such numbers. This downward trend in family size has been similarly observed in other industrialized countries.

One of the consequences of the decline in family size is that at any point in time fewer women in the childbearing years are pregnant or recovering from a current pregnancy.[7] Another consequence of low fertility is that proportionately fewer women in a society are responsible for the care of young children.

Glick and Parke (*op. cit.*) have described some of the changes in the life cycle of American families that have resulted from the changes in fertility as well as in age at marriage. The following table shows the median ages for selected groups of women at various points in the family life cycle.

Event	YEAR OF BIRTH OF WOMEN			
	1880 to 1889	1900 to 1909	1920 to 1929	1930 to 1939
First marriage	21.6	21.1	20.8	19.9
Birth of first child	22.9	22.6	23.0	21.5
Birth of last child	32.9	30.4	30.0–31.0	(NA)°
Marriage of last child	56.2	51.9	51.5–52.5	(NA)°

°Not available.

These data indicate several points of interest. First is the decline in age at first marriage. Second is the concomitant trend to an earlier age at which women have their first birth.[8] Third, and most important, is the decline in age of women at the time of the birth of their last child. Thus, for women born in the 1920s, the age at which they completed their childbearing was two to three years younger and their age at the time of marriage of their last child was some four to five years younger than the corresponding ages had been among women born in the 1880s. This shorter period of time devoted to childbearing reflects not only the decrease in family size but also, as noted earlier, the closer spacing of children. Furthermore, this means that, with the duration of marriage increasing (as previously pointed out), husbands and wives spend an increasing amount of time together after their children have left home.

Some students of the family have argued that one result of these changes has been for marriages to become more companionate in nature. Furthermore, the reduced time required for reproduction and child care has permitted married women to enter the labor force in greater numbers. In turn, this increased labor-force participation, or the possibility of it, has led to a lessened financial dependence of wives on their husbands. Therefore, the importance of the personal relationship within marriage has been further enhanced.

Davis (1950) has speculated that this increased importance of the personal relationship in marriage has contributed somewhat to the increase in divorce. It is possible also that husbands and wives, realizing that both will survive into the older ages, are more prone to seek divorce if they find their marriages unsatisfactory.

Migration

While it was the Industrial Revolution that produced the technology and, indeed, the need for high rates of mobility within societies, the shifts in mortality and fertility rates also contributed to increasing rates of migration within and between societies.

The shifts from high to low death and birth rates caused population to increase. These high rates of growth were the result of the differential timing of the changes in the death and birth rates. As a general pattern, death rates declined more rapidly than birth rates. As long as fertility remained high, the declines in mortality meant that the numbers being born were increasingly surviving to older ages.

The pressure of the increasing numbers in rural areas tended to push many young people off the land. Moreover, the attractiveness of new opportunities produced by industrialization drew the surplus rural populations to urban centers. Also, for Europeans in the eighteenth and nineteenth centuries, there was the possibility of migrating overseas to the empty lands of the New World.

Although men moved longer distances than women, the rates of mobility among women during the early stages of the Industrial Revolution were probably almost as high as among men. This was probably more true for the working classes than for the upper classes. Certainly, the high rates of employment of women in factories in the nineteenth century testify to this. If women were to work, however, they had to work outside the home, removed from the protection of their husbands and kinsmen. Indeed, it was probably these high rates of female employment in the new industrial establishments that contributed to legislation designed to protect employed females.

Although the relationship between high rates of migration and low fertility has yet to be firmly established, a number of students have speculated that smaller family size probably contributed to the ease of movement of families (cf. Kiser, Grabill, and Campbell 1968). Migration most likely also had certain implications for the familial relations of both men and women. Although both sexes no longer resided in a community surrounded by their relatives, the isolation from one's relatives was probably felt more deeply by women. No longer could women share their household and child-care problems with other relatives. Hence, more and more they had to turn to their husbands for adult companionship and emotional support.

Changes in Age and Sex Composition

Changes in the rates of births, deaths, and migration produce changes in the age and sex composition of a population. One consequence of these shifts, often overlooked, was the increased task of child rearing and child care women experienced in the early stages of the demographic transition. Because increasing proportions of infants and children were surviving, the number of children women had to rear increased, and this increase in the child-rearing tasks occurred when fathers were increasingly working away from home. As long as fertility remained high and increasing numbers of babies survived, women, no doubt, found themselves more confined to their homes. Consequently, they were less able to take advantage of the economic and social opportunities that the Industrial Revolution afforded. Only when fertility was reduced could women begin to resume an economic and social role in society.

Another consequence of changes in population structure is the phenomenon popularly referred to as the "marriage squeeze" (Akers 1961). Declines in mortality, increases in fertility, or changes in the rate of migration tend to create an imbalance between the sexes in the prime ages of marriages. Declines in mortality over a period of years, while fertility remains fairly high and stable, result in successive increases in the number of males and females surviving to marriageable ages. Since women in most societies marry men somewhat older than themselves, declines in mortality tend to produce an excess of women in the marriageable ages, the supply of potential husbands having been born in a period of higher mortality.

Likewise, an increase in the rate of male emigration from an area may create an excess of females of marriageable age. Since the rates of male migration are particularly high when men are in their late teens and early twenties, the supply of potential husbands may be considerably reduced.

Both of these phenomena—declining mortality and high rates of male emigration—were experienced by many of the industrializing countries in the West during the nineteenth century. It is not suprising, therefore, to find census data of Great Britain for the period from 1851 to 1901 indicating a surplus of women in the marriageable ages. For this period, sex ratios[9] within the marriageable ages were typically 90 or below.

It appears that in Great Britain the major accommodation to the deficit of marriageable males was an increase in the proportion of women who remained single. For example, between 1851 and 1901, the proportions of single women in Great Britain increased from 14 to 17 percent. In Sweden, between 1800 and 1910, the proportions of single women aged 45–49 rose from 12 to 22 percent. The United States during the nineteenth century had a high sex ratio as a result of heavy male immigration. Such older settled areas as New England, however, apparently suffered a shortage of males in the marriageable ages as a result of migration to the West and thus exhibited a high rate of spinsterhood.

An increase in fertility may also contribute to a marriage squeeze. Currently, the United States appears to be experiencing this phenomenon. The number of males in the marriageable ages has been decreasing as a result of the upturn in fertility that began in the late 1930s. Births continued to rise until 1947 and remained at a high level for the next decade. Whereas in 1950 the sex ratio in the prime marriage ages was 104.2, by 1956 it had dropped to 97.1, and by 1962 the sex ratio had further decreased to 85.0. By 1970, it had recovered somewhat and was 97. Not until the late 1970s, however, will the number of males exceed the number of females, as a result of the declines in fertility that began in 1957 (Goldberg 1965). The slight increase in age at marriage for females that has occurred since the late 1950s in the United States probably reflects the increased difficulty of females in finding marital partners of the suitable ages.[10] Whether or not the current marriage squeeze will result in an increase in the proportion of females remaining single in the United States remains to be seen.

The increases in the proportion of women remaining single as a result of the marriage squeeze during the nineteenth century in industrializing countries held certain implications for the roles and status of women. No longer was it certain that all girls would eventually marry. Hence, parents had to find a means of support for their daughters as well as their sons. For wealthy parents, this could be secured by ensuring the inheritance rights of their daughters. For middle-class parents, the solution lay in providing an adequate education for their daughters, to enable them to earn a living. Thus, not only were changes in laws pertaining to property rights of women enacted but an increasing concern with the education of females was voiced as the nineteenth century progressed (Klein 1965).[11] For daughters of the working class, the need was simply to work. That they found work in the factories of the expanding industrial economy is not suprising.

Increasingly, therefore, many women entered marriage with some education and some working experience. By the early part of the twentieth century, the pattern of young single women working until marriage appears to have become firmly established. Yet, it still was not accepted for married women to work after marriage. Many women, having tasted a certain amount of independence, must have found it difficult to adjust to the dependent role of wife. Thus, another element of strain in the marital relationship was introduced (Myrdal, *op. cit.*). Since the marital role itself had become less demanding, particularly in terms of childbearing, it is not suprising that women developed feelings of uselessness, felt a loss of self-esteem, and began demanding an improvement in their status. That the movement for the emancipation of women found fertile ground among the better-educated middle-class women who were restricting their family size is, therefore, not unexpected (Klein, *op. cit.*).

The Effects of Future Demographic Change

The examination of past demographic changes has indicated a number of consequences for the roles and status of women. What may be expected in the future? Here we may only speculate—although certain past trends surely will continue. Among these trends have been the increased participation of women in the economic life of societies, the intensification and increased importance of the personal relationship between husbands and wives, and the concomitant equalizing of status between the sexes. The almost exclusive assumption by males of the economic role in industrialized societies surely must be regarded as a transitional phase. Indeed, as Myrdal (*op. cit.*) pointed out, when viewed from the long perspective of history, there is nothing "normal" in such a pattern.

As more and more women resume an economic role in society, their status will eventually no longer depend on that of their husbands. Consequently, their positions in society will be judged on the basis of their occupational role. In the transitional period, however, it is probable that the rates of divorce will continue to climb, partly because of this increased independence of women. Assuredly, the structure and functions of the family will continue to change. Whether the family as we know it today will completely disappear remains to be seen. Certainly, the trend is in the direction of relationships between husbands and wives becoming more egalitarian.

Demographic changes in the future will also have an effect on the roles and status of women. Increasingly, concern is being voiced over the high rates of growth of the world's population. The eventual achievement of stability in population numbers, popularly referred to as "zero population growth," is viewed as an absolute necessity. In fact, it has been pointed out that the increase in numbers has reached a "climax" and "that a change in trend probably in this century, is inevitable" (Davis 1970).

Human societies have already attained the means of effectively controlling mortality. As current scientific and technological knowledge is applied in more and more societies, every individual will increasingly live out what is regarded as the normal life span.[12] Whether life can be extended beyond the upper limits already achieved is an open question. To do so would require major scientific breakthroughs in conquering the degenerative diseases of old age. For this reason, attention is not directed to this possible source of future demographic change. Rather, attention is focused on implications of two other imminent scientific discoveries. These are, first, the development of a perfect contraceptive technique and, second, the possibility of couples being able to predetermine the sex of their children.

The Perfect Contraceptive[13]

The most immediate consequence of the availability of perfect contraception for women would be that they would have only the number of children they want. If it may also be assumed that all illegitimate births are unwanted, one implication of perfect contraception would be the disappearance of illegitimacy. Even in the United States, where most couples do attempt to control their fertility, approximately one-fifth of all births in the period 1960–65 have been estimated to be unwanted. Moreover, it is estimated that fully two-fifths of wanted births would have occurred at another time if the women had been successful in controlling the timing of the births (Bumpass and Westoff 1970). Accordingly, the availability of a perfect contraceptive suggests a decline in family size as well as a change in the spacing of births.

Another probable consequence might be the reduction of premarital conceptions. For the period 1964–66 in the United States, 22 percent of first births occurred to women married less than eight months (U.S., Department of Health, Education, and Welfare, 1970). If many of these births are actually premarital conceptions, such conceptions are undoubtedly a factor in determining the timing of marriage. This suggests that another consequence of perfect contraception may be an increase in age at marriage.

Data from a number of studies indicate that one consequence of a premarital pregnancy for a woman is the discontinuance of her education (U.S., Department of Labor, 1966). Since the attainment of education is so crucial in achieving occupational success, its interruption or termination as a result of pregnancy most likely has a number of deleterious effects on a woman's eventual status in nonfamilial roles (Presser 1971). Moreover, early first births have been shown to affect the woman's role in decision making within the family. The longer a first birth is delayed, the more the wife participates in familial decision making (Campbell 1970).

At a more general level, it has been suggested that the delay of any birth permits a woman to acquire nonfamilial roles that may be incompatible with having a child in the future. Accordingly, the eventual result of postponing a birth may mean its postponement forever (Bumpass and Westoff, op. cit.).

The availability of a perfect contraceptive technique, however, does not necessarily imply that all women would utilize it. Nor does its availability imply that women would resort to its use for purposes of restricting their fertility. Most American couples have been reported to want a family size of 2 to 4 children (Ryder 1969). In a recent survey, wives fourteen to twenty-four years of age reported expecting an average of approximately 2.9 children (U.S., Department of Commerce, 1971). This is still well above the number of children necessary for simple population replacement (U.S., Department of Commerce, *op. cit.*). One suggestion is that governmental policies be developed to give women meaningful role alternatives to those of wife and mother (Blake 1969). The need is to reconcile the differences between the reproductive needs of society and the roles of women in society.

The Predetermination of the Sex of Children

In regard to couples being able to choose the sex of their children, the probable demographic and social consequences for women depend, first of all, on the preferred sex composition of their families. Evidence for industrialized societies indicates that the vast majority of couples want children of both sexes (Freedman, Freedman, and Whelpton 1960). On the other hand, data for developing countries, particularly non-Western cultures, indicate a strong preference for males (Pohlman 1967). It is possible, however, that as such countries industrialize, preferences will shift to a desire for children of each sex. Freedman, Freedman, and Whelpton (*op. cit.*) have argued that the preference for one sex over the other has diminished, since the economic importance of sons is no longer a relevant consideration in industrialized societies. Currently, however, the desire for at least one son appears to be a universal one.

A number of students, in noting this strong desire for male children, have attempted to estimate what the effects on the sex ratio would be if a method for predetermining the sex of a child were available. Etzioni (1968) estimates that the sex ratio would rise to 121, indicating that a serious imbalance between the sexes would eventually result. The shortage of females, he has speculated, would produce an increase in the proportion of males remaining single, an increase in the age at marriage for males, as well as an increase in prostitution and homosexuality. The likely effects on women, however, are not touched upon.

The situation of a surplus of males would, of course, be the exact opposite of the marriage squeeze phenomenon previously discussed. As suggested, the effect in the past of a surplus of females was probably to raise women's status, since many women had to seek their satisfactions outside the family. One could, of course, argue that a deficit of females in a society would lead to the attainment of a higher status, since their relative scarcity would increase their value. Nevertheless, it appears more reasonable to suggest that females would marry at earlier ages and, therefore, be cut off from the opportunities of developing the skills necessary for their participation in the economic and social life of societies.

Alternatively, if one assumes that most couples would choose to have only one or two children if they could determine the sex, sex predetermination could perhaps contribute to greater equality between the sexes. A number of studies have indicated that preference regarding the sex of children, although minor, has a significant effect on eventual family size (cf. Ridley and Kiser 1951, and Freedman, Freedman, and Whelpton, *op. cit.*). Consequently, the childbearing period must be restricted to even a shorter period of time, and thus women would be freer to pursue nonfamilial roles on a more continuous basis.

Zero Population Growth

As yet, no large population for any relatively long period of time has attained a rate of population growth that is zero or has experienced a decrease in numbers. For a population to cease growing under conditions of low mortality, the average number of children per couple must be reduced to approximately two (U.S., Department of Commerce, *op. cit.*). Hence, the attainment of zero growth would have to be coupled with the desire for a relatively small family.

There are many different paths that a population might take toward achieving such a goal. Many women could remain unmarried and presumably childless. Alternatively, substantial numbers of married women could choose to remain childless or have no more than two children.[14] Indeed, the variability in family size could be very great even in a society in which stability in numbers obtains. One may, in fact, visualize a society in which a minority of women specialize in childbearing[15] and child rearing, with the vast majority of women participating like men throughout their adult lives in economic activities. Mead (1967), in discussing such possibilities, suggests that one consequence would be that most individuals in a society "would be free to function—for the first time in history—as individuals."

Another aspect of zero population growth, not fully appreciated, is the inevitable need for women to participate more fully in economic activities than they do at present. This requirement arises from the fact that a population with zero growth is a fairly old population. Such a population under conditions of low mortality has as many people over 60 as under 15 and a median age of approximately 37 years (Coale 1968). While such a population will not place a premium on youth, as is currently done, it is improbable that such a society could cease to depend on its young as a source of new ideas. Since the proportion of young adults would be smaller than at present, society would have to create the means whereby the childbearing and child-rearing functions of women were eased to a greater extent than they are at present.

Moreover, in the transition to a stationary population, a society will be faced with a gradually smaller proportion of its population in the younger, economically productive ages of fifteen to thirty. Thus, society could ill afford the luxury of underutilizing females at these ages. Fortunately, with the lower fertility required, more women would be available for participation in the work force. It is possible, also, that the trends toward shorter work days, shorter work weeks, as well as early retirement, might well necessitate the increased employment of women.

Accordingly, child care in most societies will become more rationalized. Indeed, the current discussion of the need for increased child-care facilities in the United States points in this direction, as does the trend toward the provision of more such facilities in other industrialized countries. If child care at the earliest ages is provided for outside the family, it is probable that the lives of men and women will become more similar.[16]

Conclusions

This paper has attempted to explore some of the implications of demographic change for the roles and status of women. A number of effects of past changes have been noted; a few implications of possible future changes have been suggested. The probable consequences of social and economic changes have, however, been neglected. Certainly, social and economic changes will inhibit or facilitate many of the possible demographic effects discussed. Nevertheless, changes in the roles of both men and women appear inevitable. Indeed, the future demographic changes involved in the achievement of a zero rate of population growth suggest that societies will be required to redefine the roles and status of both women and men.

Notes

1. This discussion is based largely on a previous paper by the author (Ridley 1968).
2. Recently, this view has been succinctly argued by O'Neil (1969) on the basis of the work of the French historical demographer, Ariès (1962). The work of Demos (1970) and Greven (1966) also supports this view for colonial America. Previously, Myrdal (1941) had cogently made this point.
3. Parsons (1942), in his now classic paper in which he discusses the types of female roles to American women, identifies this lack of an independent occupational status on the part of American women as an important source of strain and stress in the relationships between the sexes in the United States.
4. A large number of factors have been identified by demographers and sociologists as contributing to the decline of fertility (cf. Freedman 1961, Ryder 1967, and Coale 1969).
5. Life expectancy at birth is the average (mean) number of years lived by a population, assuming that age-specific death rates remain constant.
6. In making these estimates, it has been assumed that marriages are not broken by divorce.
7. This statement is true only in the extent that abortion is not relied on as the principal means of fertility control.
8. The slight increase in the age at which women born in 1920–29 had their first birth probably reflects the fact that many of these women were separated from their husbands during World War II. At that time, these women were in their early twenties.
9. The sex ratio is defined as the number of males per 100 females.
10. It should be recognized that even with a serious disproportion between the sexes, most women may eventually marry. First, they may simply delay marriage and eventually marry men who have become widowed or divorced. Secondly, women may elect to marry men closer to their own age or even younger. Hence the average age differential beteewn spouses will decline. For a detailed discussion, see Hajnal (1965).
11. It should be recognized that there were other very cogent reasons for educating females in industrializing societies. As indicated, women had to assume almost completely the tasks of child rearing and home management. Since, clearly, sons had to be educated, illiterate mothers could hardly be expected to train

their sons properly. Increasingly, also, consumption within the home depended on a market economy—an illiterate housewife could not be expected to obtain the necessary provisions for the home. In addition, the trend toward companionate marriages probably had some effect. Moreover, it must be remembered that education until the Industrial Revolution was confined almost exclusively to a tiny minority of a population, namely, the upper class. Only with the advent of industrialization was it necessary for education to be extended to the lower classes. Prior to industrialization, whether or not one was educated depended more upon an individual's social-class position than upon the individual's sex.

12. There have been very few well-documented instances of individuals living much beyond one hundred years. Indeed, the decreases in mortality have been primarily concentrated in the younger ages. For further discussion, see Petersen (1969).

13. For a recent review of the status of work in the development of better contraceptive techniques, see Segal and Tietze (1969).

14. Nor should the possibility of test-tube babies be overlooked. Such a development, of course, would completely remove the reproductive function from women.

15. Such a pattern's genetic implications for a population, however, might be quite serious.

16. The view adopted here is that one consequence of zero population growth is that women may experience an improvement in their position. Nevertheless, there are a number of other social and economic consequences that are likely to be viewed as undesirable. For detailed discussions, see Coale (1968) and Notestein (1970).

References

AKERS, DONALD S. "On Measuring the Marriage Squeeze." *Demography* 4 (1961): 907–924.

ARIÈS, PHILIPPE. *Centuries of Childhood: A Social History of Family Life.* New York: Random House, Vintage, 1962.

BLAKE, JUDITH. "Population Policy for Americans: Is the Government Being Misled?" *Science* 164 (1969): 522–529.

BOGUE, DONALD J. *The Population of the United States.* Glencoe, Ill.: The Free Press, 1959.

BUMPASS, LARRY, and WESTOFF, CHARLES F. "The 'Perfect Contraceptive' Population." *Science* 169 (1970): 1177–1182.

CAMPBELL, FREDERICK L. "Family Growth and Variation in Family Role Structure." *Journal of Marriage and Family* 32 (1970): 45–53.

COALE, ANSLEY J. "Should the United States Start a Campaign for Fewer Births?" *Population Index* 34 (1968): 467–474.

———. "The Decline in Fertility in Europe from the French Revolution to World War II." In *Fertility and Family Planning*, edited by S. J. Behrman, Leslie Corsa, Jr., and Ronald Freedman. Ann Arbor: University of Michigan Press, 1969.

DAVIS, KINGSLEY. "The World Demographic Transition." *Annals of the American Academy of Political and Social Science*, vol. 237 (January 1945), pp. 1–11.

———. "Statistical Perspective on Marriage and Divorce." *Annals of the American Academy of Political and Social Science* 272 (November 1950), pp. 9–21.

———. "The Climax of Population Growth: Past and Future Perspective." *California Medicine: The Western Journal of Medicine* 113 (1970): 33–39.

DAY, LINCOLN H. "Age of Women at Completion of Childbearing." *Public Health Reports* 73 (1958): 525–532.

DEMOS, JOHN. *The Little Commonwealth: Family Life in Plymouth Colony.* New York: Oxford University Press, 1970.

DUBLIN, LOUIS I.; LOTKA, ALFRED J.; and SPIEGELMAN, MORTIMER. *Length of Life: A Study of the Life Table.* Rev. ed. New York: Ronald, 1949.

ETZIONI, AMITAI. "Sex Control, Science, and Society." *Science* 161 (1968): 1107–1112.

FREEDMAN, DEBORAH S.; FREEDMAN, RONALD; and WHELPTON, PASCAL K. "Size of Family and Preference for Children of Each Sex." *American Journal of Sociology* 66 (1960): 141–146.

FREEDMAN, RONALD. "The Sociology of Human Fertility." *Current Sociology* 10/11 (1961): 53–57.

GLASS, D. V. "Introduction." In *Population in History: Essays in Historical Demography*, edited by D. V. Glass and D. E. C. Eversley. London: Edward Arnold, 1965.

GLICK, PAUL C., and PARKE, ROBERT, JR. "New Approaches in Studying the Life Cycle of the Family." *Demography* 2 (1965): 187–202.

GOLDBERG, DAVID. "Fertility and Fertility Differentials: Some Observations on Recent Changes in the United States." In *Public Health and Population Change: Current Research Issues*, edited by Mindel C. Sheps and Jeanne Clare Ridley. Pittsburgh: University of Pittsburgh Press, 1965.

GREVEN, PHILIP J., JR. "Family Structure in Seventeenth-Century Andover, Massachusetts." *William and Mary Quarterly*, 3rd ser. 23 (1966): 234–256.

HAJNAL, J. "European Marriage Patterns in Perspective." In *Population in History: Essays in Historical Demography*, edited by Glass and Eversley. London: Edward Arnold, 1965.

KISER, CLYDE V.; GRABILL, WILSON H.; and CAMPBELL, ARTHUR A. *Trends and Variations in Fertility in the United States*. Cambridge, Mass.: Harvard University Press, 1968.

KLEIN, VIOLA. *Britain's Married Women Workers*. London: Routledge and Kegan Paul, 1965.

MEAD, MARGARET. "The Life Cycle and Its Variations: The Division of Roles." *Daedalus* 96 (1967): 871–875.

MYRDAL, ALVA. *Nation and Family: The Swedish Experiment in Democratic Family and Population Policy*. 1941. Reprint. Cambridge, Mass.: M.I.T. Press, 1968.

MYRDAL, ALVA, and KLEIN, VIOLA. *Women's Two Roles*. London: Routledge and Kegan Paul, 1956.

NOTESTEIN, FRANK. "Zero Population Growth: What Is It?" *Family Planning Perspectives* 2 (1970): 20–23.

O'NEIL, WILLIAM L. *The Woman Movement: Feminism in the United States and England*. New York: Barnes & Noble, 1969.

PARSONS, TALCOTT. "Age and Sex in the Social Structure of the United States." *American Sociological Review* 7 (1942): 604–616.

PETERSEN, WILLIAM. *Population*. New York: The Macmillan Company, 1969.

POHLMAN, EDWARD. "Some Effects of Being Able to Control Sex of Offspring." *Eugenics Quarterly* 14 (1967): 274–281.

PRESSER, HARRIET B. "The Timing of the First Birth, Female Roles and Black Fertility." *Milbank Memorial Fund Quarterly*, in press.

RIDLEY, JEANNE E. CLARE, and KISER, CLYDE V. "Preference of Children of a Given Sex in Relation to Fertility." *Milbank Memorial Fund Quarterly* 29 (1951): 440–492.

RIDLEY, JEANNE CLARE. "Demographic Change and the Roles and Status of Women." *Annals of the American Academy of Political and Social Science* 375 (1968): 15–25.

RYDER, NORMAN B. "The Character of Modern Fertility." *Annals of the American Academy of Political and Social Science* 369 (1967): 26–36.

———. "The Time Series of Fertility in the United States," forthcoming in the proceedings of the London meetings of the International Union for the Scientific Study of Population, 1969.

SEGAL, SHELDON J., and TIETZE, CHRISTOPHER. *Contraceptive Technology: Current and Prospective Methods*. Reports on Population. Family Planning, 1969.

TAEUBER, CONRAD, and TAEUBER, IRENE B. *The Changing Population of the United States*. New York: John Wiley & Sons, 1958.

TAEUBER, IRENE B. "Change and Transition in Family Structures." In *The Family in Transition*, edited by Arthur A. Campbell. Washington, D.C.: National Institutes of Health, 1971.

UNITED NATIONS. *Demographic Yearbook, 1967.* New York: United Nations Publications, 1968.

———. *Demographic Yearbook, 1969.* New York: United Nations Publications, 1970.

U.S., DEPARTMENT OF COMMERCE, BUREAU OF THE CENSUS. *Previous and Prospective Fertility: 1967.* Current Population Reports P-20, no. 211. Washington, D.C.: Government Printing Office, 1971.

U.S., DEPARTMENT OF HEALTH, EDUCATION, and WELFARE. *Vital Statistics of the United States, 1965,* vol. 11, sec. 5, Life Tables. Washington, D.C.: Government Printing Office, 1967.

———. *Interval between First Marriage and Legitimate First Birth, United States, 1964–66.* Monthly Vital Statistics Report 18, no. 12. Maryland: National Center for Health Statistics, 1970.

U.S., DEPARTMENT OF LABOR. *1965 Handbook on Women Workers.* Washington, D.C.: Government Printing Office, 1966.

Discussion

Regardless of a number of arguments and counterarguments about the "soundness" of the Women's Liberation Movement in America, about the nature of the steps that must be taken in the future in order for it to become a full-fledged social movement, and about the likely future of men and women and the family, some facts are of great significance and should not be overlooked.

First, a women's liberation movement does exist, and every man and woman, whether he or she agrees or disagrees totally or partially with its main ideological tenets or action targets, is aware of its existence, at least to some extent influenced by it, and somehow reacting to it (positively or negatively).

Second, the existence of "Women's Lib" in its present form has, mostly indirectly, brought about several important changes in the nature of the relationships between women, and between men and women. Some of these changes have not and most probably cannot be empirically proven, but most introspective men and women who have experienced them can easily pinpoint them. One of these changes is that women now can openly discuss and/or complain about inequalities they perceive in the way they are treated as workers, friends, colleagues, or even spouses without being ridiculed, ignored, or even implicitly or explicitly punished for their "aggressive" and inappropriate behavior. Instead, they are now listened to with some attention, and even when vigorous denials of the existence of any kind of discrimination are made, some modification of previous behavior or situation usually occurs, probably partly because of guilt feelings and partly because of fear of some type of organized, collective resistance or protest on the part of women who feel they have been similarly discriminated against. More women are now protesting perceived sexist discrimination publicly or privately, probably because of their own higher level of achieved awareness, but also because of the greater social acceptability of such protests, thanks to the fact that such complaints have become quite frequent, and also because of the effectiveness of such protests, which often bring tangible and satisfactory results. This change comes about as women increasingly reject the "axiom" that women are the inferior sex and that passivity is their "natural" and "feminine" characteristic. Such a change can be all-pervasive if it spreads to all types of man-woman relationships, since it could probably for the first time in history lead to a widespread truly equalitarian and companionate relationship of men and women as employers-employees, colleagues, friends, lovers, and spouses. For it is sometimes forgotten that a range of richly rewarding relationships between men and women as friends has been totally lost as a human experience because for too long men have thought of women as inferior beings not to be considered as friends. Thus, if a woman does not qualify as (or refuses to be) a girl friend or a mistress, she is to be discarded.

The relationships between men and women have to some extent changed in yet another way. Those men who were always totally or partially "liberated" about sex roles feel for the first time free to express their real feelings, thoughts, and ideas and to behave vis-à-vis women as they had always wanted to. Previously they had been inhibited and constrained because their behavior was considered "deviant," but now they can be themselves without being labeled "deviants," and they can be considered innovators and admired, at least in some intellectual circles. Partially because some men have, as a result of discussions in mass media as well as informal discussions among friends, become more sensitized to the different sex-role issues and partially because such an introspection does constitute a new trend, many more men than ever before tend to analyze their behavior, motives, feelings, and beliefs. A few go one step further in that their behavior is affected by their introspection and even fewer men go many steps further in that they actively participate in or organize men's liberation "rap sessions" and groups. Although in terms of numbers not too many men have became "liberated," those who always were freely admit it and even may feel proud for being what they are, and a considerable number of men have started to more or less question many of the "facts," beliefs that they had in the past taken for granted.

Another very important change has affected woman-to-woman relationships, in that women are now freer and are capable of initiating and maintaining true friendships with other women, rather than "limited-risk" associations that dissolve when common interests arise regarding a man. Of course, some maintain that women have always had certain deep and rewarding friendships with other women but have not wanted to admit their existence (or their rewarding nature) in order not to displease, or insult the egos of, the men they loved.[1] If this is true, then women for the first time feel free to admit that their friendship with some woman (or women) is as rewarding or sometimes even more so than their marriage or their love affair. Furthermore, for the first time, successful women in any field, instead of being hostile, uncooperative, or simply neutral toward younger women who are just starting in their field, are showing a cooperative, supportive attitude and are even starting actively to "sponsor" younger women in the manner that men have traditionally used to help other men move up in their respective fields. As a recent study of women executives clearly showed, those who had made it to the top suffered from the "Queen Bee complex," in that they could not bring themselves to assist and train women to replace them, so that each woman had to start her own struggle without any help from the men or the women at the top.[2] This kind of antagonistic attitude from women at the top of any type of occupation, which can be interpreted as a sharing of the values of the male establishment in order to achieve complete male acceptance and recognition, has been experienced by most (if not all) young women. And these are the same young women who are suddenly pleasantly surprised to experience a change of attitudes and to receive the support of established women.

Of course, there have also been more tangible changes as a direct result of the Women's Liberation Movement, but many of these tangible changes may be of less importance than the more diffuse changes just described. Such tangible results may be the greater effort on the part of many college departments and universities to recruit women, often at the continuous insistence of female graduate students; the election of women to executive bodies of professional associations (such as the recent election of women to positions on the executive council of the American Sociological Association); and the withholding of new contracts by the Department of Health, Education, and Welfare from colleges and universities against which complaints of sex discrimination have been lodged by the Women's Equity Action League.[3]

But where is the Women's Liberation Movement going? How is it going to progress and develop? Some social scientists who have analyzed the movement maintain that it cannot progress very far unless it enlists the active support of some men who are convinced that their own "liberation" as well as that of women will entail important benefits for both groups. The point has been made that since some of the worst enemies of women can be found among women, the active support of some men is necessary in order for the movement to represent a considerable portion of the population and to gain in power.[4] It is true that some of the militant members of antiliberation panels on television have been housewives, and there are some active groups of antifeminist women such as the Pussycats. It is also true that, increasingly, some men (as this becomes more socially acceptable) become more supportive of the movement as well as its goals or create separate men's liberation groups or joint liberation groups.

One question that can be raised at this point is, If "liberation" is an undoubted benefit for all women, why are some women so strongly opposed to it? The explanation may involve several different issues. First, "liberation" entails rights as well as a set of new and specific obligations for women, obligations that require women to give up some of the leisure and all the irresponsibility that they may have been enjoying up to now. These women are not willing to exchange their freedom from responsibilities and their leisure for equal status in the society or for any kind of rights. Second, these women, by voicing their antiliberation attitudes, hope to and probably do, gain by reassuring many of the threatened, traditional males (probably including their boyfriends or husbands).[5]

Actually it is interesting to note as other people have, that for at least some women actively involved in the Women's Liberation Movement the temptation may be great to use the movement for personal rather than collective advancement.[6] But up to now women have usually tried to combine the two objectives, and if anything have placed more emphasis upon collective advancement.

The eventual success of the Women's Liberation Movement will be measured not by the extent to which it has secured legal guarantees of equality but rather by the extent to which it has helped change the values and attitudes of men and women, so that they do consider and treat each other as equals. However, some laws are still crucial and must be passed, such as those pertaining to abortion at the demand of women (with the expenses covered by all standard health insurance plans), those pertaining to alimony and child support, as well as laws concerning child-care facilities. The alimony in the case of demonstrably unskilled women could take the form of a training grant that lasts only as long as is required for the woman to be trained for some kind of job.[7] And child support could be explicitly defined by law as a joint economic and psychological responsibility of both parents. The first policy (regarding alimony) would turn a number of men who presently oppose the Women's Liberation Movement into militant supporters, and the second (regarding child support) could probably lead to a greater reduction of the actual birth rate than all family planning programs have ever achieved. Finally, the establishment of sufficient child-care centers where children are taken care of throughout the day (even when ill) beginning a few weeks after birth could free those women who stay at home only because they have no one to take care of their children.

The change in the values and attitudes of men and women cannot be insured through laws. One requirement of a true state of equality between the sexes is the institutionalization of inequality on the basis of *merit* rather than *sex*, so that it is not only possible but socially acceptable for a woman (as well as for a man) to be superior to a group of men and women, on the basis of her (his) achievements and qualifications.

Attempts to change the values subscribed to by women are being made at present through consciousness-raising groups and their "rap" sessions.[8] But beyond this, all agents and media of socialization must be tapped if a definite and significant change is to come about. Thus, parents must be influenced through the messages of the different types of mass media, especially television, and through parent education courses. Parents-to-be and young people must be reached through the messages they receive from the all too popular family courses at the high school and college level and through vocational guidance counselors at both levels. For example, some committee or group within the Women's Liberation Movement in collaboration with some of the "liberated" women sociologists could go through all family textbooks and recommend only those which treat women and sex roles in a nondiscriminatory fashion. They could ask the relevant official professional bodies to approve only the selected family textbooks, while the other ones (which at present represent the majority) would have to be either withdrawn or rewritten by the authors. And, of course, with pressure from the publishers, family textbooks would be appropriately rewritten.

In another vein, women (especially white middle-class college-educated women), who are reputed to be the preferred and most frequent clientele of psychiatrists, could have a more efficient and unbiased treatment for whatever mental health problems they are afflicted with if psychiatry in the United States would accept the premise that the desire to work and achieve does not signify a rejection of femininity and motherhood and that the occasional marital difficulties ensuing stem out of the husband's unwillingness or inability to make the required modifications and redefinitions of sex roles.[9] In this case, as in many others, women as consumers (clients) could exert great influence, bringing to bear a social pressure that would facilitate a faster change of values and orientations and thus ameliorate the quality of service they receive.

Finally, several analysts of the Women's Liberation Movement, including Kyriakos M. Kontopoulos, whose article appears in this chapter, feel that it has failed to involve and attract working- and lower-class women as well as black women and that, therefore, it essentially is a movement of and for white middle-class well-educated women, who will benefit the most from the movement's success.[10] But it is not easy to distinguish the extent to which the movement in its present form is not attracting women in lower social classes or black women, and the extent to which the women in other social classes and black women are not interested in becoming "liberated." The black Muslims, for example, advocate the return of black women to their homes and their withdrawal from the labor force, since their active participation has caused the "disintegration" of the black family. Interestingly enough, some of the white myths about the black family seem to have influenced some of the militant black ideologies, probably because both stem from the traditional, male point of view.[11]

But let us suppose that the Women's Liberation Movement does succeed to a considerable extent: What will the "new" men and women be like? Before attempting to answer this question, we must come back to Alice S. Rossi's article in this chapter concerning models of sex equality. Most probably the second alternative, the "assimilation model of equality," will be at first adopted by society and the present male-dominated establishment because it tends to place most of the burden on women, who must follow the desirable present model created by men. But as the enactment of this type of equality spreads more and more, it will become evident that it is quite strenuous for spouses to live together while both share high achievement and productivity norms and have to battle continuously against time.[12] And then, the third choice, the "hybrid model of equality," will be slowly adopted after many significant changes have taken place in the occupational structure (for both men and women) and in other areas of the total social structure.[13]

But to come back to the original question: What will the "new" men and women be like? I would predict (and hope) that the "new liberated" men and women would be able to develop their potentialities and inclinations freely, without sex-related restrictions, and would have, therefore, a greater probability of becoming fulfilled and happy people. Their sexual and economic emancipation may enable them to relate to each other openly, honestly, without hypocrisy or false modesty, and without trying to dupe each other. Liberated women would not use "feminine" ruses anymore to get a man to marry them or "tie" a man down with additional familial responsibilities. Thus, women would not intentionally "forget" to take contraceptive pills in order to become pregnant before or after marriage, and they would not tolerate conventional, "empty shell" marriages that restrict their own freedom and chance for happiness as well as that of their husbands. "Liberated" men would be able to enjoy a great range of relationships with women, including sexual, intellectual, marital, or friendship relationships, and thus their lives might become more enriched with both variety and depth. And they would no longer feel that they have the sole economic and psychological responsibility for their families but rather that such responsibility as well as rights, household and family duties, and routine work was to be shared with their companions. In this way, marriage may come to represent a real and free commitment of men and women, a true companionate, an equally shared venture, and parenthood may come to be a responsible and shared experience.

But would the possible transition in the man-woman relationship from convention and permanency to sentiment and free choice of commitment lead to briefer and more insecure relationships? And would this fluidity in relationships tend to bring about serious maladjustments, or would men and women manage to adjust to a style or relating to one another that may be closer to their "natural" polygamous inclinations? If this sounds like a "Brave New World," it is because men and women will have to grope their way forward and be brave in order to achieve this new type of life, which will be both more difficult and more rewarding.

Notes

1. Jessamyn West, "On Friendship Between Women," *Holiday*, vol. 35 (March 1964), pp. 13–17.
2. Margaret Henning, "Career Development for Women Executives" (Ph.D. diss., Harvard Graduate School of Business Administration, 1971), as reported by *New York Times*, February 23, 1971.
3. "Sex Discrimination: Campuses Face Contract Loss over HEW Demands," *Science*, vol. 170 (November 20, 1970), pp. 834–835.
4. Jacques Dofny, "The Future of Women's Liberation as a Social Movement" Department of Sociology, University of Montreal, 1970 (Unpublished manuscript).
5. *Ibid.*
6. *Ibid.*
7. Barbara Bovee Polk (author of one article and coauthor of another article in this volume and an active member of the Women's Liberation Movement in Detroit and Michigan) suggested in a private conversation with the author that the husband's life insurance should also provide the wife with training grants and child support only during training, if she demonstrably has no self-supporting skills.
8. For a lively description of such a "rap" session, see Vivian Gornick, "Consciousness," *New York Times Magazine*, January 10, 1971, pp. 22–23, 77–82.
9. There is some evidence that psychiatrists in the more "liberated" countries have gone through this transition, since they tend to interpret marital difficulties as stemming from the husband's inability to accept the new role conceptions rather than from the woman's rejection of her maternal role, as many American psychiatrists would be inclined to do. See J. Knoblochova and F. Knobloch, "Family Psychotherapy," Public Health Paper no. 28 (Geneva: W. H. O. 1965); T. Lidz, *The Person* (New York: Basic Books, 1968).
10. Dofny, *op. cit.*; Gerda Lerner, "The Feminists: A Second Look," *Columbia Forum*, vol. 13, no. 3 (Fall 1970), pp. 24–30; Linda J. M. La Rue, "Black Liberation and Women's Lib," *Trans-Action*, vol. 8, no. 1/2 (November–December 1970), pp. 59–64.
11. Mary Ann Weathers, "An Argument for Black Women's Liberation as a Revolutionary Force," *No More Fun and Games*, no. 2 (February 1969), pp. 66–70.
12. See Rhona Rapoport and Robert N. Rapoport, "The Dual-Career Family: A Variant Pattern and Social Change," in Chapter 5 of this volume.
13. Jessie Bernard, "Changing Family Lifestyles: One Role, Two Roles, Shared Roles," *Issues in Industrial Society*, vol. 2, no. 1 (1971).

Biographical Notes

JESSIE BERNARD, Ph.D., is an Emeritus Professor of Sociology and one of the most productive and original family sociologists. Some of her outstanding books have been *Academic Women* (winner of the Pennsylvania State University Press award for the best manuscript in 1964); *Remarriage, a Study of Marriage* (reissued in 1971); *Dating, Mating, and Marriage; Marriage and Family Among Negroes; Women and the Public Interest: An Essay on Policy and Protest;* and the forthcoming *The Future of Marriage.* She has held numerous offices in professional societies and has been a member of many committees and boards. She always, as she says, "likes to look forward instead of back."

LAURA BERGQUIST, a native of Chicago, has had a widely diversified journalistic career. She was a senior editor at *Look* magazine for twelve years, a senior editor at *Pageant* for three years, and held editorial positions on several other publications. Her experience also includes four years of public relations work for the Mexican government as well as several years as a White House correspondent specializing in reporting on the Kennedy administration. Her book based on this coverage, *A Very Special President,* was published in 1965. She has won many awards for her outstanding journalistic achievements. In private life she is the wife of Fletcher Knebel, the well-known author.

CAROLINE BIRD is best known for her books *Born Female,* an account of the discriminations against women in business and the professions, and *The Invisible Scar,* an account of the effects of the Great Depression, chosen by the American Library Association as one of the most important books of 1966. She has been widely published in such leading magazines as the *Atlantic, New York Times Magazine, Harvard Business Review,* and *Fortune.* For many years she was with a large New York public relations firm but now devotes her full time to writing and lecturing.

DANA DENSMORE was 23 in 1968 when her life was changed by the concept of female liberation. Many of the ideas in the feminist resurgence were not new to her. The personal experience of a dissolved marriage made her feel strongly that female liberation implied much more than women convincing their husbands that they could have a job outside the home and be so fulfilled that they would be even better housekeepers. It implied a whole political analysis that suddenly made oppression understandable and solutions possible. Densmore's life now revolves around the working out of that understanding and those possibilities.

T. NEAL GARLAND is an assistant professor of sociology at the University of Akron. He received his Ph.D. in 1971 from Case Western Reserve University. He is coauthor with Margaret M. Poloma of several articles on married professional women and their husbands and of the forthcoming book, *The Dual*

393

Profession Family: A Study of High-Status Married Professionals. He was co-recipient of the 1970–1971 Lena Lake Forrest Fellowship granted by the National Federation of Business and Professional Women's Clubs.

PHILIP GOLDBERG is an associate professor of psychology at Connecticut College in New London, Connecticut. His research, which he describes as "scattered and profane," has centered on the social-clinical areas of psychology. He is presently conducting research on the cognitive and personality variables associated with voting behavior.

PATRICIA ALBJERG GRAHAM received her Ph.D. from Columbia University and is, at present, an associate professor of history and education at Barnard College and Columbia University Teachers College. She has published extensively and is currently working on a book entitled *A History of Educational Opportunity in America, 1856–1918.*

GAEL GREENE is a contributing editor and restaurant critic for *New York* magazine. As a free-lance writer, her work has appeared in *Life, Ladies' Home Journal, McCall's,* and *Cosmopolitan.* She is the author of *Bite: A New York Restaurant Strategy, Don't Come Back Without It* and *Sex and the College Girl.*

ELINA HAAVIO-MANNILA is an associate professor of sociology at the University of Helsinki. Since 1965 she has been engaged in the study of sex roles. In addition to a large book about the status and changing roles of women and men in Finland, she has written articles in several sociological journals. She is presently engaged in a cross-national family research project sponsored by the International Sociological Association.

HARRIET HOLTER received her Ph.D. from the University of Oslo. She is currently an associate professor of social psychology and affiliated with the Institute for Social Research in Oslo. She has done research in the fields of work relations, educational systems, and family life and has had a number of articles published about Scandinavian women. She is the author of a book entitled *Sex Roles and Social Structure,* published in 1970.

KYRIAKOS M. KONTOPOULOS is currently a doctoral candidate in sociology at Harvard University. He received a law degree from the University of Athens in Greece and an M.A. in sociology from Wayne State University. His interests lie basically in the areas of philosophical sociology, societal development, and the sociology of culture.

JANE LAMBIRI-DIMAKI, who received her Ph.D. from the London School of Economics, is a Greek sociologist who lives, teaches, and does research in Greece. She is, at present, lecturing at the School of Social Work of the Association for the Protection of Minors in Athens. Her research has focused upon university students and Greek university education as well as on the impact of the introduction of a large industry, employing almost exclusively women, upon the status of women in a small town. Her publications include a number of articles in both Greek and English on dowry, university education, the characteristics of university students, and a research monograph, *Social Change in a Greek Country Town.*

MARGARET B. LEFKOWITZ received an A.B. in English from the University of Kentucky and an M.A. in magazine journalism from Syracuse University in 1968. She is an editor with the *College Board Review* magazine and was formerly an editor with *Nature and Science* magazine.

MARGARET MEAD has been uninterruptedly involved in the study of man's cultural evolution since 1925, when she began her pioneering field work with primitive peoples of the South Pacific. For her tireless and imaginative pursuit of knowledge about human potentialities, Dr. Mead has won worldwide recognition both from her colleagues and the general public and has been the recipient of many honorary degrees and awards. In June 1969, Dr. Mead became Curator Emeritus of Ethnology of The American Museum of Natural History. She has continued her teaching as adjunct professor of anthropology at Columbia University and visiting professor of anthropology in the Department of Psychiatry at the University of Cincinnati's Medical College. In addition to her own books and monographs, Dr. Mead has coauthored many books with younger collaborators and writes a monthly column for *Redbook* magazine.

S. M. MILLER is a professor of sociology and education at New York University and an adviser to the President on urban affairs. He was president of the Eastern Sociological Society in 1970–1971 and he is currently chairman of the Research Committee on Poverty, Social Welfare, and Social Policy of the International Sociological Association. He is the coauthor of *The Future of Inequality* (1970) and *Social Class and Social Policy* (1968); editor of *Max Weber: A Reader* (1964); coeditor of *Applied Sociology* (1964); and author of *Comparative Social Mobility* (1960). His long-term interests are in inequality, and he has been working on the impact of economic and social policies upon social stratification.

BARBARA BOVEE POLK, Ph.D., has been an assistant professor at Wayne State University since 1968. With her colleague Dr. Robert Stein she is now in the process of writing a book applying traditional social psychological concepts and insights to the analysis of sex-role phenomena and, together with her economist husband, she and Dr. Stein are beginning a study of urban communes. As a member of the Michigan Women's Liberation Coalition since its inception, she has been active in consciousness-raising groups and the speaker's bureau, as well as participating occasionally in demonstrations and guerrilla theater. She is also faculty adviser for the Wayne Women's Liberation Organization.

MARGARET M. POLOMA received her Ph.D. in 1970 from Case Western Reserve University. She is presently an assistant professor of sociology at the University of Akron where she teaches in the areas of sociological theory, family, and religion. She has also taught courses on sex roles in modern society and served as guest editor for the Winter 1971 issue of *Sociological Focus* which dealt with sex roles. She was co-recipient of the 1970–1971 Lena Lake Forrest Fellowship awarded by the National Federation of Business and Professional Women's Clubs. She is coauthor of the forthcoming book *The Dual Profession Family: A Study of High-Status Married Professionals*.

RHONA RAPOPORT is presently codirector of the Institute of Family and Environmental Research, London, and senior social scientist at the Tavistock Institute of Human Relations. She received her undergraduate degree from the University of Capetown and her doctorate in sociology from the London School of Economics. She is an associate member of the British Psychoanalytic Society and of the International Society. She has worked in South Africa, Uganda, and England, and she has published with Michael Fogarty and Robert N. Rapoport *Sex, Career, and Family,* and with Robert N. Rapoport *Dual-Career Families.* A book on *Work and Family in Contemporary Society* is in preparation.

ROBERT N. RAPOPORT is director of the Institute of Family and Environmental Research and senior social scientist at the Tavistock Institute of Human Relations. He received his M.A. in social anthropology at the University of Chicago and his Ph.D. from the Department of Social Relations at Harvard. He has worked among the Navaho Indians and in the Canadian Maritimes as well as in England. In addition to the books he has written with Rhona Rapoport, he has also written *Community as Doctor* and *Mid-Career Development.*

LOVELLE RAY is a Ph.D. candidate in anthropology at Wayne State University. She returned to graduate school as a widow with three teen-agers and has since married a Londoner. She is interested in the cross-cultural study of the family, particularly in the examination of the effects of social change and the education of women upon the institution of the family. Her general area of interest is urban anthropology and her area specialty India, where she has recently traveled and made a film about life in an Indian village.

JEANNE CLARE RIDLEY, Ph.D., is a professor of sociology at Georgetown University. She was previously an associate professor in the School of Public Health and Administrative Medicine, and director, Division of Demography in the International Institute for the Study of Human Reproduction at Columbia University. At present, she serves on the board of directors of the Population Association of America and the American Eugenics Society. She is the author of various articles on human fertility and the changing status of American women and a coeditor with Mindel C. Sheps of *Public Health and Population Change: Current Research Issues* (1965).

PAMELA ROBY, Ph.D., is an assistant professor in the sociology department and in the Heller School for Advanced Studies in Social Welfare at Brandeis University. She is also an associate of the National Manpower Policy Task Force. She coauthored *The Future of Inequality* with S. M. Miller, edited the forthcoming *Child Care—Who Cares? Foreign and Domestic Early Childhood Policies,* and has published articles on the structure of income inequalities, strategies for reducing poverty, the use of paraprofessionals, and the historical development of prostitution laws and policies.

ALICE S. ROSSI holds a Ph.D. in sociology from Columbia University and is currently a professor of sociology at Goucher College, Baltimore, Maryland. She has served as a research sociologist at Cornell, Harvard, the University of Chicago, and the Johns Hopkins prior to her teaching appointment at Goucher College. Special areas of research interest in which she has published include sociology of the family, career development, sex roles, reproductive behavior and the history of feminism. She is national chairman of the Committee on the Status of Women in Academe in AAUP and president pro tem of Sociologists for Women in Society. Currently she is editing two books, *Academic Women on the Move* and *Essential Works of Feminism.*

CONSTANTINA SAFILIOS-ROTHSCHILD is a Greek sociologist whose first degree was in agricultural engineering. She received her Ph.D. in sociology and is, at present, director of the Family Research Center at Wayne State University. She has published many articles dealing with the options of women in different cultures and the comparative study of the dynamics of the husband-wife relationship. Her book on *Myths and Realities About the Family: A Cross-cultural Perspective* will appear in 1972.

ROBERT B. STEIN has a Ph.D. in sociology from Vanderbilt University and is currently an assistant professor of sociology at Wayne State University. In collaboration with Dr. Barbara Bovee Polk he co-teaches a course in sociology of sex roles. He is engaged in writing a core text for social psychology illustrating major concepts via their application to sex roles and is doing an extensive study of urban communes in Detroit, Michigan.

DIANA WORTMAN WARSHAY teaches sociology at the University of Toledo where she is also a member of the linguistics program. One of the founders of Sociologists for Women in Society, Dr. Warshay is an active participant in several professional committees concerned with the status of women in sociology. Her current research is in the sociology of language and nonverbal communication.

JAMES J. WHITE is a professor of law at the University of Michigan Law School. He has done much research and published several articles and a forthcoming book on consumer credit in the ghetto and on the legal problems of low-income consumers.

MARTHA STURM WHITE, Ph.D., is a social psychologist and college teacher whose published research has appeared in various professional journals and books. She is a former director of guidance at the Radcliffe Institute, author and editor of *The Next Step*—a book on opportunities for educated women—and conducts career-planning workshops for women of the San Francisco Bay Area. Currently with the Human Development Group at the University of California, San Francisco, she is engaged in research on developmental changes in women in early adult life.

Index

A B C D E F G H I J   9 8 7 6 5 4 3 2